W9-CTR-385

OOl

Josh Lockman

1995 - 1996 SCHOOL YEAR

HOMEROOM 25

100

The North American Third Edition

Cambridge Latin Course
Unit 4

Revision Editor
Ed Phinney
Chair, Department of Classics, & Faculty Director, University Foreign Language Resource Center
University of Massachusetts at Amherst, U.S.A.

Consulting Editor
Patricia E. Bell
Teacher of Latin & Assistant Head of Languages
Centennial Collegiate and Vocational Institute, Guelph, Ontario, Canada

Editorial Assistant
Barbara Romaine
Amherst, Massachusetts, U.S.A.

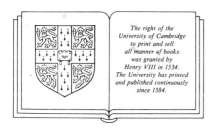

The right of the
University of Cambridge
to print and sell
all manner of books
was granted by
Henry VIII in 1534.
The University has printed
and published continuously
since 1584.

CAMBRIDGE UNIVERSITY PRESS

Cambridge

New York   Port Chester

Melbourne   Sydney

Published by the Press Syndicate of the University of Cambridge
40 West 20th Street, New York, NY 10011, USA

The Cambridge Latin Course was funded and developed by the University of Cambridge School Classics
Project and SCDC Publications, London, and is published with the sponsorship of the School Curriculum
Development Committee in London and the North American Cambridge Classics Project. The work of the
School Curriculum Development Committee has now been taken over by the National Curriculum
Council.

Library of Congress cataloging-in-publication Data
Cambridge Latin course. Unit 4. – North American 3rd ed./revision editor. Ed Phinney.
    p. cm.
    "Funded and developed by the University of Cambridge School Classics Project and
SCDC Publications. London" – T.p. verso.
    Includes indexes.
    ISBN
    1. Latin language – Grammar – 1976–   I. Phinney, Ed.   II. Cambridge School Classics Projects
(Cambridge, England)   III. SCDC Publications (Great Britain)   IV. Title: Cambridge Latin course.
Unit four.
IN PROCESS (ONLINE)   91–411
                                                                  CIP

ISBN 0 521 34380 1

Drawings by Peter Kesteven, Joy Mellor and Leslie Jones
Maps and diagrams by Reg Piggott, Jeff Edwards and Celia Hart
Picture research by Callie Kendall

DS

Acknowledgements
Thanks are due to the following for permission to reproduce photographs:
1, 8, 29, 45, 51, 77, 105, 128, 160, 201, 204, 216, Scala; **12,** Ashmolean Museum, Oxford; **21, 41, 252,
261,** Ed Phinney; **49, 165,** © Schools Council Publications; **59,** Roger Dalladay; **61, 96, 97, 113, 116,
120,** Ancient Art & Architecture Collection; **68, 127, 145, 173, 257, 260, 270,** Courtesy of the Trustees of
the British Museum; **70, 107, 185, 227, 267,** The Mansell Collection; **81, 184, 241, 254,** National
Archaeological Museum, Athens; by permission of the Ministry of Culture, **89,** Rheinisches
Landesmuseum, Trier; **109,** Photo: Bibliotheque Nationale, Paris; **124,** Fototeca Unione at the American
Academy in Rome (negs FU960, FU2281); **133,** from F.A. Brockhaus Komm.-Gesch., GmbH;
Abt. Antiquarium, Stuttgart, 1962; photos from Museum of Classical Archaeology, Cambridge; **136,**
Deutsches Archaeologisches Institut, Rome; **140,** By permission of the British Library; **149,** Viscount
Coke and the Trustees of the Holkham Estate; **152,** Somerset County Council's Museums Service; **159,**
Vatican Museums; **175,** Soprintendenza Archeologica di Roma; **176, 236,** Biblioteca Apostolica
Vaticana; **183,** Elisabeth Ayrton; **189,** Reproduced by permission of the Syndics of the Fitzwilliam
Museum, Cambridge; **196,** Musées Royaux des Beaux-Arts de Belgique, Bruxelles; **209,** Capitoline
Museum, Rome; **220,** © The University College of Wales, Aberystwyth Collection; photograph by John
Webb; **224,** Tate Gallery, London; **253,** Francis Bartlett Donation; Courtesy, Museum of Fine Arts,
Boston; **265,** The NY Carlsberg Glyptotek; **278,** The Billie Love Historical Collection; **280,**
Kunsthistorisches Museums, Vienna.

'Musée des Beaux Arts' reproduced by permission of Faber and Faber Ltd from *Collected Poems* by
W.H. Auden. Copyright 1940 and renewed 1968 by W.H. Auden; reprinted from *W.H Auden: Collected
Poems* by W.H. Auden, edited by Edward Mendelson, by permission of Random House, Inc.
Richmond Lattimore's translation of Homer's *Iliad* is reproduced by permission of the University of
Chicago Press, copyright 1951 © 1962 by the University of Chicago, all rights reserved.

Cover picture: A mosaic of Vergil, holding a scroll of the *Aeneid*, seated between the Muses of Epic and
Tragedy. From the Musée du Bardo, Tunis; photo by Roger Wood.

Contents

rūs

ex urbe

Mānius Acīlius Glabriō salūtem dīcit Lupō amīcō.
quid agis, mī Lupe, in vīllā tuā rūsticā? iamne ex istō morbō
convaluistī? quid agit Helvidius, fīlius tuus?

quotiēns dē tē tuāque vīllā cōgitō, tibi valdē invideō; nam in urbe
nūllum est ōtium, nūlla quiēs. ego quidem multīs negōtiīs cotīdiē   5
occupātus sum. prīmā hōrā ā clientibus meīs salūtor; inde ad
basilicam vel cūriam contendō; aliquandō amīcōs vīsitō, vel ab eīs
vīsitor; per tōtum diem officia prīvāta vel pūblica agō. at tū intereā
in rīpā flūminis vel in umbrā arboris ōtiōsus fortasse iacēs, et dum
ego strepitū urbis vexor, tū carmine avium dēlectāris. sed satis   10
querēlārum!

Imperātor Domitiānus triumphum heri dē Germānīs ēgit.
pompa, per tōtam urbem prōgressa, ā multīs laudābātur, ā
nōnnūllīs dērīdēbātur. aliī "spectāculum splendidissimum!"
clāmābant. "Imperātor noster, pater vērus patriae, gentēs barbarās   15
iam superāvit; Germānī per viās urbis iam in triumphō dūcuntur!"
aliī tamen "spectāculum rīdiculum!" susurrābant. "illī quī per viās
dūcuntur haudquāquam Germānī sunt, sed servī, ex prōvinciā

"dum ego strepitū urbis vexor, tū carmine avium dēlectāris." (lines 9–10)

Hispāniā arcessītī et veste Germānā indūtī! ēn splendidus
Imperātor quī, paucīs homunculīs victīs, sē dignum triumphō   20
putat!"

litterae cotīdiē ā Britanniā exspectantur, ubi Agricola bellum
contrā Calēdoniōs gerit. Calēdoniī crēduntur ferōcissimī omnium
Britannōrum esse. dē Calēdoniā ipsā omnīnō incertus sum, mī
Lupe. utrum pars est Britanniae an īnsula sēiūncta?   25

ad cōnsilium Imperātōris adesse saepe iubeor. invītus pāreō;
quotiēns enim sententiam meam ā Domitiānō rogor, difficile est
mihi respondēre; turpe vidētur mentīrī, perīculōsum vēra loquī.
nūper ego et aliī senātōrēs ab Imperātōre cōnsultī sumus dē poenā
illārum Virginum Vestālium quae incestī damnātae erant.   30
supplicium ultimum eīs dēcrēvimus; magnum erat eārum scelus, et
merita poena. at cōgitā impudentiam Domitiānī! Virginēs enim ob
incestum sevērē pūnit, ipse vītam impūrissimam vīvit.

audīvistīne umquam poētam Valerium Mārtiālem recitantem?
ego quidem recitātiōnibus eius saepe adsum; tū sī eum audīveris,   35
certē dēlectāberis. versūs eius semper ēlegantēs, nōnnumquam

quid agis?	*how are you? how are you doing?*
invideō: invidēre	*envy*
ōtium	*leisure*
prīvāta: prīvātus	*private*
arboris: arbor	*tree*
querēlārum: querēla	*complaint*
triumphum . . . ēgit: triumphum agere	*celebrate a triumph*
patriae: patria	*country, homeland*
veste: vestis	*clothing*
indūtī: indūtus	*dressed*
litterae	*letters, correspondence*
utrum . . . est . . . an?	*is it . . . or?*
sēiūncta: sēiūnctus	*separate*
cōnsilium	*council*
turpe: turpis	*shameful*
mentīrī	*lie, tell a lie*
incestī: incestum	*immorality, unchastity*
supplicium ultimum	*death penalty*
dēcrēvimus: dēcernere	*vote, decree*
impudentiam: impudentia	*shamelessness*
ob	*on account of, because of*
impūrissimam: impūrus	*immoral*
recitātiōnibus: recitātiō	*recital, public reading*
nōnnumquam	*sometimes*

scurrīlēs sunt. eum tamen ideō reprehendō, quod Imperātōrem nimium adulātur.

quandō rūre discēdēs, mī Lupe? quandō iterum tē in urbe vidēbimus? cum prīmum ad urbem redieris, mē vīsitā, quaesō; sī tē 40
mox vīderō, valdē dēlectābor. valē.

ideō . . . quod	*for the reason that, because*
reprehendō: reprehendere	*blame, criticize*
adulātur: adulārī	*flatter*
cum prīmum	*as soon as*
quaesō	*I beg,* i.e. *please*
Calēdoniōs: Calēdoniī	*Scots*
dē Germānīs	*over the Germans*

1 Who is the writer of this letter? To whom is it written? Where are they both?
2 Why does Glabrio envy Lupus? What does he imagine Lupus is doing while Glabrio is working?
3 What public event has just taken place in Rome? Why have some Romans regarded it as ridiculous?
4 From where, and from whom, is news expected? What has Glabrio heard about the Scots?
5 What request does Glabrio often receive from the Emperor? Why does he dislike obeying this request? Whose punishment has recently been discussed by the Emperor's advisers? Does Glabrio feel that the punishment was justified? Why does he feel indignant about it?
6 Whose public readings has Glabrio been attending? What criticism does he make of him?
7 What does Glabrio finally ask Lupus, and what request does he make?

About the Language

1 Study the following examples:

māne ā clientibus meīs **salūtor**.
*In the morning, **I am greeted** by my clients.*

amīcum prōdidistī; rēctē nunc **pūnīris**.
*You betrayed your friend; now **you are** rightly **punished**.*

The Latin words in boldface are *passive* forms of the 1st and 2nd persons singular.

2 Compare the active and passive forms of the 1st person singular in the following three tenses:

	ACTIVE	PASSIVE
PRESENT	**portō** *I carry*	**portor** *I am carried*
FUTURE	**portābō** *I shall carry*	**portābor** *I shall be carried*
IMPERFECT	**portābam** *I was carrying*	**portābar** *I was being carried*

Further examples:

1 laudor, laudābor, laudābar; doceor, docēbor, docēbar.
2 mittor, impedior, appellor; superābor, terrēbor, invītābor; prohibēbar, incitābar, trahēbar.

3 Compare the active and passive forms of the 2nd person singular:

	ACTIVE	PASSIVE
PRESENT	**portās** *you carry*	**portāris** *you are carried*
FUTURE	**portābis** *you will carry*	**portāberis** *you will be carried*
IMPERFECT	**portābās** *you were carrying*	**portābāris** *you were being carried*

Further examples:

1 culpāris, culpāberis; culpābāris; iubēris, iubēberis, iubēbāris.
2 spectāris, audīris, monēris; rogāberis, docēberis; neglegēbāris, salūtābāris.

---

4 Further examples of 1st and 2nd person forms:

1 nōlī dēspērāre! mox līberāberis.
2 nunc ab omnibus laudor; anteā ab omnibus culpābar.
3 heri in carcere retinēbāris; hodiē ab Imperātōre honōrāris.
4 vexor, vexāris; audiēbar, audiēbāris; dērīdēbor, dērīdēberis.

5 Compare the passive forms in paragraphs 2 and 3 with the forms of the deponent verb **cōnor**:

PRESENT	**cōnor**	*I try*	**cōnāris**	*you try*
FUTURE	**cōnābor**	*I shall try*	**cōnāberis**	*you will try*
IMPERFECT	**cōnābar**	*I was trying*	**cōnābāris**	*you were trying*

Further examples of 1st and 2nd person forms of deponent verbs:

1 cūr domum meam ingrediēbāris?
2 crās deam precābor.
3 polliceor, pollicēris; cōnspicābor, cōnspicāberis; sequēbar, sequēbāris.

---

vīta rūstica

C. Helvidius Lupus salūtem dīcit Acīliō Glabriōnī amīcō.
cum epistulam tuam legerem, mī Glabriō, gaudium et dolōrem
simul sēnsī. gaudiō enim afficiēbar, quod tam diū epistulam ā tē
exspectābam; dolēbam autem, quod tū tot labōribus opprimēbāris.

in epistulā tuā dīcis tē valdē occupātum esse. ego quoque, cum   5
Rōmae essem, saepe negōtiīs vexābar; nunc tamen vītā rūsticā
fruor. aliquandō per agrōs meōs equitō; aliquandō fundum īnspiciō.
crās in silvīs proximīs vēnābor; vīcīnī enim crēdunt aprum
ingentem ibi latēre. nōn tamen omnīnō ōtiōsus sum; nam sīcut tū ā
clientibus tuīs salūtāris atque vexāris, ita ego ā colōnīs meīs assiduē   10
vexor.

simulatque ad hanc vīllam advēnī, medicum quendam, quī prope
habitābat, arcessīvī; morbō enim valdē afflīgēbar. medicus mē iussit
vīnō abstinēre, medicīnamque sūmere. septem continuōs diēs ā
medicō vīsitābar; morbus intereā ingravēscēbat. octāvō diē   15

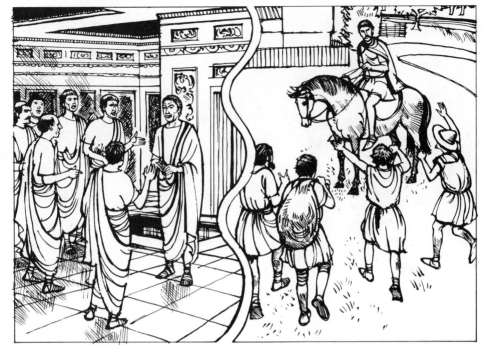

**"sīcut tū ā clientibus tuīs salūtāris atque vexāris, ita ego ā colōnīs meīs
assiduē vexor." (lines 9–10)**

medicum dīmīsī, vīnum bibere coepī, medicīnam in cloācam effūdī,
statim convaluī.

rēctē dīcis Calēdoniōs omnium Britannōrum ferōcissimōs esse.
amīcus meus Silānus, quī cum Agricolā in Britanniā nūper
mīlitābat, dīcit Calēdoniōs in ultimīs partibus Britanniae habitāre,   20
inter saxa et undās. quamquam Calēdoniī ferōcissimē pugnāre
solent, Silānus cōnfīdit exercitum nostrum eōs vincere posse. crēdit
enim Rōmānōs nōn modo fortiōrēs esse quam Calēdoniōs, sed etiam
ducem meliōrem habēre.

dē poētā Mārtiāle tēcum cōnsentiō: inest in eō multum ingenium,   25
multa ars. ego vērō ōlim versibus Ovidiī poētae maximē dēlectābar;
nunc tamen mihi epigrammata Mārtiālis magis placent.

dolēbam: dolēre	*grieve, be sad*	sūmere	*take*
fruor: fruī	*enjoy*	cloācam: cloāca	*drain*
vēnābor: vēnārī	*hunt*	cōnfīdit: cōnfīdere	*be sure, be confident*
vīcīnī: vīcīnus	*neighbor*	vērō	*indeed*
sīcut . . . ita	*just as . . . so*	epigrammata:	
colōnīs: colōnus	*tenant-farmer*	epigramma	*epigram*
abstinēre	*abstain*		

Stag hunting, from a mosaic.

in epistulā tuā Helvidium, fīlium meum, commemorās. quem
tamen rārissimē videō! nam in hāc vīllā trēs diēs mēcum morātus,
ad urbem rediit; suspicor eum puellam aliquam in urbe vīsitāre.   30
quīndecim iam annōs nātus est; nihil cūrat nisi puellās et quadrīgās.
difficile autem est mihi eum castīgāre; nam ego quoque, cum iuvenis
essem – sed satis dē hīs nūgīs.

　　nunc tū mihi graviter admonendus es, mī Glabriō. in epistulā tuā
identidem dē quōdam virō potentī male scrībis, quem nōmināre   35
nōlō. tibi cavendum est, mī amīce! perīculōsum est dē potentibus
male scrībere. virī potentēs celeriter īrāscuntur, lentē molliuntur.
·haec tibi ideō dīcō, quod patris meī cārissimī memor sum; quī cum
Vespasiānum Imperātōrem offendisset, prīmum relēgātus, deinde
occīsus est. nisi cāveris, mī Glabriō, tū quoque, sīcut pater meus,   40
damnāberis atque occīdēris. sollicitus haec scrībō; salūs enim tua
mihi magnae cūrae est. valē.

aliquam: aliquī	*some*
quadrīgās: quadrīga	*chariot*
nūgīs: nūgae	*nonsense, foolish talk*
admonendus es:	
admonēre	*warn, advise*
male	*badly, unfavorably*
nōmināre	*name, mention by name*
īrāscuntur: īrāscī	*become angry*

Practicing the Language

1 Match each adjective in the left-hand column with an adjective of the opposite meaning, taken from the right-hand column, and translate both words.

For example: **absēns** *absent*   **praesēns** *present*

absēns	parvus
dīves	multī
laetus	vīvus
longus	bonus
magnus	praesēns
malus	trīstis
mortuus	antīquus
novus	vacuus
paucī	brevis
plēnus	pauper

2 Complete each sentence with the most suitable verb from the list below, using the correct form, and then translate. Do not use any verb more than once.

terrēbit	reficiet	dabit	certābit	dūcet
terrēbunt	reficient	dabunt	certābunt	dūcent

1 hī fabrī sunt perītissimī; nāvem tuam celeriter . . . . . .
2 crās dominus lībertātem duōbus servīs . . . . . .
3 leōnēs, quī ferōciōrēs sunt quam cēterae bēstiae, spectātōrēs fortasse . . . . . .
4 sī templum vīsitāre vīs, hic servus tē illūc . . . . . .
5 frāter meus, aurīga nōtissimus, crās in Circō Maximō . . . . . .

3 With the help of paragraph 8 on page 292 of the Language Information Section, turn each of the following pairs into one sentence by replacing the word in boldface with the correct form of the relative pronoun **quī**, and then translate.

For example: prō templō erant duo tribūnī. **tribūnōs** statim agnōvī.
This becomes: prō templō erant duo tribūnī, **quōs** statim agnōvī.
*In front of the temple were two tribunes, **whom** I recognized at once.*

1 in fundō nostrō sunt vīgintī servī. **servī** in agrīs cotīdiē labōrant.
2 prope iānuam stābat nūntius. **nūntiō** epistulam trādidī.
3 in hāc vīllā habitat lībertus. **lībertum** vīsitāre volō.
4 audī illam puellam! **puella** suāviter cantat.
5 in viā erant multī puerī. **puerōrum** clāmōrēs senem vexābant.

About the Language

1 In Unit 1, you met sentences like these:

"**mercātor** multam pecūniam **habet**."
"***The merchant has** a lot of money.*"

"**servī** fraudem **parant**."
"***The slaves are preparing** a trick.*"

In each example, a statement is being *made*. These examples are known as *direct* statements. Notice the nouns **mercātor** and **servī** and the verbs **habet** and **parant**.

2 In Stage 35, you have met sentences like these:

"scīmus **mercātōrem** multam pecūniam **habēre**."
"*We know **the merchant to have** a lot of money.*"
  Or, in more natural English:
"*We know that **the merchant has** a lot of money.*"

"crēdō **servōs** fraudem **parāre**."
"*I believe **the slaves to be preparing** a trick.*"
  Or, in more natural English:
"*I believe that **the slaves are preparing** a trick.*"

In each of these examples, the statement is not being made, but is being *reported* or *mentioned*. These examples are known as *indirect* statements. Notice that the nouns **mercātōrem** and **servōs** are now in the *accusative* case, and the verbs **habēre** and **parāre** are now in the *infinitive* form.

3 Compare the following examples:

DIRECT STATEMENTS	INDIRECT STATEMENTS
"captīvī dormiunt."	centuriō dīcit **captīvōs dormīre**.
"The prisoners are asleep."	*The centurion says that **the prisoners are asleep**.*
"Lupus in vīllā rūsticā **habitat."**	audiō **Lupum** in vīllā rūsticā **habitāre**.
*"**Lupus is living** in his country villa."*	*I hear that **Lupus is living** in his country villa.*

4 Further examples of direct and indirect statements:

1 "hostēs appropinquant."
2 nūntius dīcit hostēs appropinquāre.
3 dominus crēdit fugitīvōs in fossā latēre.
4 "Agricola bellum in Calēdoniā gerit."
5 audiō Agricolam bellum in Calēdoniā gerere.
6 rhētor putat fīlium meum dīligenter labōrāre.

Country Villas

Many wealthy Romans, like Lupus on pages 2–4, owned both a town house in Rome and at least one villa in the country. There they could escape from the noise and heat of the city, especially during the unhealthy months of late summer, and relax from the pressures of private business and public duties.

Some of these country houses were fairly close to Rome; their owners could get a day's work done in the city and then travel out to their villa before nightfall. The villas were generally either on the coast, like Pliny's villa at Laurentum, or on the hills around Rome, for example at Tibur, where the Emperor Hadrian owned the most spectacular mansion of all, surrounded by specially constructed imitations of buildings that had impressed him on his travels.

But other country villas were further afield. A popular area was Campania; the coastline of the bay of Naples was dotted with the villas of wealthy men, while holiday resorts such as Baiae enjoyed a reputation for fast living and dubious morals.

Country villas naturally varied in design, but they usually contained some or all of the following features: a series of dining and reception rooms for entertaining guests, often giving extensive views of the surrounding countryside; a set of baths, heated by hypocausts, containing the full range of apodyterium, tepidarium, caldarium, and frigidarium; long colonnades where the owner and his friends might walk, or even ride, sheltered from the rain or from the direct heat of the sun; and extensive parkland, farmland, or gardens, preferably with plenty of shade and running water. In a corner of the estate there might be a small shrine, dedicated to the protecting gods.

Pliny's letters include descriptions of two of his villas; the descriptions are detailed without always being clear, and many scholars have tried to reconstruct the plans of the villas, without reaching agreement. An attempt at the plan of Pliny's Laurentine villa is shown below, together with a model based on the plan. Among the villa's special features were the heated swimming pool (10), the big semi-circular recess at the end of the chief dining-room (4), designed to provide the dinner-guests with an impressive panorama of the sea, and the covered colonnade (12) leading to Pliny's private suite (14). This suite was Pliny's own addition to the building, and it provided him with quiet and privacy; for example, at the

Model of Pliny's villa at Laurentum.

noisy mid-winter festival of the Saturnalia, Pliny could retire to his suite while his slaves enjoyed themselves in the main villa, so that he did not get in the way of their celebrations and they did not disturb his peace.

One of the most popular recreations for a wealthy Roman on his country estate was hunting. Hares, deer, or wild boars were tracked down and then pursued into nets where they could be speared to death. Long ropes, to which brightly-colored feathers were attached, were slung from trees to cut off the animal's retreat and frighten it back towards the nets. The actual chasing was often left to slaves and dogs, while the hunter contented himself with waiting at the nets and spearing the boar or deer when it had become thoroughly entangled. Pliny, for example, in reporting a successful expedition on which he caught three boars, says that he took his stylus and writing-tablets with him to the hunt and jotted ideas down under the inspiration of the woodland scene while he waited for the boars to appear. But although Pliny's description of hunting is a very peaceful one, the sport still had its dangers: a cornered boar might

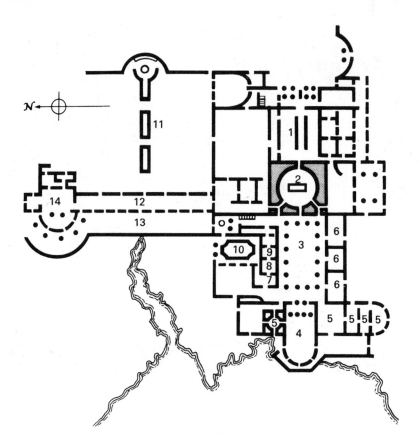

1 atrium	6 slaves' rooms	11 ornamental garden with
2 courtyard	7 tepidarium	vine pergola
3 inner courtyard	8 apodyterium	12 covered colonnade
4 dining-room	9 caldarium	13 terrace
5 bedrooms	10 heated swimming pool	14 Pliny's private suite

turn on its pursuers, and a hunter who was slow with his spear might be gashed nastily and even fatally.

Fishing was also popular, and could easily be combined with rowing or sailing, either on the sea (in the bay of Naples, for example) or on such lakes as the Lucrine lake, famous for its fish and its oysters. A lazier method of fishing is described by Martial, who refers to a villa with a bedroom directly overlooking the sea, so that the occupant could drop a fishing-line from the window and catch a fish without even getting out of bed.

Some of Pliny's letters describe his daily routine at his country villas. He spent most of his time in gentle exercise (walking, riding, or occasionally hunting), working on a speech or other piece of writing, dealing with his tenant-farmers (**colōnī**), entertaining friends, dining, or listening to a reading or music. He often spent part of the afternoon reading a Greek or Latin speech aloud "for the sake of both voice and digestion." (Pliny often spoke publicly in the law courts and the senate, and he was naturally anxious to keep his voice in good trim.)

But a country villa of this kind was not just for holiday relaxation; it was an important investment. Often there was a farm attached to the house, and the property would usually include an extensive area of land which the owner might farm himself or lease to tenant-farmers. In the ancient world, by far the commonest way of investing money was to buy land. It is not surprising that many of Pliny's letters deal with the day-to-day problems of land management. He agonizes over whether to buy a neighboring piece of land, fertile and conveniently situated but long neglected; he asks the emperor to excuse him from Rome so that he can be on one of his estates at a time when the tenancy is changing hands; and when his tenants get into difficulties and are heavily in debt, he works out a system for converting their rent from a cash sum into a proportion of their crop. He likes to present himself as an ignorant amateur with no interest in the running of his villas, but some of his comments give the impression that he was in fact enthusiastic, practical, and shrewd. He was also very successful; one of his villas alone brought him an income of 400,000 sesterces a year.

Words and Phrases Checklist

ager, agrī	*field*
an	*or*
utrum . . . an	*whether . . . or*
caveō, cavēre, cāvī	*beware*
cūrae esse	*be a matter of concern*
ideō	*for this reason*
ideō . . . quod	*for the reason that, because*
inde	*then*
īnsum, inesse, īnfuī	*be in, be inside*
magis	*more*
male	*badly, unfavorably*
mentior, mentīrī, mentītus sum	*lie, tell a lie*
meritus, merita, meritum	*deserved, well-deserved*
moror, morārī, morātus sum	*delay*
officium, officiī	*duty*
puto, putāre, putāvī	*think*
quandō?	*when?*
quidem	*indeed*
quotiēns	*whenever*
rēctē	*rightly, properly*
relēgō, relēgāre, relēgāvī, relēgātus	*exile*
rūs, rūris	*country, countryside*
simul	*at the same time*
supplicium, suppliciī	*punishment, penalty*
vīcīnus, vīcīnī	*neighbor*
virgō, virginis	*virgin*

Word Search

Match each definition with one of the words given below.

merit, moratorium, officious, putative, relegate, rural, vicinity

1 . . . . .: supposed, conjectural
2 . . . . .: proximity, state of nearness
3 . . . . .: to earn, deserve
4 . . . . .: pertaining to the country, rustic
5 . . . . .: a deferment, delay
6 . . . . .: to send or consign, especially to a remote place or obscure condition
7 . . . . .: meddlesome; overeager to offer one's services

Stage 36

recitātiō

Marcus Valerius Mārtiālis

I

in audītōriō exspectant multī cīvēs. adsunt ut Valerium Mārtiālem, poētam nōtissimum, recitantem audiant. omnēs inter sē colloquuntur. subitō signum datur ut taceant; audītōrium intrat poēta ipse. audītōribus plaudentibus, Mārtiālis scaenam ascendit ut versūs suōs recitet.

Mārtiālis: salvēte, amīcī. *(librum ēvolvit.)* prīmum recitāre volō   5
        versūs quōsdam nūper dē Sabidiō compositōs.
complūrēs audītōrēs sē convertunt ut Sabidium, quī in ultimō sellārum ōrdine sedet, spectent.

Mārtiālis: nōn amo tē, Sabidī, nec possum dīcere quārē.
        hoc tantum possum dīcere – nōn amo tē.   10

audītor: *(cum amīcīs susurrāns)* illōs versūs nōn intellegō. cūr poēta
        dīcere nōn potest quārē Sabidium nōn amet?
prīmus amīcus: *(susurrāns)* scīlicet poēta ipse causam nescit.
secundus amīcus: *(susurrāns)* immō, poēta optimē scit quārē
        Sabidium nōn amet: sed tam foeda et obscēna est causa   15
        ut poēta eam patefacere nōlit.
aliī audītōrēs: st! st!
prīmus amīcus: hem! audītōrēs nōbīs imperant ut taceāmus.
Mārtiālis: nunc de Laecāniā et Thāide, fēminīs "nōtissimīs":
        (audītōrēs sibi rīdent.)   20

        Thāis habet <u>nigrōs</u>, niveōs Laecānia <u>dentēs</u>.*
        quae ratiō est? . . .

audītor: *(interpellāns)*   . . . ēmptōs haec habet, illa suōs!

Mārtiālis, interpellātiōne valdē īrātus, dē scaenā dēscendit ut audītōrem vituperet.   25
Mārtiālis: ego poēta sum, tū tantum audītor. ego hūc invītātus sum
        ut recitem, tū ut audiās. *(subitō audītōrem agnōscit.)* hem!
        scio quis sīs. tū Pontiliānus es, quī semper mē rogās ut
        libellōs meōs tibi mittam. at nunc, mī Pontiliāne, tibi

---

*Some noun-and-adjective phrases, in which an adjective is separated by one
  word or more from the noun which it describes, have been underlined.

Mārtiālis, interpellātiōne valdē īrātus, dē scaenā dēscendit ut audītōrem vituperet. (lines 24–5)

       dīcere possum quārē semper mittere recūsem. (*ad*   30
       scaenam reversus, recitātiōnem renovat.)

     cūr nōn mitto <u>meōs</u> tibi, Pontiliāne, <u>libellōs</u>?
     nē mihi tū mittās, Pontiliāne, tuōs!

omnēs praeter Pontiliānum rīdent. Pontiliānus autem tam īrātus est ut ē sellā   35
surgat. ad scaenam sē praecipitāre cōnātur ut Mārtiālem pulset, sed amīcī eum
retinent.

audītōriō: audītōrium	*auditorium, hall (used for public readings)*
colloquuntur: colloquī	*talk, chat*
audītōribus: audītor	*listener, (pl.) audience*
ēvolvit: ēvolvere	*unroll, open*
complūrēs	*several*
obscēna: obscēnus	*obscene, disgusting*
st!	*hush!*
Thāide	*ablative of* Thāis
quae?: quī?	*what?*
ratiō	*reason*
haec . . . illa	*this one (Laecania) . . . that one (Thais)*
interpellātiōne:	
interpellātiō	*interruption*
renovat: renovāre	*continue, resume*

II

Mārtiālis, quī iam ūnam hōram recitat, ad fīnem librī appropinquat.

Mārtiālis: amīcī meī dīcunt poētam quendam, Fīdentīnum nōmine, meōs libellōs quasi suōs recitāre. nunc igitur Fīdentīnō hoc dīcere volō:

> quem recitās <u>meus</u> est, ō Fīdentīne, <u>libellus</u>. 5
>
> sed male cum recitās, incipit esse tuus.

complūrēs audītōrēs, Fīdentīnī amīcī, sibilant; cēterī rīdent.

Mārtiālis: postrēmō pauca dē prīncipe nostrō, Domitiānō Augustō, dīcere velim. aliquōs versūs nūper dē illā aulā ingentī composuī quae in monte Palātīnō stat: 10

> aethera contingit <u>nova</u> nostrī prīncipis <u>aula</u>;
>
> clārius in <u>tōtō</u> sōl videt <u>orbe</u> nihil.
>
> <u>haec</u>, Auguste, tamen, quae vertice sīdera pulsat,
>
> pār <u>domus</u> est caelō sed minor est dominō.

plērīque audītōrēs vehementissimē plaudunt; animadvertunt enim 15
Epaphrodītum, Domitiānī lībertum, in audītōriō adesse. ūnus audītor tamen,
M'. Acīlius Glabriō, tālī adulātiōne offēnsus, nōn modo plausū abstinet sed ē
sellā surgit et ex audītōriō exit. quā audāciā attonitus, Mārtiālis paulīsper
immōtus stat; deinde ad extrēmam scaenam prōcēdit ut plausum excipiat. ūnus
tamen audītor exclāmat: 20

audītor: sed quid dē mē, Mārtiālis? epigramma dē mē compōnere nunc potes?

Mārtiālis: dē tē, homuncule? quis es et quālis?

audītor: nōmine Diaulus sum. artem medicīnae nūper exercēbam . . . 25

alius audītor: . . . at nunc vespillō es!

(omnēs rīdent; rīdet praesertim Mārtiālis.)

Mārtiālis: bene! nunc epigramma accipe, mī Diaule:

> nūper erat medicus, nunc est vespillo Diaulus.
>
> quod vespillo facit, fēcerat et medicus. 30

cachinnant multī; ērubēscit Diaulus. Mārtiālis, recitātiōne ita perfectā, ex
audītōriō ēgreditur, omnibus praeter Diaulum plaudentibus. servī ingressī
audītōribus vīnum cibumque offerunt.

Palace of Domitian, Palatine Hill, from the Circus Maximus.

sibilant: sibilāre	*hiss*
prīncipe: prīnceps	*emperor*
composuī: compōnere	*compose, make up*
aethera	*accusative of* aethēr *sky, heaven*
contingit: contingere	*touch*
clārius . . . nihil	*nothing more splendid*
orbe: orbis	*globe, world*
vertice: vertex	*top, peak*
sīdera: sīdus	*star*
pār	*equal*
minor . . . dominō	*smaller than its master*
adulātiōne: adulātiō	*flattery*
ad extrēmam scaenam	*to the edge of the stage*
vespillō	*undertaker*
quod = id quod	*what*
et = etiam	*also*
monte Palātīnō: mōns Palātīnus	*the Palatine hill*
M'. = Mānius	

About the Language

1 In Unit 3, you met the *imperfect* and *pluperfect* tenses of the subjunctive:

imperfect
haruspex aderat ut victimam **īnspiceret**.
*The soothsayer was there in order that **he might examine** the victim.*
   Or, in more natural English:
*The soothsayer was there **to examine** the victim.*

pluperfect
rēx prīncipēs rogāvit num discordiam **composuissent**.
*The king asked the chieftains whether **they had settled** their quarrel.*

2 In Stage 36, you have met sentences like these:

cīvēs conveniunt ut poētam **audiant**.
*The citizens are gathering in order that **they may hear** the poet.*
   Or, in more natural English:
*The citizens are gathering **to hear** the poet.*

Mārtiālis dīcere nōn potest quārē Sabidium nōn **amet**.
Martial is unable to say why **he does** not **like** Sabidius.

The Latin form of the verb in boldface is the *present* tense of the subjunctive.

3 Further examples:

   1 cognōscere volō quid illī fabrī aedificent.
   2 tam saevus est dominus noster ut servōs pūnīre numquam dēsinat.
   3 in agrīs cotīdiē labōrō ut cibum līberīs meīs praebeam.
   4 nōn intellegimus quārē dēspērētis.

4 Compare the present subjunctive with the present indicative:

	PRESENT INDICATIVE (3RD PERSON SINGULAR AND PLURAL)	PRESENT SUBJUNCTIVE (3RD PERSON SINGULAR AND PLURAL)
FIRST CONJUGATION	**portat**	**portet**
	portant	**portent**
SECOND CONJUGATION	**docet**	**doceat**
	docent	**doceant**

THIRD CONJUGATION	**trahit**	**trahat**
	trahunt	**trahant**
THIRD CONJUGATION -iō	**capit**	**capiat**
	capiunt	**capiant**
FOURTH CONJUGATION	**audit**	**audiat**
	audiunt	**audiant**

The present subjunctive of all four conjugations is set out in full on p.298 of the Language Information Section.

5 For the present subjunctive of irregular verbs, see p.308.

---

epigrammata Mārtiālia

The following epigrams, and also the ones which appeared in "recitātiō" on pages 18–21, were written by Marcus Valerius Martialis (Martial) and published between A.D. 86 and 101.

I   *dē Tuccā, quī Mārtiālem saepe ōrat ut libellōs sibi dōnet*

   exigis ut <u>nostrōs</u> dōnem tibi, Tucca, <u>libellōs</u>.
      nōn faciam: nam vīs vēndere, nōn legere.

   dōnet: dōnāre *give*   exigis: exigere *demand*   nostrōs: noster = meus *my*

   Why does Martial refuse Tucca's request?

II   *dē Sextō, iuvene glōriōsō*

   dīcis amōre tuī <u>bellās</u> ardēre <u>puellās</u>,
      quī faciem sub aquā, Sexte, natantis habēs.

   glōriōsō: glōriōsus *boastful*   bellās: bellus *pretty*   faciem: faciēs *face*

   Judging from Martial's description, what impression do you have of Sextus' appearance?

   discipulīs: discipulus   *student*
   languēbam: languēre   *feel weak, feel sick*
   prōtinus   *immediately*
   tetigēre = tetigērunt:
      tangere   *touch*

III *dē Symmachō medicō discipulīsque eius centum*

languēbam: sed tū comitātus prōtinus ad mē
    vēnistī <u>centum</u>, Symmache, <u>discipulīs</u>.
centum mē tetigēre <u>manūs</u> Aquilōne <u>gelātae</u>;
    nōn habuī febrem, Symmache: nunc habeō.

gelātae: gelāre	*freeze*
febrem: febris	*fever*
Aquilōne: Aquilō	*North Wind*

Why do you think Martial repeats the word "centum" (lines 2–3)
and uses the phrase "Aquilōne gelātae" (line 3)?

IV *dē Catullō, quī saepe dīcit Mārtiālem hērēdem sibi esse*

hērēdem tibi mē, Catulle, dīcis.
nōn crēdam nisi lēgerō, Catulle.

When will Martial believe Catullus' promise? Why do you think he
will believe it then, but not believe it earlier?

"centum mē tetigēre manūs Aquilōne gelātae." (III, line 3)

V   *dē Quīntō, quī Thāida lūscam amat*

"Thāida Quīntus amat." "quam Thāida?" "Thāida lūscam."
ūnum oculum Thāis nōn habet, ille duōs.

lūscam: lūscus *one-eyed*
quam?: quī? *which?*
Thāida *accusative of* Thāis

What do the last two words suggest about (a) Quintus, (b) Thais?

VI   *dē Vacerrā, quī veterēs poētās sōlōs mīrātur*

mīrāris <u>veterēs</u>, Vacerra, sōlōs
nec laudās nisi mortuōs <u>poētās</u>.
ignōscās petimus, Vacerra: tantī
nōn est, ut placeam tibī, perīre.

mīrātur: mīrārī   *admire*
ignōscās petimus = petimus ut nōbīs ignōscās
tantī nōn est . . . perīre *it is not worth dying*

Do people like Vacerra still exist nowadays?

About the Language

1 From Stage 3 onwards, you have met phrases in which an adjective is placed next to the noun it describes:

ad **silvam obscūram**   *to **the dark woods***
contrā **multōs hostēs**   *against **many enemies***
in **magnā nāve**   *in **a big ship***

2 In Unit 3, you met phrases in which an adjective is separated by a preposition from the noun which it describes:

tōtam per **urbem**   *through **the whole city***
omnibus cum **mīlitibus**   *with **all the soldiers***
hōc ex **oppidō**   *from **this town***

3 In Stage 36, you have met sentences like these:

cūr nōn mitto **meōs** tibi, Pontiliāne, **libellōs**?
*Why do I not send you **my writings**, Pontilianus?*

---

aethera contingit **nova** nostrī prīncipis **aula**.
*The **new palace** of our emperor touches the sky.*

This kind of word order, in which an adjective is separated by one or more words from the noun which it describes, is particularly common in poetry.

Further examples:

1 dēnique centuriō **magnam** pervēnit ad **urbem**.
2 nox erat, et **caelō** fulgēbat lūna **serēnō**. (*from a poem by Horace*)
3 flūminis in rīpā nunc **noster** dormit **amīcus**.

4 In each of the following examples, pick out the Latin adjective and say which noun it is describing:

1 atque iterum ad Trōiam magnus mittētur Achillēs. (*Vergil*)
   And great Achilles will be sent again to Troy.
2 ergō sollicitae tū causa, pecūnia, vītae! (*Propertius*)
   Therefore you, money, are the cause of an anxious life!
3 rōbustus quoque iam taurīs iuga solvet arātor. (*Vergil*)
   Now, too, the strong plowman will unfasten the yoke from the bulls.

5 Translate the following examples:

1 *On a journey:*
   cōnspicimus montēs atque altae moenia Rōmae.
2 *Cries of pain:*
   clāmōrēs simul horrendōs ad sīdera tollit. (*Vergil*)
3 *A foreigner:*
   hic posuit nostrā nūper in urbe pedem. (*Propertius*)
4 *Preparations for battle:*
   tum iuvenis validā sustulit arma manū.
5 *The foolishness of sea travel:*
   cūr cupiunt nautae saevās properāre per undās?

moenia	*city walls*
horrendōs : horrendus	*horrifying*
properāre	*hurry*

Pick out the adjective in each example and say which noun it is describing.

Practicing the Language

1 Study the form and meaning of the following nouns and adjectives and give the meaning of the untranslated words:

ōtium	*leisure, idleness*	ōtiōsus	*idle, at leisure*
spatium	*space*	spatiōsus	*spacious, large*
fōrma	*beauty*	fōrmōsus	
līmus	*mud*	līmōsus	
herba		herbōsus	*grassy*
bellum		bellicōsus	*aggressive, warlike*
pretium	*price, value*	pretiōsus	
perīculum		perīculōsus	
fūror	*madness, rage*	fūriōsus	
damnum		damnōsus	*harmful, damaging*

Match each of the following Latin adjectives with the correct English translation:

Latin: fūmōsus, iocōsus, ventōsus, perfidiōsus, annōsus
English: *treacherous, smoky, fond of jokes, old, blown by the winds*

2 Complete each sentence with the right word and then translate.

1 Mārtiālis versum dē Imperātōre compōnere . . . . . . (cōnābātur, ēgrediēbātur)
2 Glabriō amīcum . . . . . ut ad urbem revenīret. (cōnspicābātur, hortābātur)
3 mīlitēs ducem ad ultimās regiōnēs Britanniae . . . . . . (sequēbantur, suspicābantur)
4 omnēs senātōrēs dē victōriā Agricolae . . . . . . (adipīscēbantur, loquēbantur)
5 pauper, quī multōs cāsūs . . . . ., nihilōminus contentus erat. (patiēbātur, precābātur)
6 clientēs, quī patrōnum ad forum . . . . ., viam complēbant. (comitābantur, proficīscēbantur)

3 Translate each sentence; then, with the help of the tables on pages 284–285 and 286 of the Language Information Section, change the words in boldface from singular to plural, and translate again.

1 tribūnus **centuriōnem callidum** laudāvit.
2 frāter meus, postquam **hoc templum** vīdit, obstupefactus est.

3 senex **amīcō dēspērantī** auxilium tulit.
4 ubi **est puella**? **eam** salūtāre volō.
5 iuvenis, **hastā ingentī** armātus, ad vēnātiōnem contendit.
6 **puer**, **quem** heri pūnīvī, hodiē labōrāre nōn **potest**.

4 Complete each sentence with the most suitable verb from the list below, using the correct form, and then translate. Do not use any verb more than once.

exstīnxit	accēpit	iussit	recitāvit	dūxit
exstīnxērunt	accēpērunt	iussērunt	recitāvērunt	dūxērunt
exstīnctus est	acceptus est	iussus est	recitātus est	ductus est
exstīnctī sunt	acceptī sunt	iussī sunt	recitātī sunt	ductī sunt

1 ignis tandem ā mīlitibus . . . . . .
2 poēta multōs versūs dē Imperātōre . . . . . .
3 captīvī per viās urbis in triumphō . . . . . .
4 clientēs pecūniam laetissimē . . . . . .
5 lībertus ad aulam contendere . . . . . .

Recitātiōnes

The easiest and commonest way for a Roman author to bring his work to the notice of the public was to read it aloud to them. For example, a poet might choose a convenient spot, such as a street corner, a barbershop, or a colonnade in the forum, and recite his poems to anyone who cared to stop and listen. Like any kind of street performance or sales-talk, this could be very entertaining or very annoying for the passers-by. In an exaggerated but colorful complaint, Martial claims that a poet called Ligurinus used to recite continually at him, whether he was eating dinner, hurrying along the street, swimming in the baths, or using the public lavatories, and that even when he went to sleep, Ligurinus woke him up and began reciting again.

Often, however, a writer's work received its first reading in a more comfortable place than the street corner, with a carefully chosen group of listeners rather than a casual collection of passers-by. A natural audience for a writer was his patron, if he had one, and his patron's family and friends. For example, Vergil read sections of his poem the *Aeneid* to the

Emperor Augustus and to Augustus' sister Octavia, who is said to have fainted when Vergil reached a part of the poem which referred to her dead son Marcellus. A writer might also invite friends to his house and read his work to them there, perhaps inviting them to make comments or criticisms before he composed a final version of the work. This kind of reading sometimes took place at a dinner-party. If the host was an accomplished and entertaining writer, this would add to the guests' enjoyment of the meal; but some hosts made great nuisances of themselves by reading boring or feeble work to their dinner-guests.

The public reading of a writer's work often took place at a special occasion known as a **recitātiō**, like the one on pages 18–21, in which an invited audience had a chance to hear the author's work and could decide whether or not to buy a copy or have a copy made. The recitatio might be given at the writer's house, or more often the house of his patron; or a hall (**audītōrium**) might be specially rented for the purpose. Invitations were sent out. Cushioned chairs were set out at the front for the more distinguished guests; benches were placed behind them, and, if the recitatio was a very grand occasion, tiered seats on temporary scaffolding. Slaves gave out programs to the audience as they arrived,

Relief showing a Roman reading from a book.

and if the writer was unscrupulous or over-anxious, one or two friends might be stationed at particular points in the audience with instructions to applaud at the right moments.

When all was ready, the reading started. Generally the author himself read his work, though there were exceptions. (Pliny, for example, knew that he was bad at reading poetry; so although he read his speeches himself, he had his poems read by a freedman.) The writer, specially dressed for the occasion in a freshly laundered toga, stepped forward and delivered a short introduction (**praefātiō**) to his work, then sat to read the work itself. The recital might be continued on a second and third day, sometimes at the request of the audience.

Things did not always go smoothly at recitationes. The Emperor Claudius, when young, embarked on a series of readings from his own historical work, but disaster struck when an enormously fat man joined the audience and sat down on a flimsy bench, which collapsed beneath him; in the general mirth it became impossible for the reading to continue. Pliny records a more serious incident during the reign of Trajan. A historian, who had announced that he would continue his reading in a few days' time, was approached by a group of people who begged him not to read the next installment because they knew it would be dealing with some fairly recent events in which they had been concerned, and which they did not want read out in public. It is possible that the author concerned was the historian Tacitus, describing the past misdeeds of the Emperor Domitian and his associates. The historian granted the request and canceled the next installment of the reading. However, as Pliny pointed out, canceling the recitatio did not mean that the men's misdeeds would stay unknown: people would be all the more curious to read the history, in order to find out why the recitatio had been canceled.

Pliny, who gave **recitātiōnes** of his own work and also regularly attended those of other people, was very shocked at the frivolous way in which some members of the audience behaved: "Some of them loiter and linger outside the hall, and send their slaves in to find out how far the recitatio has gotten; then, when the slaves report that the author has nearly finished his reading, they come in at last – and even then they don't always stay, but slip out before the end, some of them sheepishly and furtively, others boldly and brazenly."

Some Roman writers are very critical of recitationes. Seneca, for example, says that when the author says to the audience, "Shall I read some more?" they usually reply, "Yes, please do," but privately they are praying for the man to be struck dumb. Juvenal sarcastically includes recitationes among the dangers and disadvantages of life in Rome, together with fires and falling buildings. In fact, the work read out must have varied enormously in quality: occasional masterpieces, a sprinkling of good-to-middling work, and plenty of trash. A more serious criticism of recitationes is that they encouraged writers to think too much about impressing their audience. One author admitted: "Much of what I say is said not because it pleases me but because it will please my hearers."

However, in first-century Rome, when every copy of a book had to be produced individually by hand, recitationes filled a real need. They enabled the author to bring his work to the notice of many people without the expense and labor of creating large numbers of copies. Recitationes were also useful from the audience's point of view. It was far harder in Roman than in modern times to go into a bookstore, run one's eye over the titles and covers, sample the contents of a few likely-looking books, and make one's choice. The physical nature of a Roman book (see illustration on p.29) meant that there was no such thing as a cover; the title was printed not on a convenient part of the book but on a label attached to it, which was often lost; and the act of unrolling and reading a book, then rerolling it ready for the next reader, was so laborious that sampling and browsing were virtually impossible. The recitatio allowed the author to present his work to an audience conveniently, economically, and (if he was a good reader) attractively.

Words and Phrases Checklist

animadvertō, animadvertere, animadvertī, animadversus	*notice, take notice of*
arma, armōrum	*arms, weapons*
causa, causae	*reason, cause*
discipulus, discipulī	*student, pupil*
dōnō, dōnāre, dōnāvī, dōnātus	*give*
extrēmus, extrēma, extrēmum	*farthest*
fīnis, fīnis	*end*
ignis, ignis	*fire*
mīror, mīrārī, mīrātus sum	*admire, wonder at*
nē	*that . . . not, in order that . . . not*
niger, nigra, nigrum	*black*
offendō, offendere, offendī, offēnsus	*displease, offend*
pār, *gen.* paris	*equal*
plērīque, plēraeque, plēraque	*most, the majority*
praesēns, *gen.* praesentis	*present, ready*
praesertim	*especially*
praeter	*except*
recitō, recitāre, recitāvī, recitātus	*recite, read out*
regiō, regiōnis	*region*
tangō, tangere, tetigī, tāctus	*touch*
vacuus, vacua, vacuum	*empty*
vetus, *gen.* veteris	*old*

Word Search

Match each definition with one of the words given below.

disciple, evacuate, finite, ignite, inveterate, recital, tactile

1 . . . . .: a follower
2 . . . . .: limited; capable of being enclosed
3 . . . . .: long-established; habitual
4 . . . . .: used for or pertaining to touch
5 . . . . .: a narrative or musical performance of something memorized
6 . . . . .: to set fire to, kindle
7 . . . . .: to withdraw; to create a void

cōnsilium

Agricola, Calēdoniīs victīs, epistulam nūntiō dictat. in hāc epistulā Agricola victōriam Rōmānōrum Imperātōrī nūntiat.

"exercitus Rōmānus Calēdoniōs superāvit!"

Agricola dīcit exercitum Rōmānum Calēdoniōs superāvisse.

"multī hostēs periērunt, paucī effūgērunt."

Agricola dīcit multōs hostēs periisse, paucōs effūgisse.

"aliae gentēs nūntiōs iam mīsērunt quī pācem petant."

Agricola dīcit aliās gentēs nūntiōs mīsisse quī pācem petant.

epistula

Cn. Iūlius Agricola Domitiānō Imperātōrī salūtem dīcit.
septimus annus est, domine, ex quō pater tuus, dīvus Vespasiānus,
ad prōvinciam Britanniam mē mīsit, ut barbarōs superārem. tū
ipse, audītīs precibus meīs, iussistī Calēdoniōs quoque in populī
Rōmānī potestātem redigī. nunc tibi nūntiō exercitum Rōmānum   5
magnam victōriam rettulisse. bellum est cōnfectum; Calēdoniī sunt
victī.
    initiō huius aestātis, exercitus noster ad ultimās partēs Britanniae
pervēnit. hostēs, adventū nostrō cognitō, prope montem Graupium
sē ad proelium īnstrūxērunt. ibi mīlitēs nostrī, spē glōriae adductī,   10

in . . . potestātem redigī:
   in potestātem redigere   *bring under the control*
victōriam rettulisse:
   victōriam referre   *win a victory*
initiō: initium   *beginning*
aestātis: aestās   *summer*
proelium   *battle*

victōriam nōmine tuō dignam rettulērunt. nōn satis cōnstat quot hostēs perierint; sciō tamen paucissimōs effūgisse. explōrātōrēs meī affirmant nōnnūllōs superstitēs, salūte dēspērātā, etiam casās suās incendisse atque coniugēs līberōsque manū suā occīdisse.

dē bellō satis dīxī. nunc bellōrum causae tollendae sunt; nunc pāx firmanda est. omnibus eīs pepercī quī sē dēdidērunt. per tōtam prōvinciam centuriōnēs frūmentum ac tribūtum mollius exigere iussī sunt. ego ipse Britannōs hortātus sum ut templa, fora, domōs exstruant; fīliīs prīncipum persuāsī ut linguam Latīnam discant. mōrēs Rōmānī ā Britannīs iam adsūmuntur; ubīque aspiciuntur togae.

ūna cūra tamen mē sollicitat. timeō nē inquiēta sit Britannia, dum Hibernia īnsula in lībertāte manet. quod sī Hibernōs superāverimus, nōn modo pācem in Britanniā habēbimus, sed etiam magnās dīvitiās comparābimus; audiō enim ex mercātōribus metalla Hiberniae aurum multum continēre. equidem crēdō hanc īnsulam legiōne ūnā obtinērī posse. mīlitēs sunt parātī; signum Imperātōris alacriter exspectātur. valē.

satis cōnstat	*it is generally agreed*	sollicitat: sollicitāre	*worry*
affirmant: affirmāre	*declare*	timeō nē	*I am afraid that*
coniugēs: coniūnx	*wife*	inquiēta: inquiētus	*unsettled*
firmanda est: firmāre	*strengthen, establish*	quod sī	*but if*
pepercī: parcere	*spare*	aurum	*gold*
sē dēdidērunt: sē dēdere	*surrender,*	equidem	*I indeed*
	give oneself up	obtinērī: obtinēre	*hold*
tribūtum	*tribute, tax*		
mollius: molliter	*gently, leniently*	Cn. = Gnaeus	
adsūmuntur: adsūmere	*adopt*	Hibernia	*Ireland*

When you have read this, answer the questions at the end.

amīcī prīncipis

diē illūcēscente, complūrēs senātōrēs in aulam Domitiānī
conveniēbant. nam Domitiānus cōnsilium suum ad aulam arcessī
iusserat. senātōrēs, dum Imperātōrem exspectant, anxiī inter sē
colloquēbantur. in angulō ātriī L. Catullus Messālīnus, vir
maximae auctōritātis, cum Q. Vibiō Crispō, senātōre septuāgintā   5
annōs nātō, susurrābat.

Messālīnus: cūr adeō perturbāris, mī Crispe? nōn intellegō quārē
             anxius sīs.
Crispus: nōn sine causā perturbor. ego enim prīmus ā
             Domitiānō sententiam rogābor, quia cōnsulāris sum   10
             nātū maximus. at nisi sciam quārē Domitiānus nōs
             cōnsulere velit, sententiam bene meditātam prō-
             pōnere nōn poterō.
Messālīnus: difficile est mihi tē adiuvāre, mī amīce. nescio enim
             quārē Domitiānus nōs arcessīverit. aliī dīcunt   15
             nūntium ē Britanniā advēnisse; aliī putant Germānōs
             rebellāvisse; aliī crēdunt ministrōs Epaphrodītī
             coniūrātiōnem dēprehendisse. nōn tamen tibi tim-
             endum est; tū enim es senātor summae auctōritātis.
Crispus: id quod dīcis fortasse vērum est. nihilōminus mihi   20
             semper difficile est intellegere quāle respōnsum
             Domitiānus cupiat. sēnsūs enim vērōs dissimulāre

solet. sī tamen tū mē adiūveris, sēcūrus erō. vīsne, quicquid dīxerō, sententiam similem prōpōnere?

Messālīnus: minimē! perīculum mihi ipsī facere haudquāquam   25
volō. nihil dīcam priusquam Epaphrodītī sententiam audīverō.

Crispus: sed –

Messālīnus: tacē, mī amīce! adest Imperātor.

cōnsulāris	*ex-consul*	quicquid	*whatever*
meditātam: meditārī	*consider*	similem: similis	*similar*
dēprehendisse: dēprehendere	*discover*	Q. = Quīntus	
sēnsūs: sēnsus	*feeling*		

1 At what time of day does this conversation take place?
2 In lines 4–6, find two words or phrases which suggest that Crispus and Messalinus are anxious not to be overheard.
3 Why is Crispus agitated?
4 What three guesses have been made about Domitian's reason for calling this meeting?
5 What favor does Crispus ask from Messalinus? Is his request granted?
6 By what tactics does Messalinus hope to keep out of trouble at the meeting?

About the Language

1 Compare the following direct and indirect statements:

DIRECT STATEMENTS	INDIRECT STATEMENTS
"servus **fūgit**."	dominus crēdit servum **fūgisse**.
*"The slave **has fled**."*	*The master believes the slave **to have fled**.*
	Or, in more natural English:
	*The master believes that the slave **has fled**.*
"Rōmānī multa oppida **dēlēvērunt**."	audiō Rōmānōs multa oppida **dēlēvisse**.
*"The Romans **have destroyed** many towns."*	*I hear that the Romans **have destroyed** many towns.*

The Latin form of the verb in boldface is known as the *perfect active infinitive*.

2 Further examples:

1 scio servōs cēnam splendidam parāvisse.
2 "Rōmānī magnam victōriam rettulērunt."
3 in hāc epistulā Agricola nūntiat Rōmānōs magnam victōriam rettulisse.
4 clientēs putant patrōnum ex urbe discessisse.
5 "hostēs castra in rīpā flūminis posuērunt."
6 centuriō dīcit hostēs castra in rīpā flūminis posuisse.

3 Compare the perfect active infinitive with the perfect active indicative:

PERFECT ACTIVE INDICATIVE (1ST PERSON SINGULAR)		PERFECT ACTIVE INFINITIVE	
portāvī	*I have carried*	**portāvisse**	*to have carried*
docuī	*I have taught*	**docuisse**	*to have taught*
trāxī	*I have dragged*	**trāxisse**	*to have dragged*
audīvī	*I have heard*	**audīvisse**	*to have heard*

cōnsilium Domitiānī

I

dum senātōrēs anxiī inter sē colloquuntur, ingressus est Domitiānus vultū ita compositō ut nēmō intellegere posset utrum īrātus an laetus esset. eum sequēbātur Epaphrodītus, epistulam manū 5 tenēns.

Domitiānus, ā senātōribus salūtātus, "nūntius," inquit, "nōbīs epistulam modo attulit, ā Cn. Iūliō Agricolā missam. in hāc epistulā Agricola nūntiat exercitum 10 Rōmānum ad ultimās partēs Britanniae pervēnisse et magnam victōriam rettulisse. Epaphrodīte, epistulam recitā."

epistulā recitātā, Domitiānus, ad Crispum statim conversus,

modo *just now*

"quid," inquit, "dē hāc Agricolae epistulā putās? quid mihi   15
suādēs?"

Crispus diū tacēbat; superciliīs contractīs quasi
rem cōgitāret, oculōs humī dēfīxit. dēnique:
"moderātiōnem," inquit, "suādeō."
Domitiānus "breviter," inquit, "et commodē   20
locūtus es. tua tamen sententia amplius est
explicanda."

priusquam Crispus respondēret, A. Fabricius Vēientō, cēterīs
paulō audācior, interpellāvit. veritus tamen nē Domitiānum
offenderet, verbīs cōnsīderātīs ūsus est: 25

"cognōvimus, domine, Cn. Iūlium Agricolam
Calēdoniōs tandem superāvisse. ille tamen victōriā
nimis ēlātus est. Agricola crēdit īnsulam Hiberniam
facile occupārī posse; ego autem puto Agricolam
longē errāre; Hibernī enim et ferōcēs et validī sunti. sī   30
cōpiae nostrae trāns mare in Hiberniam ductae
erunt, magnō perīculō obicientur."

deinde P. Cornēlius Fuscus, praefectus praetōriō:

"Aulus Fabricius," inquit, "commodē et sapienter
nōs admonuit. mīsit Agricola nōbīs litterās verbō   35
speciōsās, rē vērā inānēs. iste septem annōs
Britanniae iam praeest. mīsitne tribūtum septem
annōrum ad aerārium? minimē! ipse in suā epistulā
dīcit centuriōnēs iussōs esse tribūtum mollius
exigere; addit sē fīliīs prīncipum persuāsisse ut   40

linguam Latīnam discant. scīlicet Agricola putat sē ad Britanniam
missum esse ut puerōs doceat, nōn ut barbarōs superet! revocandus
est Agricola et pūniendus."

tum M'. Acīlius Glabriō, hāc sententiā incēnsus,

"Cornēlī Fusce," inquit, "tū sine causā   45
Agricolam culpās. eī invidēs quod rēs tam
splendidās gessit. equidem valdē gaudeō
Calēdoniōs superātōs esse. sī Hibernia quoque
ab Agricolā victa erit, tōtam Britanniam in
potestāte nostrā habēbimus. absurdum est   50
Agricolam revocāre priusquam Britannōs
omnīnō superet! quis nostrōrum ducum est

melior quam Agricola? quis dignior est triumphō?"

suādēs: suādēre	*advise, suggest*	ēlātus	*excited, carried away*
superciliīs contractīs:			
supercilia contrahere	*draw eyebrows together, frown*	cōpiae	*forces*
		obicientur: obicere	*put in the way of, expose to*
moderātiōnem: moderātiō	*moderation, caution*		
breviter	*briefly*	praefectus praetōriō	*commander of the praetorian guard*
commodē	*appropriately*		
amplius	*more fully*	sapienter	*wisely*
veritus: verērī	*be afraid, fear*	speciōsās: speciōsus	*impressive*
cōnsīderātīs:		aerārium	*treasury*
cōnsīderātus	*careful, well-considered*	A. = Aulus	
ūsus est: ūtī	*use*		

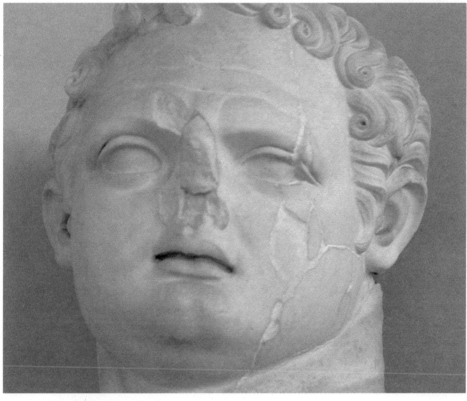

Head of Domitian from Ephesus.

II

cēterī, audāciā Glabriōnis obstupefactī, oculōs in Imperātōrem dēfīxōs tenēbant nec quicquam dīcere audēbant. ille tamen nec verbō nec vultū sēnsūs ostendit. deinde Epaphrodītus, ad Glabriōnem conversus,

"num comparās," inquit, "hanc inānem Agricolae victōriam cum rēbus splendidīs ab Imperātōre nostrō gestīs? nōnne audīvistī, mī Glabriō, Imperātōrem ipsum proximō annō multa mīlia Germānōrum superāvisse? num oblītus es prīncipēs Germānōs, catēnīs vīnctōs, per viās urbis in triumphō dēductōs esse?"

tum Messālīnus, simulatque haec Epaphrodītī verba audīvit, occāsiōne ūsus,

"satis cōnstat," inquit, "nūllōs hostēs ferōciōrēs Germānīs esse, nūllum ducem Domitiānō Augustō esse meliōrem. scīmus etiam Agricolam in prōvinciā septem annōs mānsisse. ipse affirmat tam fidēlēs sibi legiōnēs esse ut ad Hiberniam sine timōre prōgredī possit. cavendum est nōbīs! quis nostrum Sulpiciī Galbae exemplum nescit? omnēs meminimus Galbam quoque prōvinciam septem annōs rēxisse; omnēs scīmus Galbam cupīdine imperiī corruptum esse; scīmus Galbam dēnique bellum contrā patriam suam gessisse. num Glabriō cupit Agricolam fierī Imperātōrem? Agricola, meā sententiā, revocandus, laudandus, tollendus est."

Glabriō nihil respondit. nōn enim dubitābat quīn Imperātōrem graviter offendisset. Messālīnī sententiam cēterī senātōrēs alacriter secūtī sunt.

Domitiānus autem nūllum signum dedit neque odiī neque gaudiī neque invidiae. cōnsiliō tandem dīmissō, in ātriō sōlus mānsit; multa in animō dē Glabriōne atque Agricolā volvēbat.

nec . . . nec	*neither . . . nor*	cupīdine:		
comparās:		cupīdō	*desire*	
comparāre	*compare*	imperiī:		
gestīs: gerere	*achieve*	imperium	*power*	
proximō:		fierī	*to become, to be made*	
proximus	*last*	nōn . . .		
oblītus es:		dubitābat quīn	*did not doubt that*	
oblīvīscī	*forget*	odiī: odium	*hatred*	
meminimus	*we remember*	invidiae:		
rēxisse:		invidia	*jealousy, envy*	
regere	*rule*			

About the Language

1 Compare the following direct and indirect statements:

DIRECT STATEMENTS	INDIRECT STATEMENTS
"captīvī *lībertī sunt*."	scio captīvōs **līberātōs esse**.
*"The prisoners **have been freed**."*	*I know the prisoners **to have been freed**.*
	Or, in more natural English:
	*I know that the prisoners **have been freed**.*
"nūntius ab Agricolā **missus est**."	Domitiānus dīcit nūntium ab Agricolā **missum esse**.
*"A messenger **has been sent** by Agricola."*	*Domitian says that a messenger **has been sent** by Agricola.*

The Latin form of the verb in boldface is known as the *perfect passive infinitive*.

2 Further examples:

1 "multī Calēdoniī occīsī sunt."
2 in hāc epistulā Agricola nūntiat multōs Calēdoniōs occīsōs esse.
3 audiō lībertātem omnibus servīs datam esse.
4 nauta crēdit quattuor nāvēs tempestāte dēlētās esse.
5 "templum novum in forō exstrūctum est."
6 mercātōrēs dīcunt templum novum in forō exstrūctum esse.

3 Compare the perfect passive infinitive with the perfect passive indicative:

PERFECT PASSIVE INDICATIVE (1ST PERSON SINGULAR)	PERFECT PASSIVE INFINITIVE
portātus sum *I have been carried*	**portātus esse** *to have been carried*
doctus sum *I have been taught*	**doctus esse** *to have been taught*
tractus sum *I have been dragged*	**tractus esse** *to have been dragged*
audītus sum *I have been heard*	**audītus esse** *to have been heard*

Notice that the perfect passive infinitive contains a participle (**portātus**, etc.) which changes its ending in the usual way to agree with the noun it describes:

videō **cibum parātum** esse. *I see that **the food has been prepared**.*
videō **victimās parātās** esse. *I see that **the victims have been prepared**.*

Practicing the Language

1 Complete each sentence with the most suitable word from the list below, and then translate.

audītō, exstruēbātur, prōcēdere, imperātōrī, esset

1 in summō monte novum templum . . . . . .
2 nūntius, simulatque advēnit, ... epistulam trādidit.
3 strepitū . . . . ., cōnsul ē lectō surrēxit.
4 facile cognōvī quis auctor fraudis . . . . . .
5 putō pompam per forum iam . . . . . .

2 In each pair of sentences, translate sentence (a); then, with the help of pages 296–7 of the Language Information Section, express the same idea by completing the verb in sentence (b) with a passive form, and translate again.

For example: (a) senātōrēs Domitiānum timent.
              (b) Domitiānus ā senātōribus timē. . . .
Translated and completed, this becomes:
(a) senātōrēs **Domitiānum timent**.
   The senators **fear Domitian**.
(b) **Domitiānus** ā senātōribus *timētur*.
   Domitian is feared *by the senators*.

1a dux equitēs iam incitat.
1b equitēs ā duce iam incitā. . . .
2a exercitus noster oppidum mox dēlēbit.
2b oppidum ab exercitū nostrō mox dēlē. . . .

In sentences 3–6, nouns as well as verbs have to be completed. Refer if necessary to the table of nouns on pp.284–5.

3a multī cīvēs lūdōs spectābunt.
3b lūdī ā multīs cīv. . . spectā. . . .
4a puellae ātrium ōrnābant.
4b ātrium ā puell. . . ōrnā. . . .
5a puer victimās ad āram dūcēbat.
5b victimae ad āram ā puer. . . dūcē. . . .
6a mercātor servum accūsābat.
6b serv. . . ā mercātor. . . accūsā. . . .

3 Translate each sentence into Latin by selecting correctly from the list of Latin words.

1 *The enemy have been surrounded by our army.*

    hostēs   ad exercitum   nostrō   circumventus est

    hostibus   ab exercitū   noster   circumventī sunt

2 *A certain senator is trying to deceive you.*

    senātōrī   quīdam   tē   dēcipit   cōnātur

    senātor   quidem   tuī   dēcipere   cōnantur

3 *He was lying hidden, in order to hear the old men's conversation.*

    latēbat   ut   sermōnem   senem   audīvisset

    latuerat   nē   sermō   senum   audīret

4 *The same clients will be here tomorrow.*

    eōsdem   cliēns   crās   aderunt

    eīdem   clientēs   cotīdiē   aberunt

5 *The originator of the crime did not want to be seen in the forum.*

    auctor   scelerī   in forum   vidēre   volēbat

    auctōrem   sceleris   in forō   vidērī   nōlēbat

The Emperor's Council

Among the people who took part in the government of the empire were the members of the emperor's **cōnsilium** (*council*), often referred to as **amīcī** (*friends*) of the emperor.

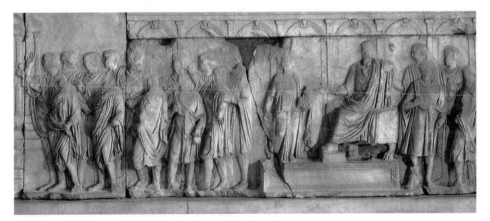

Relief showing an emperor dealing with affairs of state, seated on a platform in front of the Basilica Julia in the forum.

The consilium did not have a fixed membership; it was simply made up of those people whom the emperor invited to advise him on any particular occasion. Some men were regularly asked to meetings of the consilium; others were asked occasionally. Many would be experienced and distinguished men of senatorial rank, who had reached the top of the career described on pp.47–9. Some men of equestrian rank might also be invited, such as the commander of the praetorian guard. When there was a change of emperor, the new emperor usually invited some new members to meetings of the consilium, but also found it convenient to continue using some of the previous emperor's advisers. Often the new emperor had himself been a member of the previous emperor's consilium.

The matters on which the emperor asked his consilium for advice were naturally varied. The consilium might, for example, be summoned in moments of crisis, such as the discovery of a conspiracy against the emperor's life; or it might be consulted on the delicate question: "Who should be the emperor's heir?" Sometimes the emperor would want advice about military decisions or foreign affairs. The story on pp.00–0, in which Domitian asks his advisers about Agricola's letter from Britain, is fictitious, but it would not have been odd or unusual for the consilium to have discussed such a question.

However, the commonest task of the amici was to advise the emperor while he was administering the law. For example, they might join him when he was hearing an appeal by a condemned prisoner, or settling a property dispute between two or more parties. After the people concerned had stated their case, the emperor would ask for the **sententia** (*opinion*) of each member of the consilium in turn; he would then perhaps retire for further thought, and finally announce his decision. He was not bound to follow the majority opinion of the consilium, and could even ignore their advice altogether. In theory, the amici were free to give their opinions firmly and frankly; but under some emperors, it could be dangerous to speak one's mind too openly. During Domitian's reign a number of amici used their position as members of the consilium to increase their own power and to spread rumors and accusations about their enemies; it was said of one man that he could "slit a throat with a whisper."

Some of the cases which were heard by the Emperor Trajan are described by Pliny, who was sometimes invited to Trajan's consilium. They include a charge of adultery against a military tribune's wife and a centurion, and a dispute in a small town in Gaul where the local mayor had abolished the town's annual games. It is clear from Pliny's account that even quite trivial cases were sometimes referred to the emperor for decision; most Roman emperors were kept very busy, and needed the help of their amici in order to cope with the workload.

The Senatorial Career

Most of the amici taking part in the discussion on pages 39–42 would have successfully followed a career known as the senatorial **cursus honōrum** (*series of honors* or *ladder of promotion*) in which members of the senatorial class competed with each other for official positions in the Roman government. These official positions were arranged in a fixed order, and as a man worked his way through them, his responsibilities and status steadily increased. Some positions were compulsory, so that a man who had not held a particular position was not allowed to proceed to a higher one, except by special favor of the emperor. The most successful men got to the top, and the rest dropped out at various points along the way.

Some officials, such as the consuls, were chosen by the emperor; others were elected by the senate. Even in those positions where the choice was made by the senate, the emperor still had great influence, since he could "recommend" particular candidates to the senate for election.

By the time of Domitian, the most important stages in the cursus honorum were as follows:

1 **vīgintīvir** Every year twenty young men were chosen as vīgintīvirī, and served for a year in Rome as junior officials, assisting with such tasks as the management of the law courts and prisons, and the minting of the Roman coinage.

2 **tribūnus mīlitum** In the following year, each of the young men went abroad on military service as an officer in a legion.

3 **quaestor** On returning to Rome, a man who wanted to progress further in the cursus honorum would aim at the quaestorship. This position involved the management of sums of public money and was usually (but not always) held in Rome. It lasted for one year and was important because it qualified a man for entry into the senate, which met regularly to discuss and decide government business.

4 **tribūnus plēbis** or **aedīlis** After a compulsory interval of a year, an ex-quaestor who wanted further promotion had a choice. He might aim

to become one of the ten tribunes of the people, whose original responsibility had been to act as helpers and advisers of the common people (**plēbs**), but whose tasks had been greatly reduced by the time of Domitian. Alternatively, he could try to be appointed as one of the six aediles, who were responsible for the upkeep of public buildings, baths, sewers, and roads.

5 **praetor** The chief task of the praetors was to run the Roman law courts. A man who had held the praetorship also became eligible for certain important positions abroad; for example, he might command a legion, or govern one of the twenty-eight provinces (except for the ten most important ones). Governorships of provinces were normally held for a period of three years.

6 **cōnsul** The highest position in the cursus honorum was the consulship. There were only two consuls at any one time, but they changed at intervals during the year. They presided at meetings of the senate, and had a general responsibility for supervising government business. The ablest ex-consuls became governors of the ten most important provinces; some men, through exceptional ability or by favor of the emperor, achieved further distinctions, including second or even third consulships.

This system enabled the emperor to see who the ablest men were. It also showed him whether a man had any special skills which made him suitable for a particular job or province. For example, Agricola was a good soldier, while Pliny was an expert in financial matters; each man was given work that offered him opportunities to use his particular gifts.

Relief showing a magistrate in a mule-drawn chariot, followed by men carrying his sedan-chair.

The careers of both men are given overleaf. They differ from each other in the early stages, because Agricola did not become a vigintivir and had an unusually long period as a military tribune. Pliny's career looks somewhat fuller than Agricola's; this is partly because Agricola's governorship of Britain was exceptionally lengthy, and partly because Agricola held no position at all between his recall from Britain and his death.

Pliny's cursus.

Career of Agricola		Career of Pliny	
A.D.		A.D.	
40	birth	61 or 62	birth
		?82	vigintivir (with responsibility for one of the law courts)
58–61	tribunus militum in Britain	?83	tribunus militum in Syria
64	quaestor in Asia	90	quaestor in Rome
66	tribunus plebis	92	tribunus plebis
68	praetor	93	praetor
70–73	legatus legionis XX in Britain	94–96	praefectus aerarii militaris (in charge of the military treasury)
74–76	legatus (governor) of Aquitania	98–100	praefectus aerarii Saturni (in charge of the treasury of the god Saturn)
77	consul	100	consul
78–84	legatus (governor) of Britain	103	augur (honorary priesthood, held simultaneously with other positions)
		104–106	curator Tiberis (responsible for flood precautions, drainage, etc., in connection with river Tiber)
		109–111	legatus Augusti in Bithynia (a special governorship by personal appointment of the emperor)
93	death	111	death

Several of the above dates, especially in the early part of Pliny's career, are approximate and uncertain.

Words and Phrases Checklist

amplius	*more fully, at greater length*
amplissimus, amplissima, amplissimum	*very great*
aurum, aurī	*gold*
complūrēs, complūra	*several*
coniūnx, coniugis	*wife*
culpō, culpāre, culpāvī	*blame*
dignus, digna, dignum	*worthy, appropriate*
discō, discere, didicī	*learn*
dīvus, dīvī	*god*
dubitō, dubitāre, dubitāvī	*hesitate, doubt*
ēlātus, ēlāta, ēlātum	*excited, carried away*
exemplum, exemplī	*example*
exercitus, exercitūs	*army*
fīō, fierī, factus sum	*become, be made*
inānis, ināne	*empty, meaningless*

incēnsus, incēnsa, incēnsum	*inflamed, angered*
initium, initiī	*beginning*
invideō, invidēre, invīdī	*envy, be jealous of*
oblīvīscor, oblīvīscī, oblītus sum	*forget*
occāsiō, occāsiōnis	*opportunity*
odium, odiī	*hatred*
patria, patriae	*country, homeland*
paulō	*a little*
perturbō, perturbāre, perturbāvī, perturbātus	*alarm, disturb*
praefectus, praefectī	*commander*
proelium, proeliī	*battle*
revocō, revocāre, revocāvī, revocātus	*recall, call back*
satis cōnstat	*it is generally agreed*
sēcūrus, sēcūra, sēcūrum	*without a care*
validus, valida, validum	*strong*

Word Search

Match each definition with one of the words given below.

conjugal, culpability, invidious, irrevocable, oblivion, odious, validate

1 . . . . .: offensive; tending to rouse envy
2 . . . . .: to substantiate, confirm
3 . . . . .: forgetfulness
4 . . . . .: blameworthiness
5 . . . . .: hateful, nasty
6 . . . . .: beyond recall; unchangeable
7 . . . . .: pertaining to marriage or a marital relationship

Scene from the Aldobrandine fresco.

nūptiae

When you have read this, answer the questions at the end.

Imperātōris sententia

*in aulā Domitiānī, T. Flāvius Clēmēns, adfīnis Imperātōris, cum Domitiānō
anxius colloquitur. Clēmēns semper cum Imperātōre cōnsentīre solet; verētur
enim nē idem sibi accidat ac frātrī Sabīnō, quī iussū Imperātōris occīsus est.*

Domitiānus: decōrum est mihi, mī Clēmēns, līberōs tuōs honōrāre, nōn modo propter adfīnitātem nostram sed   5
etiam ob virtūtēs tuās. ego ipse, ut scīs, līberōs nūllōs
habeō quī imperium post mortem meam exerceant.
cōnstituī igitur fīliōs tuōs in familiam meam ascīscere.
cognōmina "Domitiānum" et "Vespasiānum" eīs
dabō; praetereā rhētorem nōtissimum eīs praeficiam,   10
M. Fabium Quīntiliānum. prō certō habeō
Quīntiliānum eōs optimē doctūrum esse.

"prō certō habeō Quīntiliānum eōs optimē doctūrum esse." (lines 11–12)

Clēmēns:	grātiās maximās tibi agō, domine, quod fīliōs meōs tantō honōre afficis. ego semper –	
Domitiānus:	satis! pauca nunc dē Pōllā, fīliā tuā, loquī velim. crēdō Pōllam quattuordecim annōs iam nātam esse. nōnne nōs oportet eam in mātrimōnium collocāre?	15
Clēmēns:	domine –	
Domitiānus:	virum quendam cognōvī quī omnī modō fīliā tuā dignus est. commendō tibi Sparsum, senātōrem summae virtūtis quī magnās dīvitiās possidet.	20
Clēmēns:	at, domine, iam quīnquāgintā annōs nātus est Sparsus.	
Domitiānus:	ita vērō! aetāte flōret.	
Clēmēns:	at bis mātrimōniō iūnctus, utramque uxōrem repudiāvit.	25
Domitiānus:	prō certō habeō eum numquam cognātam Imperātōris repudiātūrum esse. quid multa? prōmittō Sparsum tibi generum grātissimum futūrum esse. haec est sententia mea, quam sī dissēnseris mūtābō. sed prius tibi explicandum erit quārē dissentiās.	30

adfinis	*relative, relation by marriage*	quattuordecim	*fourteen*
idem . . . ac	*the same . . . as*	aetāte flōret: aetāte flōrēre	*be in the prime of life*
propter	*because of*	bis	*twice*
adfīnitātem: adfīnitās	*relationship*	iūnctus: iungere	*join*
virtūtēs: virtūs	*virtue*	utramque: uterque	*each, both*
ascīscere	*adopt*	repudiāvit: repudiāre	*divorce*
cognōmina: cognōmen	*surname, additional name*	cognātam: cognāta	*relative (by birth)*
		quid multa?	*in brief, in short*
		generum: gener	*son-in-law*
		grātissimum: grātus	*acceptable, pleasing*
afficis: afficere	*treat*	mūtābō: mūtāre	*change*

1 Why does Clemens normally take care to agree with Domitian?

2 What decision has Domitian made about Clemens' sons? What arrangements does he intend to make about their education?

3 How old is Clemens' daughter Polla? What suggestion does Domitian make about her? Whom does he recommend, and on what grounds?

4 What two doubts does Clemens raise about Sparsus' suitability? How does Domitian answer Clemens' second objection?

Pōlla

Pōlla, fīlia Clēmentis, fortūnam suam queritur; māter Flāvia eam cōnsōlārī cōnātur.

Pōlla: quam crūdēlis est pater meus, quī mē Sparsō nūbere iussit! quid faciam, māter? num putās mē illī senī umquam nūptūram esse? scīs mē alium quendam amāre.   5

Flāvia: ō dēliciae, nōlī lacrimāre! dūra est vīta; necesse est pārēre eīs quī nōs regunt. crēdō tamen Sparsum satis grātum et benignum tibi futūrum esse.

Pōlla: cūr mē ita dēcipis? scīs eum esse senem minimae venustātis. scīs etiam eum duās uxōrēs iam repudiāvisse. at   10 tū, māter, sententiā Imperātōris nimis movēris; nihil dē mē cūrās, nihil dē Helvidiō quem amō.

Flāvia: num tū tam audāx es ut istī amōrī indulgeās? iste enim Helvidius gentī nostrae est odiō. num oblīta es avum eius, cum Vespasiānum Imperātōrem graviter offendisset, in   15 exiliō occīsum esse? prūdēns estō, mea Pōlla! melius est cēdere quam frūstrā resistere.

queritur: querī	*lament, complain about*
cōnsōlārī	*console*
nūbere	*marry*
quid faciam?	*what am I to do?*
venustātis: venustās	*charm*
movēris: movēre	*move, influence*
avum: avus	*grandfather*
estō!	*be!*

About the Language

1 Compare the following direct and indirect statements:

DIRECT STATEMENTS
"hostēs mox **pugnābunt**."

"*The enemy **will fight** soon.*"

INDIRECT STATEMENTS
crēdimus hostēs mox **pugnātūrōs esse**.

*We believe the enemy **to be going to fight** soon.*
　　Or, in more natural English:
*We believe that the enemy **will fight** soon.*

"senex **perībit**."

"*The old man **will die**.*"

medicus dīcit senem **peritūrum esse**.

*The doctor says that the old man **will die**.*

The form of the verb in boldface is known as the *future active infinitive*.

2 Further examples:

1 "multī āthlētae crās certābunt."
2 praecō dīcit multōs āthlētās crās certātūrōs esse.
3 "novae cōpiae mox advenient."
4 mīlitēs crēdunt novās cōpiās mox adventūrās esse.
5 suspicor ancillam tē dēceptūram esse.
6 mercātor spērat sē magnās dīvitiās comparātūrum esse.

3 Study the way in which the future active infinitive is formed:

portātūrus esse　　*to be about to carry*
doctūrus esse　　　*to be about to teach*
tractūrus esse　　　*to be about to drag*
audītūrus esse　　　*to be about to hear*

Notice that the future active infinitive contains a participle (**portātūrus**, etc.) which changes its ending in the usual way to agree with the noun it describes:

puer dīcit **imperātōrem** crās **reventūrum** esse.
*The boy says that **the emperor will return** tomorrow.*

puer dīcit **fēminās** crās **reventūrās** esse.
*The boy says that **the women will return** tomorrow.*

prīdiē nūptiārum

nox est. crās nūptiae Pōllae et Sparsī celebrābuntur. Pōlla per hortum patris errat. crēdit sē sōlam esse; ignōrat Helvidium advēnisse. quī, hortum clam ingressus, Pōllam querentem audit; inter arborēs immōtus stat.

Pōlla: quid faciam? Helvidius trēs diēs iam abest, neque sciō
    quō ille ierit. intereā tōtam domum nostram videō ad   5
    nūptiās meās odiōsās parārī. ō Helvidī, ēripe mē ex hīs
    malīs!

Helvidius: *(subitō prōgressus)* id libenter faciam. nēmō mē
    prohibēbit.

Pōlla: *(gaudiō et pavōre commōta)* Helvidī! quō modō hūc vēnistī?   10
    sī hīc captus eris, interficiēris. fuge, priusquam pater
    meus tē cōnspiciat!

Helvidius: fugiam vērō, sed nōn sine tē. fuge mēcum, mea Pōlla! tē
    ex hīs malīs ēripiam, sīcut tū modo precābāris.

Pōlla: quō modō fugere possumus? tū ipse scīs mē semper   15
    custōdīrī. nūptiās crāstinās nūllō modō vītāre possum.
    parentēs, Imperātor, lēgēs mē iubent cōguntque Sparsō
    nūbere.

Helvidius: minimē, mea Pōlla! tibi polliceor mē prius moritūrum
    esse quam ille senex tē uxōrem dūcat. nōbīs procul ex   20
    hāc urbe fugiendum est, ubi parentēs tuī nōs invenīre
    numquam poterunt.

Pōlla: distrahor et excrucior. hūc amor, illūc pietās mē trahit.

Helvidius: nōlī timēre, mea Pōlla! tē numquam dēseram, semper
    servābō.   25

Flāvia: *(intrā domum)* Pōlla! Pōlla, ubi es?

Pōlla: ēheu! ā mātre vocor. brevissimē dīcendum est. Helvidī,
    tē amō, tē semper amābō. fugere tamen tēcum nōn
    possum. crās mē Sparsus uxōrem dūcet.

Helvidius: *(īrā et amōre incēnsus)* ēn haec fidēs! simulās tē mē amāre,   30
    rē vērā Sparsum amās. scīlicet dīvitiīs Sparsī corrupta
    es; amōrem meum floccī nōn facis.

Flāvia: *(intus)* Pōlla! ubi es, Pōlla?

Pōlla: *(dolōre paene cōnfecta)* audī, mī Helvidī! haec ultima verba
    tibi dīcō; nōn enim puto mē umquam tē iterum vīsūram   35
    esse. crās ego Sparsō nūbam. est mihi nūlla spēs fugae.

sed quamquam Sparsus mē uxōrem ductūrus est, mī
Helvidī, iūrō mē tē sōlum amāre, iūrō mē . . . . .
(*lacrimās retinēre frūstrā cōnātur.*) tē semper amātūram . . .
amātū. . . . (*vōx dēficit.*)   40

Helvidius: (*dextram Pōllae arripiēns*) Pōlla, dēsine mē tēque torquēre!
deōs testor Sparsum tē uxōrem numquam ductūrum
esse. cōnfīde mihi, mea Pōlla! (*Pōllam ardenter amplexus,
Helvidius abit.*)

Pōlla: (*Helvidium abeuntem spectāns, utrum spēret an timeat incerta*)   45
dea Fortūna, servā eum!

prīdiē	*the day before*	pietās	*duty*
ignōrat: ignōrāre	*not known (about)*	intrā	*inside*
errat: errāre	*wander*	simulās: simulāre	*pretend*
odiōsās: odiōsus	*hateful*	iūrō: iūrāre	*swear*
ēripe: ēripere	*rescue, snatch away*	dēficit: dēficere	*fail, die away*
crāstinās: crāstinus	*tomorrow's*	dextram: dextra	*right hand*
prius . . . quam	*before*	arripiēns: arripere	*seize*
uxōrem dūcat: uxōrem dūcere	*take as a wife, marry*	testor: testārī	*call to witness*
distrahor: distrahere	*tear apart, tear in two*	ardenter	*passionately*
hūc . . . illūc	*this way . . . that way, one way . . . another way*		

Lovers from an Arretine vase.

About the Language

1 In Stage 36, you met the *present* subjunctive:

incertus sum ubi Mārtiālis hodiē **recitet**.
*I am not sure where Martial **is reciting** today.*

2 In Stages 37 and 38, you have met sentences like these:

cognōscere volō quārē Domitiānus nōs **arcessīverit**.
*I want to find out why Domitian **has sent** for us.*

Pōlla nescit quō Helvidius **ierit**.
*Polla does not know where Helvidius **has gone**.*

The Latin form of the verb in boldface is the *perfect* tense of the subjunctive.

3 Further examples:

1 centuriō scīre vult num senex equum cōnspexerit.
2 crās cognōscēmus quantam pecūniam parentēs nōbīs relīquerint.
3 uxor mē cotīdiē rogat quārē hanc vīllam ēmerim.
4 incertī sumus utrum nautae perierint an superfuerint.

4 Compare the perfect subjunctive with the perfect indicative:

PERFECT INDICATIVE	PERFECT SUBJUNCTIVE
portāvī	**portāverim**
portāvistī	**portāverīs**
portāvit	**portāverit**
portāvimus	**portāverīmus**
portāvistis	**portāverītis**
portāvērunt	**portāverint**

Perfect subjunctive forms of **doceō**, **trahō**, **capiō**, and **audiō** are given on p.000 of the Language Information Section.

5 For the perfect subjunctive of irregular verbs, see p.308.

cōnfarreātiō

I

diēs nūptiārum adest. Pōlla, veste nūptiālī ōrnāta, in cubiculō suō stat. māter eam īnspicit.

Flāvia: nunc tē verte ad mē, Pōlla! flammeum firmē capitī superpositum est? (*Pōllam lacrimāre videt.*) ō mea fīlia, tibi haud lacrimandum est; diē   5 nūptiārum nōn decet lacrimāre.

servus Clēmentis: (*ingressus*) domina, iussus sum vōs ad sacrificium arcessere. dominus meus dīcit victimam iam ēlēctam esse, haruspicēs parātōs adstāre. nūntius quoque iam adest, quī dīcit Imper-   10 ātōrem, comitante Sparsō, mox adventūrum esse.

Wedding ceremony, second century A.D.

Sparsus Pōllam perturbārī animadvertit. (line 29)

Flāvia: bene! nūntiā dominō tuō nōs statim ad ātrium
                              prōcessūrās esse.

Flāvia et Pōlla ad ātrium prōcēdunt, ubi multī amīcī, familiārēs, clientēs iam   15
adsunt. subitō ingēns clāmor oritur:
spectātōrēs: euge! euge! advenit Imperātor! advenit Sparsus!
intrat Sparsus, multīs comitantibus servīs; deinde ingreditur ipse Domitiānus.
spectātōrēs: fēlīciter! fēlīciter!
Pōlla, valdē commōta, ad Sparsum dūcitur; dextrās sollemniter iungunt. deinde   20
Domitiānus, ut Pontifex Maximus, prōcēdit ut sacrificium Iovī faciat.
Sparsus: cōnsīde in hāc sellā, mea Pōlla. tē fessam esse
                              videō. mox pontifex fīnem sacrificiīs faciet. tum
                              uxor mea fīēs.

in mediō ātriō, victima ā Domitiānō sacrificātur; precēs Iovī et Iūnōnī   25
offeruntur. Pōlla tamen adeō perturbātur ut precēs audīre vix possit; in mente
eius haerent illa verba ultima Helvidiī: "deōs testor Sparsum tē uxōrem
numquam ductūrum esse."

                                          Stage 38

Sparsus:	(*Pōllam perturbārī animadvertit.*) nōlī timēre, mea
	Pōlla! nunc cōnfarreātiōnem celebrābimus.	30
Domitiānus:	(*lībum farreum Sparsō et Pōllae offerēns*) hoc lībum
	sacrum cōnsūmite!

Sparsus et Pōlla, iuxtā sedentēs, lībum sacrum cōnsūmunt.

Domitiānus:	tacēte vōs omnēs, quī adestis! (*omnēs tacent.*) vōbīs
	prōnūntiō hanc virginem nunc in manum huius	35
	virī convenīre.
spectātōrēs:	fēlīciter! fēlīciter!
Domitiānus:	nunc cēdite testibus! tabulae nūptiālēs
	signandae sunt.

tabulīs signātīs, omnēs ad triclīnium prōcēdunt, ubi cēna sūmptuōsa parāta est.   40

cōnfarreātiō	*wedding ceremony*	lībum farreum	*cake made from*
nūptiālī: nūptiālis	*wedding*		*grain*
flammeum	*veil*	iuxtā	*side by side*
superpositum est:		in manum . . . convenīre	*pass into*
superpōnere	*place on*		*the hands of*
oritur: orīrī	*rise up*	tabulae nūptiālēs	*marriage contract,*
fēlīciter!	*good luck!*		*marriage tablets*
Iūnōnī: Iūnō	*Juno (goddess of*		
	marriage)		

II

sōle occidente, servī Pōllam domum Sparsī dēdūcere parant, ubi Sparsus, prior profectus, iam eam exspectat. chorus musicōrum carmen nūptiāle cantāre incipit.

chorus: ō Hymēn Hymenaee, iō!
      ō Hymēn Hymenaee!

Flāvia: mea fīlia, sīc tē amplexa valedīcō. valē, mea Pōlla, valē!   5
servī, ut mōs est, puellam ā mātre abripiunt. duo puerī, quī facēs ardentēs ferunt, Pōllam forās dēdūcunt. magnā comitante turbā pompa per viās prōgreditur.

chorus: tollite, ō puerī, facēs!
      flammeum videō venīre.   10
      ō Hymēn Hymenaee, iō!
      ō Hymēn Hymenaee!

occidente: occidere	*set*	abripiunt: abripere	*tear away from*
prior	*earlier*	forās	*out of the house*
chorus	*chorus, choir*	Hymēn	
musicōrum: musicus	*musician*	Hymenaee: Hymenaeus	} *Hymen (god of weddings)*

III

tandem pompa domum Sparsī, flōribus ōrnātam, advenit. quī, domō ēgressus,
Pōllam ita appellat:

Sparsus: siste! quis es tū? quō nōmine hūc venīs?

Pōlla: ubi tū Gāius, ibi ego Gāia.

quibus verbīs sollemnibus dictīs, Pōlla postēs iānuae oleō unguit, ut   5
fascinātiōnem āvertat. Sparsus intereā, prō iānuā stāns, grātulātiōnēs iocōsque
spectātōrum accipit. subitō magnus clāmor audītur; ē mediā turbā ērumpit
iuvenis, pugiōne armātus, quī praeceps in Sparsum ruit.

iuvenis: nunc morere, Sparse! (*Sparsum ferōciter pugiōne petit; quī*
          tamen, ācriter sē dēfendēns, bracchium iuvenis prēnsāre cōnātur.)   10

Sparsus: subvenīte! subvenīte!

ingēns strepitus oritur; servī accurrunt; aliī spectātōrēs Sparsō servīsque
subveniunt, aliī immōtī et obstupefactī stant. Pōlla tamen, iuvene Helvidiō
agnitō, pallēscit.

Sparsus: (*cum Helvidiō lūctāns*) festīnāte! festīnāte!   15

servī Helvidium, tandem comprehēnsum, firmē retinent.

Sparsus: (*exclāmāns*) illum agnōscō! Helvidius est, homō
         īnfestissimus gentī Imperātōris. eum ad Imperātōrem
         dūcite! prō certō habeō Domitiānum eī poenam

aptissimam excōgitātūrum esse. (*Pōlla horrēscit.*) nōlī   20
timēre, mea Pōlla! ille iuvenis īnsānus numquam iterum
nōs vexābit. nunc tibi tempus est domum tuam novam
intrāre.

Sparsus Pōllam bracchiīs tollit ut eam trāns līmen portet. Helvidius ad
Domitiānum abdūcitur.   25

siste: sistere	*stop, halt*
sollemnibus: sollemnis	*solemn, traditional*
postēs: postis	*post, doorpost*
fascinātiōnem: fascinātiō	*the evil eye*
āvertat: āvertere	*avert, turn away*
morere!	*die!*
lūctāns: lūctārī	*struggle*
excōgitātūrum esse: excōgitāre	*invent, think up*
horrēscit: horrēscere	*shudder*
abdūcitur: abdūcere	*lead away*

About the Language

1 In Stage 34, you met the *present passive infinitive*, used in sentences like
these:

laudārī volō.   sonitus **audīrī** nōn poterat.
*I want **to be praised**.*   *The sound was unable **to be heard**.*
                                     Or, in more natural English:
                                     *The sound could not **be heard**.*

2 In Stage 38, you have met the present passive infinitive in indirect
statements. Study the following examples:

DIRECT STATEMENTS   INDIRECT STATEMENTS
"vexāris."   scio tē **vexārī**.
"*You are annoyed*."   *I know you **to be annoyed**.*
                                 Or, in more natural English:
                                 *I know that you **are annoyed**.*

"multī mīlitēs *exercentur*."   audīmus multōs mīlitēs
                                    exercērī.
"*Many soldiers are being trained*."   *We hear that many soldiers **are being**
                                          trained.*

3 Further examples:

1 prō certō habeō cēnam splendidam in vīllā iam parārī.
2 "cōnsul morbō gravī afflīgitur."
3 senātōrēs dīcunt cōnsulem morbō gravī afflīgī.
4 "fīliī Clēmentis ā Quīntiliānō cotīdiē docentur."
5 audiō fīliōs Clēmentis ā Quīntiliānō cotīdiē docērī.
6 amīcus meus affirmat tē numquam ab Imperātōre laudārī, saepe culpārī.

Practicing the Language

1 Complete each sentence with the right word and then translate.

1 cognōscere volō ubi fīlius vester . . . . . . (habitet, habitent)
2 tot gemmās ēmistī ut nūllam pecūniam iam . . . . . . (habeās, habeātis)
3 strēnuē labōrāmus ut opus ante lūcem . . . . . . (perficiam, perficiāmus)
4 tam fessus est amīcus meus ut longius prōgredī nōn . . . . . . (possit, possint)
5 senex nescit quārē puerī in viā . . . . . . (clāmēs, clāmet, clāment)
6 iterum vōs rogō num hunc virum . . . . . . (agnōscam, agnōscās, agnōscātis)

2 In each pair of sentences, translate sentence (a); then change it from a direct statement to an indirect statement by completing sentence (b), and translate again.

For example: (a) puer labōrat.
                (b) dominus putat puerum labōr. . . .
Translated and completed, this becomes:
(a) puer **labōrat**.   *The boy **is working**.*
(b) dominus putat puerum **labōrāre**.
    *The master thinks that the boy **is working**.*

1a multae vīllae ardent!
1b senex dīcit multās vīllās ard. . . .
2a centuriō appropinquat.
2b mīlitēs putant centuriōnem appropinqu. . . .

3a medicus tēcum cōnsentit.
3b crēdō medicum tēcum cōnsent. . . .

In sentences 4–6, nouns as well as verbs have to be completed. Refer if necessary to the table of nouns on pp.284–5 of the Language Information Section.

4a rēx in illā aulā habitat.
4b sciō rēg. . . in illā aulā habit. . . .
5a servī iam dormiunt.
5b fūr crēdit serv. . . iam dorm. . . .
6a puella dentēs nigrōs habet.
6b Mārtiālis dīcit puell. . . dentēs nigrōs hab. . . .

Marriage

The average age for a Roman girl to marry was about thirteen or fourteen; men usually married in their late teens or early twenties. If the husband had been married previously, like Sparsus in the story on pp.61–5, there might be a wide age-gap between him and his wife.

The husband was normally chosen for the girl by her father or guardian. The law laid down that if the girl did not agree to the marriage, it could not take place; but probably few daughters would have found it very easy to defy their father's wishes. The girl's father would also negotiate with the family of her future husband about the **dōs** (*dowry*); this was a payment (in money or property or both) made by the bride's family to the husband.

At the ceremony of betrothal or engagement (**spōnsālia**), the husband-to-be made a promise of marriage, and the father of the bride promised on his daughter's behalf; gifts were exchanged, and a ring was placed on the third finger of the girl's left hand, as in many countries nowadays. (There was a widespread belief that a nerve ran directly from this finger to the heart.) Family and friends were present as witnesses, and the ceremony was followed by a party.

Under Roman law, there were two different sorts of marriage. In the first, which was known as marriage **cum manū**, the bride ceased to be a member of her father's family and passed completely into the **manus** (*control*) of her husband; any property she possessed became her

Gold betrothal ring.

husband's, and although he could divorce her, she could not divorce him. A couple could enter into marriage "cum manū" in various ways; one was by an ancient ceremony known as **cōnfarreātiō**, in which the bride and bridegroom together ate a sacred cake made of **far** (*grain*). This ceremony was only used by a few aristocratic families and had almost died out by the end of the first century A.D.; however, on pages 61–5, Polla is married by confarreatio because she is related to the Emperor Domitian.

By the first century, marriage "cum manū" had become far less common than the other type of marriage, which was known as marriage **sine manū**. In this type of marriage, the bride did not pass into the "manus" of her husband; legally, she was still regarded as a member of her father's family (even though she was now no longer living with them); she could possess property of her own and she could divorce her husband. It was very easy for a couple to enter into marriage "sine manū"; all they needed to do was to live together after declaring their intention of being man and wife.

Whether a couple became married "cum manū" or "sine manū," they usually celebrated their wedding with some of the many customs and ceremonies that were traditional among the Romans. Some of these are mentioned in the story of Polla's wedding to Sparsus on pages 61–5: the flame-colored bridal veil (**flammeum**); the symbolic joining of hands (**iūnctiō dextrārum**); the sacrifice; the signing of the marriage contract, witnessed by the wedding guests; the wedding feast at the bride's house; the ancient custom of pretending to pull the bride away from her mother by force; the torch-lit procession to the bridegroom's house; the wedding song; the traditional words spoken by the bride to her husband, **ubi tū Gāius, ego Gāia** (*Where you are Gaius, I am Gaia*); the anointing of the doorposts with oil; the calling out of noisy greetings and coarse jokes to the bridegroom; and the custom of carrying the bride across the threshold of her new home. Other traditions and ceremonies included the careful arrangement of the bride's hair, parted with the point of a spear and then divided into six plaits; the presentation of fire and water by the bridegroom to the bride; and the undressing of the bride by **mātrōnae ūnivirae** (*women who had had only one husband*).

The chief purpose of Roman marriage, as stated in marriage contracts and in various laws, was the obvious one of producing and bringing up children. The Roman government often made efforts to encourage marriage and large families; in particular, the Emperor Augustus introduced a law which imposed penalties on those who remained unmarried (for example, by forbidding them to receive legacies) and offered special privileges to married couples who produced three or more children. Nevertheless, the birthrate in Rome dropped steadily from the second century B.C. onwards, especially among the senatorial class.

A Roman wife had fewer legal rights than her husband. In the eyes of the law, she was under the authority of either her husband or her father (or guardian), depending on whether she had been married **cum manū** or **sine manū**. She could not vote in elections, take an active part in public or political life, sit on a jury, or plead in court. But in some ways a first-century Roman wife had more freedom than women in other countries, and enjoyed a higher status than they did. She was not restricted to the home, but could visit friends, go to the theater and the baths, and accompany her husband to dinner-parties (unlike the women of classical Athens, for example). Her traditional day-to-day task – the running of the household – was regarded by most Romans as important and valuable, and a woman could gain great prestige and respect for the way in which this task was carried out; in many aristocratic and wealthy families, running the house was a highly complicated and demanding job, involving the management and supervision of a large number of domestic slaves.

Our knowledge of Roman married life is very incomplete. We know far less about the poor than about the wealthy upper classes, and have hardly any information on married life from the wife's point of view, because most of what is written in Latin was written by men. Nevertheless, the writings of Roman authors include many references to married life. The following letter, for example, was written by Pliny to his wife Calpurnia:

"The strength of my longing for you is hard to believe. Love is the reason above all others. Another reason is that we are not used to being separated. I spend most of the night awake, picturing you. During the

Relief showing a mother suckling her child while the father looks on.

day, at the times when I usually come to see you, my feet guide me to your room; then I turn sadly back, sick at heart."

Calpurnia was Pliny's third wife. At the time of their marriage, she was about fifteen and he was in his early forties. In another letter, he writes about Calpurnia:

"From sheer affection for me, she keeps copies of my speeches, reads them over and over again and even learns them by heart. She is tortured with worry when I appear in court, and is overcome with relief when the case is over. Whenever I give a recitatio, she listens from behind a curtain waiting eagerly for comments of approval. As for my poems, she sets them to music and sings them, taught not by some musician but by love, the best of teachers."

A letter by Cicero describes an incident from the stormy relationship between his brother Quintus and Quintus' wife Pomponia:

"We lunched at Arcanum. When we got there, Quintus said, perfectly politely, 'Pomponia, you invite the women, and I'll get the slave-boys together.' There was nothing to be cross about, as far as I could see, either in what he said or the way he said it. But, within everyone's hearing, Pomponia replied, "What, me? I'm only a stranger here!" – just because Quintus had made arrangements for the lunch without telling her, I suppose. "There you are," said Quintus. "That's what I have to put up with every day." I hid my feelings. We sat down to eat; she refused to join us. Quintus sent her some food from the table; she sent it back. The following day, Quintus told me that she had refused to sleep with him and had continued to behave as she had done at lunch-time."

Roman married life is also referred to in numerous inscriptions, set up in memory of husbands and wives. For example:

"Here lies Amymone, wife of Marcus, most good and most beautiful, wool-spinner, dutiful, modest, careful, chaste, home-loving."

"I have written these words so that those who read them may realize how much we loved each other."

"To my dearest wife, with whom I lived two years, six months, three days, ten hours."

Words and Phrases Checklist

aptus, apta, aptum	*suitable*
bracchium, bracchiī	*arm*
certus, certa, certum	*certain, infallible*
prō certō habēre	*know for certain*
clam	*secretly, in private*
commendō, commendāre,	
commendāvī, commendātus	*recommend*
cōnfectus, cōnfecta, cōnfectum	*worn out, exhausted, overcome*
cōpiae, cōpiārum	*forces*
dextra, dextrae	*right hand*
ēripiō, ēripere, ēripuī, ēreptus	*rescue, snatch away*
familia, familiae	*household*
grātus, grāta, grātum	*acceptable, pleasing*
ignōrō, ignōrāre, ignōrāvī	*not know about*
intrā	*inside*
iungō, iungere, iūnxī, iūnctus	*join*
lēx, lēgis	*law*
līmen, līminis	*threshold, doorway*
mēns, mentis	*mind*
nūbō, nūbere, nūpsī	*marry*
orior, orīrī, ortus sum	*rise, arise*
polliceor, pollicērī,	
pollicitus sum	*promise*
pontifex, pontificis	*priest*
prohibeō, prohibēre,	
prohibuī, prohibitus	*prevent*
queror, querī, questus sum	*lament, complain about*
regō, regere, rēxī, rēctus	*rule*
trāns	*across*
unguō, unguere, ūnxī, ūnctus	*anoint, smear*
vereor, verērī, veritus sum	*be afraid, fear*
vērō	*indeed*
vestis, vestis	*clothing*

Word Search

Match each definition with one of the words given below.

aptitude, subliminal, legislation, pontificate, querulous, revere, unguent

1 . . . . .: below the level of conscious perception, subconscious
2 . . . . .: to hold in awe, venerate
3 . . . . .: facility for learning; appropriateness
4 . . . . .: the act of lawmaking
5 . . . . .: an ointment
6 . . . . .: to speak in a pompous or self-important manner
7 . . . . .: peevish, fretful

studia

hērēdēs prīncipis

I

in aulā Imperātōris, duo puerī in studiīs litterārum sunt occupātī. alter puer,
Titus nōmine, fābulam nārrāre cōnātur; alter, nōmine Pūblius, intentē audit.
adest quoque puerōrum rhētor, M. Fabius Quīntiliānus. Titus Pūbliusque,
fīliī Clēmentis ac frātrēs Pōllae, nūper hērēdēs Imperātōris factī sunt.

Titus: (*fābulam nārrāns*) deinde Iuppiter, rēx deōrum, 5
sceleribus hominum valdē offēnsus, genus mortāle
dēlēre cōnstituit. prīmō eī placuit dē caelō fulmina
spargere, quae tōtam terram cremārent. haesitāvit
tamen Iuppiter. "sī enim," sibi inquit, "flammae ad
caelum ā terrā ascenderint, nōnne nōs deī ipsī 10
eōdem ignī cremābimur?" dīversam ergō poenam
impōnere māluit; nimbōs ingentēs dē caelō
dēmittere cōnstituit ut genus mortāle dīluviō
perderet.

"bonā causā perturbāmur." (line 27)

Titō nārrante, iānua subitō aperitur. ingreditur Epaphrodītus. puerī anxiī inter   15
sē aspiciunt; Quīntiliānus, cui Epaphrodītus odiō est, nihilōminus eum cōmiter
salūtat.

Quīntiliānus: libenter tē vidēmus, Epaphro –

Epaphrodītus: (*interpellāns*) salvēte, puerī. salvē tū, M. Fabī. hūc
              missus sum ut mandāta prīncipis nūntiem. prīnceps   20
              vōbīs imperat ut ad sē quam celerrimē contendātis.

Quīntiliānus: verba tua, mī Epaphrodīte, nōn intellegō. cūr nōs
              ad Imperātōrem arcessimur?

Epaphrodītus, nūllō respōnsō datō, puerōs Quīntiliānumque per aulam ad
Imperātōris tablīnum dūcit. puerī, timōre commōtī, extrā tablīnum haesitant.   25

Quīntiliānus: (*timōrem suum dissimulāns*) cūr perturbāminī, puerī?

Pūblius: bonā causā perturbāmur. Imperātor enim nōs sine
              dubiō castīgābit vel pūniet.

Quīntiliānus: nimis timidus es, Pūblī. sī prūdenter vōs gesseritis,
              neque castīgābiminī neque pūniēminī.   30

studiīs: studium	*study*
litterārum: litterae	*literature*
genus mortāle	*the human race*
fulmina: fulmen	*thunderbolt*
cremārent: cremāre	*burn, destroy by fire*
dīversam: dīversus	*different*
nimbōs: nimbus	*rain-cloud*
dīluviō: dīluvium	*flood*
perderet: perdere	*destroy*
prūdenter	*prudently, sensibly*
vōs gesseritis: sē gerere	*behave, conduct oneself*

II

Quīntiliānus et puerī, tablīnum ingressī, Domitiānum ad mēnsam sedentem muscāsque stilō cōnfīgere temptantem inveniunt. Domitiānus neque respicit neque quicquam dīcit. puerī pallēscunt.

Domitiānus: (*tandem respiciēns*) nōlīte timēre, puerī. vōs nōn pūnitūrus sum – nisi mihi displicueritis. (*muscam*   5 *aliam cōnfīgit; dēnique, stilō dēpositō, puerōs subitō interrogat:*) quam diū discipulī M. Fabiī iam estis?

Titus: (*haesitāns*) d-duōs mēnsēs, domine.

Domitiānus: nōbīs ergō tempus est cognōscere quid didiceritis. (*ad Pūblium repente conversus*) Pūblī, quid heri   10 docēbāminī?

Pūblius: versūs quōsdam legēbāmus, domine, quōs Ovidius poēta dē illō dīluviō fābulōsō composuit.

Domitiānus: Ovidius? fācundus vērō erat ille poēta. meritō tamen ex Ītaliā relēgātus est; nam nōn modo vītam   15 impūram ēgit sed etiam prīncipem offendit. (*Epaphrodītus rīdet.*) itaque, versibus Ovidiānīs heri lēctīs, quid hodiē facitis?

Pūblius: hodiē cōnāmur eandem fābulam verbīs nostrīs atque ōrātiōne solūtā nārrāre.   20

Quīntiliānus: ubi tū nōs arcessīvistī, domine, Titus dē īrā Iovis nārrātūrus erat.

Domitiānus: fābula scīlicet aptissima! eam audīre velim. Tite, nārrātiōnem tuam renovā!

Titus: (*fābulam cūnctanter renovāns*) Iu-Iuppiter igitur   25 Aquilōnem in ca-cavernīs Aeoliīs inclūsit, et Notum līberāvit. quī madidīs ālīs ēvolāvit; ba-barba nimbīs

muscās: musca	*fly*
cōnfīgere	*stab, skewer*
respicit: respicere	*look up*
displicueritis: displicēre	*displease*
didiceritis: discere	*learn*
repente	*suddenly*
fābulōsō: fābulōsus	*legendary, famous*
fācundus	*fluent, eloquent*
meritō	*deservedly, rightly*
Ovidiānīs: Ovidiānus	*of Ovid*
ōrātiōne solūtā: ōrātiō solūta	*prose speech (i.e. instead of verse)*
nārrātiōnem: nārrātiō	*narration*
cūnctanter	*slowly, hesitantly*
cavernīs: caverna	*cave, cavern*
inclūsit: inclūdere	*shut up*

gravābātur, undae dē capillīs fluēbant. simulatque
Notus ēvolāvit, nimbī dēnsī ex aethere cum ingentī
fragōre effūsī sunt. sed tanta erat Iovis īra ut   30
imbribus caelī contentus nōn esset; auxilium ergō ā
frātre Neptūnō petīvit. quī cum terram tridente
percussisset, illa valdē tremuit viamque patefēcit ubi
undae fluerent. statim flūmina ingentia per campōs
apertōs ruēbant.   35

Domitiānus: satis nārrāvistī, Tite. nunc tū, Pūblī, nārrātiōnem
             excipe.

Pūblius: iamque inter mare et tellūrem nūllum discrīmen
             erat; mare ubīque erat, neque ūlla lītora habēbat.
             hominēs exitium effugere cōnābantur. aliī montēs   40
             ascendērunt; aliī, in nāvibus sedentēs, per agrōs illōs
             rēmigāvērunt quōs nūper arābant; hic suprā segetēs
             aut tēcta vīllārum mersārum nāvigāvit; ille in
             summīs arboribus piscēs invēnit. lupī inter ovēs
             natābant; leōnēs fulvī undīs vehēbantur. avēs,   45
             postquam terram diū quaerēbant ubi cōnsistere
             possent, tandem in mare fessīs ālīs dēcidērunt.
             capellae gracilēs –

Pūbliō hoc nārrantī Domitiānus manū significat ut dēsistat. diū tacet, puerīs
anxiīs exspectantibus; tandem loquitur.   50

gravābātur: gravāre	*load, weigh down*
imbribus: imber	*rain*
tridente: tridēns	*trident*
campōs: campus	*plain*
excipe: excipere	*take over*
tellūrem: tellūs	*land, earth*
discrīmen	*boundary, dividing line*
rēmigāvērunt: rēmigāre	*row*
arābant: arāre	*plow*
hic . . . ille	*this man . . . that man, one*
	man . . . another man
suprā	*over, on top of*
aut	*or*
mersārum: mergere	*submerge*
piscēs: piscis	*fish*
ovēs: ovis	*sheep*
fulvī: fulvus	*tawny, light brown*
capellae: capella	*she-goat*
gracilēs: gracilis	*graceful*
causās . . . dīxeritis:	*plead a case*
causam dīcere	

Fresco of Ovid.

| Domitiānus: | fortūnātī estis, Pūblī ac Tite; nam, ut decet prīncipis hērēdēs, ab optimō rhētore docēminī, quī optima exempla vōbīs prōposuit. sī vōs, puerī, causās vestrās tam fācundē dīxeritis quam Ovidius versūs composuit, saepe victōrēs ē basilicā discēdētis; ab omnibus laudābiminī. | 55 |
| Titus: | (*timōre iam dēpositō*) nōnne ūna rēs tē fallit, domine? nōs sumus hērēdēs tuī; nōnne igitur nōs, cum causās nostrās dīxerimus, nōn saepe sed semper victōrēs discēdēmus et ab omnibus laudābimur? | 60 |

Quīntiliānus ērubēscit. Domitiānus, audāciā Titī obstupefactus, nihil dīcit. tandem, rīdēns vel rīsum simulāns, puerōs rhētoremque dīmittit; deinde, stilō resūmptō, muscās iterum captāre incipit.

fācundē	*fluently, eloquently*
fallit: fallere	*escape notice of, slip by*
resūmptō: resūmere	*pick up again*
captāre	*try to catch*

Aeoliīs: Aeolius	*Aeolian*
Notum: Notus	*South Wind*
Neptūnō: Neptūnus	*Neptune (god of the sea)*

"ab omnibus laudābiminī." (lines 55–6)

About the Language

1 Study the following examples:

"hērēdēs prīncipis" nunc **appellāmur**.
We are now *called* "heirs of the emperor."

cavēte, cīvēs! ab hostibus **dēcipiminī**.
Be careful, citizens! **You are being fooled** *by the enemy.*

The Latin words in boldtype are passive forms of the 1st and 2nd persons plural.

2 Compare the active and passive forms of the 1st person plural:

	ACTIVE	PASSIVE
PRESENT	**portāmus**	**portāmur**
	we carry	*we are carried*
FUTURE	**portābimus**	**portābimur**
	we shall carry	*we shall be carried*
IMPERFECT	**portābāmus**	**portābāmur**
	we were carrying	*we were being carried*

Further examples:

1 superāmur, superābimur, superābāmur; monēmur, monēbimur, monēbāmur.
2 iubēmur, invītāmur, pūnīmur; servābimur, prohibēbimur, salūtābimur; dūcēbāmur, laudābāmur, terrēbāmur.

3 Compare the active and passive forms of the 2nd person plural:

	ACTIVE	PASSIVE
PRESENT	**portātis**	**portāminī**
	you carry	*you are carried*
FUTURE	**portābitis**	**portābiminī**
	you will carry	*you will be carried*
IMPERFECT	**portābātis**	**portābāminī**
	you were carrying	*you were being carried*

Further examples:

1 docēminī, docēbiminī, docēbāminī; laudāminī, laudābiminī, laudābāminī.
2 incitāminī, mittiminī, monēminī; rogābiminī, iubēbiminī; audiēbāminī, superābāminī.

4 Further examples of 1st and 2nd person plural forms:

1 ā clientibus nostrīs cotīdiē salūtāmur.
2 hodiē dērīdēminī; crās honōrābiminī.
3 ab omnibus comitibus dēserēbāmur.
4 terrēmur, terrēminī; culpābimur, culpābiminī; mittēbāmur, mittēbāminī.

5 Compare the passive forms in paragraphs 1 and 2 with the forms of the deponent verb **cōnor**:

PRESENT	**cōnāmur**	*we try*	**cōnāminī**	*you try*
FUTURE	**cōnābimur**	*we shall try*	**cōnābiminī**	*you will try*
IMPERFECT	**cōnābāmur**	*we were trying*	**cōnābāminī**	*you were trying*

Further examples of 1st and 2nd person plural forms of deponent verbs:

1 ubi vōs proficīscēbāminī, nōs regrediēbāmur.
2 templum ipsum mox cōnspicābimur.
3 loquimur, loquiminī; pollicēbimur, pollicēbiminī; precābāmur, precābāminī.

The story of the flood, told by Publius and Titus on pages 74–8 above, is based on the following lines written by the poet Ovid. When you have read them, answer the questions at the end. At the start of the extract, the god Jupiter is about to punish the human race for its wickedness.

versūs Ovidiānī

iamque erat in <u>tōtās</u> sparsūrus fulmina <u>terrās</u>*:
sed timuit, nē forte <u>sacer</u> tot ab ignibus <u>aethēr</u>
conciperet flammās, <u>longusque</u> ardēsceret <u>axis</u>.
<u>poena</u> placet <u>dīversa</u>, genus mortāle sub undīs
perdere et ex <u>omnī</u> nimbōs dēmittere <u>caelō</u>.   5

---

* Some noun-and-adjective phrases, in which an adjective is separated by one word or more from the noun which it describes, have been underlined.

Statue of Poseidon.

conciperet flammās:	
concipere flammās	*burst into flames*
ardēsceret: ardēscere	*catch fire, blaze up*
axis	*(arched) vault of heaven*

prōtinus Aeoliīs Aquilōnem claudit in antrīs.
ēmittitque Notum; madidīs Notus ēvolat ālīs;
barba gravis nimbīs, cānīs fluit unda capillīs.
fit fragor; hinc dēnsī funduntur ab aethere nimbī.

nec caelō contenta suō est Iovis īra, sed illum   10
caeruleus frāter iuvat auxiliāribus undīs.
ipse tridente suō terram percussit, at illa
intremuit mōtūque viās patefēcit aquārum.
exspatiāta ruunt per apertōs flūmina campōs.

iamque mare et tellūs nūllum discrīmen habēbant: 15
omnia pontus erant, dēerant quoque lītora pontō.
occupat hic collem, cumbā sedet alter aduncā
et dūcit rēmōs illīc, ubi nūper arābat;
ille suprā segetēs aut mersae culmina vīllae
nāvigat, hic summā piscem dēprendit in ulmō.   20

nat lupus inter ovēs, fulvōs vehit unda leōnēs,
quaesītīsque diū terrīs, ubi sistere possit,
in mare lassātīs volucris vaga dēcidit ālīs.
et, modo quā gracilēs grāmen carpsēre capellae,
nunc ibi dēfōrmēs pōnunt sua corpora phōcae.   25

antrīs: antrum	cave	illīc	there, in that place
cānīs: cānus	white	culmina: culmen	roof
fit: fierī	be made, occur	ulmō: ulmus	elm-tree
hinc	then, next	nat: nāre	swim
caeruleus	from the deep blue sea	lassātīs: lassāre	tire, weary
iuvat: iuvāre	help, assist	volucris	bird
auxiliāribus: auxiliāris	additional	vaga: vagus	wandering
intremuit: intremere	shake	quā	where
exspatiāta: exspatiārī	extend, spread out	grāmen	grass
pontus	sea	carpsēre =	chew, nibble, crop
dēerant: dēesse	be lacking, be missing	carpsērunt: carpere	
collem: collis	hill	dēfōrmēs: dēfōrmis	ugly, inelegant
cumbā: cumba	boat	phōcae: phōca	seal
aduncā: aduncus	curved		

1 How did Jupiter at first intend to punish the human race? Why did he change his mind?
2 What action does Jupiter take in line 6 and the beginning of line 7 (prōtinus . . . Notum)? Why?
3 What happened when Neptune struck the earth with his trident?

4 Which detail or incident in lines 17–23 do you find you can picture most vividly?
5 Which word in line 25 is used by Ovid to contrast with "gracilēs" in line 24?
6 Which seems to you to be the better description of Ovid's account: "serious" or "light-hearted"? Why?

About the Language

1 In Stage 36, you met verse sentences like this:

exigis ut **nostrōs** dōnem tibi, Tucca, **libellōs**.
*You demand that I should give you **my books**, Tucca.*

The adjective **nostrōs** is separated from the noun which it describes (**libellōs**).

2 In Stage 39, you have met sentences in which one noun-and-adjective phrase is followed by another:

caeruleus frāter iuvat **auxiliāribus undīs**.
His brother from the deep blue sea *helps him* **with additional waves**.

Further examples:

1 *arbore* sub *magnā* **parva** latēbat **avis**.
2 *vertice* dē *summō* **liquidōs** mōns ēvomit **ignēs**.

liquidōs: liquidus *liquid*
ēvomit: ēvomere *spit out, spew out*

Study the pattern formed by the pairs of noun-and-adjective phrases in each of the above sentences. Similar patterns are often formed in English verses by rhymes at the ends of lines. For example:

> The panther is like a *leopard*,
> Except it hasn't been *peppered*.
> Should you behold a panther **crouch**,
> Prepare to say **Ouch**.
> Better yet, if called by a **panther**,
> Don't **anther**.
>
> (*Ogden Nash*)

3 You have also met sentences in which one noun-and-adjective phrase is placed inside another one:

nunc ibi **dēfōrmēs** pōnunt *sua corpora* **phōcae.**
*Now the **ugly seals** rest their bodies there.*

Further examples:

1 in **mediōs** vēnit *iuvenis fortissimus* **hostēs.**
2 cōnstitit ante **oculōs** *pulchra puella* **meōs.**

Compare the arrangement of the noun-and-adjective phrases in the above sentences with the arrangement of the rhyming lines in such verses as the following:

Then he climbed the tower of the Old North **church,**
By the wooden stairs, with stealthy *tread,*
To the belfry-chamber *overhead,*
And startled the pigeons from their **perch**.

(Henry Wadsworth Longfellow)

4 In each of the following examples, pick out the Latin adjectives and say which nouns they are describing:

1 aure meā ventī murmura rauca sonant.
The hoarse murmurs of the wind sound in my ear.
2 iam nova prōgeniēs caelō dēmittitur altō. (*Vergil*)
Now a new generation is being sent down from high heaven.
3 nōn fuit ingeniō Fāma maligna meō. (*Ovid*)
Fame has not been unkind to my talent.
4 agna lupōs audit circum stabula alta frementēs. (*Ovid*)
The lamb hears the wolves howling around the tall sheepfolds.
5 atque opere in mediō laetus cantābat arātor.
And the happy plowman was singing in the middle of his work.
6 vincuntur mollī pectora dūra prece. (*Tibullus*)
Hard hearts are won over by soft prayer.

5 Translate the following examples:

1 *A cry for help*:
at puer īnfēlīx mediīs clāmābat in undīs.
2 *An echo*:
reddēbant nōmen concava saxa meum.

3 *Travel plans*:

nunc mare per longum mea cōgitat īre puella. (*Propertius*)

4 *Evening*:

maiōrēsque cadunt altīs dē montibus umbrae. (*Vergil*)

concava: concavus *hollow*

Pick out the adjectives in each example, and say which nouns they are describing.

Practicing the Language

1 Study the form and meaning of each of the following verbs and nouns and give the meaning of the untranslated words:

nōmināre	*nominate, name*	nōmen	*name*
volvere	*turn, roll*	volūmen	*roll of papyrus, scroll*
certāre	*compete*	certāmen	
crīmināre	*accuse*	crīmen	
fluere		flūmen	
unguere	*anoint, smear*	unguentum	*ointment*
arguere	*prove, argue*	argūmentum	*proof, argument*
impedīre		impedīmentum	*hindrance, nuisance*
vestīre	*clothe, dress*	vestīmenta	
ōrnāre		ōrnāmentum	
torquēre		tormentum	

Match each of the following Latin nouns with the correct English translation:

Latin: blandīmentum, incitāmentum, cōnāmen, mūnīmentum, sōlāmen

English: *effort, flattery, encouragement, comfort, defense*

2 In each sentence, replace the noun in boldface with the correct form of the noun in parentheses, and then translate. Refer if necessary to the table of nouns on pp.284–5 of the Language Information Section; you may also need to consult pp.284–5 to find out the genitive singular of 3rd declension nouns, as a guide to forming the other cases.

1 subitō Pōlla **Flāviam** vīdit. (māter)
2 nūntius **senī** epistulam trādidit. (dominus)
3 senātōrēs ad aulam **Domitiānī** contendēbant. (imperātor)

4 iuvenis **Agricolae** tōtam rem nārrāvit. (dux)

5 ingēns multitūdō **Rōmānōrum** in amphitheātrō conveniēbat. (cīvis)

6 poēta **audītōribus** paucōs versūs recitāvit. (fēmina)

3 Complete each sentence with the right word and then translate.

1 fessus sum! cotīdiē ā centuriōne labōrāre . . . . . . (iubeor, teneor)

2 tū semper bene recitās; semper ā rhētore . . . . . . (parāris, laudāris)

3 nōlī dēspērāre, mī amīce! mox . . . . . . (spectāberis, līberāberis)

4 maximē gaudeō; crās enim ab Imperātōre . . . . . . (honōrābor, vituperābor)

5 cum in urbe habitārem, strepitū continuō . . . . . . (audiēbar, mittēbar, vexābar)

6 medicus tē sānāvit, ubi morbō gravī . . . . . . (afficiēbāris, dēcipiēbāris, dūcēbāris)

4 In each pair of sentences, translate sentence (a); then change it from a direct statement to an indirect statement by completing sentence (b), and translate again.

For example: (a) hostēs advēnērunt.

(b) nūntius dīcit hostēs advēn. . . .

Translated and completed, this becomes:

(a) hostēs **advēnērunt**.   *The enemy **have arrived**.*

(b) nūntius dīcit **hostēs advēnisse**.

*The messenger says that the enemy **have arrived**.*

In sentences 1–3, a perfect *active* infinitive is required. For examples of the way in which this infinitive is formed, see p.295, paragraph 5.

1a   Imperātor sententiam mūtāvit.

1b   cīvēs crēdunt Imperātōrem sententiam mūtāv. . . .

2a   nautae nāvem ingentem comparāvērunt.

2b   mercātor dīcit nautās nāvem ingentem comparāv. . . .

3a   fabrī mūrum optimē refēcērunt.

3b   putō fabr. . . mūrum optimē refēc. . . .

In sentences 4–6, a perfect *passive* infinitive is required. For examples of the way in which it is formed, see p.297, paragraph 3. Note that the first part of this infinitive (e.g. **parātus** in **parātus esse**) changes its ending to agree with the noun it describes.

For example: (a) epistulae missae sunt.
             (b) crēdō epistulās miss. . . . . . .
Translated and completed, this becomes:
  (a) epistulae **missae sunt**.   *The letters* **have been sent**.
  (b) crēdō epistulās **missās esse**.
     I believe that the letters **have been sent**.

4a victima ā pontifice ēlēcta est.
4b spectātōrēs putant victimam ā pontifice ēlēct. . . . . . .
5a multī amīcī ad cēnam vocātī sunt.
5b scio multōs amīcōs ad cēnam vocāt. . . . . . .
6a captīvus occīsus est.
6b mīlitēs dīcunt captīv. . . occīs. . . . . . .

Authors, Readers and Listeners

After a Roman writer had recited his work to his patron or friends, or to a wider audience at a recitatio, as decribed in Stage 36, he had to decide whether or not to make it available to the general public. If he decided to go ahead, his next step was to have several copies made. If he or his patron owned some sufficiently educated slaves, they might be asked to make copies for the author to distribute among his friends; or the author might offer his work to the booksellers, whose slaves would make a number of copies for sale to the public.

Most Roman booksellers had their shops in the Argiletum, a street which ran between the forum and the Subura. Books were fairly cheap; a small book of poems might cost 5 sesterces if it were an ordinary copy, 20 sesterces if it were a deluxe edition made of high-quality materials. After the work had been copied, all money from sales of the book belonged to the booksellers, not to the author. We do not know whether the booksellers ever paid anything to an author for letting them copy his work.

One result of these arrangements for copying and selling books was that there was no such thing in Rome as a professional writer; no author could hope to make a living from his work. Some of the people who wrote books were wealthy amateurs like Pliny, who made most of his money as a landowner and wrote as a hobby; others like Martial, depended on patrons for support.

Sometimes the emperor became an author's patron. For example, the poets Vergil and Horace were helped and encouraged first by the Emperor Augustus' friend Maecenas, and then by Augustus himself. Other authors, however, got into trouble with the emperor. Ovid, for instance, was sent into exile by Augustus because he had been involved in a mysterious scandal in the emperor's own family, and because he had written a poem entitled *Ars Amatoria* (*The Art of Love*), a witty and light-hearted guide for young men on the conduct of love affairs. The *Ars Amatoria* greatly displeased Augustus, who had introduced a number of laws for the encouragement of respectable marriage (see p.69), and Ovid was exiled to a distant part of the empire for the rest of his life. Under later emperors such as Domitian, it was safest for an author to publish nothing at all, or else to make flattering remarks about the emperor in his work, like Martial in the story on p.20 (lines 11–14).

Some works of Latin literature reached a wide public. For example, thousands of people saw the comic plays of Plautus when they were performed in the theater. But most Roman authors wrote for a small, highly educated group of readers who were familiar not only with Latin literature, but also with the literature of the Greeks.

Relief showing a rhetor and his students.

In this school, the students have high-backed chairs like the teacher, instead of the usual wooden benches. Notice the two partly-unrolled papyrus scrolls, the case of writing materials held by the right-hand boy, and the low platform for the teacher. Suggest a reason for the rather apologetic attitude of the right-hand boy.

Schoolboys like Publius and Titus in the story on pp.76–8 were introduced by their teachers to the study of both Greek and Roman authors. Quintilian, who wrote a book called *The Education of an Orator*, gives a long list of recommended authors, adding comments on each one. For example, he says that: "Ovid is light-hearted even on serious subjects, and too fond of his own cleverness, but parts of his work are excellent."

In this way, Latin literature played an important part in Roman education. Roman education, in turn, played an important part in the writing of Latin literature. Most Roman authors had received a thorough training from a rhetor, who taught them how to express themselves persuasively, how to choose words that would have maximum effect on an audience, and how to organize a speech in accordance with fixed rules. This training had a great influence on the way Latin literature was written.

The most important difference between Latin and modern literature is that modern literature (except drama) is usually written for silent reading, whereas Latin literature was normally written to be read aloud. Two reasons for this have been mentioned already: first, the easiest way for an author to tell the public about his work was to read it aloud to them; second, most authors had received a long training in public speaking when they were young, and this affected the way they wrote. There is also a third reason: when a Roman read a book, he normally read it aloud, even if he was reading it to himself. (Reading silently was unusual. Saint Augustine was amazed when he saw it done, and wrote a brief description of it: "cum legebat, oculi ducebantur per paginas et cor intellectum rimabatur, vox autem et lingua quiescebant." – "When he was reading, his eyes glided over the pages, and his heart searched out the meaning, but his voice and tongue were at rest.")

The fact that Latin literature was written for speaking aloud, and not for silent reading, made a great difference to the way Roman authors wrote. They expressed themselves in ways that would sound effective when heard, not just look effective when read. For example, suppose a Roman author wished to say, in the course of a story:

"*The unfortunate boy did not see the danger.*"

He might express this quite straightforwardly:

"puer īnfēlīx perīculum nōn vīdit."

But he might, especially in poetry, prefer a more dramatic way of expressing himself. For instance, he might address the character in the story as if he were physically present, and put a question to him:

"heu, puer īnfēlīx! nōnne perīculum vidēs?"
"Alas, unfortunate boy! Do you not see the danger?"

On the printed page, especially in English translation, this style of writing may sometimes appear rather overheated and exaggerated to a modern reader, but when read aloud in Latin the effect can be very different. To read Latin literature silently is like looking at the score of a piece of music: the reader gets some idea of what the piece is like, but it needs to be performed aloud for full effect.

Drawing (based on a relief) of a reader choosing a book from a shelf.

Words and Phrases Checklist

arbor, arboris	*tree*
aut	*or*
cadō, cadere, cecidī	*fall*
campus, campī	*plain*
capillī, capillōrum	*hair*
discrīmen, discrīminis	*(1) dividing line, (2) crisis*
ergō	*therefore*
fallō, fallere, fefellī, falsus	*deceive, escape notice of, slip by*
fragor, fragōris	*crash*
genus, generis	*race*
hinc	*from here, then, next*
iuvō, iuvāre, iūvī	*help, assist*
littera, litterae	*letter (of alphabet)*
litterae, litterārum	*letter, letters (correspondence)*

mēnsis, mēnsis	*month*					

mēnsis, mēnsis   *month*
ōrātiō, ōrātiōnis   *speech*
perdō, perdere, perdidī,
    perditus   *destroy*
respiciō, respicere, respexī   *look back, look up*
simulō, simulāre, simulāvī,
    simulātus   *pretend*
spargō, spargere, sparsī,
    sparsus   *scatter*
stilus, stilī   *pen (pointed stick for writing on wax tablet), stylus*
studium, studiī   *enthusiasm, study*
suprā   *over, on top of*
ūllus, ūlla, ūllum   *any*

Numbers

ūnus	*one*	sēdecim	*sixteen*	prīmus	*first*
duo	*two*	septendecim	*seventeen*	secundus	*second*
trēs	*three*	duodēvīgintī	*eighteen*	tertius	*third*
quattuor	*four*	ūndēvīgintī	*nineteen*	quārtus	*fourth*
quīnque	*five*			quīntus	*fifth*
sex	*six*	vīgintī	*twenty*	sextus	*sixth*
septem	*seven*	trīgintā	*thirty*	septimus	*seventh*
octō	*eight*	quadrāgintā	*forty*	octāvus	*eighth*
novem	*nine*	quīnquāgintā	*fifty*	nōnus	*ninth*
decem	*ten*	sexāgintā	*sixty*	decimus	*tenth*
		septuāgintā	*seventy*		
ūndecim	*eleven*	octōgintā	*eighty*		
duodecim	*twelve*	nōnāgintā	*ninety*		
trēdecim	*thirteen*	centum	*a hundred*		
quattuordecim	*fourteen*	ducentī	*two hundred*		
quīndecim	*fifteen*				

Word Search

Match each definition with one of the words given below.

arboreal, cadence, illiterate, discriminate, perdition, simulate, sparse

1 . . . . .: dispersed, thinly spread
2 . . . . .: to differentiate; divide
3 . . . . .: rhythm or meter; lowering, decline
4 . . . . .: treelike; pertaining to trees
5 . . . . .: unable to read or write
6 . . . . .: ruin, desolation
7 . . . . .: to imitate; feign

Stage 40

iūdicium

ingēns senātōrum multitūdō in cūriā convēnerat, ubi Gāius
Salvius Līberālis accūsābātur.

"multa scelera ā Salviō in Britanniā
     commissa sunt."

prīmus accūsātor affirmāvit
multa scelera ā Salviō in
Britanniā commissa esse.

"Salvius testāmentum rēgis fīnxit."

secundus accūsātor dīxit
Salvium testāmentum rēgis
fīnxisse.

"innocēns sum."

Salvius respondit sē innocentem
esse.

accūsātiō

I

septimō annō Domitiānī prīncipātūs, C. Salvius Līberālis, quī priōre annō fuerat cōnsul, ab Acīliō Glabriōne falsī accūsātus est. quā rē imprōvīsā perturbātus, amīcōs statim cōnsuluit utrum accūsātiōnem sperneret an dēfēnsiōnem susciperet.

Salviō rogantī quid esset agendum, aliī alia suādēbant. aliī   5
affirmāvērunt nūllum perīculum īnstāre quod Salvius vir magnae auctōritātis esset. aliī exīstimābant Domitiānī īram magis · timendam esse quam minās accūsantium; Salvium hortābantur ut ad Imperātōrem īret veniamque peteret. amīcīs dīversa mon-
entibus, Salvius exspectāre cōnstituit, dum cognōsceret quid   10
Domitiānus sentīret.

interim Glabriō et aliī accūsātōrēs causam parābant. eīs magnō auxiliō erat L. Mārcius Memor, haruspex et Salviī cliēns, quī, socius quondam scelerum Salviī, nunc ad eum prōdendum adductus est, spē praemiī vel metū poenārum. quō testimōniō ūsī,   15
accūsātōrēs rem ad Imperātōrem rettulērunt.

Domitiānus, ubi verba accūsātōrum audīvit, cautē sē gessit; bene enim sciēbat sē ipsum sceleribus Salviī implicārī. interim, ut sollicitūdinem dissimulāret et speciem amīcitiae praebēret, Salvium dōnīs honōrāvit, ad cēnam invītāvit, cōmiter excēpit.   20

accūsātiō	*accusation*	īnstāre	*be pressing, threaten*
prīncipātūs:		minās: minae	*threats*
prīncipātus	*principate, reign*	interim	*meanwhile*
falsī: falsum	*forgery*	accūsātōrēs:	
imprōvīsā:		accūsātor	*accuser, prosecutor*
imprōvīsus	*unexpected, unforeseen*	socius	*companion, partner*
sperneret: spernere	*ignore*	ad eum prōdendum	*to betray him*
dēfēnsiōnem:		testimōniō:	
dēfēnsiō	*defense*	testimōnium	*evidence*
aliī alia . . .	*different people . . .*	implicārī: implicāre	*implicate, involve*
	different things; some . . .	speciem: speciēs	*appearance*
	one thing, some . . . another		

II

Domitia autem, iam ab exiliō revocāta atque in favōrem Domitiānī restitūta, intentē ultiōnem adversus Salvium meditābātur. patefēcerat enim Myropnous pūmiliō Salvium auctōrem fuisse exiliī Domitiae, Paridis mortis. Myropnous nārrāvit Salvium domum Hateriī falsīs litterīs Domitiam Paridemque invītāvisse; Salviō 5 auctōre, Domitiam in īnsulā duōs annōs relēgātam esse, Paridem occīsum esse.

accūsātōrēs igitur, ā Domitiā incitātī, cognitiōnem senātūs poposcērunt. invidia Salviī aucta est suspīciōne Cogidubnum venēnō necātum esse. fāma praetereā vagābātur reliquiās corporum 10 in thermīs Aquārum Sūlis repertās esse, dēfīxiōnēs quoque nōmine Cogidubnī īnscrīptās. quibus audītīs, multī crēdēbant Salvium animās inimīcōrum dīs īnferīs cōnsecrāvisse.

tum dēmum Salvius perīculōsissima esse haec crīmina intellēxit. veste ergō mūtātā, domōs circumiit amīcōrum, quī in tantō perīculī 15 sibi auxiliō essent. omnibus autem abnuentibus, domum rediit, spē omnī dēiectus.

restitūta: restituere	*restore*
adversus	*against*
domum Hateriī	*to Haterius' house*
cognitiōnem senātūs:	
cognitiō senātūs	*trial by the senate*
invidia	*unpopularity*
fāma	*rumor*
vagābātur: vagārī	*spread, go around*
reliquiās: reliquiae	*remains*
repertās esse: reperīre	*find*
dēfīxiōnēs: dēfīxiō	*curse*
animās: anima	*soul*
dīs īnferīs: dī īnferī	*gods of the Underworld*
veste . . . mūtātā:	
vestem mūtāre	*change clothing, i.e. put on mourning clothes*
circumiit: circumīre	*go around*
abnuentibus:	
abnuere	*refuse*

Coin of Domitian.

cognitiō

diē dictā, magna senātōrum multitūdō ad causam audiendam in
cūriā convēnit. Salvius, iam metū cōnfectus, ad cūriam lectīcā
vectus est; fīliō comitante, manibus extentīs, Domitiānō lentē ac
suppliciter appropinquāvit. quī Salvium vultū compositō excēpit;
crīminibus recitātīs, pauca dē Salviō ipsō addidit: eum Vespasiānī   5
patris amīcum fuisse, adiūtōremque Agricolae ā sē missum esse ad

dictā: dictus   *appointed*
ad causam audiendam   *to hear the case, for the purpose of the case being heard*
suppliciter   *like a suppliant, humbly*
adiūtōrem: adiūtor   *assistant*

Head of Vespasian.

Britanniam administrandam. dēnique L. Ursum Serviānum, senātōrem clārissimum, ēlēgit quī cognitiōnī praeesset.

primō diē cognitiōnis Glabriō crīmina levia et inānia exposuit. dīxit Salvium domī statuam suam in locō altiōre quam statuam   10
prīncipis posuisse; imāginem dīvī Vespasiānī quae aulam rēgis Cogidubnī ōrnāvisset ā Salviō vīlī pretiō vēnditam esse; et multa similia. quibus audītīs, Salvius spērāre coepit sē ē manibus accūsātōrum ēlāpsūrum esse.

postrīdiē tamen appāruit accūsātor novus, Quīntus Caecilius   15
Iūcundus. vōce ferōcī, vultū minantī, oculīs ardentibus, verbīs īnfestissimīs Salvium vehementer oppugnāvit. affirmāvit Salvium superbē ac crūdēliter sē in Britanniā gessisse; cōnātum esse necāre Ti. Claudium Cogidubnum, rēgem populō Rōmānō fidēlissimum et amīcissimum; rēge mortuō, Salvium testāmentum fīnxisse; poenās   20
maximās meruisse.

Quīntō haec crīmina expōnentī ācriter respondit Salvius: "id quod dīcis absurdum est. quō modō venēnum Cogidubnō darī potuit, tot spectātōribus adstantibus? quis tam stultus est ut crēdat mē mortem rēgis octōgintā annōrum efficere voluisse? etiam rēgēs   25
mortālēs sunt." dēnique servōs suōs ad tormenta obtulit; dē testāmentō nihil explicāvit.

subitō extrā cūriam īnfestae vōcēs sunt audītae clāmantium sē ipsōs Salvium interfectūrōs esse sī poenam scelerum effūgisset. aliī effigiem Salviī dēreptam multīs contumēliīs in Tiberim iēcērunt; aliī   30
domum eius circumventam secūribus saxīsque pulsāre coepērunt. tantus erat strepitus ut ēmitteret prīnceps per urbem mīlitēs praetōriānōs quī tumultum sēdārent.

interēa Salvius, lectīcā vectus, ā tribūnō domum dēductus est; utrum tribūnus custōs esset an carnifex, nēmō sciēbat.   35

levia: levis	*trivial*
exposuit: expōnere	*set out, explain*
imāginem: imāgō	*image, bust*
crūdēliter	*cruelly*
amīcissimum: amīcus	*friendly*
fīnxisse: fingere	*forge*
meruisse: merērī	*deserve*
dēreptam: dēripere	*tear down*
sēdārent: sēdāre	*quell, calm down*

About the Language

1 From Stage 35 onwards, you have met sentences in which indirect statements are introduced by a verb in the present tense, such as **dīcit**, **spērant**, **audiō**, etc.:

DIRECT STATEMENT	INDIRECT STATEMENT
"custōs **revenit**."	puer *dīcit* custōdem **revenīre**.
"*The guard **is returning**.*"	*The boy says that the guard **is returning**.*
"puella **recitābit**."	*spērant* puellam **recitātūram esse**.
"*The girl **will recite**.*"	*They hope that the girl **will recite**.*
"vīllae **dēlētae sunt**."	*audiō* vīllās **dēlētās esse**.
"*The villas **have been destroyed**.*"	*I hear that the villas **have been destroyed**.*

2 In Stage 40, you have met sentences in which indirect statements are introduced by a verb in the perfect or imperfect tense, such as **dīxit**, **spērābant**, **audīvī**, etc.:

DIRECT STATEMENT	INDIRECT STATEMENT
"custōs **revenit**."	puer *dīxit* custōdem **revenīre**.
"*The guard **is returning**.*"	*The boy said that the guard **was returning**.*

"puella **recitābit**."	*spērābant* puellam **recitātūram esse**.
"*The girl **will recite**.*"	*They hoped that the girl **would recite**.*
"vīllae **dēlētae sunt**."	*audīvī* vīllās **dēlētās esse**.
"*The villas **have been destroyed**.*"	*I heard that the villas **had been destroyed**.*

Compare the indirect statements in paragraph 1 with the indirect statements in paragraph 2.

3 Further examples:

1 "Salvius multa scelera commīsit."
2 accūsātōrēs affirmāvērunt Salvium multa scelera commīsisse.
3 "mīlitēs urbem facile capient."
4 centuriō crēdēbat mīlitēs facile urbem captūrōs esse.
5 "Agricola iniūstē revocātus est."
6 multī senātōrēs putābant Agricolam iniūstē revocātum esse.
7 "frāter tuus in Britanniā iam habitat."
8 nūntius dīxit frātrem meum in Britanniā illō tempore habitāre.
9 "Domitiānus timōre coniūrātiōnis saepe perturbātur."
10 cīvēs sciēbant Domitiānum timōre coniūrātiōnis saepe perturbārī.

When you have read section I, answer the questions that follow it.

dēspērātiō

I

intereā Rūfilla, Salviī uxor, dum spēs eius firma manēbat, pollicēbātur sē sociam cuiuscumque fortūnae futūram esse. cum autem sēcrētīs Domitiae precibus veniam ā prīncipe impetrāvisset, Salvium dēserere cōnstituit; dēnique mediā nocte ē marītī cubiculō ēgressa domum patris suī rediit.   5

tum dēmum Salvius dēspērābat. fīlius Vitelliānus identidem affirmāvit senātōrēs numquam eum damnātūrōs esse; Salvium hortābātur ut animō firmō dēfēnsiōnem postrīdiē renovāret. Salvius autem respondit nūllam iam spem manēre: īnfestōs esse senātōrēs, prīncipem nūllō modō lēnīrī posse.   10

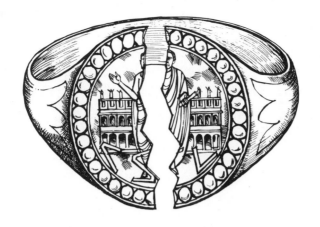

illō tempore saepe in manibus Salviī vīsa est epistula quaedam.
multī putābant mandāta sēcrēta Imperātōris in hāc epistulā
continērī; fāma enim vagābātur Domitiānum ipsum Salviō
imperāvisse ut Cogidubnum interficeret. amīcī Salvium
incitāvērunt ut hanc epistulam apud senātōrēs recitāret; ille tamen,   15
fīliī salūtis memor, hoc cōnsilium reiēcit.

postulāvit tabulās testāmentī. quās signātās lībertō trādidit. tum
frēgit ānulum suum, nē posteā ad aliōs accūsandōs ūsuī esset.
postrēmō litterās in hunc modum compositās ad prīncipem mīsit:

"opprimor, domine, inimīcōrum coniūrātiōne mendācibusque   20
testibus, nec mihi licet innocentiam meam probāre. deōs
immortālēs testor mē semper in fidē adversus tē mānsisse. hoc
ūnum ōrō ut fīliō meō innocentī parcās. nec quicquam aliud
precor."

dē Rūfillā nihil scrīpsit.   25

dēspērātiō	*despair*
dum	*so long as*
firma: firmus	*firm*
sociam: socia	*companion, partner*
cuiuscumque:	
quīcumque	*any, any whatever*
impetrāvisset:	
impetrāre	*obtain*
reiēcit: reicere	*reject*
ūsuī esset: ūsuī esse	*be of use*
mihi licet	*I am allowed*
innocentiam:	
innocentia	*innocence*

1 In what way did Rufilla's behavior change? What caused this change? What effect did it have on Salvius?
2 What did Salvius' friends urge him to do, in order to clear himself of blame for Cogidubnus' death? Explain why he rejected their advice.
3 What did Salvius do after sealing and handing over his will? Explain his reason for doing this.
4 What was Salvius' only request in his last letter to the Emperor?

II

cum advesperāsceret, Salvius aliīs servīs pecūniam, aliīs lībertātem dedit. deinde mortem sibi cōnscīscere parāvit. venēnō ūtī nōn potuit; nam corpus iam diū antidotīs mūniēbātur. cōnstituit ergō vēnās pugiōne incīdere. quō factō, in balneum inlātus mox exanimātus est.   5

at prīnceps, simulac mortem ā Salviō cōgitārī per ministrōs cognōvit, tribūnum mīlitēsque domum eius ēmīsit. mandāvit eīs ut Salviī mortem prohibērent; ipse enim crūdēlis vidērī nōlēbat. mīlitēs igitur, ā tribūnō iussī, Salvium ē balneō extrāxērunt, dēligāvērunt bracchia vulnerāta, sanguinem suppressērunt.   10

antidotīs: antidotum	*antidote, remedy*
mūniēbātur: mūnīre	*protect, immunize*
vēnās: vēna	*vein*
incīdere	*cut open*
suppressērunt: supprimere	*staunch, stop flow*

damnātiō

postrīdiē Ursus Serviānus, quī cognitiōnī praefuerat, sententiam prōnūntiāvit: nōmen Salviī Fāstīs ērādendum esse; bonōrum eius partem pūblicandam, partem fīliō trādendam; Salvium ipsum quīnque annōs relēgandum.

ille igitur, vulneribus sānātīs, Rōmā discessit. eōdem diē mīrum fideī exemplum oculīs populī Rōmānī obiectum est. Q. Haterius Latrōniānus, quī favōrem Salviī flōrentis semper quaerēbat, eum

rēbus adversīs oppressum nōn dēseruit, sed in exilium comitātus
est.

paucīs post diēbus Domitiānus accūsātōribus honōrēs ac praemia
distribuit. Glabriōnī sacerdōtium dedit; plūrimī autem
exīstimābant Glabriōnem rē vērā Domitiānum hāc accūsātiōne   15
graviter offendisse. Quīntō Caeciliō prīnceps favōrem suum ad
honōrēs petendōs pollicitus est; simul autem eum monuit nē nimis
ēlātus vel superbus fieret. pūmiliōnī Myropnoō, quī Salviī scelera
Domitiae patefēcerat, lībertātem obtulit; quam tamen ille recūsāvit.
"quid mihi cum lībertāte?" rogāvit; "satis est mihi amīcum   20
mortuum vindicāvisse." et tībiīs dēmum resūmptīs, exsultāns
cantāre coepit.

damnātiō	*condemnation*
sententiam: sententia	*sentence*
prōnūntiāvit:	
prōnūntiāre	*announce*
bonōrum: bona	*goods, property*
pūblicandam:	
pūblicāre	*confiscate*
flōrentis: flōrēre	*flourish*
distribuit:	
distribuere	*distribute*
dēmum	*at last*
Fāstīs: Fāstī	*the list of consuls*

About the Language

1 In Stage 32, you met sentences like these:

mihi fābula **nārranda est**.   Haterius **laudandus est**.
*I **must tell*** a story.   *Haterius **should be praised***.

In these examples, the gerundives **nārranda** and **laudandus** are being
used with **est** to indicate that (in the speaker's opinion) something
ought to be done ("the story *ought* to be sold," "Haterius *ought* to be
praised").

2 In Stage 40, you have met the gerundive used with **ad**, meaning *for the purpose of* . . .:

deinde Quīntus **ad Salvium accūsandum** surrēxit.
Then Quintus stood up **for the purpose of Salvius being accused**.
   Or, in more natural English:
Then Quintus stood up **to accuse Salvius**.

mercātōrēs in portū **ad nāvem reficiendam** manēbant.
The merchants stayed in port **for the purpose of their ship being repaired**.
   Or, in more natural English:
The merchants stayed in port **to repair their ship**.

3 Further examples:

1 Calēdoniī nūntiōs ad pācem petendam mīsērunt.
2 sculptor ingentem marmoris massam ad statuās faciendās comparāvit.
3 poēta ad versūs recitandōs scaenam ascendit.
4 Memor ad scelera Salviī patefacienda adductus est.
5 servōs in agrōs ad frūmentum colligendum ēmīsī.

Practicing the Language

1 Match each adjective in the left-hand column with an adjective of the opposite meaning, taken from the right-hand column, and translate both words.

benignus	stultus
callidus	levis
dūrus	pessimus
falsus	malignus
fidēlis	dīligēns
gravis	mollis
lātus	nūllus
neglegēns	perfidus
optimus	angustus
ūllus	vērus

2 Translate each sentence into Latin by selecting correctly from the list of Latin words.

1 *I was being cared for by a very experienced doctor.*

ā medicō	perītiōre	cūrābam
prope medicum	perītissimō	cūrābar

2 *The commander hopes that the messengers will return soon.*

lēgātus	spērō	nūntiī	mox	revenīre
lēgātī	spērat	nūntiōs	nūper	reventūrōs esse

3 *We hear that a new house is being built.*

audīmus	domus	nova	aedificāre
audīvimus	domum	novam	aedificārī

4 *The soothsayer advises you not to leave the city.*

haruspex	tū	monet	ut	urbī	discēdās
haruspicem	tē	monēbat	nē	ex urbe	discessissēs

5 *After the conspiracy had been revealed* (two words only), *very many senators were condemned.*

coniūrātiōnem	patefactā	plūrimī	senātōrī	damnātī sunt
coniūrātiōne	patefactam	maximī	senātōrēs	damnātus est

Detail from the Cancelleria Reliefs, which provide a record of the Emperor Domitian's life.

3 With the help of paragraph 8 on page 292 of the Language Information Section, turn each of the following pairs into one sentence by replacing the word in boldface with the correct form of the relative pronoun **quī** and adjusting the word order so that the relative pronoun comes at the *beginning* of the relative clause; then translate. Check the gender of the noun if necessary by referring to the vocabulary at the end of the book.

For example: intrāvit medicus. senex **medicum** arcessīverat.
This becomes: intrāvit medicus, **quem** senex arcessīverat.
> *In came the doctor, **whom** the old man had sent for.*

1 templum nōtissimum vīsitāvimus. Domitiānus ipse **templum** exstrūxerat.
2 prō domō cōnsulis stābat pauper. praecō **pauperī** sportulam trādēbat.
3 ille vir est Quīntus. pater **Quīntī** mēcum negōtium agere solēbat.
4 tribūnus catēnās solvit. captīvus **catēnīs** vīnctus erat.
5 praemium illīs puerīs dabitur. auxiliō **puerōrum**, fūr heri comprehēnsus est.

Roman Law Courts

At the beginning of the first century A.D., there were several different law courts in Rome, for handling different sorts of cases. If a Roman was charged with a criminal offense, he might find himself in one of a group of jury courts known as **quaestiōnēs** (*commissions of inquiry*), each responsible for judging a particular crime, such as treason, murder, adultery, misconduct by governors of provinces, forgery, and election bribery. If he was involved in a civil (i.e. non-criminal) case, such as a dispute over a legacy, or an attempt to gain compensation from his next-door neighbor for damage to property, he would go first of all to a praetor. The praetor would inquire into the cause and nature of the dispute, then either appoint an individual judge (**iūdex**) to hear the case, or refer it to an appropriate court; inheritance cases, for example, usually went to the court of the centumviri.

By the time of Domitian, some further ways of handling law cases had

Statue of a Roman making a speech.

been added. For example, a senator charged with a crime could be tried in the senate by his fellow-senators, like Salvius in the story on pages 95–103; and the emperor himself took an increasingly large part in administering the law (see pp.45–6). But the courts described in the previous paragraph continued to operate alongside these new arrangements.

In modern times, someone who has committed an offense is liable to be charged by the police and prosecuted by a lawyer who acts on behalf of the state; the system is supervised by a government department. In

Rome, however, there were no charges by the police, no state lawyers, and no government department responsible for prosecutions. If a man committed a crime, he could be prosecuted only by a private individual, not by a public official. Any citizen could bring a prosecution, and if the accused man was found guilty, there was sometimes a reward for the prosecutor.

The courts played an important part in the lives of many Romans, especially senators and their sons. Success as a speaker in court was one of the aims of the long training which they had received from the rhetor. In the courts, a Roman could make a name for himself with the general public, play his part as a patron by looking after any clients who had gotten involved with the law, and catch the eye of people (such as the emperor and his advisers) whose support might help him gain promotion in the cursus honorum.

Fame and prestige usually mattered more than financial reward to the men who conducted cases in the courts. For a long time, they were forbidden to receive payment at all from their clients. Later, they were permitted to accept a fee for their services, but this fee was regarded as an unofficial "present", or donation, which the client was not obliged to pay and the lawyer was not supposed to ask for.

Roman courts were probably at their liveliest in the first century B.C., when rival politicians fought each other fiercely in the courts as part of their struggle for power. By the time of Domitian, some of the glamour had faded; now that Rome was ruled by an emperor, there was less political power to be fought for. Nevertheless, the contests in court still mattered to the speakers and their clients, and attracted enthusiastic audiences. Pliny gives a vivid description of a case that aroused particularly lively interest:

"There they were, one hundred and eighty jurors, a great crowd of lawyers for both plaintiff and defendant, dozens of supporters sitting on the benches, and an enormous circle of listeners, several rows deep, standing around the whole courtroom. The platform was packed solid with people, and in the upper galleries of the basilica men and women were leaning over in an effort to hear, which was difficult, and see, which was rather easier."

The writings of Martial, Pliny, and Quintilian are full of casual details which convey the liveliness and excitement of the courts: the gimmicky lawyer who always wears an eye-patch while pleading a case; the claque of spectators who applaud at the right moments in return for payment;

the successful speaker who wins a standing ovation from the jury; the careful allocation of time for each side, measured by the water-clock; the lawyer with the booming voice, whose speech is greeted by applause not only in his own court but also from the court next door; the windbag who is supposed to be talking about the theft of three she-goats, but goes off into long irrelevant ramblings about Rome's wars with Carthage three hundred years ago; and the anxious wife who sends messengers to court every hour to find out how her husband is doing.

It is difficult to say how fair Roman justice was. Some of the tactics used in Roman law courts had very little to do with the rights and wrongs of the case. An accused man might dress up in mourning or hold up his little children to the jury to arouse their pity. A speaker whose client was in the wrong might ignore the facts altogether, and try to win his case by appealing to the jury's emotions or prejudices, or by using irrelevant arguments. Sometimes a man might be accused and found guilty for political reasons; there were a number of "treason trials" under Domitian, in which innocent men were condemned. However, the writings of such men as Pliny and Quintilian show that at least some Roman judges made an honest effort to be fair and just. Fairness in a Roman court was partly the result of the laws themselves. Roman law developed over several centuries, and at its best it was careful, practical, and immensely detailed; it became the basis of many present-day legal systems in North America and Europe.

This coin illustrates voting in the senate: in the center, under a canopy, the presiding magistrate's chair; on the right the tablets used by the jurors (A and C); and on the left the urn into which they were cast.

Words and Phrases Checklist

adversus	*against*
affirmō, affirmāre, affirmāvī	*declare*
amīcitia, amīcitiae	*friendship*
augeō, augēre, auxī, auctus	*increase*
auxiliō esse	*be a help, be helpful*
cōnsul, cōnsulis	*consul (senior magistrate)*
crīmen, crīminis	*charge*
cūria, cūriae	*senate-house*
dēmum	*at last*
tum dēmum	*then at last, only then*
exilium, exiliī	*exile*
exīstimō, exīstimāre, exīstimāvī	*think, consider*
fāma, fāmae	*rumor*
fingō, fingere, finxī, fictus	*pretend, invent, forge*
flōreō, flōrēre, flōruī	*flourish*
interim	*meanwhile*
invidia, invidiae	*jealousy, envy, unpopularity*
levis, leve	*light, slight, trivial*
meditor, meditārī,	
meditātus sum	*consider*
minor, minārī, minātus sum	*threaten*
mūtō, mūtāre, mūtāvī, mūtātus	*change*
obiciō, obicere, obiēcī, obiectus	*present, put in the way of, expose to*
probō, probāre, probāvī	*prove*
prōdō, prōdere, prōdidī,	
prōditus	*betray*
similis, simile	*similar*
socius, sociī	*companion, partner*
suādeō, suādēre, suāsī	*advise, suggest*
tumultus, tumultūs	*riot*
ūtor, ūtī, ūsus sum	*use*
videor, vidērī, vīsus sum	*seem*

Word Search

Match each definition with one of the words given below.

augment, fiction, immutable, incriminate, infamy, levity, probation

1 . . . . .: frivolity; lightheartedness
2 . . . . .: unalterable
3 . . . . .: to enlarge, expand
4 . . . . .: evil reputation
5 . . . . .: something imagined or made up; a falsehood
6 . . . . .: to accuse of a crime or offense, indict
7 . . . . .: a trial period

Bīthȳnia

For about four hundred and fifty years, the Romans controlled an empire that stretched from the Atlantic Ocean to the edge of Russia and from Scotland to the Sahara Desert. The empire's provinces were ruled by an enormous and complicated organization of governors and their staffs.

As a rule, we know very little about the day-to-day running of this vast network; but in one case we have an unusually large amount of information because the provincial governor's letters to the emperor have survived, together with the emperor's replies. In about A.D. 110, Gaius Plinius Caecilius Secundus (Pliny) was appointed by the Emperor Trajan to govern the province of Bithynia et Pontus (roughly equivalent to northern Turkey). It was an abnormal governorship: Pliny had been personally chosen by the emperor himself; he was given special authority and status, and he had a special job to do. Stage 41 contains five of Pliny's official letters to Trajan, together with Trajan's replies.

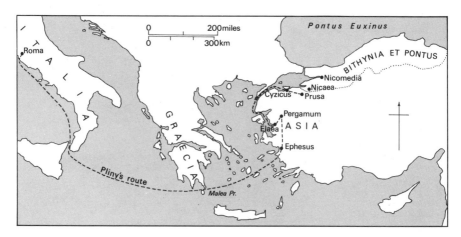

Pliny's route.

---

adventus

I
GĀIUS PLĪNIUS TRĀIĀNŌ IMPERĀTŌRĪ

nāvigātiō mea, domine, usque Ephesum salūberrima erat; inde, postquam vehiculīs iter facere coepī, gravissimīs aestibus atque etiam febriculīs afflīgēbar; Pergamī igitur ad convalēscendum substitī. deinde, cum nāvem iterum cōnscendissem, contrāriīs 5 ventīs retentus sum; itaque Bīthȳniam intrāvī aliquantō tardius quam spērāveram, id est XV Kal. Octōbrēs.

nunc ratiōnēs Prūsēnsium excutiō; quod mihi magis ac magis necessārium vidētur. multae enim pecūniae, variīs ex causīs, ā prīvātīs cīvibus retinentur; praetereā quaedam pecūniae sine iūstā   10

nāvigātiō	*voyage*	excutiō: excutere	*examine, investigate*
usque Ephesum	*as far as Ephesus*	necessārium:	
salūberrima: salūbris	*comfortable*	necessārius	*necessary*
vehiculīs: vehiculum	*carriage*	pecūniae: pecūnia	*sum of money*
gravissimīs: gravis	*severe*	iūstā: iūstus	*proper, right*
aestibus: aestus	*heat*	impenduntur:	
febriculīs: febricula	*slight fever*	impendere	*spend*
ad convalēscendum	*for the purpose of getting better, in order to get better*		
		Pergamī	*at Pergamum*
		Prūsēnsium:	
substitī: subsistere	*halt, stop*	Prūsēnsēs	*people of Prusa*
aliquantō	*somewhat, rather*		
XV Kal. Octōbrēs	*September 17th (literally "fifteen days before October 1st")*		

Theater at Ephesus, first century A.D., and the Arcadian Way.

causā impenduntur. dispice, domine, num necessārium putēs
mittere hūc mēnsōrem, ad opera pūblica īnspicienda; crēdō enim
multās pecūniās posse revocārī ā cūrātōribus pūblicōrum operum,
sī mēnsūrae fidēliter agantur. hanc epistulam tibi, domine, in ipsō
adventū meō scrīpsī.   15

dispice: dispicere	*consider*	cūrātōribus: cūrātor	*supervisor,*
mēnsōrem: mēnsor	*surveyor*		*superintendent*
opera: opus	*work, building*	mēnsūrae: mēnsūra	*measurement*
revocārī: revocāre	*recover*	fidēliter	*faithfully, reliably*
ā	*from*		

1 How did Pliny travel to Ephesus?
2 What change in his method of traveling did he make when he got
   there?
3 Why was he forced to stop at Pergamum?
4 What method of travel did he use for the final stage of his journey?
   What delayed him?
5 What is Pliny doing at Prusa? From lines 8–10 find two reasons why
   Prusa is short of public money.
6 What kind of assistant does Pliny ask Trajan for?
7 What job does Pliny want this assistant to do?
8 What impression does Pliny give by the words "nunc" (line 8) and "in
   ipsō adventū" (lines 14–15)? Can you suggest any reason why Pliny is
   so anxious to impress Trajan in this way – is it, for example, to make
   up for any failure on his part?

II

TRĀIĀNUS PLĪNIŌ

cognōvī litterīs tuīs, Secunde cārissime, quō diē in Bīthȳniam
pervēnissēs. brevī tempore, crēdō, Bīthȳnī intellegent prōvinciam
mihi esse cūrae: nam ego tē ēlēgī quī ad eōs meī locō mittāris; tū
efficiēs ut benignitās mea sit manifesta illīs.   5

    prīmum autem tibi ratiōnēs pūblicae sunt excutiendae; nam satis
cōnstat eās vexātās esse.

    mēnsōrēs vix sufficientēs habeō etiam eīs operibus quae aut
Rōmae aut in proximō fiunt. sed in omnī prōvinciā inveniuntur
mēnsōrēs quibus crēdere possīmus; et ideō nōn vereor nē tibi dēsint.   10
sī tū dīligenter excutiēs, inveniēs.

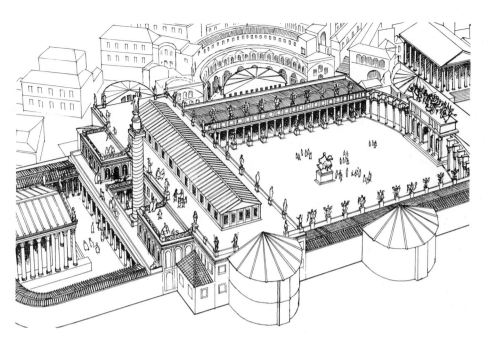

mēnsōrēs vix sufficientēs habeō etiam eīs operibus quae aut Rōmae aut in proximō fiunt. (lines 8–9)

meī locō	*in my place*
efficiēs ut: efficere ut	*bring it about that,*
	see to it that
benignitās	*concern, kindly interest*
vexātās: vexātus	*confused, in chaos*
sufficientēs:	
sufficiēns	*enough, sufficient*
aut . . . aut	*either . . . or*
in proximō	*nearby*
omnī: omnis	*every*
dēsint: dēesse	*be lacking, be unavailable*
Bīthȳnī	*Bithynians*

1 What phrase does Trajan use to emphasize that Pliny's job in Bithynia is an important one?

2 What impression of himself does Trajan want the Bithynians to have?

3 Why is Trajan unable to agree to Pliny's request for a surveyor? What steps does he suggest Pliny should take instead?

4 On the evidence of this pair of letters, what special task has Pliny been sent to Bithynia to perform? Can you suggest reasons why Trajan should have chosen Pliny for this task?

carcer

I

GĀIUS PLĪNIUS TRĀIĀNŌ IMPERĀTŌRĪ

rogō, domine, ut mē tuō cōnsiliō adiuvēs: incertus enim sum utrum carcerem custōdīre dēbeam per pūblicōs servōs (quod usque adhūc factum est) an per mīlitēs. sī enim servīs pūblicīs ūtar, vereor nē parum fidēlēs sint; sī mīlitibus ūtar, vereor nē hoc officium magnum numerum mīlitum distringat. interim pūblicīs servīs paucōs mīlitēs addidī. videō tamen in hōc cōnsiliō perīculum esse nē utrīque neglegentiōrēs fiant; nam sī quid adversī acciderit, culpam mīlitēs in servōs, servī in mīlitēs trānsferre poterunt.   5

usque adhūc	*until now*	utrīque	*both groups of people*
parum	*too little, not . . . enough*	sī quid	*if anything*
fidēlēs: fidēlis	*reliable, trustworthy*	adversī: adversus	*unfortunate, undesirable*
officium	*task, duty*	culpam: culpa	*blame*
distringat: distringere	*distract, divert*	trānsferre	*transfer, put*

1 What problem is causing Pliny difficulty? What disadvantage does each of his two alternatives have?
2 What step has Pliny taken for the moment?
3 Is Pliny satisfied with his present solution? If not, why not?
4 What reply would you expect from Trajan? Would you expect him to agree with what Pliny has done? or to prefer another solution? or to snap at Pliny for bothering him with trivialities?

II

TRĀIĀNUS PLĪNIŌ

nihil opus est, mī Secunde cārissime, mīlitēs ad carcerem
custōdiendum convertere. melius est persevērāre in istīus
prōvinciae cōnsuētūdine, et pūblicīs servīs ad vigilandum in carcere
ūtī; tū enim, sevēritāte ac dīligentiā tuā, potes efficere ut servī   5
fidēliter hoc faciant. nam, sī mīlitēs servīs pūblicīs permiscentur,
rēctē verēris nē utrīque neglegentiōrēs sint; sed nōs semper oportet
hoc meminisse: mīlitēs Rōmānōs in prōvinciīs nostrīs positōs esse
nōn ad carcerēs custōdiendōs, sed ad pugnandum.

nihil opus est	*there is no need*	ad vigilandum	*for keeping watch*
convertere	*divert*	sevēritāte: sevēritās	*strictness, severity*
persevērāre	*continue*	permiscentur:	
cōnsuētūdine:		permiscēre	*mix with*
cōnsuētūdō	*custom*		

1 In Trajan's view, who ought to guard the prisoners?
2 Why had Pliny been reluctant to adopt this solution, and how does
   Trajan answer his objection?
3 Which of Pliny's fears does Trajan agree with?
4 What aspect of the problem does Trajan seem to feel most strongly
   about? Is it the unreliability of the public slaves, the disadvantage of
   sharing the work, or some other aspect?

About the Language

1 In Stage 40, you met the gerundive used with **ad**, meaning *for the purpose of . . .*:

Quīntus **ad Salvium accūsandum** surrēxit.
*Quintus stood up **for the purpose of Salvius being accused**.*
   Or, in more natural English:
*Quintus stood up in order **to accuse Salvius**.*

iuvenēs **ad pompam spectandam** advēnērunt.
*The young men arrived **for the purpose of the procession being watched**.*
   Or, in more natural English:
*The young men arrived **to watch the procession**.*

2 In Stage 41, you have met sentences like these:

pontifex **ad sacrificandum** aderat.
*The priest was present **for the purpose of sacrificing**.*
   Or, in more natural English:
*The priest was present **in order to sacrifice**.*

līberī **ad lūdendum** exiērunt.
*The children went out **for the purpose of playing**.*
   Or, in more natural English:
*The children went out **to play**.*

The word in boldface is known as a *gerund*.

Further examples:

1 puer in fossam ad latendum dēsiluit.
2 senex ad cēnandum recumbēbat.

3 Further examples of sentences containing gerunds and gerundives:

1 mīlitēs **ad imperātōrem salūtandum** īnstrūctī erant. (*gerundive*)
2 mīlitēs **ad pugnandum** īnstrūctī erant. (*gerund*)
3 Plīnius **ad convalēscendum** in oppidō manēbat. (*gerund*)
4 haruspicēs **ad victimās īnspiciendās** prōcessērunt. (*gerundive*)
5 servus **ad labōrandum** ē lectō surrēxit. (*gerund*)
6 dominus **ad pecūniam numerandam** in tablīnō sedēbat. (*gerundive*)

7 clientēs **ad patrōnōs vīsitandōs** per viās contendēbant.
8 amīcus meus **ad dormiendum** abiit.
9 multī āthlētae **ad certandum** aderant.
10 cīvēs aquam **ad incendium exstinguendum** quaerēbant.

In sentences 7–10, which of the words in boldface are gerundives, and which are gerunds?

---

aquaeductus

I

GĀIUS PLĪNIUS TRĀIĀNŌ IMPERĀTŌRĪ

in aquaeductum, domine, Nīcomēdēnsēs impendērunt sestertium
$\overline{\text{XXX}}$ CCCXVIII, quī, imperfectus adhūc, nōn modo omissus sed
etiam dēstrūctus est; deinde in alium aquaeductum impēnsa sunt
$\overline{\text{CC}}$. hōc quoque relictō, novō impendiō opus est, ut aquam habeant,   5
postquam tantam pecūniam perdidērunt. ipse pervēnī ad fontem
pūrissimum, ex quō vidētur aqua dēbēre perdūcī (sīcut initiō
temptātum erat), arcuātō opere, nē tantum ad humilēs regiōnēs
oppidī perveniat. manent adhūc paucissimī arcūs; possunt etiam

aquaeductus	*aqueduct*
$\overline{\text{XXX CCCXVIII}}$ 3,318,000: $\boxed{}$ = *multiply by 100,000;* $\overline{}$ = *multiply by 1,000*	
imperfectus	*unfinished*
adhūc	*still*
omissus = omissus est: omittere	*abandon*
dēstrūctus est: dēstruere	*destroy, demolish*
$\overline{\text{CC}}$	*200,000*
impendiō: impendium	*expense, expenditure*
opus est	*there is need of (literally "there is work (to be done) with")*
perdidērunt: perdere	*waste, lose*
perdūcī: perdūcere	*bring, carry*
arcuātō: arcuātus	*arched*
humilēs: humilis	*low-lying*

exstruī arcūs complūrēs lapide quadrātō quī ex priōre opere   10
dētractus est; aliqua pars, ut mihi vidētur, testāceō opere agenda
erit (id enim et facilius et vīlius est). sed in prīmīs necessārium est
mittī ā tē vel aquilegem vel architēctum, nē id quod prius accidit
rūrsus ēveniat. ego quidem cōnfīdō et ūtilitātem operis et
pulchritūdinem prīncipātū tuō esse dignissimam.   15

quadrātō: quadrātus	*squared, in blocks*
testāceō opere: testāceum opus	*brick work*
in prīmīs	*in the first place*
vel . . . vel	*either . . . or*
aquilegem: aquilex	*water engineer, hydraulic engineer*
ēveniat: ēvenīre	*occur*
ūtilitātem: ūtilitās	*usefulness*
pulchritūdinem: pulchritūdō	*beauty*
Nīcomēdēnsēs	*people of Nicomedia*

Aqueduct at Pont du Gard.

1 What happened to the Nicomedians' first aqueduct?
2 What has happened to their second attempt?
3 Why does the aqueduct have to be carried on arches?
4 What three suggestions does Pliny make in lines 0–00 ("manent . . . agenda erit") for the providing of arches?
5 What request does he make to Trajan?
6 How does Pliny attempt to make his idea more persuasive to Trajan?

II

TRĀIĀNUS PLĪNIŌ

cūrandum est, ut aqua in oppidum Nīcomēdīam perdūcātur. cōnfīdō tē summā dīligentiā hoc opus effectūrum esse. sed medius fidius! necesse est tibi eādem dīligentiā ūtī ad cognōscendum quōrum vitiō tantam pecūniam Nīcomēdēnsēs perdiderint; 5 suspicor eōs ideō tot aquaeductūs incohāvisse et relīquisse, ut inter sē grātificentur. quicquid cognōveris, perfer in nōtitiam meam.

cūrandum est	*steps must be taken*	grātificentur: grātificārī	*do favors*
medius fidius!	*for goodness sake!*	perfer: perferre	*bring*
vitiō: vitium	*fault, failure*	nōtitiam: nōtitia	*notice*
incohāvisse: incohāre	*begin*		

1 Does Trajan give permission for the new aqueduct?
2 What is Trajan especially concerned about? What does he suspect?
3 What does Trajan do about Pliny's request for a water engineer?

lapis quadrātus.

testāceum opus.

supplicium

I

GĀIUS PLĪNIUS TRĀIĀNŌ IMPERĀTŌRĪ

Semprōnius Caeliānus, ēgregius iuvenis, duōs servōs inter tīrōnēs repertōs mīsit ad mē; quōrum ego supplicium distulī, ut tē cōnsulerem dē modō poenae. ipse enim ideō maximē dubitō, quod hī servī, quamquam iam sacrāmentum dīxērunt, nōndum in numerōs distribūtī sunt. rogō igitur, domine, ut scrībās quid facere dēbeam, praesertim cum pertineat ad exemplum. 5

ēgregius	*excellent, outstanding*
tīrōnēs: tīrō	*recruit*
distulī: differre	*postpone*
sacrāmentum dīxērunt:	
sacrāmentum dīcere	*take the military oath*
numerōs: numerī	*military units*
cum	*since, because*
pertineat ad exemplum:	
pertinēre ad exemplum	*involve a precedent*

1 What has Sempronius Caelianus discovered? What action has he taken?
2 What does Pliny want Trajan to decide?
3 Why is Pliny particularly hesitant?
4 Why does he think the case is important?

II

TRĀIĀNUS PLĪNIŌ

rēctē mīsit Semprōnius Caeliānus ad tē eōs servōs, quī inter tīrōnēs repertī sunt. nunc tē oportet cognōscere num supplicium ultimum meruisse videantur. rēfert autem utrum vōluntāriī vēnerint an lēctī sint vel etiam vicāriī ab aliīs datī. sī lēctī sunt, illī peccāvērunt quī ad mīlitandum eōs ēlēgērunt; sī vicāriī datī sunt, culpa est penes eōs quī dedērunt; sī ipsī, quamquam habēbant condiciōnis suae cōnscientiam, nihilōminus vēnērunt, sevērē pūniendī erunt. neque multum rēfert, quod nōndum in numerōs distribūtī sunt. illō enim diē, quō prīmum probātī sunt, vēritās condiciōnis eōrum patefacienda erat. 5

10

rēfert: rēferre	*make a difference*
voluntāriī: voluntārius	*volunteer*
vēnerint: venīre	*come forward*
lēctī sint	*have been chosen, have been conscripted*
vicāriī: vicārius	*substitute*
datī: dare	*put forward*
peccāvērunt: peccāre	*do wrong, be to blame*
penes	*with*
condiciōnis: condiciō	*status*
cōnscientiam: cōnscientia	*awareness, knowledge*
prōbātī sunt: prōbāre	*examine (at time of enrollment)*
vēritās	*truth*

1 What punishment are the slaves liable to suffer if they are found guilty?
2 Trajan refers to three possible explanations for the situation. What are they? What action does he think should be taken in each case?
3 When ought the status of the recruits to have been discovered?
4 Who seems to have the better grasp of the problem, Pliny or Trajan?

About the Language

1 Study the following pairs of sentences:

puerī clāmōrem faciunt.
The boys are making a noise.

clāmor **fit**.
*A noise **is being made**.*

Nerō multa et dīra faciēbat.
Nero was doing many terrible things.

multa et dīra **fīēbant**.
*Many terrible things **were being done**.*

The Latin words in boldface are forms of the irregular verb **fīō** (*I am made*).

2 The verb **faciō** (*I make, I do*) has no passive forms in the present, future and imperfect tenses. Instead, the Romans used the following forms of **fīō**:

PRESENT		PRESENT INFINITIVE	
fīō	*I am made*	**fierī**	*to be made*
fīs	*you are made*		
fit	*he is made*	PRESENT SUBJUNCTIVE	
fīunt	*they are made*	**fīam**	
		fīās	*etc.*

FUTURE (*I shall be made, etc.*)
fīam
fīēs   *etc.*

IMPERFECT	IMPERFECT SUBJUNCTIVE
(*I was being made, etc.*)	
fīēbam	**fierem**
fīēbās *etc.*	**fierēs** *etc.*

Note: See Language Information Section, p.309, for complete tables.

Translate the following pairs of sentences:

1a mīlitēs impetum mox facient.
1b impetus mox fīet.

2a servus nihil in culīnā faciēbat.
2b nihil in culīnā fīēbat.

3a ignōrābāmus quid senātōrēs in cūriā facerent.
3b ignōrābāmus quid in cūriā fieret.

3 Notice some of the different ways in which **fīō** can be translated:

aliquid mīrī **fīēbat.**
*Something strange **was being done**.*
Or *Something strange **was happening**.*

ecce! deus **fīō.**
Look! ***I'm being made*** *into a god,* Or *Look!* ***I'm becoming*** *a god.*

Further examples:

1 crās nōs cōnsulēs fīēmus.
2 salvē, Mārce! quid in fundō tuō hodiē fit?
3 tam timidē hostēs resistēbant ut peditēs nostrī audāciōrēs fierent.

   peditēs   *foot soldiers, infantry*

4 The perfect, future perfect, and pluperfect tenses of the passive of **faciō** are formed in the normal way. Study the following pairs of sentences and notice some of the different ways of translating **factus est**, etc.

   mīlitēs Claudium imperātōrem **fēcērunt**.
   *The soldiers **made** Claudius emperor.*

   Claudius imperātor **factus est**.
   *Claudius **was made** emperor,* Or *Claudius **became** emperor.*

   haruspex rem rīdiculam **fēcerat**.
   The soothsayer had done a silly thing.

   rēs rīdicula **facta erat**.
   *A silly thing **had been done**,* Or *A silly thing **had happened**.*

incendium

I
GĀIUS PLĪNIUS TRĀIĀNŌ IMPERĀTŌRĪ

cum dīversam partem prōvinciae circumīrem, vāstissimum incendium Nīcomēdiae coortum est. nōn modo multās cīvium prīvātōrum domōs dēlēvit, sed etiam duo pūblica opera, Gerūsiān et templum Īsidis. flammae autem lātius sparsae sunt, prīmum   5

vāstissimum: vāstus	*great, large*
coortum est: coorīrī	*break out*
lātius: lātē	*widely*
coortum est: coorīrī	*break out*

violentiā ventī, deinde inertiā hominum, quī ōtiōsī et immōtī
adstābant, neque quicquam ad adiuvandum fēcērunt. praetereā,
nūllus est usquam pūblicus sīpō, nūlla hama, nūllum omnīnō
īnstrūmentum ad incendia exstinguenda. et haec quidem
īnstrūmenta, ut iam praecēpī, parābuntur; tū, domine, dispice num   10
putēs collēgium fabrōrum esse īnstituendum, dumtaxat hominum
CL. ego efficiam nē quis nisi faber in hoc collēgium admittātur, nēve
fabrī hōc iūre in aliud ūtantur; nec erit difficile custōdīre tam
paucōs.

sparsae sunt: spargere	*spread*	dumtaxat	*not exceeding*
violentiā: violentia	*violence*	nē quis	*that nobody*
inertiā: inertia	*laziness, idleness*	nēve	*and that . . . not*
sīpō	*fire-pump*	iūre: iūs	*right, privilege*
hama	*fire-bucket*	in aliud	*for any other purpose*
īnstrūmentum	*equipment*	Nīcomēdīae	*at Nicomedia*
praecēpī: praecipere	*instruct, order*		
collēgium	*brigade*	Gerūsiān	*Greek accusative of*
fabrōrum: faber	*fireman*		Gerūsia *the Gerusia*
īnstituendum:			*(club for wealthy*
īnstituere	*set up*		*elderly men)*

A1 What has happened in Nicomedia?
 2 Where was Pliny at the time?
 3 How extensive was the damage?
 4 What was the attitude of the bystanders?
 5 In what way was the city ill-prepared for such a disaster?
 6 What preventive measure is Pliny taking?
 7 What further suggestion does he make to the emperor?

B1 Why does Pliny mention his whereabouts at the time of the disaster?
 2 Do the words "ōtiōsī et immōtī adstābant" (lines 0–0) merely
     describe the scene, or do they also convey Pliny's attitude towards
     the bystanders? If so, what *is* his attitude?
 3 Does Pliny's suggestion to the emperor seem to you a reasonable
     one? What reply would you expect to this letter?
 4 Do lines 11–14 (from "dumtaxat hominum" to the end) indicate
     Pliny's confidence that the emperor will agree to his suggestion, or
     does he think the emperor may disapprove?

Bronze water-pump.

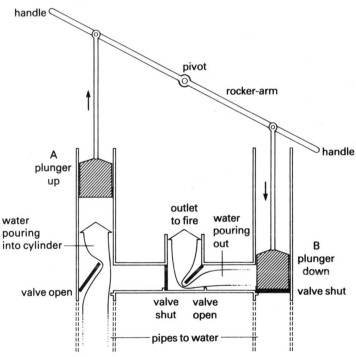

How the pump worked.

Head of Trajan.

II

TRĀIĀNUS PLĪNIŌ

tibi in mentem vēnit collēgium fabrōrum apud Nīcomēdēnsēs
īnstituere, sīcut in aliīs prōvinciīs factum est. sed nōs oportet
meminisse prōvinciam istam et praecipuē urbēs factiōnibus eius
modī saepe vexātās esse. quodcumque nōmen dederimus eīs quī in   5
idem contractī erunt, hetaeriae brevī tempore fient. melius igitur est
comparāre ea quae ad incendia exstinguenda auxiliō esse possint;
admonendī quoque sunt dominī praediōrum ut ipsī flammās
exstinguere cōnentur; dēnique, sī opus est, auxilium ā spectantibus
est petendum.   10

in mentem vēnit:
   in mentem venīre   *occur, come to mind*
praecipuē   *especially*
factiōnibus: factiō   *organized group*
quodcumque   *whatever*
in idem   *for a common purpose, for the same purpose*
contractī erunt: contrahere *bring together, assemble*
hetaeriae: hetaeria   *political club*
dominī: dominus   *owner*
praediōrum: praedium   *property*

admonendī quoque sunt dominī praediōrum ut ipsī flammās exstinguere cōnentur. (lines 8–9)

1 What decision does Trajan give?
2 How has the previous history of Bithynia affected Trajan's decision?
3 What three suggestions does Trajan make?
4 To what extent do you agree with the following opinion?
"Trajan seems more concerned with politics than with the safety of his subjects; his advice to Pliny is vague and unhelpful. He appears not to realize the seriousness of fires in large towns."

About the Language

1 Study the following examples:

tam stultus est ille puer ut ā cēterīs discipulīs semper **dērīdeātur**.
*That boy is so stupid that **he is** always **laughed** at by the other students.*

medicus ignōrat quārē hōc morbō **afflīgāris**, mī amīce.
*The doctor does not know why **you are stricken** with this illness, my friend.*

The Latin form of the verb in boldface is the *present subjunctive passive*.

Further examples:

1 scīre velim quot captīvī in illō carcere retineantur.
2 tot clientēs habēmus ut in viīs semper salūtēmur.
3 arma semper gerō nē ā latrōnibus interficiar.

2 Compare the active and passive forms of the present subjunctive of **portō**:

PRESENT SUBJUNCTIVE ACTIVE	PRESENT SUBJUNCTIVE PASSIVE
portem	**porter**
portēs	**portēris**
portet	**portētur**
portēmus	**portēmur**
portētis	**portēminī**
portent	**portentur**

Present subjunctive passive forms of **doceō**, **trahō**, **capiō**, and **audiō** are given on p.299 of the Language Information Section.

3 Study the following examples:

nescio quid iuvenis efficere **cōnētur**.
*I do not know what the young man **is trying to achieve**.*

crās equōs cōnscendēmus ut **proficīscāmur**.
*Tomorrow we will mount our horses in order **to set out**.*

The Latin words in boldface are *present subjunctive* forms of *deponent* verbs.

Further examples:

1 tam timidī sunt servī meī ut etiam umbrās vereantur.
2 dīcite mihi quārē illōs senēs sequāminī.

The present subjunctive of the deponent verbs **cōnor**, **vereor**, **loquor**, **ēgredior**, and **mentior** is set out in full on p.000.

Practicing the Language

1 The following list contains the 3rd person singular present and perfect forms of seven verbs, jumbled together. Sort them into pairs, writing the present form first and then the perfect, and give the meaning of each form.

For example: **portat** *he carries*   **portāvit** *he carried*

portat, facit, tulit, est, cōgit, fēcit, fert, ēgit, fuit, vēnit, coēgit, venit, agit, portāvit.

2 Complete each sentence with the right word and then translate.

1 ego vōs servāvī, ubi ab inimīcīs . . . . . .
(accūsābāminī, fingēbāminī)

2 difficile erat nōbīs prōcēdere, quod ā turbā . . . . . .
(dīcēbāmur, impediēbāmur)

3 audīte, meī amīcī! nōs ad aulam contendere . . . . . .
(regimur, iubēmur)

4 rēctē nunc . . . . . ., quod ā proeliō heri fūgistis.
(culpāminī, agnōsciminī)

5 epistulam ad prīncipem hodiē mittam, mīlitēs, ut facta nostra nūntiem; sine dubiō ab illō . . . . . . (rogābimur, laudābimur)

6 iūdex "facinus dīrum commīsistis" inquit. "crās . . . . . ."
(amābiminī, necābiminī)

3 This exercise is based on the letters on pp.336–42. Refer to the letters where necessary, and complete each of the sentences below with one of the following groups of words; then translate. Use each group of words once only.

Plīnium rem dīligenter effectūrum esse
quamquam multam pecūniam impenderant
quod servī erant
num servī supplicium ultimum meruissent
ut architēctum ad Bīthȳniam mitteret

1 Nīcomēdēnsēs, ..., nūllam aquam habēbant.
2 Plīnius imperātōrī persuādēre cōnābātur . . . . . .
3 Trāiānus cōnfīdēbat . . . . . .
4 Semprōnius duōs tīrōnēs ad Plīnium mīsit . . . . . .
5 Plīnius incertus erat . . . . . .

The Government of the Roman Provinces

The map opposite shows the provinces of the Roman empire at the time of its greatest extent, during the reign of the Emperor Trajan. The Romans obtained these territories gradually during several centuries, starting with the island of Sicily in the third century B.C., and ending with Trajan's conquests in Dacia (modern Romania) and the east. Some provinces, such as Britain, became part of the empire as a result of a successful Roman invasion. Others were given to the Romans by their previous rulers; Bithynia, for example, was bequeathed to Rome by its king in his will.

A number of provinces (whose names are marked on the map in italics) were known as "imperial provinces"; their governor was chosen by the emperor, and his official title was **lēgātus Augustī** (*emperor's deputy*). The other provinces (whose names are in boldface) were known as "senatorial provinces"; their governor was appointed by the senate and his official title was **prōcōnsul**. Occasionally the emperor stepped in and picked the governor of a senatorial province himself, as Trajan did when he appointed Pliny as governor of Bithynia, instead of leaving the choice to the senate.

Both the senate and the emperor took trouble to select suitable people for governorships. No senator could become the governor of a province unless he had previously held the praetorship, and some important provinces could be governed only by men who had been consul. The senate and emperor kept a lookout for men who had shown special skill or talent during the earlier part of their career. For example both Agricola and Pliny were sent to provinces where they could put their particular qualities and experience to good use.

A small group of imperial provinces was governed by members of the equestrian class, who were known as **praefectī**. The most important of these provinces was Egypt, whose governorship was one of the highest honors that an eques could hope for. Another province with an equestrian governor was Judaea, one of whose praefecti was the best-known of all Roman governors, Pontius Pilatus (Pilate), who offended the Jews with his harshness and tactlessness and became notorious among Christians for the crucifixion of Jesus.

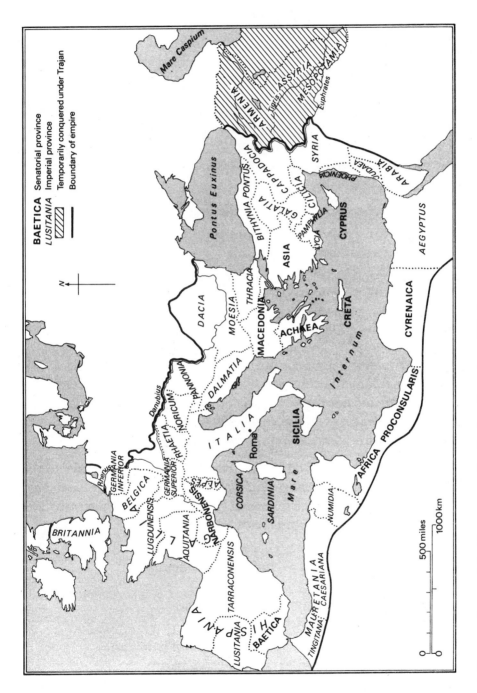

The provinces of the Roman empire during the reign of Trajan.

BAETICA Senatorial province
LUSITANIA Imperial province
Temporarily conquered under Trajan
Boundary of empire

N

Mare Caspium

ARMENIA ASSYRIA MESOPOTAMIA
Tigris Euphrates

SYRIA
PHOENICIA
JUDAEA
ARABIA

BITHYNIA PONTUS
CAPPADOCIA
GALATIA
PAMPHYLIA CILICIA
LYCIA
CYPRUS

ASIA

AEGYPTUS

Pontus Euxinus

DACIA

MOESIA
THRACIA
MACEDONIA
ACHAEA

CRETA

CYRENAICA

Mare Internum

Danubius

PANNONIA
NORICUM
DALMATIA
RHAETIA
GERMANIA SUPERIOR
ALPES
ITALIA

Roma

SICILIA

AFRICA PROCONSULARIS

Rhenus
GERMANIA INFERIOR
BELGICA
LUGDUNENSIS
AQUITANIA
NARBONENSIS

BRITANNIA

CORSICA

SARDINIA

Mare

NUMIDIA

TARRACONENSIS

LUSITANIA
HISPANIA
BAETICA

MAURETANIA
TINGITANA CAESARIENSIS

500 miles
1000 km

A governor's first and most important duty was a military one, to protect his province against attack from outside and rebellion from inside. Under his command were one or more legions or **auxilia**. He might, like Agricola in Scotland, use these troops to conquer further territory; he could also use them, if necessary, to deal with nuisances such as bandits or pirates. A small number of soldiers were taken away from their legions or auxilia to serve as officials on the governor's staff, but the governor was not supposed to use soldiers for jobs that could be done by civilians. (Trajan reminded Pliny firmly about this when Pliny thought of using soldiers as prison warders; see "carcer" II, p.117.) Although the governor was not a professional soldier, he would not be completely inexperienced in army matters, because normally he would have served as a military tribune in the early part of his career, and in most cases he would have commanded a legion after his praetorship.

The governor's other main task was to administer the law, by traveling around his province and acting as judge in the towns' law courts. He had supreme power, and his decisions could not be challenged, with one exception: any Roman citizen who was sentenced to death or flogging had the right to appeal to the emperor against the governor's decision. One man who appealed in this way was Saint Paul, who was arrested in the province of Judaea. The Jews wished to try him in their own court,

Diagrammatic map of the sort used in the Roman empire. It shows travelers the road system and accommodations available using standard symbols. The places marked are roughly in the correct relationship to each other but their shapes are distorted to get the map on a narrow continuous roll for easy reference.

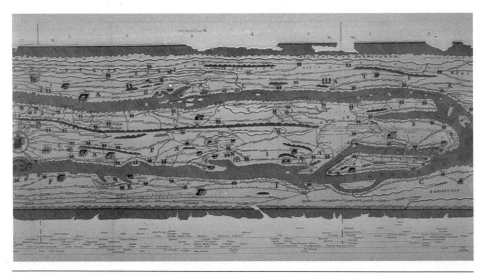

but Paul not only insisted on being tried in a Roman court but also appealed to the emperor. The following extract from *Acts of the Apostles* describes the confrontation between Paul and the Roman governor Festus:

"But Paul said to Festus, 'Against the Jews I have committed no offense, as you very well know. If I am guilty of any capital crime, I do not ask to escape the death penalty; but if there is no truth in the charges which these men bring against me, no one has any right to hand me over to them. I appeal to Caesar!'

Then Festus, after consulting his council of advisers, replied, 'You have appealed to Caesar; to Caesar you shall go.'"

(Paul was then handed over to a centurion and put on board a ship. After many adventures, including a shipwreck, he eventually reached Rome, where he may have been put to death during Nero's persecution of Christians after the great fire.)

Sometimes, especially in imperial provinces, the governor was too busy with his military tasks to carry out his other duty of administering the law. When this happened, the emperor could send out another official, known as a **iūridicus**, to take charge in the law courts while the governor carried on with the fighting. For example, Salvius acted as a iuridicus in the south of Britain while Agricola was busy campaigning in Scotland.

A governor appointed by the emperor was normally given **mandāta** (*instructions*) about the work he was to do in the province. Pliny, for example, was instructed in his mandata to make a public announcement

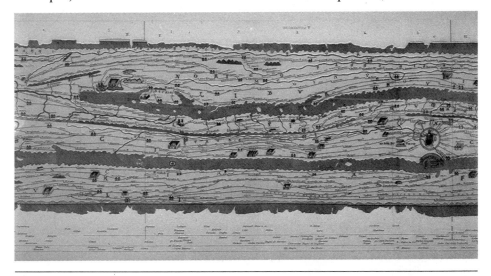

Relief showing official dispatch carrier.

banning political clubs. It is likely that he was also under orders to report back to Trajan about any proposals for public building in his province. (The Bithynians had been spending large sums of money on projects of this kind, and the results had often been disastrous.) Several of Pliny's letters deal with building projects; for example, he writes to Trajan about an aqueduct in Nicomedia ("aquaeductus" I, p.119), public baths at Prusa, a theater at Nicaea, and a smelly and unhygienic sewer at Amastris.

In the first century B.C., Roman governors were often feared and hated for their greed and cruelty; the people of the provinces generally believed, with good reason, that the Romans were only interested in their empire for what they could get out of it. By the time of Trajan, there may have been some improvement. (Most of our information, however, comes from the Romans themselves, rather than the people whom they governed.) Pliny's letters often express concern for the Bithynians' well-being (e.g. in "aquaeductus" and "incendium," pp.119 and 125); and in one of Trajan's replies (p.114, line 4), the emperor stresses his **benignitās** (*kindly feelings*) towards the people. Tacitus, in his account of Agricola's life, claims that a deliberate attempt was made to introduce the Britons to some benefits of the Roman way of life:

"Agricola encouraged individuals and gave help to local communities for the building of temples, forums, and houses. He also provided an education for the sons of the chieftains. Those who had recently refused to use the Roman language were now eager to make speeches in it. Roman clothing became a sign of status, and togas were often to be seen."

Roman governors may have behaved in this way partly from kindness, partly from self-interest; if people are comfortable and contented, they are less likely to make trouble for their rulers. Tacitus follows his description of Agricola's policy with a cynical comment:

"The Britons were gradually led astray by the temptations of idleness and luxury – colonnades, baths, and elegant dinner parties. In their innocence, the Britons referred to this as 'civilization'; in fact it was part of their slavery."

Many people, however, were bitterly hostile to the Romans and their empire. In the following extract, Tacitus imagines the speech which might have been made by a Scottish chieftain whose homeland was being invaded:

"The Romans plunder the whole world; when there is no land left for them to devastate, they search the sea as well. If their enemy is rich, they are greedy for wealth; if he is poor, they are eager for glory. They describe robbery and slaughter with the deceptive name of "empire"; they make a desert and call it 'peace.'"

Words and Phrases Checklist

dīversus, dīversa, dīversum	*different*
factum, factī	*deed, achievement*
glōria, glōriae	*glory*
incendium, incendiī	*fire*
lūdō, lūdere, lūsī	*play*
mereō, merēre, meruī	*deserve*
nōndum	*not yet*
opus est	*there is need*
peditēs, peditum	*foot soldiers, infantry*
perdō, perdere, perdidī, perditus	*waste, lose*
sī quis	*if anyone*
sī quid	*if anything*
vīlis, vīle	*cheap*
vitium, vitiī	*sin, fault, vice*

Give the meaning of each of the following:

incendere, lūdus, vīlitās, vitiōsus.

Synonym Search

Using the Words and Phrases Checklist above, find a synonym for each of the following words. The number in parentheses refers to the Stage Checklist in which each word appeared. The meaning of non-Checklist words should be inferred from the Checklist words given in parentheses.

āmittere (12), ardor (cf. ardēre, 27), error (cf. errāre, 23), inūtilis (cf. ūtilis, 11).

Stage 42

MVSA MIHI
CAVSAS MEMORA
QVO NVMINE
LAESO QVIDVE

carmina

Phaedrus

Phaedrus, who lived in the first half of the first century A.D., was originally a slave of the emperor, and became a "lībertus Augustī." He composed five books of verse mainly based on the animal fables of Aesop, such as the following fable of the wolf and the lamb:

> ad rīvum eundem lupus et agnus vēnerant
> sitī compulsī; superior stābat lupus
> longēque īnferior agnus. tunc fauce improbā
> latrō incitātus iūrgiī causam intulit.
> "quārē" inquit "<u>turbulentam</u> fēcistī mihi
> <u>aquam</u>* bibentī?" lāniger contrā timēns:
> "quī possum, quaesō, facere quod quereris, lupe?
> ā tē dēcurrit ad meōs haustūs liquor."
> repulsus ille vēritātis vīribus:

*Some noun-and-adjective phrases, in which an adjective is separated by one word or more from the noun which it describes, have been underlined.

A scene from Aesop's *Fables*.

"ante hōs sex mēnsēs male" ait "dīxistī mihi."
respondit agnus: "equidem nātus nōn eram."
"pater hercle tuus" ille inquit "male dīxit mihi";
atque ita correptum lacerat, iniūstā nece.

rīvum: rīvus	*stream*
sitī: sitis	*thirst*
compulsī: compellere	*drive, compel*
superior	*higher, farther upstream*
īnferior	*lower, farther downstream*
tunc	*then*
fauce	*(ablative singular) hunger (literally "throat")*
improbā: improbus	*wicked, relentless*
latrō	*the robber, i.e. the wolf*
iūrgiī: iūrgium	*argument, dispute*
causam intulit: causam īnferre	*make an excuse, invent an excuse*
turbulentam: turbulentus	*disturbed, muddy*
lāniger	*the woolly one, i.e. the lamb*
contrā	*in reply*
quī?	*how?*
dēcurrit: dēcurrere	*run down*
haustūs: haustus	*drinking, drinking-place*
liquor	*water*
repulsus	*repelled, taken aback*
vīribus: vīrēs	*forces, strength*
male . . . dīxistī: male dīcere	*insult*
ait	*said*
correptum: corripere	*seize*
lacerat: lacerāre	*tear apart*
iniūstā: iniūstus	*unjust*
nece: nex	*slaughter*

1 Where had the wolf and lamb come to, and why? Where did they stand?
2 Who started the argument? What excuse did he invent?
3 What reason did the lamb give for saying that the wolf must be wrong?
4 What accusation did the wolf then make? What was the lamb's reply?
5 How did the wolf then change his accusation? What did he do next?
6 Suggest a moral (or a title) for this fable. Then compare your moral with the one which Phaedrus wrote:

> haec propter illōs scrīpta est hominēs fābula
> quī fictīs causīs innocentēs opprimunt.

Catullus   *poetic device*

Gaius Valerius Catullus came from Verona in the north of Italy. He was
born in about 84 B.C. and died not long after 54 B.C. His poems, mostly
short, vary from tender and loving to insulting and obscene. Stage 42
contains two poems by Catullus in very contrasting styles.

I

Egnātius, quod <u>candidōs</u> habet <u>dentēs,</u>
renīdet usque quāque. sī ad reī ventum est
subsellium, cum ōrātor excitat flētum,
renīdet ille; sī ad <u>piī</u> rogum <u>filī</u>
lūgētur, <u>orba</u> cum flet ūnicum <u>māter,</u>   5
renīdet ille. quidquid est, ubicumque est,
quodcumque agit, renīdet: hunc habet morbum,
neque ēlegantem, ut arbitror, neque urbānum.
quārē monendum est tē mihi, bone Egnātī.
sī urbānus essēs aut Sabīnus aut Tīburs   10
aut pinguis Umber aut obēsus Etruscus
aut quīlibet, quī pūriter lavit dentēs,
tamen renīdēre usque quāque tē nōllem:
nam rīsū ineptō <u>rēs</u> ineptior <u>nūlla</u> est.

candidōs: candidus	*bright, gleaming white*	ubicumque	*wherever*
renīdet: renīdēre	*grin, smirk*	arbitror: arbitrārī	*think*
usque quāque	*on every possible occasion*	urbānum: urbānus	*(line 8) refined*
reī: reus	*defendant*	quārē	*therefore*
ventum est	*people have come (literally "there has been an arrival")*	urbānus	*(line 10) a city-dweller, a man from Rome*
subsellium	*bench (for prisoner in court)*	pinguis	*plump*
ōrātor	*speaker (in court), pleader*	quīlibet	*anyone at all*
flētum: flētus	*weeping, tears*	pūriter	*decently, with clean water*
piī: pius	*good, pious*		
lūgētur	*mourning is taking place, mourning is in progress*	nōllem	*I would not want*
		ineptō: ineptus	*silly*
orba: orbus	*bereaved*	Sabīnus	*a Sabine*
flet: flēre	*weep for*	Tīburs	*a man from Tibur*
ūnicum: ūnicus		Umber	*an Umbrian*
(fīlius)	*one and only (son)*	Etruscus	*an Etruscan*
quidquid est	*whatever is happening*		

sī ad reī ventum est subsellium, cum ōrātor excitat flētum, renīdet ille. (lines 2–4)

1 Why, according to Catullus, does Egnatius grin so continually?
2 What is happening in lines 2–5 (a) in court (b) at the funeral pyre? What does Egnatius do on each occasion? Suggest reasons why Catullus includes the words "cum ōrātor excitat flētum" (line 3) and "orba cum flet ūnicum māter" (line 5) in his description of the scenes.
3 Suggest a reason why the verb "renīdet" is repeated so often (lines 2,4,6,7 and "renīdēre" in line 13).
4 How does Catullus describe Egnatius' habit in lines 7–8?
5 What does Catullus say he must do to Egnatius in line 9?
6 Study the long sentence in lines 10–13. Does Catullus imply that Egnatius in fact comes from any of these places? Does he imply that Egnatius cleans his teeth "pūriter"?
7 According to line 14, why would Catullus still object to Egnatius' smile, no matter where he came from?

II

multās per gentēs et multa per aequora vectus,
    adveniō <u>hās miserās</u>, frāter, ad <u>īnferiās</u>,
ut tē postrēmō dōnārem mūnere mortis
    et <u>mūtam</u> nēquīquam adloquerer <u>cinerem</u>.
quandoquidem fortūna mihī tētē abstulit ipsum,   5
    heu miser indignē frāter adēmpte mihī,
nunc tamen intereā haec*, <u>prīscō</u> quae <u>mōre</u> parentum
    trādita sunt trīstī mūnere ad īnferiās,
accipe* <u>frāternō</u> multum mānantia <u>flētū</u>,
    atque in perpetuum, frāter, avē atque valē.   10

aequora: aequor	sea
vectus: vehī	be carried (e.g. by horse or ship), travel
īnferiās: īnferiae	tribute to the dead
postrēmō: postrēmus	last
mūnere: mūnus	gift
mūtam: mūtus	silent
nēquīquam	in vain
(ut) adloquerer	(so that) I might speak to
quandoquidem	seeing that, since
mihī	from me
tētē = tē	
heu = ēheu	
indignē	unfairly
adēmpte: adēmptus	taken away
haec	these things, these gifts
prīscō . . . mōre	by the ancient custom
parentum: parentēs	ancestors, forefathers
trīstī mūnere	as a sad gift, by way of a sad gift
frāternō: frāternus	of a brother, fraternal
multum mānantia	drenched
avē atque valē	hail and farewell

1 How does Catullus emphasize the distance he has traveled?
2 Why has he made this journey? Why do you think he emphasizes its length?
3 Explain "nēquīquam" in line 4. Is your explanation supported by any other word in the same line?
4 Is there any indication in the poem that Catullus believes or disbelieves in an afterlife?
5 Where in the poem does the emotion seem to be most intense? What, in your opinion, is the mood of the final line?

* These two words go closely together.

Roman cinerary urn.

Mārtiālis

A number of Martial's epigrams were included in Stage 36. Martial (Marcus Valerius Martialis) was originally a native of Spain, and lived from about A.D.40 to about A.D.104. Pliny said of him: "He was a talented man, sharp and shrewd, whose epigrams had plenty of salt and vinegar in them."

I

tū Sētīna quidem semper vel Massica pōnis,
    Pāpyle, sed rūmor tam bona vīna negat:
dīceris hāc factus caelebs quater esse lagōnā.
    nec puto nec crēdō, Pāpyle, nec sitiō.

pōnis: pōnere	*serve*
rūmor	*rumor*
negat: negāre	*deny, say that . . . not*
tam bona vīna negat =	negat ea esse tam bona vīna
caelebs	*widower*
quater	*four times*
lagōnā: lagōna	*bottle*
sitiō: sitīre	*be thirsty*

Sētīna = vīna Sētīna	*Setian wine (a good wine)*
Massica = vīna Massica	*Massic wine (another good wine)*

II

Eutrapelus tōnsor dum circuit ōra Lupercī
expingitque genās, altera barba subit.

Eutrapelus tōnsor dum = dum Eutrapelus tōnsor
circuit = circumit
expingit: expingere *paint, put paint onto*
genās: gena   *cheek*
subit: subīre   *come up*

III

nūbere Paula cupit nōbīs, ego dūcere Paulam
nōlō: anus est. vellem, sī magis esset anus.

nōbīs = mihi
dūcere   *marry*
vellem   *I would be willing*

About the Language

1 From Unit 2 onwards, you have met sentences like these:

sī illud dīxistī, errāvistī.
If you said that, *you were wrong.*

sī fīlius meus mortuus est, fundum lībertīs lēgō.
If my son is dead, *I leave the farm to the freedmen.*

The group of Latin words in boldface is known as a *conditional clause*, and sentences which contain a conditional clause are known as *conditional sentences*.

2 Translate the following examples, and pick out the conditional clause in each sentence:

1 sī Mārcō crēdis, īnsānus es.
2 sī Salvius tālia facinora commīsit, pūniendus est.
3 sī illum servum magnō pretiō ēmistī, vēnālīcius tē dēcēpit.

3 From Stage 33 onwards, you have met sentences in which a conditional clause refers to the future:

sī **respexeris**, aliquid mīrī **vidēbis**.
*If **you look behind you**, **you will see*** something amazing.

sī mīlitēs bene **pugnābunt**, hostēs **terrēbunt**.
*If the soldiers **fight well**, **they will terrify*** the enemy.

Notice again how the verb in the Latin conditional clause is put either into the future perfect tense (as in the first example, **respexeris**) or the future tense (as in the second example, **pugnābunt**). English, however, normally uses a present tense (*look behind you, fight*).

Further examples:

1 sī pecūniam meam reppereritis, vōbīs praemium ingēns dabō.
2 sī pompam spectābis, dēlectāberis.
3 sī Virginēs Vestālēs ignem sacrum neglexerint, dī populum Rōmānum pūnient.
4 sī tū mihi nocueris, ego tibi nocēbō.

4 Notice how the word **nisi** (*unless* or *if . . . not*) is used in conditional clauses:

nisi tacueritis, ē tabernā ēiciēminī.
***Unless you are quiet**, you will be thrown out of the inn.*
   Or, in more natural English:
***If you aren't quiet**, you'll be thrown out of the inn.*

Further examples:

1 nisi prīnceps mē līberābit, in exiliō relīquam vītam manēbō.
2 nisi cāveris, custōdēs tē invenient.

5 In Stage 42, you have met a slightly different type of conditional sentence:

sī urbānus **essēs**, tamen renīdēre usque quāque tē **nōllem**.
*If you **were** a city-dweller, **I** still **wouldn't want** you to be forever grinning.*

sī magis **esset** anus, Mārtiālis eam dūcere **vellet**.
*If she **were** older, Martial **would be willing** to marry her.*

Notice that in these sentences, Latin uses the subjunctive and English uses the word *would*.

Ovidius

Illustration from a medieval manuscript showing Doctor Ovid Lecturing in a Garden of Lovers.

Stage 39 included a short extract from the *Metamorphoses* of Ovid (Publius Ovidius Naso, 43 B.C. – A.D.17). The following lines are taken from Ovid's *Ars Amatoria* or *Art of Love*, of which the first two sections (or "books") give advice to young men on how to find, win, and keep a girlfriend. Here, Ovid is telling his reader what to do if a girl ignores him and sends his love-messages back without reading them:

> sī nōn accipiet scrīptum inlēctumque remittet,
> > lēctūram spērā prōpositumque tenē.
> tempore <u>difficilēs</u> veniunt ad arātra <u>iuvencī</u>,
> > tempore <u>lenta</u> patī <u>frēna</u> docentur equī.
> <u>ferreus</u> assiduō cōnsūmitur <u>ānulus</u> ūsū,   5
> > interit assiduā vōmer aduncus humō.
> quid magis est saxō dūrum, quid mollius undā?
> > <u>dūra</u> tamen mollī <u>saxa</u> cavantur aquā.
> Pēnelopēn ipsam, perstā modo, tempore vincēs:
> > <u>capta</u> vidēs sērō <u>Pergama</u>, capta tamen.   10

inlēctum: inlēctus	*unread*
lēctūram spērā = spērā eam id lēctūram esse	
prōpositum	*intention, resolution*
tenē: tenēre	*keep to, hold on to*
difficilēs: difficilis	*obstinate*
arātra: arātrum	*plow*
iuvencī: iuvencus	*bullock, young ox*
lenta: lentus	*supple*
frēna	*reins*
ferreus	*iron, made of iron*
assiduō: assiduus	*continual*
interit: interīre	*wear away, wear out*
vōmer	*plowshare*
cavantur: cavāre	*hollow out*
sērō	*late, after a long time*
Pēnelopēn	*Greek accusative of* Pēnelopē

1 What is Ovid's advice to the young man? What arguments does he use to support his advice? Do these arguments actually prove Ovid's point? If not, why does he include them?

2 Using a Classical Dictionary if necessary, find out what or where Pergama (line 10) was, and how long a time is referred to by "sērō" (line 10). Then (using the dictionary again if needed), find out who Penelope was, and suggest reasons why Ovid uses her as his example in line 9.

Vergilius

The chief work of Vergil (Publius Vergilius Maro, 70–19 B.C.) was the *Aeneid*, an epic poem in nearly ten thousand lines, which related the adventures of Aeneas, the legendary ancestor of the Romans. The following lines form a tiny but complete episode in this huge poem; Aeneas, who is describing his earlier wanderings to Dido, Queen of Carthage, tells of a storm that hit him and his Trojan companions as they sailed westwards from the island of Crete.

postquam altum tenuēre ratēs nec iam amplius ūllae	
appārent terrae, caelum undique et undique pontus,	
tum mihi <u>caeruleus</u> suprā caput adstitit <u>imber</u>	
noctem hiememque ferēns, et inhorruit unda tenebrīs.	
continuō ventī volvunt mare magnaque surgunt	5
aequora, dispersī iactāmur gurgite vāstō;	
involvēre diem nimbī et nox ūmida caelum	
abstulit, ingeminant abruptīs nūbibus ignēs.	
excutimur cursū et <u>caecīs</u> errāmus in <u>undīs</u>.	
ipse* diem noctemque negat discernere caelō	10
nec meminisse viae <u>mediā</u> Palinūrus* in <u>undā</u>.	
<u>trēs adeō incertōs</u> caecā cālīgine <u>sōlēs</u>	
errāmus pelagō, totidem sine sīdere noctēs.	
<u>quārtō</u> terra <u>diē</u> prīmum sē attollere tandem	
vīsa, aperīre procul montēs ac volvere fūmum.	15

altum	*deep sea, open sea*
tenuēre = tenuērunt:	
tenēre	*occupy, be upon*
ratēs: ratis	*boat*
amplius	*any more*
caeruleus	*dark*
adstitit: adstāre	*stand*
imber	*storm-cloud*
noctem: nox	*darkness*
hiemem: hiems	*storm*
inhorruit:	
inhorrēscere	*shudder*
continuō	*immediately*

*These two words go closely together.

volvunt: volvere	*(line 5) set rolling,* *turn to billows*
dispersī: dispergere	*scatter*
gurgite: gurges	*whirlpool, swirling water*
involvēre =	
involvērunt: involvere	*envelop, swallow up*
ūmida: ūmidus	*rainy, stormy*
ingeminant:.	
ingemināre	*redouble*
abruptīs: abrumpere	*split, tear apart*
ignēs: ignis	*lightning*
excutimur: excutere	*shake off, drive* *violently off*
caecīs: caecus	*(line 9) unseen* *(literally "blind")*
negat = negat sē posse	
discernere	*distinguish*
trēs adeō	*as many as three, three entire*
caecā: caecus	*(line 12) impenetrable*
cālīgine: cālīgō	*darkness, gloom*
sōlēs: sōl	*day*
pelagō: pelagus	*sea*
totidem	*the same number*
prīmum	*for the first time*
sē attollere	*raise itself, rise up*
aperīre	*reveal*
volvere	*(line 15) send rolling upwards*
Palinūrus	*Palinurus (the Trojans' helmsman)*

A 1 Where were the boats when the storm broke?

  2 Were they within sight of land? What were they surrounded by?

  3 What was the first sign of trouble? Where was it? What did it bring with it?

  4 What did the winds do to the ocean (line 5)? What happened to the Trojans?

  5 What was the effect of the rain-clouds (line 7)? What further detail of the storm does Vergil give in line 8?

  6 What was the next thing that happened to the Trojans?

  7 What does Palinurus say he cannot do in line 10? What other difficulty is he having?

  8 For how long did the Trojans wander? What was unusual about the "noctēs" (line 13)?

  9 When did they finally catch sight of land?

  10 List the three stages in which the Trojans got an increasingly detailed view of land in lines 14–15.

Ships from the mosaic at a villa in Low Ham (Somerset, England).

B1 What idea is most strongly emphasized in lines 1–2? In what way is it relevant to the storm that follows?

2 What does Vergil suggest in line 4 about the appearance of the sea?

3 Compare the following translations of "continuō ventī volvunt mare magnaque surgunt aequora" (lines 5–6):

(a) "The ruffling winds the foamy billows raise."

(John Dryden, 1697)

(b) "The winds quickly set the sea-surface rolling and lifted it in great waves." *(W.F. Jackson Knight, 1956)*

(c) "Winds billowed the sea at once, the seas were running high."

(C. Day Lewis, 1952)

(d) "The winds roll up the sea, great waters heave."

(Allen Mandelbaum, 1981)

(e) "Soon the winds
Made the sea rise and big waves came against us."

(Robert Fitzgerald, 1983)

Which of the translations is most successful in conveying the feeling of Vergil's words? Which gives the most vivid picture?

4 What is the point of "ipse" (line 10)?

5 Compare the following translations of lines 12–13:

(a) "Three starless nights the doubtful navy strays
Without distinction, and three sunless days." *(Dryden)*

(b) "For three whole days, hard though they were to reckon, and as many starless nights, we wandered in the sightless murk over the ocean." *(Jackson Knight)*

(c) "Three days, three days befogged and unsighted by the darkness,
We wandered upon the sea, three starless nights we wandered." *(Day Lewis)*

(d) "We wander for three days in sightless darkness and for as many nights without a star." *(Mandelbaum)*

(e) "Three days on the deep sea muffled in fog,
Three starless nights we wandered blind." *(Fitzgerald)*

Relief showing slaves serving wine.

About the Language

1 In Stage 39, you met sentences in which one noun-and-adjective phrase is placed inside another one:

cōnstitit ante *oculōs* **pulchra puella** *meōs*.
A beautiful girl stood before my eyes.

2 In Stage 42, you have met sentences like this, in which two noun-and-adjective phrases are intertwined with each other:

dura tamen **mollī** *saxa* cavantur **aquā**.
Nevertheless, hard stones are hollowed out by soft water.

Further examples:
1 **parva** necat morsū *spatiōsum* **vīpera** *taurum*. (*Ovid*)
2 *frīgidus* **ingentēs** irrigat *imber* **agrōs.**

morsū: morsus	*bite, fangs*
spatiōsum: spatiōsus	*huge*
vīpera	*viper*
frīgidus	*cold*
irrigat: irrigāre	*to water*

3 Compare the intertwining of the noun-and-adjective phrases in paragraph 2 with the intertwining of rhymed lines in such verses as the following:

> Oh, life is a glorious cycle of *song*,
> A medley of **extemporanea**;
> And love is a thing that can never go *wrong*;
> And I am Marie of **Roumania**.
> > (*Dorothy Parker*)

4 In each of the following examples, pick out the Latin adjectives and say which nouns they are describing:

1 impiaque aeternam timuērunt saecula noctem. (*Vergil*)
   The evil generations were in fear of endless night.
2 molliaque immītēs fīxit in ōra manūs. (*Propertius*)
   It fastened its cruel hands on her soft face.

5 Translate the following examples:

1 *Poets and poverty:*
   Maeonidēs nūllās ipse relīquit opēs. (*Ovid*)
2 *A poet's epitaph on himself:*
   hīc iacet immītī cōnsūmptus morte Tibullus. (*Tibullus*)
3 *Ovid congratulates Cupid on his forthcoming victory procession:*
   haec tibi magnificus pompa triumphus erit. (*Ovid*)

Maeonidēs = Homer, the greatest of Greek poets

Practicing the Language

1 Notice again that there are often several different ways of translating a Latin word, and that you always have to choose the most suitable translation for the particular sentence you are working on.

For example, the vocabulary at the end of the book gives the following meanings for **ēmittō**, **petō**, and **referō**:

ēmittō *throw, send out*
petō *make for, attack; seek, beg for, ask for*
referō *bring back, carry, deliver, tell, report*

Translate the following sentences, using suitable translations of **ēmittō**, **petō**, and **referō** chosen from the above list:

1 dux trīgintā equitēs ēmīsit.
2 duo latrōnēs, fūstibus armātī, senem petīvērunt.
3 nūntius tōtam rem rettulit.
4 nautae, tempestāte perterritī, portum petēbant.
5 subitō mīlitēs hastās ēmittere coepērunt.
6 mercātor nihil ex Āfricā rettulit.
7 captīvus, genibus ducis haerēns, lībertātem petīvit.

2 Complete each sentence with the right word and then translate.

1 corpora mīlitum mortuōrum crās . . . . . . (sepeliētur, sepelientur)
2 nōlīte timēre, cīvēs! ā vestrīs equitibus . . . . . . (dēfendēris, dēfendēminī)
3 sī custōdēs mē cēperint, ego sine dubiō . . . . . . (interficiar, interficiēmur)
4 fābula nōtissima in theātrō . . . . . . (agētur, agentur)
5 difficile erit tibi nāvigāre; nam ventīs et tempestātibus . . . . . . (impediēris, impediēminī)
6 nisi fortiter pugnābimus, ab hostibus . . . . . . (vincar, vincēmur)

3 In each pair of sentences, translate sentence (a), then change it from a direct statement to an indirect statement by completing sentence (b), and translate again.

For example: (a) equī hodiē exercentur.
                    (b) audiō equ. . . hodiē exerc. . . .

Translated and completed, this becomes:

(a) **equī** hodiē **exercentur.** *The **horses are being exercised** today.*

(b) audiō **equōs** hodiē **exercērī.**
    *I hear that the **horses are being exercised** today.*

In sentences 1–3, a present passive infinitive is required. For examples of the way in which this infinitive is formed, see paragraph 6 on p.000.

1a patrōnus ā clientibus cotīdiē salūtātur.
1b sciō patrōn. . . ā clientibus cotīdiē salūt. . . .
2a duae puellae in hōc carcere retinentur.
2b centuriō putat du. . . puell. . . in hōc carcere retin. . . .
3a vīlla nova prope montem aedificātur.
3b agricola dīcit . . . . prope montem . . . . . .

In sentences 4–6, a future active infinitive is required. For examples of the way in which this infinitive is formed, see paragraph 9 on page 000. Note that the first part of this infinitive (e.g. **parātūrus** in **parātūrus esse**) changes its ending to agree with the noun it describes.

For example: (a) puella ad nōs scrībet.
                    (b) spērō puell. . . ad nōs scrīp. . . . .

Translated and completed, this becomes:

(a) **puella** ad nōs **scrībet.** *The **girl will write** to us.*

(b) spērō **puellam** ad nōs **scrīptūram esse.**
    *I hope that **the girl will write** to us.*

4a gladiātor crās pugnābit.
4b exīstimō gladiāt. . . crās pugnā. . . . .
5a nostrī mīlitēs vincent.
5b dux crēdit nostr. . . mīl. . . vic. . . . .
6a discipulī crās recitābunt.
6b rhētor pollicētur . . . . . crās . . . .

Time chart

This time chart shows the dates of the five Roman poets represented in Stage 42, together with some events in Roman history.

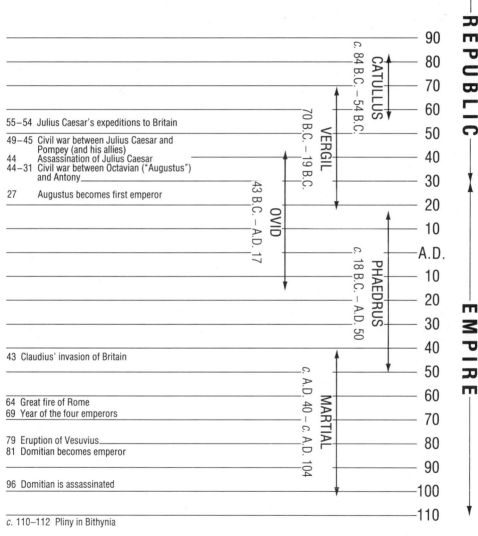

REPUBLIC

	90
	80
	70
	60
55–54 Julius Caesar's expeditions to Britain	50
49–45 Civil war between Julius Caesar and Pompey (and his allies)	40
44   Assassination of Julius Caesar
44–31 Civil war between Octavian ("Augustus") and Antony	30
27 Augustus becomes first emperor	20
	10
	A.D.

c. 84 B.C. – 54 B.C.   CATULLUS

70 B.C. – 19 B.C.   VERGIL

43 B.C. – A.D. 17   OVID

c. 18 B.C. – A.D. 50   PHAEDRUS

c. A.D. 40 – *c.* A.D. 104   MARTIAL

	10
	20
	30
43 Claudius' invasion of Britain	40
	50
64 Great fire of Rome	60
69 Year of the four emperors	70
79 Eruption of Vesuvius	80
81 Domitian becomes emperor	90
96 Domitian is assassinated	100
	110

c. 110–112 Pliny in Bithynia

EMPIRE

Words and Phrases Checklist

adloquor, adloquī,
    adlocūtus sum — *speak to, address*
caecus, caeca, caecum — *(1) blind, (2) invisible, unseen*
genū, genūs — *knee*
longē — *far, a long way*
lūgeō, lūgēre, lūxī — *lament, mourn*
meminī, meminisse — *remember*
mollis, molle — *soft*
nec (*also spelled* neque) — *and not, nor*
    nec . . . nec — *neither . . . nor*
quīcumque, quaecumque — *whoever*
    quodcumque — *whatever*
reperiō, reperīre, repperī,
    repertus — *find*
sepeliō, sepelīre, sepelīvī, sepultus — *bury*
sīdus, sīderis — *star*

Give the meaning of each of the following:

caecitās, mollīre, repertor, sepulcrum.

Synonym Search

Numbers in parentheses refer to Stage Checklists.

invenīre (10), obscūrus (29), procul (34).

ūnivira

mātrōna Ephesia

Versions of the following story have been found all over the world. Its first appearance in Latin is in the fables of Phaedrus, and it was particularly popular in the Middle Ages; numerous versions exist in Latin, French, Italian, English, German, Russian, Chinese, and Hebrew, and in 1946 it was turned into a stage play (*A Phoenix Too Frequent*) by Christopher Fry. The following version is based closely on the *Satyrica* by Petronius, who is probably the same man as Gaius Petronius Arbiter, Nero's "arbiter ēlegantiae" (adviser on taste and fashion) who was eventually ordered by Nero to commit suicide in A.D. 66.

Façades of two Roman "house" tombs.

I

mātrōna quaedam, quae Ephesī habitābat, ita nōta erat propter
pudīcitiam ut ab omnibus fēminīs illīus locī laudārētur. haec ergō,
marītō mortuō, tantō dolōre affecta est ut sine eō vīvere nōllet; nōn
modo fūnus eius, ut mōs erat, passīs crīnibus et veste scissā
prōsecūta est, sed etiam servīs imperāvit ut ipsa in sepulcrō eōdem   5
ūnā cum corpore marītī clauderētur. ibi corpus eius custōdīre ac
flēre tōtās noctēs diēsque coepit; neque cibum neque vīnum
accipere volēbat; precēs parentum, propinquōrum, etiam
magistrātuum, repudiāvit; cōnstituerat enim mortem inediā iuxtā
corpus marītī obīre.   10

quīntum iam diem mātrōna sine cibō agēbat, cīvibus
affirmantibus eam vērum pudīcitiae amōrisque exemplum omnibus
uxōribus praestitisse.

interim lēgātus prōvinciae trēs latrōnēs iussit crucibus affīgī
prope illud sepulcrum ubi mātrōna lūgēbat. proximā ergō nocte,   15
mīles quīdam, ad crucēs custōdiendās ēlēctus, nē corpora ad
sepultūram ā propinquīs latrōnum dētraherentur, lūmine inter
sepulcra cōnspectō et gemitū lūgentis audītō, statim contendit ad
cognōscendum quid ibi fieret. sepulcrum ingressus, vīsāque
mātrōnā pulcherrimā, attonitus cōnstitit; deinde, cum corpus   20
marītī vīdisset lacrimāsque mātrōnae, intellēxit eam dēsīderium
mortuī nōn posse patī; ad sepulcrum igitur cēnulam suam attulit,
coepitque hortārī lūgentem nē in dolōre inānī persevērāret;

ita	*so*
pudīcitiam: pudīcitia	*chastity, virtue, purity*
fūnus	*funeral procession*
passīs: passus	*loose, disheveled*
prōsecūta est: prōsequī	*follow, escort*
propinquōrum: propinquus	*relative*
repudiāvit: repudiāre	*reject*
inediā: inedia	*starvation*
crucibus: crux	*cross*
crucibus affīgī: cruce affīgere	*nail to a cross, crucify*
sepultūram: sepultūra	*burial*
lūmine: lūmen	*light*
dēsīderium	*loss, longing*
cēnulam: cēnula	*little supper*

omnibus enim mortālibus tandem pereundum esse. "quid tibi
prōderit" inquit "sī inediā perieris, sī tē vīvam sepelīveris?" et   25
cibum vīnumque mātrōnae obtulit. quae, inediā paene cōnfecta,
tandem passa est superārī pertināciam suam.

at mīles, quī mātrōnam esse pulcherrimam prius animadverterat,
in sepulcrō multās hōrās manēbat, et eīsdem blanditiīs pudīcitiam
eius aggredī coepit, quibus eam anteā incitāverat ut cibum   30
acciperet. multa dē pulchritūdine eius locūtus est, multa dē amōre
suō. postrēmō mīles mātrōnae persuāsit ut illam noctem ibi in
sepulcrō sēcum iacēret.

quid . . . prōderit?	*what good will it do?*
passa est: patī	*allow*
pertināciam: pertinācia	*obstinacy, determination*
aggredī	*assail, make an attempt on*
Ephesī: Ephesus	*Ephesus (city in Asia Minor)*

II

mediā autem nocte, cum mīles et fēmina in sepulcrō ūnā iacērent,
parentēs ūnīus latrōnum crucibus affīxōrum, ubi vīdērunt nēminem
crucēs custōdīre, corpus clam dē cruce dētractum ad rīte
sepeliendum abstulērunt.

postrīdiē māne mīles, ē sepulcrō ēgressus, ubi vīdit ūnam sine   5
corpore crucem esse, supplicium ultimum sibi verēbātur. mātrōnae
quid accidisset exposuit; negāvit sē iūdicis sententiam
exspectātūrum esse; potius sē ipsum neglegentiam suam pūnitūrum
esse. "trāde mihi pugiōnem" inquit "ut ego hīc in marītī tuī sepulcrō
moriar atque sepeliar." mātrōna tamen, quae nōn minus misericors   10
quam pudīca erat, "nē illud deī sinant" inquit "ut eōdem tempore
corpora duōrum mihi cārissimōrum hominum spectem. mālō
mortuum impendere quam vīvum occīdere." quibus verbīs dictīs,
imperāvit ut ex arcā corpus marītī suī tollerētur atque illī quae
vacābat crucī affīgerētur. itaque mīles cōnsiliō prūdentissimae   15
mātrōnae libenter ūsus est, et postrīdiē populus mīrābātur quō
modō mortuus in crucem ascendisset.

rīte	*properly*
neglegentiam: neglegentia	*carelessness*
minus	*less*
misericors	*tender-hearted, full of pity*
pudīca: pudīcus	*chaste, virtuous*
nē illud deī sinant!	*heaven forbid! (literally "may the gods not allow it")*

mātrōnae quid accidisset exposuit. (lines 6–7)

impendere — *make use of*
arcā: arca — *coffin*
vacābat: vacāre — *be unoccupied*

1 What happened outside the tomb in the middle of the night?
2 What did the soldier see next morning when he came out of the tomb? What did he fear would happen to him? Rather than wait for this fate, what did he say he would do?
3 What did he ask the lady to do? What were his intentions?
4 What reason did the lady give for objecting violently to the soldier's request?
5 Whom did she mean by "mortuum" and "vīvum" (line 13)?
6 What did she tell the soldier to do?
7 Why were the people puzzled next day?
8 Do you approve of the lady's decision?
9 Why do you think this story has been so popular and been retold so often?

About the Language

1 Study the following examples:

lēgātus prōvinciam tam bene regēbat ut ab omnibus **dīligerētur**.
*The governor ruled the province so well that **he was loved** by everybody.*

nesciēbāmus utrum ā sociīs nostrīs **adiuvārēmur** an **impedīrēmur**.
*We did not know whether **we were being helped** or **hindered** by our companions.*

The form of the Latin verb in boldface is the *imperfect subjunctive passive*.

Further examples:

1 intellegere nōn poteram quārē fēminae līberīque in oppidō relinquerentur.
2 tam ignāvus erat coquus ut ā cēterīs servīs contemnerētur.
3 ferōciter resistēbāmus nē ā barbarīs superārēmur.

2 Compare the active and passive forms of the imperfect subjunctive of **portō**:

IMPERFECT SUBJUNCTIVE ACTIVE	IMPERFECT SUBJUNCTIVE PASSIVE
portārem	**portārer**
portārēs	**portārēris**
portāret	**portārētur**
portārēmus	**portārēmur**
portārētis	**portārēminī**
portārent	**portārentur**

Imperfect subjunctive passive forms of **doceō**, **trahō**, **capiō**, and **audiō** are given on p.299.

3 Study the following examples:

tantus erat fragor ut omnēs nautae **verērentur**.
*So great was the crash that all the sailors **were afraid**.*

iūdex mē rogāvit num **mentīrer**.
*The judge asked me whether **I was lying**.*

The Latin words in boldface are *imperfect subjunctive* forms of *deponent* verbs.

Further examples:

1 cum ēgrederēmur, amīcus meus subitō cōnstitit.
2 pontifex cīvibus imperāvit ut deōs immortālēs precārentur.

Imperfect subjunctive forms of the deponent verbs **cōnor**, **vereor**, etc. are given on p.298.

Woman of the Flavian period.

Tūria

The funeral ceremony of a Roman noble often included a **laudātiō**, or speech in praise of the dead person, which might later be inscribed on the tomb. The following passages are based on one of these speeches, which survives (in an incomplete form) on a number of stone fragments. It is not known who the speaker was but we refer to him in this Stage as "Vespillo," and to his wife (the subject of the inscription) as "Turia." As often in such speeches, the dead woman is addressed directly by her husband as "you," as if her **mānēs** (*departed spirit*) could hear the speech or read it on the inscription.

I

Vespillo and Turia lived through a time of great violence, when the Romans' system of republican government was collapsing in ruins, and Italy was torn by a series of horrible civil wars. Vespillo's laudatio in praise of Turia mentions three separate incidents which reflect the violence of the period. The first occurred on the eve of Vespillo and Turia's wedding:

orba repente facta es ante nūptiārum diem, utrōque parente in rūsticā sōlitūdine occīsīs. per tē maximē (quod ego in Macedoniam abieram) mors parentum nōn inulta mānsit. tū officium tuum tantā dīligentiā et tantā pietāte ēgistī, efflāgitandō et investīgandō et ulcīscendō, ut ego ipse, sī adfuissem, nōn amplius efficere   5
potuissem.

orba	*orphan*
sōlitūdine: sōlitūdō	*lonely place*
pietāte: pietās	*piety, family feeling*
efflāgitandō	*by demanding justice*
investīgandō:	
investīgāre	*investigate*
ulcīscendō: ulcīscī	*take vengeance*
nōn . . . potuissem	*would not have been able*

In 49 B.C., civil war broke out between Julius Caesar and Pompey the Great. Vespillo had to flee for his life, and he describes the help he received from Turia on that occasion:

mihi fugientī tū maximō auxiliō fuistī; omne aurum margarītaque corporī tuō dētracta trādidistī quae ferrem mēcum; callidē dēceptīs inimīcīs nostrīs, mihi absentī servōs et pecūniam et alia bona subinde praebuistī.

10

margarīta: margarītum *pearl*   callidē   *cleverly*
dētracta: dētrahere   *take off*   subinde   *regularly*

tanta erat virtūs tua ut mē dēfendere assiduē cōnārēris. (lines 14–15)

In 43 B.C., civil war was again raging and Vespillo was in still greater danger; his name was published in a list of "public enemies" and a reward was offered for killing him. Vespillo evidently wanted to make a bold dash for escape, but Turia persuaded him otherwise:

ubi amīcī nostrī mē ad imminentia perīcula vītanda excitābant, tuō cōnsiliō servātus sum. tū enim mē audāciā meā efferrī nōn passa es, sed latebrās tūtās parāvistī; mē inter cameram et tēctum cubiculī cēlātum ab exitiō servāvistī. tanta erat virtūs tua ut mē dēfendere assiduē cōnārēris, nōn sine magnō perīculō tuō.

15

efferrī: efferre *carry away*   cameram: camera *ceiling*

II

After the civil wars were over, Vespillo and Turia could at last enjoy peace and prosperity. But in their private life, they had one cause of great unhappiness:

pācātō orbe terrārum, restitūtā rēpūblicā, tandem contigit nōbīs ut temporibus quiētīs fruerēmur. magis ac magis līberōs optābāmus, quōs diū sors nōbīs invīderat. sī precibus nostrīs fortūna fāvisset, quid ultrā cupīvissēmus? annīs tamen lābentibus, spēs nostrae ēvānēscēbant.　　　　　　　　　　　　　　　　　　　　　　　　5

diffīdēns fēcunditātī tuae et dolēns orbitāte meā, timēbās nē ego, tenendō tē in mātrimōniō, spem habendī līberōs dēpōnerem atque ideō fierem īnfēlīx; dīvortium igitur prōpōnere ausa es. dīxistī tē vacuam domum nostram alicui fēminae fēcundiōrī trāditūram esse; tē ipsam mihi dignam uxōrem quaesītūram, ac futūrōs līberōs prō　　10 tuīs habitūram esse.

quibus verbīs audītīs, adeō cōnsiliō tuō incēnsus sum ut vix redderer mihi. num mihi erat tanta cupiditās aut necessitās habendī līberōs, ut proptereā fidem fallerem, mūtārem certa dubiīs? sed quid plūra? mānsistī apud mē; nōn enim cēdere tibi sine dēdecore meō et　　15 commūnī dolōre poteram.

pācātō: pācāre	*make peaceful*
rēpūblicā: rēspūblica	*"the republic" (i.e. republican government, which Augustus, the first Roman emperor, claimed to have restored)*
contigit nōbīs ut . . .	*it was our good fortune that . . .*
	we had the good fortune to . . .
optābāmus: optāre	*pray for, long for*
sors	*fate, one's lot*
invīderat: invidēre	*begrudge*
ultrā	*more, further*
cupīvissēmus	*would have wanted*
lābentibus: lābī	*pass by, slide by*
ēvānēscēbant: ēvānēscere	*die away, vanish*
fēcunditātī: fēcunditās	*fertility*
orbitāte: orbitās	*childlessness*
dēpōnerem: dēpōnere	*give up, abandon*
dīvortium	*divorce*
ausa es	*you dared, you ventured*
fēcundiōrī: fēcundus	*fertile*
futūrōs: futūrus	*future*
prō	*as*
habitūram esse:	
habēre	*regard*
redderer mihi: sibi reddī	*be restored to one's senses, be restored to oneself*

cupiditās	*desire*
necessitās	*need*
proptereā	*for that reason*
fidem fallerem: fidem fallere	*break one's word*
dubiīs: dubius	*uncertain*
quid plūra?	*why say more?*
dēdecore: dēdecus	*disgrace*
commūnī: commūnis	*shared (by both of us)*

III

Vespillo praises Turia for being faithful, obedient, and loving; he says she was conscientious in her weaving and spinning (two traditional tasks of Roman wives), elegant without being showy, and religious without being superstitious. Finally, he speaks of Turia's death and his own bereavement:

contigit nōbīs ut ad annum XXXXI sine ūllā discordiā mātrimōnium nostrum perdūcerētur. iūstius erat mihi, ut maiōrī annīs, priōrī mortem obīre. tū tamen praecucurristī; mihi dolōrem dēsīderiumque lēgāvistī. aliquandō dēspērō; sed exemplō tuō doctus, dolōrī resistere cōnor. fortūna mihi nōn omnia ēripuit;   5
adhūc enim est mihi memoria tuī.

optō ut dī mānēs tē quiētam iacēre patiantur atque tueantur.

perdūcerētur: perdūcere	*continue*
iūstius erat	*it would have been fairer, more proper*
praecucurristī:	
praecurrere	*go on ahead, run ahead*
dī mānēs	*the spirits of the dead*
tueantur: tuērī	*watch over, protect.*

About the Language

1 In Stage 41, you met the gerund used with **ad** meaning *for the purpose of* . . . in sentences like these:

ego et frāter meus **ad certandum** missī sumus.
*My brother and I were sent **for the purpose of competing**.*
  Or, in more natural English:
*My brother and I were sent **to compete**.*

In these examples, the gerund is in the *accusative* case, because it is being used with the preposition **ad**.

2 In Stage 43, you have met the *genitive* and *ablative* cases of the *gerund*, used in sentences like these:

GENITIVE nūlla spēs **habendī** līberōs iam manet.
      *No hope **of having children** remains now.*

      in omnibus āthlētīs ingēns cupīdō **vincendī** inest.
      *In all athletes, there is an immense love **of winning**.*

ABLATIVE **investīgandō**, Tūria cognōvit quid accidisset.
      ***By investigating**, Tūria found out what had happened.*

      nūntius, celerrimē **currendō**, Rōmam prīmā lūce pervēnit.
      *The messenger, **by running** very fast, reached Rome at dawn.*

      cases of the gerund are listed in full on p.302.

3 Further examples of the gerund used in the accusative, genitive, and ablative cases:

1 cōnsul ōs ad respondendum aperuit; nihil tamen dīcere poterat.
2 optimam occāsiōnem effugiendī nunc habēmus.
3 ad bene vīvendum, necesse est magnās opēs possidēre.
4 cantandō et saltandō, puellae hospitēs dēlectāvērunt.
5 poētae nihil dē arte nāvigandī sciunt.
6 et Agricola et mīlitēs magnam glōriam adeptī sunt, ille imperandō, hī pārendō.

Practicing the Language

1 Match each word in the left-hand column with a word of similar meaning taken from the right-hand column.

For example: aedificāre   exstruere

aedificāre	ergō
epistula	supplicium
festīnāre	autem
fīdus	colloquium
igitur	interficere
metus	litterae
nihilōminus	exstruere
occīdere	iterum
poena	contendere
rūrsus	coniūnx
sermō	timor
uxor	fidēlis

2 Complete each sentence with the most suitable word from the list below, and then translate.

erit, reperiēmus, necābunt, gaudēbit, poteritis, dabit

1 sī mēcum domum revēneris, frāter meus . . . . . .
2 sī dīligenter quaesīverimus, equum āmissum mox . . . . . .
3 sī mea fīlia huic senī nūpserit, semper miserrima . . . . . .
4 mīlitēs sī urbem oppugnāverint, multōs cīvēs . . . . . .
5 sī patrōnus meus tē ad cēnam invītāverit, vīnum optimum tibi
. . . . . .
6 sī ad forum hodiē ieritis, pompam spectāre . . . . . .

3 Translate each sentence into Latin by selecting correctly from the list of Latin words.

1 *We were being hindered by shortage of water.*
    inopiae   aquae   impediēmur
    inopiā   aquā   impediēbāmur
2 *They were afraid that the robbers would return next day.*
    timēbant   nōn   latrōnī   postrīdiē   revenīrent
    timēbunt   nē   latrōnēs   cotīdiē   reveniēbant

3 *As the enemy approached, I heard strange noises.*

     hostibus   appropinquantibus   sonitum   mīrōs audītī

     hostēs   appropinquantēs   sonitūs   mīrum audīvī

4 *We tried to set out at first light.*

     prīmam   lūcem   proficīscī   cōnātus erāmus

     prīmā   lūce   proficīscimur   cōnātī   sumus

5 *Why do you promise what you cannot carry out?*

     cūr   pollicēmur   id quod   suscipere   nōn   vultis

     ubi   pollicēminī   is quī   efficere   nusquam potestis

About the Language

1 Study the following examples:

dīcō testem mentīrī.
__I say__ that the witness is lying.

rogāvimus quis cibum relīquum cōnsūmpsisset.
__We asked__ who had eaten the rest of the food.

dux **nūntiāvit** sociōs nōbīs mox subventūrōs esse.
The leader __announced__ that our companions would soon come to our help.

Each sentence contains

1 a *verb of speaking, asking, etc.*, e.g. **dīcō**, **rogāvimus**,
2 an indirect statement or indirect question.

Notice that in each example, the verb of speaking, asking, etc. is placed at the *beginning* of the sentence.

2 Compare the examples in paragraph 1 with the following sentences:

multōs barbarōs **dīcimus** in proeliō cecidisse.
__We say__ that many barbarians fell in the battle.

quid prīnceps cupiat, numquam **sciō**.
I never __know__ what the emperor wants.

haruspex deōs nōbīs favēre **affirmāvit**.
The soothsayer __declared__ that the gods favored us.

In these examples, the verb of speaking, asking, knowing, etc. is placed in the *middle* or at the *end* of the sentence.

3 Read through each of the following sentences, noticing the position the verb of speaking, asking, etc.; then translate the sentence.

1 nūntius hostēs in eōdem locō manēre dīcit.
2 quārē familiam convocāverīs, omnīnō ignōrō.
3 togam tuam vīdī scissam esse.
4 fabrōs opus iam perfēcisse audīvimus.
5 ubi rēx exercitum suum collocāvisset, incertum erat.
6 ego vērō et gaudeō et gaudēre mē dīcō. (*Pliny*)

convocāverīs: convocāre   *call together*

A Roman couple.

Divorce and Remarriage

The Romans believed that the first divorce in Rome took place in about 230 B.C., when the senator Spurius Carvilius, although he loved his wife deeply, divorced her because she was unable to have children.

The story of Carvilius' divorce may be partly or entirely fiction; it certainly cannot have happened in 230 B.C., because by that date laws about divorce had already been in existence for two hundred years. But the reason for Carvilius' divorce is a very typical one; it is the same reason as the one put forward by "Turia" on p.168. Roman marriage was supposed to produce children; and when a marriage ended in divorce, childlessness was the reason in many cases.

There were, of course, many other reasons why a husband or wife, or both, might decide to end a marriage. Continual bickering and disagreement, or objectionable behavior such as unfaithfulness or brutality, could all lead to divorce. Divorces were sometimes arranged for political reasons, especially in the first century B.C.; for example, an ambitious man might divorce his wife in order to remarry into a wealthier or more powerful family.

If a wife was under the legal control (**manus**) of her husband, he could divorce her but she could not divorce him. But if the marriage had taken place **sine manū** and the wife was free from her husband's legal control, husband and wife each had the power to divorce the other.

The only thing necessary for divorce, in the eyes of the law, was that the husband or wife, or both, had to demonstrate that they regarded the marriage as finished and intended to live separately in future; if one partner moved out of the marital house and began to live somewhere else, nothing else was legally required. But the husband and wife could also follow certain procedures, in action or in writing, to emphasize that they intended their separation to be permanent. In the early years of Rome's history, a husband could divorce his wife by addressing her, in front of witnesses, with the phrase **tuās rēs tibi agitō** (*take your things and go*), or by demanding the return of the keys of the house. By the first century A.D., these picturesque customs were no longer in common use; instead, one partner might send the other a written notification of divorce, or the husband and wife might make a joint declaration, either spoken before witnesses or put in writing, as in the following agreement, which was discovered on an Egyptian papyrus:

Part of the inscription on which the story of Vespillo and Turia is based.

"Zois daughter of Heraclides and Antipater son of Zeno agree that they have separated from each other, ending the marriage which they made in the seventeenth year of Augustus Caesar, and Zois acknowledges that she has received from Antipater by hand the goods which he was previously given as dowry, namely clothes to the value of 120 drachmas and a pair of gold earrings. Hereafter it shall be lawful both for Zois to marry another man and for Antipater to marry another woman without either of them being answerable."

It is difficult to discover how common divorce was in Rome. Among the richer classes, it may perhaps have reached a peak in the first century B.C., and then declined during the following century. (Nothing is known about the divorce rate of Rome's poor.) Some Roman writers speak as if divorce was rare in early Roman history but common in their own times. Juvenal says of one woman that she "wears out her wedding veil as she flits from husband to husband, getting through eight men in five years." But it is impossible to tell how much truth there is in Juvenal's description, and how much is exaggeration; nor do we know how typical such women were. Any husband who was thinking of divorcing his wife had to bear in mind that he would have to return all or part of her **dōs**, or *dowry* (payment of money or property made by the bride's family to the husband at the time of marriage), as in the papyrus document quoted above; this may have made some husbands have second thoughts about going ahead with the divorce.

Remarriage after divorce was frequent. "They marry in order to divorce; they divorce in order to marry," said one Roman writer. Remarriage was also common after the death of a husband or wife, especially if the surviving partner was still young. For example, a twelve-year-old girl who married an elderly husband might find herself widowed in her late teens, and if a wife died in childbirth, a man might

Dido and Aeneas.

become a widower within a year or two of the marriage, perhaps while he himself was still in his early twenties; in this situation, the idea of remarriage was often attractive and sensible for the surviving partner.

Nevertheless, the Romans had a special respect for women who married only once. They were known as **ūnivirae** and had certain religious privileges; for a long time, they were the only people allowed to worship at the temple of Pudicitia (Chastity), and it was a Roman tradition for a bride to be undressed by ūnivirae on her wedding night. Some women took great pride in the idea that they were remaining faithful to a dead husband, and the description **ūnivira** is often found on tombstones.

The idea of being **ūnivira** is sometimes used by Roman authors for the purposes of a story or poem. For example, the lady in the story on pp.160–162 is so determined to remain loyal to her dead husband that she refuses to go on living after his death, until a twist in the story persuades her to change her mind. A similar idea provides the starting-point of Book Four of Vergil's poem, the *Aeneid*. In an earlier part of the poem, the Trojan prince Aeneas has landed in Africa and been hospitably received by Dido, Queen of Carthage. The two are strongly attracted to each other, and Dido is very much moved by Aeneas' account of his adventures (a short extract from his story appeared in Stage 42, p.150). Aeneas, however, is under orders from the gods to seek a new home in Italy, while Dido has sworn an oath of loyalty to her dead husband, binding herself like a Roman **ūnivira** never to marry again; and so, although a love affair quickly develops between Dido and Aeneas, it ends in disaster and death.

Words and Phrases Checklist

aggredior, aggredī, aggressus sum	*attack, make an attempt on*
bona, bonōrum	*goods, property*
contemnō, contemnere, contempsī, contemptus	*despise, disregard*
efferō, efferre, extulī, ēlātus	*carry out, carry away*
ēlātus	*carried away, excited*
fīdus, fīda, fīdum	*loyal, trustworthy*
inopia, inopiae	*shortage, scarcity, poverty*
iuxtā	*next to*
magistrātus, magistrātūs	*elected government official*
negō, negāre, negāvī	*deny, say . . . not*
possideō, possidēre, possēdī, possessus	*possess*
propter	*because of*
repente	*suddenly*
ulcīscor, ulcīscī, ultus sum	*avenge, take revenge on*

Give the meaning of each of the following:

opēs, repentīnus, ultiō, ultor.

Synonym Search

fidēlis (14), oppugnāre (24), paucitās (cf. paucī, 17), rēs (*pl.*) (6), spernere (29), subitō (6), tenēre (15).

Daedalus
et Īcarus

The following story is taken from Ovid's poem, the *Metamorphoses*, an immense collection of myths, legends, and folk-tales which begins with the creation of the world and ends in Ovid's own day.

I

Daedalus, who was famous as a craftsman and inventor, came from Athens to the island of Crete at the invitation of King Minos. The king, however, had a dispute with him and refused to allow him and his son Icarus to leave the island.

> Daedalus intereā Crētēn longumque perōsus
> exilium, tāctusque locī nātālis amōre,
> clausus erat pelagō. "terrās licet" inquit "et undās
> obstruat, at caelum certē patet; ībimus illāc!

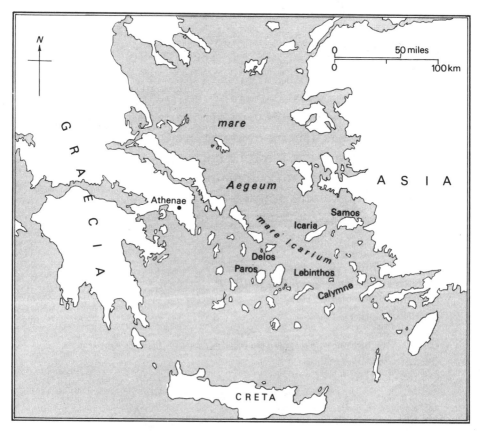

Crete and the Greek islands.

omnia possideat, nōn possidet āera Mīnōs."
dīxit et ignōtās animum dīmittit in artēs,
nātūramque novat. nam pōnit in ōrdine pennās,
ut clīvō crēvisse putēs; sīc rūstica quondam
fistula disparibus paulātim surgit avēnīs.

perōsus	*hating*
tāctus: tangere	*touch, move*
locī nātālis: locus nātālis	*place of birth, native land*
clausus erat: claudere	*cut off*
licet	*although*
obstruat	*he (i.e. Minos) may block my way through*
at	*yet*
certē	*at least*
patet: patēre	*lie open*
illāc	*by that way*
omnia possideat	*he may possess everything (else)*
āera:	*accusative of* āēr *air*
dīmittit: dīmittere	*turn, direct*
novat: novāre	*change, revolutionize*
pennās: penna	*feather*
clīvō: clīvus	*slope*
crēvisse: crēscere	*grow*
crēvisse = pennās crēvisse	
putēs	*you would think*
sīc	*in the same way*
rūstica: rūsticus	*of a countryman*
quondam	*sometimes*
fistula	*pipe*
disparibus: dispār	*of different length*
surgit: surgere	*grow up, be built up*
avēnīs: avēna	*reed*
Crētēn	*accusative of* Crētē *Crete*

1 Why was Daedalus eager to leave Crete?
2 Why was it difficult for him to get away?
3 What method of escape did he choose?
4 How did he set about preparing his escape?
5 What did the arrangement of feathers resemble?

II

tum līnō mediās et cērīs adligat īmās,
atque ita compositās parvō curvāmine flectit,
ut vērās imitētur avēs. puer Īcarus ūnā
stābat et, ignārus <u>sua</u> sē tractāre <u>perīcla</u>,
ōre renīdentī modo, quās vaga mōverat aura,   5
captābat plūmās, flāvam modo pollice cēram
mollībat, lūsūque suō mīrābile patris
impediēbat opus. postquam manus ultima coeptō
imposita est, geminās <u>opifex</u> lībrāvit in ālās
<u>ipse</u> suum corpus mōtāque pependit in aurā.   10

līnō: līnum	*thread*
mediās (pennās)	*the middle (of the feathers)*
īmās (pennās)	*the bottom (of the feathers)*
curvāmine: curvāmen	*curve*
flectit: flectere	*bend*
ūnā	*with him*
sua . . . perīcla	*cause of danger for himself (literally "his own danger")*
tractāre	*handle, touch*
ōre renīdentī	*with smiling face*
modo . . . modo	*now . . . now, sometimes . . . sometimes*
aura	*breeze*
plūmās: plūma	*feather*
flāvam: flāvus	*yellow, golden*
mollībat = molliēbat: mollīre	*soften*
lūsū: lūsus	*play, games*
manus ultima	*final touch*
coeptō: coeptum	*work, undertaking*
geminās . . . ālās	*the two wings*
opifex	*inventor, craftsman*
lībrāvit: lībrāre	*balance*
mōtā: mōtus	*moving (literally "moved," i.e. by the wings)*

1 What materials did Daedalus use to fasten the feathers together? Where did he fasten them? What did he then do to the wings?
2 In line 4, what was Icarus failing to realize?
3 How did Icarus amuse himself while his father was working? Judging from lines 5–8, what age would you imagine Icarus to be?
4 What actions of Daedalus are described in lines 9–10? Has the journey begun at this point?

Daedalus winged: bronze by Michael Ayrton.

Fragment of Greek painted vase.

III

īnstruit et nātum, "mediō" que "ut līmite currās,
Īcare," ait "moneō, nē, sī dēmissior ībis,
unda gravet pennās, sī celsior, ignis adūrat.
inter utrumque volā! nec tē spectāre Boōtēn
aut Helicēn iubeō strictumque Ōrīonis ēnsem: 5
mē duce carpe viam!" pariter praecepta volandī
trādit et ignōtās umerīs accommodat ālās.

īnstruit: īnstruere	*equip, fit (with wings)*
nātum: nātus	*son*
īnstruit et nātum = et īnstruit nātum	
mediō . . . līmite	*middle course*
currās: currere	*go, fly*
ait	*says*
dēmissior	*lower (than you should), i.e. too low*
pennās: penna	*wing*
celsior	*higher (than you should), i.e. too high*
ignis	*fire, heat of sun*
adūrat: adūrere	*burn*
volā: volāre	*fly*
strictum: stringere	*draw, unsheathe*
ēnsem: ēnsis	*sword*
carpe: carpere	*hasten upon*
pariter	*at the same time*
praecepta: praeceptum	*instruction*
accommodat: accommodāre	*fasten*
Boōtēn	*accusative of* Boōtēs *Herdsman (constellation)*
Helicēn	*accusative of* Helicē *Great Bear, Big Bear (constellation)*
Ōrīonis: Ōrīon	*Orion, the Hunter (constellation)*

Wall-painting from Pompeii.

About the Language

1 Study the following example:

> fūr per fenestram intrāvit. circumspexit; sed omnia tacita erant. subitō
> sonitum **audit**; ē tablīnō canis **sē praecipitat**. fūr effugere **cōnātur**;
> **lātrat** canis; **irrumpunt** servī et fūrem **comprehendunt**.

> *A thief entered through the window. He looked around; but all was silent.*
> *Suddenly he **hears** a noise; a dog **hurtles** out of the study. The thief **tries** to*
> *escape; the dog **barks**; the slaves **rush in** and **seize** the thief.*

2 Notice that all the verbs in the above example, after the first two
sentences, are in the *present* tense, even through the event obviously
happened in the past. This is known as the *historical* use of the present
tense (*"historical present"* for short); it is often used by Roman writers to
make the narration rather more lively and vivid, as if the action were
happening before the reader's (or listener's) eyes.

3 A historical present in Latin can be translated *either* by an English
present tense (as in the example in paragraph 1), *or* by a past tense.

4 Look again at lines 6–7 of Part I on p.181. Which verbs in these two
lines are in the historical present tense, and which in the perfect tense?

5 You have already met examples of the historical present in sentences
containing the word **dum** (meaning *while*):

> dum equitēs **morantur**, nūntius prīncipia irrūpit.
> *While the cavalry **were delaying**, a messenger burst into headquarters.*

IV

inter opus monitūsque genae maduēre senīlēs,
et patriae tremuēre manūs. dedit ōscula nātō
nōn iterum repetenda suō pennīsque levātus
ante volat, comitīque timet, velut āles, ab <u>altō</u>
quae teneram prōlem prōdūxit in āera <u>nīdō</u>;   5
hortāturque sequī, damnōsāsque ērudit artēs,

et movet ipse <u>suās</u> et nātī respicit <u>ālās</u>.
hōs* aliquis, <u>tremulā</u> dum captat <u>harundine</u> piscēs,
aut pāstor baculō stīvāve innīxus arātor
vīdit* et obstipuit, quīque aethera carpere possent
crēdidit esse deōs.

inter	*during*
monitūs: monitus	*warning, advice*
maduēre = maduērunt:	
madēscere	*become wet*
senīlēs: senīlis	*old*
patriae: patrius	*of the father*
tremuēre = tremuērunt	
nōn iterum repetenda	*never to be repeated, never to be sought again*
levātus: levāre	*raise, lift up*
ante	*in front*
velut	*like*
āles	*bird*
teneram: tener	*tender, helpless*
prōlem: prōlēs	*offspring, brood*
prōdūxit: prōdūcere	*bring forward, bring out*
damnōsās: damnōsus	*ruinous, fatal*
ērudit: ērudīre	*teach*
tremulā: tremulus	*quivering*
harundine: harundō	*rod*
baculō: baculum	*stick, staff*
stīvā: stīva	*plow-handle*
-ve	*or*
innīxus: innītī	*lean on*
obstipuit: obstipēscere	*gape in amazement*
carpere	*hasten through, fly through*

*These two words go closely together.

A1 What signs of emotion did Daedalus show while speaking to Icarus?
  2 What was his last action before the journey began?
  3 What is Daedalus compared to as he sets out on his flight?
  4 Who witnessed the flight? What did they think of Daedalus and Icarus, and why?

B1 What do you think caused Daedalus' agitation in lines 1–2?
  2 In what ways is the comparison in lines 4–5 appropriate?
  3 Does Ovid suggest in any way that the journey will end in disaster?

V

et iam Iūnōnia laevā
parte Samos (fuerant Dēlosque Parosque relictae),
dextra Lebinthos erat fēcundaque melle Calymne,
cum puer audācī coepit gaudēre volātū

The Fall of Icarus, by Allegrini.

déseruitque ducem, caelīque cupīdine tractus   5
altius ēgit iter. rapidī vīcīnia sōlis
mollit odōrātās, pennārum vincula, cērās.
tābuerant cērae; nūdōs quatit ille lacertōs,
rēmigiōque carēns nōn ūllās percipit aurās.
ōraque caeruleā patrium clāmantia nōmen   10
excipiuntur aquā, quae nōmen trāxit ab illō.
at pater īnfēlīx nec iam pater "Īcare" dīxit,
"Īcare," dīxit, "ubi es? quā tē regiōne requīram?"
Īcare," dīcēbat; pennās aspexit in undīs,
dēvōvitque suās artēs corpusque sepulcrō   15
condidit, et tellūs ā nōmine dicta sepultī.

laevā parte	*on the left hand*
-que . . . -que	*both . . . and*
dextrā: dexter	*on the right*
fēcunda . . . melle	*rich in honey*
gaudēre	*be delighted*
volātū: volātus	*flying, flight*
tractus: trahere	*draw on, urge on*
altius	*higher (than he should), i.e. too high*
ēgit iter: iter agere	*make one's way, travel*
rapidī: rapidus	*blazing, consuming*
vīcīnia	*nearness*
odōrātās: odōrātus	*sweet-smelling*
vincula	*fastenings*
tābuerant: tābēscere	*melt*
nūdōs: nūdus	*bare*
quatit: quatere	*shake, flap*
lacertōs: lacertus	*arm*
rēmigiō: rēmigium	*wings (literally "oars")*
carēns: carēre	*lack, be without*
percipit: percipere	*take hold of, get a grip on*
ōra	*mouth*
caeruleā: caeruleus	*dark blue, dark green*
trāxit: trahere	*draw, derive*
nec iam	*no longer*
requīram: requīrere	*search for*
aspexit: aspicere	*catch sight of*
dēvōvit: dēvovēre	*curse*
condidit: condere	*bury*
dicta =dicta est: dīcere	*call, name*
sepultī: sepultus	*the one who was buried*
Iūnōnia: Iūnōnius	*sacred to Juno*

A1 On the map on p.180, find the point reached by Daedalus and Icarus in lines 1–3.

2 What mistake did Icarus make?

3 What effect did this have on his wings?

4 Where did he fall? What was he doing as he fell?

5 How did Daedalus learn of his son's fate? What did he do then?

B1 Why did Icarus not obey his father's instructions?

2 Why is Daedalus described as "pater . . . nec iam pater" in line 12?

3 After reading this story, what impression do you have of the different personalities of Daedalus and Icarus?

About the Language

1 From Stage 13 onwards, you have met sentences like this:

Britannī cibum **laudāvērunt**, Rōmānī vīnum.
*The Britons praised the food, the Romans (**praised**) the wine.*

2 From Stage 15 onwards, you met a slightly different type of sentence:

Britannī cibum, Rōmānī vīnum **laudāvērunt**.

3 Compare the examples in paragraphs 1 and 2 with a longer way of expressing the same idea:

Britannī cibum **laudāvērunt**, Rōmānī vīnum **laudāvērunt**.

This kind of sentence is grammatically correct, but is not often used in Latin; the Romans would normally prefer the shorter versions in paragraphs 1 and 2, to avoid repeating the word **laudāvērunt**.

4 Sentences similar to the ones in paragraphs 1 and 2 are very common in Latin. Study the following examples, which you have met in Stages 36 and 44:

Thāis **habet** nigrōs, niveōs Laecānia dentēs.
*Thais **has** black teeth, Laecania **has** white ones.*
(Compare this with a longer way of expressing the same idea:
Thāis dentēs nigrōs **habet**, Laecānia dentēs niveōs **habet**.)

et movet ipse suās et nātī respicit **ālās**.
*He both moves his own **wings** himself and looks back at the **wings** of his son.*
(Compare: et ipse suās **ālās** movet et **ālās** nātī respicit.)

5 Further examples:

1 centuriō gladium, mīles hastam gerēbat.
  (Compare: centuriō gladium gerēbat, mīles hastam gerēbat.)
2 hic caupō vēndit optimum, ille vīnum pessimum.
  (Compare: hic caupō vīnum optimum vēndit, ille caupō vīnum pessimum vēndit.)
3 nōs in urbe, vōs prope mare habitātis.
4 altera fēmina quīnque līberōs habēbat, altera nūllōs.
5 dīvitiās quaerit senex, spernit iuvenis.
6 ēnumerat mīles vulnera, pāstor ovēs. (*Propertius*)
7 culpāvit dominus, laudāvit domina vīlicum.
8 nōn semper viātōrēs ā latrōnibus,. aliquandō latrōnēs ā viātōribus occīduntur.

> ēnumerat: ēnumerāre   *count*   viātōrēs: viātor *traveler*

Practicing the Language

1 In Stage 42, the different ways of translating **ēmittere**, **petere**, and **referre** were practiced. Another verb with a wide variety of translations is **solvere**, which you have often met with the meaning *untie* but which can be translated in many other ways as well. Match each of the phrases in the left-hand column with the correct English translation from the right-hand column.

nāvem solvere	*relaxed by the wine*
catēnās ex aliquō solvere	*to discharge a promise made to the gods*
vīnō solūtus	*to set out on a voyage*
aenigma solvere	*to settle a debt*
margarītam in acētō solvere	*to free somebody from chains*
pecūniam solvere	*to solve a puzzle*
vōtum solvere	*to dissolve a pearl in vinegar*

Suggest reasons why the Romans used **solvere** in all these phrases: is there any connection in meaning between them?

2 Complete each sentence by describing the word in boldface with a suitable adjective chosen from the list below, using paragraphs 1 and 2 on pages 286–7 to help you put your chosen adjective into the correct form. Do not use any adjective more than once. The gender of the word in boldface is given after each sentence. (An adjective which indicates size or quantity is usually placed *before* the noun it describes; other adjectives *after*. But the Romans did not observe this as a strict rule.)

īrātus, ingēns, fortis, pulcher, magnus, fēlīx, longus, audāx, gravis

1 dominus **ancillās** arcessīvit. (f.)
2 iuvenis pecūniam **senī** reddidit. (m.)
3 sacerdōtēs **templum** intrāvērunt. (n.)
4 dux virtūtem **mīlitum** laudāvit. (m.)
5 cīvēs **spectāculō** dēlectātī sunt. (n.)
6 centuriō, **hastā** armātus, extrā carcerem stābat. (f.)

3 In each pair of sentences, translate sentence (a); then with the help of pages 296–7 express the same idea in a passive form by completing the noun and verb in sentence (b) in the correct way, and translate again.

For example: (a) hostēs nōs circumveniēbant.
                (b) ab host. . . circumveni. . . .
Translated and completed, this becomes:
   (a) hostēs **nōs circumveniēbant**.
        The enemy **were surrounding us**.
   (b) ab **hostibus circumveniēbāmur**.
        We were being surrounded *by the enemy*.

1a cūr centuriō tē culpābat?
1b cūr ā centuriō. . . culp. . . ?
2a optimē labōrāvistis, puerī; vīlicus vōs certē laudābit.
2b optimē labōrāvistis, puerī; ā vīlic. . . certē laud. . . .
3a moritūrus sum; amīcī mē in hōc locō sepelient.
3b moritūrus sum; ab amīc. . . in hōc locō sepel. . . .
4a medicus mē cotīdiē vīsitat.
4b ā med. . . cotīdiē vīsit. . . .
5a barbarī nōs interficient.
5b ā barbar. . . interfici. . . .

4 Complete each sentence with the right infinitive or group of words from the list below, and then translate.

nūllam pecūniam habēre
per hortum suum flūxisse
scrīptam esse
aedificārī
equum occīsūrōs esse

1 nūntius sciēbat epistulam ab Imperātōre . . . . . .
2 senex affirmāvit sē . . . . . .
3 rēx crēdēbat leōnēs . . . . . .
4 agricola querēbātur multam aquam . . . . . .
5 puer dīxit novum templum . . . . . .

About the Language

1 In Stage 6, you met the 3rd person plural of the perfect tense:

cīvēs gladiātōrem **incitāvērunt**.
*The citizens **urged** the gladiator **on**.*

2 From Stage 36 onwards, you have met examples like this:

centum mē **tetigēre** manūs.   clientēs patrōnum **salūtāvēre**.
*A hundred hands **touched** me.*   *The clients **greeted** their patron.*

In these examples, the 3rd person plural of the perfect tense ends in **-ēre** instead of **-ērunt**. The meaning is unchanged. This way of forming the 3rd person plural of the perfect is especially common in poetry.

3 Translate the following:

1 servī contrā dominum coniūrāvēre.
2 in illō proeliō multī barbarī periēre.
3 coniūnxēre; ēripuēre; perdidēre; respexēre; studuēre.

Icarus in Art

The tale of Daedalus and Icarus has attracted many artists. The oldest surviving version of the story in picture form comes from Greece; a small fragment of a painted vase (see p.184) shows the lower edge of a tunic, two legs wearing winged boots, and the inscription $IKAPO\Sigma$ (Icarus). The vase was made in the middle of the sixth century B.C., more than five hundred years earlier than Ovid's version of the story.

Daedalus and Icarus also appear in wall-paintings excavated at Pompeii. One of these paintings is shown on p.185. The figure of Daedalus flying in the center has been almost entirely lost, because of the hole in the painting, and only the wing tips are visible. Icarus, however, appears twice, once at the top near the sun, and again at the bottom. The bystanders gaze skywards in wonder, as in Ovid's account (p.187, lines 10–11). The sun is shown not as a ball of fire but as a god driving his chariot and horses across the sky.

The work reproduced on p.183 is by the twentieth-century artist Michael Ayrton. Ayrton was fascinated by the story of Daedalus and Icarus, and came back to it again and again during a period of several years. He created a large number of drawings, reliefs, and sculptures dealing not only with the making of the wings and the fall of Icarus, but also with other details of the Daedalus story, such as the maze which Daedalus built in Crete, and the monstrous half-man, half-bull known as the Minotaur, who lived at the center of the maze. Ayrton also retold the Daedalus story in his own words in two short novels.

In about 1555, Pieter Bruegel painted the picture which is reproduced on p.196. Some of the details of his painting are very close to Ovid's account; the plowman leaning on his plow, the shepherd with his staff, and the fisherman (p.187, lines 8–9) are all there. In other ways, however, Bruegel's treatment of the story is unusual and at first sight surprising; for example the bystanders in Bruegel's picture are behaving very differently from those in the painting by Allegrini, reproduced on p.188.

In this way, the story of Daedalus and Icarus, as told by Ovid and other writers, became a subject for Bruegel and other artists. Bruegel's painting, in turn, became the subject of the following poem by W.H. Auden. Auden's title, *Musée des Beaux Arts*, refers to the gallery in Brussels where *Icarus* and other paintings by Bruegel are hung.

Musée des Beaux Arts

About suffering they were never wrong,
The Old Masters: how well they understood
Its human position; how it takes place
While someone else is eating or opening a window or just walking
    dully along;
How, when the aged are reverently, passionately waiting
For the miraculous birth, there always must be
Children who did not specially want it to happen, skating
On a pond at the edge of the wood:
They never forgot
That even the dreadful martyrdom must run its course
Anyhow in a corner, some untidy spot
Where the dogs go on with their doggy life and the torturer's horse
Scratches its innocent behind on a tree.

In Bruegel's *Icarus*, for instance: how everything turns away
Quite leisurely from the disaster; the ploughman may
Have heard the splash, the forsaken cry,
But for him it was not an important failure; the sun shone
As it had to on the white legs disappearing into the green
Water; and the expensive delicate ship that must have seen
Something amazing, a boy falling out of the sky,
Had somewhere to get to and sailed calmly on.

The Fall of Icarus, by Pieter Bruegel.

Words and Phrases Checklist

aspiciō, aspicere, aspexī,
    aspectus   *look towards, catch sight of*
coniungō, coniungere,
    coniūnxī, coniūnctus   *join*
coniūrō, coniūrāre, coniūrāvī   *conspire, plot*
crēscō, crēscere, crēvī   *grow*
cupīdō, cupīdinis   *desire*
fēlīx, *gen.* fēlīcis   *lucky, happy*
licet, licēre   *be allowed*
    mihi licet   *I am allowed*
paulātim   *gradually*
studeō, studēre, studuī   *study*
tellūs, tellūris   *land, earth*
ūnā cum   *together with*
uterque, utraque, utrumque   *both, each of two*
vinculum, vinculī   *fastening, chain*

Give the meaning of each of the following:

coniūrātiō, cupere, fēlīcitās, vincīre.

Synonym Search

augērī (cf. augēre, 40), catēna (31), fortūnātus (cf. fortūna, 18), spectāre (5), terra (12).

Lesbia

Some of Catullus' most famous poems are concerned with a woman to whom he gave the name "Lesbia." Stage 45 contains eight of the Lesbia poems.

I

ille mī pār esse deō vidētur,
ille, sī fās est, superāre dīvōs,
quī sedēns adversus identidem tē
    spectat et audit

dulce rīdentem, <u>miserō</u> quod omnēs   5
ēripit sēnsūs <u>mihi</u>: nam simul tē,
Lesbia, aspexī, nihil est super mī
    vōcis in ōre,

lingua sed torpet, tenuis sub artūs
flamma dēmānat, sonitū suōpte   10
tintinant aurēs, <u>geminā</u> teguntur
    lūmina <u>nocte</u>.

ōtium, Catulle, tibi molestum est:
ōtiō exsultās nimiumque gestīs:
ōtium et rēgēs prius et beātās   15
    perdidit urbēs.

mī = mihi		sub	*to the depths of*
fās	*right*	artūs: artus	*limb*
superāre	*surpass*	dēmānat: dēmānāre	*flow down*
adversus	*opposite*	suōpte = suō	
dulce	*sweetly*	tintinant: tintināre	*ring*
quod	*(a thing) which*	geminā: geminus	*twofold, double*
sēnsūs: sēnsus	*sense*	teguntur: tegere	*cover*
simul = simulac		lūmina	*eyes*
nihil . . . vōcis	*no voice*	exsultās: exsultāre	*get excited*
est super = superest:		gestīs: gestīre	*become restless*
superesse	*remain, be left*	prius	*before now*
torpet: torpēre	*be paralyzed*	beātās: beātus	*prosperous, wealthy*
tenuis	*thin, subtle*		

1 Why does Catullus regard "ille" (lines 1 and 2) as fortunate? Why does he regard himself as "miserō" (line 5)?
2 "omnēs ēripit sēnsūs" (lines 5–6): give an example of this from lines 7–12.
3 What warning does Catullus give himself in lines 13–16? Do you think these lines follow on naturally from lines 1–12, or are they a separate poem?

Wall-painting from Herculaneum showing lovers on a couch.

II

vīvāmus, mea Lesbia, atque amēmus,
rūmōrēsque senum sevēriōrum
omnēs ūnius aestimēmus assis!
sōlēs occidere et redīre possunt:
nōbīs, cum semel occidit brevis lūx,   5
nox est perpetua ūna dormienda.
dā mī bāsia mīlle, deinde centum,
dein mīlle altera, dein secunda centum,
deinde usque altera mīlle, deinde centum,
dein, cum mīlia multa fēcerīmus,   10
conturbābimus illa, nē sciāmus,
aut nē quis malus invidēre possit,
cum tantum sciat esse bāsiōrum.

vīvāmus	*let us live*
rūmōrēs	*gossip*
sevēriōrum: sevērior	*over-strict*
ūnius . . . assis	*at a single "as" (smallest Roman coin)*
aestimēmus: aestimāre	*value*
semel	*once*
est . . . dormienda	*must be slept through*
bāsia: bāsium	*kiss*
dein = deinde	
usque altera	*yet another*
conturbābimus: conturbāre	*mix up, lose count of*
nē quis	*in case anyone*
invidēre	*cast an evil eye*
tantum	*so much, such a large number*

1 Who, according to Catullus, might be making comments about him
   and Lesbia? What does he think he and Lesbia should do about these
   comments?
2 What contrast does Catullus draw between "sōlēs" (line 4) and "nōs"
   ("nōbīs," line 5)?
3 What have lines 7–9 got to do with lines 4–6?
4 Why does Catullus suggest in line 11 that he and Lesbia should
   deliberately lose count?

vīvāmus, mea Lesbia, atque amēmus! (line 1, page 202).

About the Language

1 Study the following examples:

vīvāmus atque amēmus!	*Let us live and let us love!*
nē **dēspērēmus**!	*Let us not despair!*
aut **vincāmus** aut **vincāmur**!	*Let us either conquer or be conquered!*

In these sentences, the speaker is ordering or encouraging himself and one or more other people to do something. The 1st-person plural form (*we*) is used, and the verb is in the present tense of the subjunctive. This is known as the *jussive* use of the *subjunctive*. Further examples:

1 in mediam pugnam ruāmus!   2 nē haesitēmus!
3 sociōs nostrōs adiuvēmus.   4 opus perficiāmus.
5 gaudeāmus igitur, iuvenēs dum sumus.
6 flammās exstinguere cōnēmur!

2 The *jussive subjunctive* can also be used in a 3rd-person form of the verb (*he, she, it,* or *they*):

omnēs captīvī **interficiantur**!	*Let all the prisoners be killed!* Or, *All the prisoners are to be killed.*
nē **respiciat**!	*Let him not look back!* Or, *He is not to look back.*

Further examples:

1 statim redeat!   2 sit amīcitia inter nōs et vōs.
3 prīmum taurus sacrificētur; deinde precēs Iovī adhibeantur.

3 Occasionally, the jussive subjunctive is used in a 2nd-person form (*you*):

dēsinās querī.   *You should stop complaining.*

But it is far more common for Latin to use the imperative:

dēsine querī!   *Stop complaining!*

III

lūgēte, ō Venerēs Cupīdinēsque,
et quantum est hominum venustiōrum!
passer mortuus est meae puellae,
passer, dēliciae meae puellae,
quem plūs illa oculīs suīs amābat.   5
nam mellītus erat suamque nōrat
ipsam tam bene quam puella mātrem,
nec sēsē ā gremiō illius movēbat,
sed circumsiliēns modo hūc modo illūc
ad sōlam dominam usque pīpiābat;   10
quī nunc it per iter tenebricōsum
illūc, unde negant redīre quemquam.
at vōbīs male sit, malae tenebrae
Orcī, quae omnia bella dēvorātis:
tam bellum mihi passerem abstulistis.   15
ō factum male! ō miselle passer!
tuā nunc operā, meae puellae
flendō turgidulī rubent ocellī.

quantum est	*all the company (literally "as much as there is")*
venustiōrum: venustus	*tender, loving*
passer	*sparrow*
mellītus	*sweet as honey*
nōrat = nōverat	
ipsam: ipsa	*mistress*
tam . . . quam	*as . . . as*
sēsē = sē	

Wall-painting from Herculaneum showing cupids at play.

gremiō: gremium	*lap*
circumsiliēns: circumsilīre	*hop around*
usque	*continually*
tenebricōsum: tenebricōsus	*dark, shadowy*
quemquam: quisquam	*anyone*
vōbīs male sit	*curses on you*
ō factum male!	*Oh dreadful deed! (literally "Oh dreadfully done!")*
miselle: misellus	*wretched little*
tuā . . . operā	*by your doing, because of you*
turgidulī: turgidulus	*swollen*
rubent: rubēre	*be red*
ocellī: ocellus	*poor eye, little eye*
Venerēs Cupīdinēsque	*gods and goddesses of love, Venuses and Cupids*
Orcī: Orcus	*the Underworld, Hell*

1 What has happened?
2 Who are asked to mourn in line 1? Why are they appropriate mourners on this occasion?
3 Is Catullus chiefly concerned about the death, or about something else?
4 Why does he speak as if *he* had been bereaved ("mihi," line 15)?
5 Compare the two descriptions of the sparrow in (*a*) lines 8–10, (*b*) lines 11–12. Do they sound equally serious, or is one of the descriptions slightly comic? How serious is the poem as a whole?

IV

nūllī sē dīcit mulier mea nūbere mālle
    quam mihi, nōn sī sē Iuppiter ipse petat.
dīcit: sed mulier <u>cupidō</u> quod dīcit <u>amantī</u>,
    in ventō et rapidā scrībere oportet aquā.

nūllī:	*used as dative of* nēmō
mulier	*woman*
nōn sī	*not even if*
sed mulier . . . quod dīcit	= sed quod mulier . . . dīcit
cupidō: cupidus	*eager, passionate*
amantī: amāns	*lover*
rapidā: rapidus	*rushing, racing*

1 What does Lesbia say in lines 1–2? Why does the mention of Jupiter imply a compliment to Catullus?
2 What would be the best translation for the first "dīcit" in line 3?
    (a) "She says"
    (b) "She says so"

(c) "That's what she *says*"

(d) "*That's* what she says"

or none of these?

3 What comment does Catullus then make about Lesbia's remark?

4 What does he mean? Does he mean, for example, that women can't be trusted? Or is he suggesting something more precise than that? Is Catullus being cynical or fair-minded?

V

dīcēbās quondam <u>sōlum</u> tē nōsse <u>Catullum</u>,
    Lesbia, nec prae mē velle tenēre Iovem.
dīlēxī tum tē nōn tantum ut vulgus amīcam,
    sed pater ut gnātōs dīligit et generōs.
nunc tē cognōvī: quārē etsī impēnsius ūror,   5
    multō mī tamen es vīlior et levior.
quī potis est, inquis? quod amantem iniūria tālis
    cōgit amāre magis, sed bene velle minus.

nōsse = nōvisse	
prae	*instead of, rather than*
tenēre	*possess*
vulgus	*the ordinary man, common man*
amīcam: amīca	*mistress, girlfriend*
gnātōs = nātōs	
quārē	*and so, wherefore*
etsī	*although, even if*
impēnsius: impēnsē	*strongly, violently*
ūror: ūrere	*burn*
levior: levis	*worthless*
quī potis est?	*how is that possible?*
	how can that be?
bene velle	*like, be friendly*

1 What statement by Lesbia does Catullus recall in lines 1–2? What were his feelings about her at that time, according to lines 3–4?

2 What is the point of the comparison in line 4?

3 Explain what Catullus means by "nunc tē cognōvī" (line 5). In what way has his discovery affected his feelings for Lesbia? Why has it had this effect?

About the Language

1 From Unit 3 onwards, you have met sentences in which forms of the pronoun **is** are used as antecedents of the relative pronoun **quī**:

is *quī nūper servus erat* nunc dīvitissimus est.
He *who was recently a slave* is now extremely rich.

id *quod mihi nārrāvistī* numquam patefaciam.
That *which you have told me* I shall never reveal.
Or, in more natural English:
I shall never reveal **what** *you have told me.*

dominus **eōs** pūniet *quī pecūniam āmīsērunt.*
The master will punish **those** *who lost the money.*

Notice that in these sentences the antecedent (in boldface) comes *before* the relative clause (italicized).

Further examples:

1 id quod dīcis vērum est.
2 is quī rēgem vulnerāvit celeriter fūgit.
3 nūllum praemium dabitur eīs quī officium neglegunt.

2 You have also met sentences like these, in which the antecedent comes *after* the relative clause:

quī auxilium mihi prōmīsērunt, **eī** mē iam dēserunt.
Those *who promised me help* are now deserting me.

quod potuimus, **id** fēcimus.
That *which we could do,* we did.
Or, in more natural English:
We did **what** *we could.*

Further examples:

1 quod saepe rogāvistī, ecce! id tibi dō.
2 quōs per tōtum orbem terrārum quaerēbam, eī in hāc urbe inventī sunt.

3 In Stages 41–45 you have met sentences in which the antecedent is omitted altogether:

quod mulier dīcit amantī, in ventō scrībere oportet.
What a woman says to her lover should be written on the wind.

quī numquam timet stultus est.
He *who is never frightened* is a fool.

quī speciem amīcitiae praebent nōn semper fidēlēs sunt.
Those *who put on an appearance of friendship* are not always faithful.

Further examples:

1 quod suscēpī, effēcī.
2 quae tū mihi heri dedistī, tibi crās reddam.
3 quī multum habet plūs cupit.
4 quod sentīmus loquāmur.
5 quī rēs adversās fortiter patiuntur, maximam laudem merent.

    laudem: laus   *praise, fame*

VI

ōdī et amō. quārē id faciam, fortasse requīris.
   nescio, sed fierī sentiō et excrucior.

requīris: requīrere   *ask*

Do the first three words of this poem make sense? Does Catullus mean that he hates at some times and loves at others, or that he hates and loves simultaneously?

VII

miser Catulle, dēsinās ineptīre,
et quod vidēs perīsse perditum dūcās.
fulsēre quondam candidī tibi sōlēs,
cum ventitābās quō puella dūcēbat
amāta nōbīs quantum amābitur nūlla.   5
ibi illa multa cum iocōsa fiēbant,
quae tū volēbās nec puella nōlēbat,
fulsēre vērē candidī tibi sōlēs.

nunc iam illa nōn volt: tū quoque impotēns nōlī,
nec quae fugit sectāre, nec miser vīve,   10
sed obstinātā mente perfer, obdūrā.

valē, puella. iam Catullus obdūrat,
nec tē requīret nec rogābit invītam.
at tū dolēbis, cum rogāberis nūlla.
scelesta, vae tē, quae tibi manet vīta?   15
quis nunc tē adībit? cui vidēberis bella?
quem nunc amābis? cuius esse dīcēris?
quem bāsiābis? cui labella mordēbis?
at tū, Catulle, dēstinātus obdūrā.

ineptīre	*be a fool*
perditum: perditus	*completely lost, gone forever*
dūcās: dūcere	*consider*
candidī: candidus	*bright*
ventitābās: ventitāre	*often go, go repeatedly*
nōbīs = mihi	*by me*
quantum	*as, as much as*
ibi	*then, in those days*
illa multa cum . . . fiēbant = cum illa multa . . . fiēbant
iocōsa	*moments of fun, moments of pleasure*
vērē	*truly*
nunc iam	*now however, as things are now*
volt = vult	
impotēns	*being helpless, being powerless*
sectāre	*imperative of* sectārī *chase after*
perfer: perferre	*endure*
obdūrā: obdūrāre	*be firm*
requīret: requīrere	*go looking for*
nūlla: nūllus	*not at all*
scelesta: scelestus	*wretched*
vae tē!	*alas for you!*
bāsiābis: bāsiāre	*kiss*

labella: labellum   *lip*
mordēbis: mordēre   *bite*
dēstinātus   *determined*

1 Explain the advice which Catullus gives himself in lines 1–2. What English proverb corresponds to the idea expressed in line 2?
2 Does line 3 simply mean that it was fair weather?
3 Which word in line 9 contrasts with "quondam" (line 3)?
4 What future does Catullus foresee in lines 14–15?
5 On the evidence of lines 12–19, does Catullus seem capable of following his own advice? Give reasons for your view.
6 What is the mood of the poem? Sad, angry, bitter, determined, resigned? Does the mood change during the course of the poem? If so, where and in what way?

VIII

In the first four verses of this poem, given here in translation, Catullus describes the loyalty and friendship of Furius and Aurelius:

Furius and Aurelius, comrades of Catullus,
whether he journeys to furthest India,
whose shores are pounded by far-resounding
    Eastern waves,

or whether he travels to soft Arabia,
to Persia, Scythia, or the arrow-bearing Parthians,
or the plains which are darkened by the seven mouths
    of the river Nile,

or whether he crosses the lofty Alps,
visiting the scene of great Caesar's triumphs,
over the Rhine and the ocean, to Britain on the
    edge of the world,

ready to join in any adventure,
whatever the will of the gods may bring,
carry a few bitter words
    to my girl.

The poem's last two verses are Catullus' message:

cum suīs vīvat valeatque moechīs,
quōs simul complexa tenet trecentōs,
nūllum amāns vērē, sed identidem omnium
    īlia rumpēns;

nec meum respectet, ut ante, amōrem,   5
quī illius culpā cecidit velut prātī
ultimī flōs, praetereunte postquam
    tāctus arātrō est.

valeat: valēre	*thrive, prosper*	respectet: respectāre	*look towards, count on*
moechīs: moechus	*lover, adulterer*	illius culpā	*through her fault, thanks to her*
complexa: complectī	*embrace*	cecidit: cadere	*die*
trecentōs: trecentī	*three hundred*	prātī: prātum	*meadow*
īlia	*groin*	ultimī: ultimus	*farthest, at the edge*
rumpēns: rumpere	*burst, rupture*		

1 Why does Catullus spend so much of this poem describing Furius' and
   Aurelius' loyalty?
2 What is the gist of the message which he asks them to deliver?
3 Do any phrases or words in lines 17 and 19 remind you of other poems
   by Catullus that you have read?
4 "His final goodbye to Lesbia." Do you think this is an accurate
   description of the last two verses?

Practicing the Language

1 Match each word in the left-hand column with a word of the opposite meaning, taken from the right-hand column.

amor	tollere
celeriter	adiuvāre
dare	gaudēre
dēmittere	paulō
hiems	odium
impedīre	perīculum
incipere	lūx
lūgēre	dēsinere
multō	aestās
poena	accipere
salūs	lentē
tenebrae	praemium

2 In each pair of sentences, translate sentence (a); then change it from a direct question to an indirect question by completing sentence (b) with the correct form of the present subjunctive active or passive, and translate again.

For example: (a) cūr semper errātis?
                    (b) dīcite nōbīs cūr semper . . . . . .
Completed and translated, sentence (b) becomes:
  dīcite nōbīs cūr semper **errētis**.
  *Tell us why you are always **wandering around***.

The active and passive forms of the present subjunctive are given on pp.298–9. You may also need to consult the vocabulary at the end to find which conjugation a verb belongs to.

1a ubi habitās?
1b dīc mihi ubi . . . . . .
2a quō captīvī illī dūcuntur?
2b scīre volō quō captīvī illī . . . . . .
3a quot fundōs possideō?
3b oblītus sum quot fundōs . . . . . .
4a quid quaerimus?
4b tibi dīcere nōlumus quid . . . . . .
5a novumne templum aedificātur?

5b incertus sum num novum templum . . . . . .
6a cūr in hōc locō sedētis?
6b explicāte nōbīs cūr in hōc locō . . . . . .

3 Complete each sentence with the right word or phrase and then translate.

1 dēnique poēta . . . . . surrēxit. (ad recitandum, ad dormiendum)
2 nūntius, celeriter . . . . ., mox ad castra pervēnit. (scrībendō, equitandō)
3 captīvī, quī nūllam spem . . . . . habēbant, dēspērābant. (coquendī, effugiendī)
4 omnēs hospitēs in triclīnium . . . . . contendērunt. (ad cēnandum, ad pugnandum)
5 senex, quī procul ā marī habitābat, artem . . . . . numquam didicerat. (nāvigandī, spectandī)
6 pater meus, dīligenter . . . . ., tandem magnās dīvitiās adeptus est. (labōrandō, bibendō)

About the Language

1 In Stage 9, you met the dative used in sentences like this:

pater **nōbīs** dōnum ēmit.   *Father bought a present **for us**.*

This use of the dative is sometimes described as the *dative of advantage*.

2 In Stages 41–45, you have met the dative used in sentences like these:

Fortūna **mihi** frātrem ēripuit.   *Fortune has snatched my brother away* **from me**.

tenebrae Orcī **eī** passerem abstulērunt.   *The shades of Hell stole the sparrow* **from her**.

This use of the dative is sometimes described as the *dative of disadvantage*.

Further examples:

1 fūr mihi multam pecūniam abstulit.
2 barbarī eīs cibum ēripuērunt.
3 Rōmānī nōbīs lībertātem auferre cōnantur.

Clodia

The real identity of "Lesbia" is uncertain, but there are reasons for thinking that she was a woman named Clodia. Clodia came from the aristocratic family of the Claudii (who used a different spelling of their name), and was married to Metellus, a wealthy and distinguished noble. She was an attractive, highly educated woman, whose colorful lifestyle caused continual interest and gossip at Rome. Among the other rumors that regularly circulated around her, she was said to have murdered her husband and commited incest with her brother.

One of Clodia's lovers was the lively and talented Marcus Caelius Rufus. Their relationship lasted for about two years, before being broken off by Caelius. There was a violent quarrel; and Clodia, furious and humiliated, was determined to revenge herself. She launched a prosecution against Caelius, alleging (among other things) that he had robbed her and attempted to poison her.

Clodia, in spite of her doubtful reputation, was a powerful and dangerous enemy, with many influential friends, and the prosecution was a serious threat to Caelius. To defend himself against her charges, he turned to various friends, including Rome's leading orator, Cicero. Not only was Cicero a close friend of Caelius, but he had a bitter and long-running feud with Clodia's brother Clodius.

Some of the charges were dealt with by other speakers for the defense; Cicero's job was to deal with Clodia's allegations of theft and poisoning. It would not be enough to produce arguments and witnesses; Clodia herself had to be discredited and (if possible) made to look ridiculous, if a verdict of "not guilty" was to be achieved.

The following paragraphs are from Cicero's speech in defense of Caelius:

> Two charges in particular have been made: theft and attempted murder, and both charges involve the same individual. It is alleged that the gold was stolen from Clodia, and that the poison was obtained for administering to Clodia. The rest of the chief prosecutor's speech was not a list of charges, but a string of insults, more suitable to a vulgar slanging-match than a court of law. When the prosecutor calls my client "adulterer, fornicator, swindler," these are not accusations, but mere abuse. Such charges have no foundation; they are wild mud-

slinging, by an accuser who has lost his temper and has no one to back him up.

But when we come to the charges of theft and attempted murder, we have to deal not with the prosecutor but with the person behind him. In speaking of these charges, gentlemen of the jury, my concern is wholly with Clodia, a lady who possesses not only nobility of birth but also a certain notoriety. However, I shall say nothing about her except

Dancing-girls on a mosaic from Sicily.

Stage 45

in connection with the charges against my client. I should be more energetic and forceful in speaking about Clodia, but I do not wish to seem influenced by my political dispute with her husband – I mean her *brother*, of course (I'm always making that mistake). I shall speak in moderate language, and will go no further than I am obliged by my duty to my client and the facts of the case: for I have never felt it right to argue with a woman, especially with one who has always been regarded not as any man's enemy but as *every* man's friend . . .

I shall name no names, but suppose there were a woman, unmarried, blatantly living the life of a harlot both here in the city and in the public gaze of the crowded resort of Baiae, flaunting her behavior not only by her attitude and her appearance, not only by her passionate glances and her insolent tongue, but by lustful embraces, drinking-sessions, and beach-parties, so that she seemed to be not merely a harlot, but a harlot of the lewdest and most lascivious description – suppose that a young man, like my client, were to associate with such a woman; do you seriously claim that he would be seducing an innocent victim? . . .

I was present, gentlemen, and indeed it was perhaps the saddest and bitterest occasion of my whole life, when Quintus Metellus, who only two days previously had been playing a leading part in the political life of our city, a man in the prime of his years, in the best of health and at the peak of his physical strength, was violently, suddenly, shockingly taken from us. How can the woman, who comes from that house of crime, now dare to speak in court about the rapid effects of poison?

Caelius was acquitted. Nothing is known of Clodia's later fate.

Words and Phrases Checklist

aestās, aestātis	*summer*
candidus, candida, candidum	*bright, shining*
culpa, culpae	*blame*
fleō, flēre, flēvī	*weep*
modo . . . modo	*now . . . now, sometimes . . . sometimes*
mulier, mulieris	*woman*
orbis, orbis	*circle, globe*
orbis terrārum	*world*
ōtium, ōtiī	*leisure*
quisquam, quicquam	*anyone, anything*
rumpō, rumpere, rūpī, ruptus	*break, split*
speciēs, speciēī	*appearance*
tegō, tegere, tēxī, tēctus	*cover*
tenuis, tenue	*thin*

Give the meaning of each of the following:

candor, culpāre, ērumpere, flētus, irrumpere.

Synonym Search

clārus (23), fēmina (5), frangere (18), lacrimāre (7), tellūs (44).

clādēs

"Eruption of Vesuvius" by Joseph Wright of Derby.

Pliny wrote two letters to the historian Tacitus giving an eye-witness account of the eruption of Mount Vesuvius, which had taken place in August A.D. 79 when Pliny was seventeen. In the first letter, he described the death of his uncle (Pliny the Elder), who went too near the danger zone on a rescue mission, and was choked to death by the fumes. In the second letter, on which the passages in this Stage are based, Pliny describes the adventures which he and his mother had at Misenum after Pliny the Elder had departed on his mission.

tremōrēs

I

profectō avunculō, ipse reliquum tempus studiīs impendī (ideō enim remānseram); deinde balneum, cēna, somnus inquiētus et brevis. per multōs diēs priōrēs, tremor terrae sentiēbātur, minus fōrmīdolōsus quia Campāniae solitus; sed illā nocte ita invaluit, ut nōn movērī omnia sed ēvertī vidērentur. irrūpit cubiculum meum   5
māter; surgēbam ipse, ad eam excitandam sī dormīret. cōnsēdimus in āreā domūs, quae mare ā tēctīs modicō spatiō dīvidēbat; ego, ut timōrem mātris meā sēcūritāte lēnīrem, poposcī librum et quasi per ōtium legere coepī. subitō advenit amīcus quīdam avunculī, quī ubi mē et mātrem sedentēs, mē vērō etiam legentem videt, vituperat   10
illīus patientiam, sēcūritātem meam. ego nihilōminus intentus in librum manēbam.

iam hōra diēī prīma; sed adhūc dubia lūx. iam quassātīs proximīs tēctīs, magnus et certus ruīnae metus. tum dēmum fugere cōnstituimus; nam sī diūtius morātī essēmus, sine dubiō   15
periissēmus. ultrā tēcta prōgressī, ad respīrandum cōnsistimus. multa ibi mīrabilia vidēmus, multās fōrmīdinēs patimur.

avunculō: avunculus	*uncle*
remānseram: remanēre	*stay behind*
somnus	*sleep*
fōrmīdolōsus	*alarming*
solitus	*common, usual*
invaluit: invalēscere	*become strong*
tēctīs: tēctum	*building*
spatiō: spatium	*space, distance*
dīvidēbat: dīvidere	*separate*
sēcūritāte: sēcūritās	*unconcern, lack of anxiety*
per ōtium	*at leisure, free from care*
quassātīs: quassāre	*shake violently*
ruīnae: ruīna	*collapse*
ultrā	*beyond*
respīrandum: respīrāre	*recover one's breath, get one's breath back*
fōrmīdinēs: fōrmīdō	*fear, terror*
Campāniae	*in Campania*

II

nam vehicula, quae prōdūcī iusserāmus, quamquam in plānissimō
campō, in contrāriās partēs agēbantur, ac nē lapidibus quidem fulta
in eōdem locō manēbant. praetereā mare in sē resorbērī vidēbāmus,
quasi tremōre terrae repulsum esset. certē prōcesserat lītus,
multaque maris animālia siccīs arēnīs dētinēbantur. ab alterō latere   5
nūbēs ātra et horrenda in longās flammārum figūrās dēhīscēbat,
quae et similēs et maiōrēs fulguribus erant. tum vērō ille amīcus
avunculī vehementius nōs hortātus est ut effugere cōnārēmur: "sī
frāter" inquit, "tuus, tuus avunculus, vīvit, salūtem vestram cupit;
sī periit, superstitēs vōs esse voluit; cūr igitur cūnctāminī?"   10

plānissimō: plānus	*level, flat*
campō: campus	*ground*
partēs: pars	*direction*
agēbantur: agī	*move, roll*
fulta: fulcīre	*prop up, wedge*
resorbērī: resorbēre	*suck back*
siccīs: siccus	*dry*
arēnīs: arēna	*sand*
dētinēbantur:	
dētinēre	*hold back,*
	strand
latere: latus	*side*
dēhīscēbat:	
dēhīscere	*gape open*
fulguribus: fulgur	*lightning*
cūnctāminī: cūnctārī	*delay, hesitate*

The area
affected by
ashfall after
the eruption
of Vesuvius
in A.D.79.

Relief from House of Caecilius showing effects of earthquake at Pompeii, A.D.62.

respondimus nōs salūtī nostrae cōnsulere nōn posse, dum dē illō
incertī essēmus. nōn morātus ultrā, sē convertit et quam celerrimē ē
perīculō fūgit.

nec multō post, illa nūbēs ātra dēscendit in terrās, operuit maria;
cēlāverat Capreās, Mīsēnī prōmunturium ē cōnspectū abstulerat.   15
tum māter mē ōrāre hortārī iubēre, ut quōquō modō fugerem;
affirmāvit mē, quod iuvenis essem, ad salūtem pervenīre posse; sē,
quae et annīs et corpore gravārētur, libenter moritūram esse, sī mihi
causa mortis nōn fuisset. ego respondī mē nōlle incolumem esse nisi
illa quoque effūgisset; deinde manum eius amplexus, addere   20
gradum cōgō. pāret invīta, castīgatque sē, quod mē morētur.

cōnsulere	*take thought for, give consideration to*
operuit: operīre	*cover*
prōmunturium	*promontory*
ōrāre hortārī iubēre = ōrābat hortābātur iubēbat	
quōquō: quisquis	*whatever (i.e. whatever possible)*
incolumem: incolumis	*safe*
amplexus: amplectī	*grasp, clasp*
addere gradum	*go forward step by step (literally "add one step (to another)")*
Capreās: Capreae	*Capri*
Mīsēnī: Mīsēnum	*Misenum*

1 What strange things were happening to (*a*) Pliny's carriages, (*b*) the
  sea and shore, (*c*) the sea-creatures?
2 Describe what Pliny saw in the sky (lines 5–7).
3 What did the friend of Pliny's uncle urge Pliny and his mother to do?
  What reason did they give for refusing? What did the friend then do?
4 What were the effects of the black cloud, as described in lines 14–15?

5 Why did Pliny's mother think they should separate? What action did Pliny take in response to her entreaties?

6 What impression do you have of the character of (*a*) the friend of Pliny's uncle, (*b*) Pliny and his mother, as shown by their behavior during the eruption?

About the Language

1 In Stage 30, you met the pluperfect indicative passive:

omnēs servī **dīmissī erant**.
*All the slaves **had been sent away**.*

2 In Stage 46, you have met sentences like these:

cum omnēs servī **dīmissī essent**, ad āream rediimus.
*When all the slaves **had been sent away**, we returned to the courtyard.*

Plīnius scīre voluit num avunculus **servātus esset**.
*Pliny wanted to know whether his uncle **had been saved**.*

The Latin form of the verb in boldface is the *pluperfect subjunctive passive*.

Further examples:

1 ancilla cognōvit quid in testāmentō dominī scrīptum esset.
2 cum victimae sacrificātae essent, pontifex pauca verba dīxit.
3 amīcī vestrī ignōrābant quārē comprehēnsī essētis.

3 Compare the indicative and subjunctive forms of the pluperfect passive of **portō**:

PLUPERFECT INDICATIVE PASSIVE	PLUPERFECT SUBJUNCTIVE PASSIVE
portātus eram	**portātus essem**
portātus erās	**portātus essēs**
portātus erat	**portātus esset**
portātī erāmus	**portātī essēmus**
portātī erātis	**portātī essētis**
portātī erant	**portātī essent**

Pluperfect subjunctive passive forms of **doceō**, **trahō**, **capiō**, and **audiō** are given on p.300.

4 Study the following examples:

iūdex rogāvit quantam pecūniam mercātor mihi **pollicitus esset**.
*The judge asked how much money the merchant **had promised** me.*

cum Rōmam **regressus essem**, prīnceps mē arcessīvit.
*When **I had returned** to Rome, the emperor sent for me.*

The Latin words in boldface are *pluperfect subjunctive* forms of *deponent* verbs.

Further examples:

1 cum multās gemmās adeptī essēmus, domum revēnimus.
2 memineram quid māter mea locūta esset.

Pluperfect subjunctive forms of **cōnor**, **vereor**, etc. are given on p.305.

---

tenebrae

---

iam dēcidēbat cinis, adhūc tamen rārus. respiciō; dēnsa cālīgō, tergīs nostrīs imminēns, nōs sequēbātur quasi ingēns flūmen ātrum in terram effūsum esset. "dēflectāmus" inquam, "dum vidēmus, nē in viā sternāmur et in tenebrīs ā multitūdine fugientium obterāmur." vix cōnsēderāmus, cum dēscendit nox dēnsissima,   5
quasi omnia lūmina in conclāvī clausō exstīncta essent. sī adfuissēs, audīvissēs ululātūs fēminārum, īnfantum vāgītūs, clāmōrēs virōrum; aliī vōcibus parentēs requīrēbant, vōcibusque nōscitābant, aliī līberōs, aliī coniugēs; hī suum cāsum, aliī suōrum lūgēbant; nōnnūllī metū mortis mortem precābantur; multī ad deōs   10
manūs tollēbant, plūrēs nusquam iam deōs ūllōs esse affirmābant.

paulum relūxit, quod nōn diēs nōbīs, sed appropinquantis ignis indicium vidēbātur. ignis tamen procul substitit; deinde tenebrae rūrsus, cinis rūrsus, multus et gravis. nisi identidem surrēxissēmus et cinerem excussissēmus, sine dubiō opertī atque etiam oblīsī   15
pondere essēmus.

tandem cālīgō tenuāta ac dissolūta est, sīcut fūmus vel nebula. mox diēs rediit; sōl etiam fulgēbat, pallidus tamen. attonitī vīdimus

omnia mūtāta altōque cinere tamquam nive operta. regressī
Mīsēnum, noctem spē ac metū exēgimus. metus praevalēbat; nam   20
tremor terrae persevērābat. nōbīs tamen nūllum cōnsilium abeundī
erat, dōnec cognōscerēmus num avunculus servātus esset.

rārus	*occasional*
dēflectāmus:	
dēflectere	*turn aside,*
	turn off the road
sternāmur: sternere	*knock over*
obterāmur: obterere	*trample to death*
ululātūs: ululātus	*shriek*
vāgītūs: vāgītus	*wailing, crying*
nōscitābant: nōscitāre	*recognize*
paulum	*a little, to a slight extent*
relūxit: relūcēscere	*become light again*
opertī = opertī	
essēmus: operīre	*bury*
oblīsī . . . essēmus:	
oblīdere	*crush*
pondere: pondus	*weight*
tenuāta: tenuāre	*thin out*
dissolūta est: dissolvere	*disperse, dissolve*
nebula	*mist*
nive: nix	*snow*
exēgimus: exigere	*spend*
praevalēbat: praevalēre	*prevail, be uppermost*
dōnec	*until*
Mīsēnum	*to Misenum*

Petrified bodies.

About the Language

1 Study the following conditional sentences:

sī iuvenis **respexisset**, latrōnem **vīdisset**.
*If the young man **had looked round**, he **would have seen** the robber.*

sī mē **vocāvissēs**, statim **vēnissem**.
*If you **had called me**, I **would have come** at once.*

nisi canis **lātrāvisset**, servī **effūgissent**.
*If the dog **had** not **barked**, the slaves **would have escaped**.*

sī imperātor ipse hanc rem **iūdicāvisset**, **damnātī essētis**.
*If the emperor himself **had judged** this case, **you would have been condemned**.*

Notice that:

1 the Latin verbs are in the *pluperfect* tense of the *subjunctive*;
2 the English translations contain the words *had . . .*, followed by *would have . . . .*

2 Further examples:

1 sī nautae in portū mānsissent, tempestātem vītāvissent.
2 sī satis pecūniae obtulissētis, agricola vōbīs equum vēndidisset.
3 sī centuriō tergum vertisset, minus graviter vulnerātus esset.
4 sī fīlia tua illī senī nūpsisset, miserrima fuisset.
5 sī exercitus noster superātus esset, prīnceps novās cōpiās ēmīsisset.
6 nisi pater mē prohibuisset, tibi subvēnissem.

Practicing the Language

1 Translate each sentence; then, referring if necessary to the table of nouns on pages 284–5 and to the vocabulary at the end of the book, change the *number* of the words in boldface (i.e. change singular words to plural, and plural words to singular) and translate again.

1 centuriō barbarōs **catēnīs** vīnxit.
2 fūr vestēs **amīcī tuī** abstulit.
3 sacerdōs ad **templa** ambulābat.
4 multitūdō artem **gladiātōris** mīrābātur.
5 pāstōrēs strepitum **canum** audīvērunt.
6 puer cum **ancillīs** et **iuvenibus** stābat.
7 **mercātōrī** pecūniam trādidit.
8 ego callidior **meīs inimīcīs** sum.

2 This exercise is based on lines 1–12 of "tremōrēs," Part I on page 222. Read the lines again, then translate the following sentences into Latin. All necessary vocabulary can be found on page 222 in lines 1–12, but you will need to make various alterations to the word-endings, e.g. by changing a verb form from 1st person to 3rd person, or a noun from the nominative to the genitive; refer to the appropriate pages of the Language Information Section where necessary.

1 Plinius spent the remaining time *on dinner*[1] and *sleep*[1].
2 Throughout those days, tremors were being felt.
3 Plinius began to read a book, in order that he might calm *his*[2] mother's fear.
4 They *saw*[3] his uncle's friend arriving.
5 Plinius, having been scolded *by the friend*[4], was nevertheless remaining in the courtyard.

[1]dative   [2]omit   [3]use either perfect or historical present
[4]"ab" + ablative

3 Translate each pair of sentences; then replace the word in boldface with the correct form of the relative pronoun **quī**, using the table in paragraph 8 on page 292 and adjusting the word order if necessary so that the relative pronoun comes at the beginning of the second sentence; then translate again. Do NOT join the two sentences together, but translate the relative pronoun as a "connecting relative," i.e. as **he**, **she**, **it**, **this**, etc.

For example: in mediā urbe stābat templum. simulatque **templum** intrāvī, attonitus cōnstitī.
In the middle of the city stood a temple. As soon as I entered the **temple**, *I halted in amazement.*

This becomes: in mediā urbe stābat templum. **quod** simulatque intrāvī, attonitus cōnstitī.
In the middle of the city stood a temple. As soon as I entered **it**, *I halted in amazement.*

The gender of the word in boldface is given after each sentence. For ways of translating the connecting relative, see paragraph 8 on p.292.

1 subitō appāruērunt duo lupī. cum **lupōs** vīdissent, pāstōrēs clāmōrem sustulērunt. (m.)
2 agricola uxōrem monuit ut fugeret. **uxor** tamen obstinātē recūsāvit. (f.)
3 rēx epistulam celeriter dictāvit. cum servus **epistulam** scrīpsisset, nūntius ad Imperātōrem tulit. (f.)
4 fūr ātrium tacitē intrāvit. **fūre** vīsō, canis lātrāvit. (m.)
5 Quīntus "Salvium perfidiae accūsō," inquit. **verbīs** audītīs, Salvius tacuit. (n.)
6 "ubi est pecūnia mea?" rogāvit mercātor. nēmō **mercātōrī** respondēre audēbat. (m.)
7 hominēs clāmāre coepērunt. clāmōribus **hominum** excitātus, surrēxī. (m.)
8 crās pontifex sacrificium faciet. ut **sacrificium** videās, tē ad templum dūcam. (n.)

About the Language

1 From Unit 1 onwards, you have met sentences like these, containing various forms of the verb **esse** (*to be*):

nihil tam ferōx **est** quam leō.
*Nothing **is** as ferocious as a lion.*

postrīdiē discessimus; sed iter longum et difficile **erat**.
*We left next day; but the journey **was** long and difficult.*

2 Sometimes, however, the various forms of **esse** are omitted, especially in verse or fast-moving narrative. In Stages 41–46 of this Unit you have met sentences like these:

nihil tam terribile quam incendium.
*Nothing **is** as frightening as a fire.*

caelum undīque et pontus.
*On every side **was** sky and sea.*

subitō fragōrem audīvimus; deinde longum silentium.
*Suddenly we heard a crash; then **there was** a long silence.*

3 Translate again lines 13–14 of "tremōrēs," Part I (p.222), from "iam" to "metus." How many times does the Latin omit the word **erat** where the English translation contains the word *was*?

Time Chart of Roman Authors

The chart below shows the dates of eight Roman authors who appear in Unit 4, Stages 41–48 (in Latin or in translation), together with a brief indication of their work.

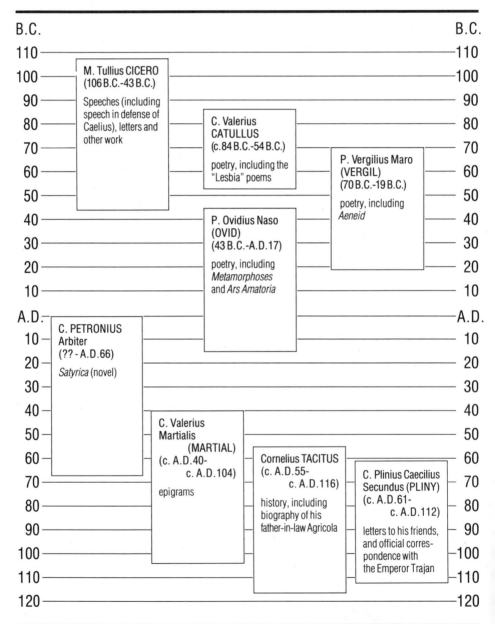

Words and Phrases Checklist

clādēs, clādis	*disaster*
iūdicō, iūdicāre, iūdicāvī, iūdicātus	*judge*
lapis, lapidis	*stone*
lūmen, lūminis	*light*
minus	*less*
paulum	*a little, slightly*
quisquis	*whoever*
quidquid (*also spelled* quicquid)	*whatever*
reliquus, reliqua, reliquum	*remaining, the rest*
requīrō, requīrere, requīsīvī	*ask, seek*
somnus, somnī	*sleep*
sternō, sternere, strāvī, strātus	*lay low, knock over*
tēctum, tēctī	*building*
ultrā	*further*

Give the meaning of each of the following:

iūdex, iūdicium, lapillus.

Synonym Search

aedificium (13), dēlēre (14), longius (cf. longē, 18), lūx (29), petere (18), quodcumque (42), saxum (15).

lūdī

The following narrative, told partly in Latin and partly in translation, comes from Book Five of Vergil's *Aeneid*.

certāmen

During their wanderings after the destruction of Troy, Aeneas and his Trojan followers have arrived at the island of Sicily, where Aeneas' father Anchises is buried. They decide to mark the anniversary of Anchises' death by holding a festival of games in his honor.

immōtā . . . attollitur undā. (II, line 4).

I

First is a race between four ships,
Picked from the whole fleet, well-matched with heavy oars:
The speedy *Pristis*, with a keen crew led by Mnestheus;
Massive *Chimaera*, huge as a city, commanded by Gyas;
The large *Centaur*, which carries Sergestus,
And sea-blue *Scylla*, with Cloanthus as captain.

II

est procul in pelagō saxum spūmantia contrā
lītora, quod <u>tumidīs</u> summersum tunditur ōlim
<u>flūctibus</u>, hībernī condunt ubi sīdera Cōrī;
tranquillō silet immōtāque attollitur undā.
hīc viridem <u>Aenēās</u> frondentī ex īlice mētam   5
cōnstituit signum nautīs <u>pater</u>, unde revertī
scīrent et longōs ubi circumflectere cursūs.

spūmantia: spūmāre	*foam*
contrā	*opposite*
tumidīs: tumidus	*swollen*
tunditur: tundere	*beat, buffet*
ōlim	*sometimes*
flūctibus: flūctus	*wave*
hībernī: hībernus	*wintry, of winter*
condunt: condere	*hide*
hībernī condunt ubi = ubi hībernī . . . condunt	
tranquillō: tranquillum	*calm weather*
attollitur: attollī	*rise*
viridem: viridis	*green*
frondentī: frondēns	*leafy*
īlice: īlex	*oak tree*
cōnstituit: cōnstituere	*set up, place*
circumflectere cursūs:	
circumflectere cursum	*turn one's course around*
clāra: clārus	*loud (literally "clear")*

inde ubi clāra dedit sonitum tuba, fīnibus omnēs
(haud mora) prōsiluēre suīs; ferit aethera clāmor
nauticus, adductīs spūmant freta versa lacertīs.   10
    effugit ante aliōs prīmīsque ēlābitur undīs
turbam inter fremitumque Gyās; quem deinde Cloanthus
cōnsequitur, melior rēmīs, sed pondere pīnus
tarda tenet. post hōs aequō discrīmine Pristis
Centaurusque locum tendunt superāre priōrem;   15
et nunc Pristis habet, nunc victam praeterit ingēns
Centaurus, nunc ūnā ambae iūnctisque feruntur
frontibus et longā sulcant vada salsa carīnā.

fīnibus: fīnis	*starting-place*
ferit: ferīre	*strike*
nauticus	*made by the sailors*
adductīs: addūcere	*pull, draw up (to the chest)*
freta: fretum	*water, sea*
versa: vertere	*churn up*
fremitum: fremitus	*noise, din*
cōnsequitur: cōnsequī	*follow, chase*
pīnus	*pine tree, i.e. boat (made of pine wood)*
tarda: tardus	*slow*
tenet: tenēre	*hold back*
aequō discrīmine	*at an equal distance (from the leaders)*
tendunt: tendere	*strain, strive*
superāre	*achieve, win*
iūnctīs: iūnctus	*side by side*
frontibus: frōns	*prow*
sulcant: sulcāre	*plow through*
vada: vadum	*water*
salsa: salsus	*salty*
carīnā: carīna	*keel*
Cōrī: Cōrus	*Northwest Wind*

1 Where is the rock? What happens to it when the weather is stormy?
  What happens in calm weather?
2 What does Aeneas place on the rock? Why? Which noun in lines 5–7
  emphasizes Aeneas' position of responsibility?
3 What is the starting-signal? What do the words "haud mora" and
  "prōsiluēre" (line 9) indicate about the manner in which the
  competitors move off?
4 What does Vergil say in lines 9–10 about (*a*) the shouting of the
  sailors? (*b*) the appearance of the sea? (*c*) the movements of the
  oarsmen?
5 Who takes the lead?

6 Who comes next? What advantage does he have, and what disadvantage?
7 Which two ships are struggling for third place? What is happening at each of the three stages of the struggle, introduced by "nunc . . . nunc . . . nunc" (lines 16–17)?
8 The verb "sulcāre" ("sulcant," line 18) literally means "to drive a furrow." In what way is it appropriate to the description of the ships' course?

Gyās et Cloanthus

I

They were nearing the rock, close to the turning-point,
When Gyas, leading at the halfway mark,
Cried out to his helmsman Menoetes: "What are you doing?
Don't wander so far to the right! Keep over this way!
Run close to the rock, let the oars on the port side graze it!

The rest can stay out at sea, if they want." But Menoetes,
Fearing a hidden reef, turned the prow to the open water.
"Where are you off to?" cried Gyas again. "Make for the rock!"
And looking around as he shouted, he saw Cloanthus,
Hard on his tail, cutting in between him and the rock.
Cloanthus, scraping through on the inside, took the lead
And reached safe water, leaving the turning-post far behind.

II

    tum vērō exarsit iuvenī dolor ossibus ingēns
nec lacrimīs caruēre genae, sēgnemque Menoetēn
in mare praecipitem puppī dēturbat ab altā;
ipse gubernāclō rēctor subit, ipse magister
hortāturque virōs clāvumque ad lītora torquet.   5
at gravis ut fundō vix tandem redditus īmō est
iam senior madidāque fluēns in veste Menoetēs
summa petit scopulī siccāque in rūpe resēdit.
illum et lābentem Teucrī et rīsēre natantem
et salsōs rīdent revomentem pectore flūctūs.   10

exarsit: exardēre	*blaze up*
ossibus: os	*bone*
sēgnem: sēgnis	*timid, unenterprising*
puppī: puppis	*stern, poop*
dēturbat: dēturbāre	*push, send flying*
gubernāclō: gubernāclum	*helm, steering-oar*
rēctor	*helmsman*
subit: subīre	*take over*
magister	*pilot*
clāvum: clāvus	*tiller, helm*
torquet: torquēre	*turn*
ut	*when*
fundō: fundus	*depth*
vix tandem	*at long last*
īmō: īmus	*lowest*
senior	*elderly*
fluēns	*dripping, streaming*
scopulī: scopulus	*rock*
resēdit: resīdere	*sit down, sink down*
revomentem: revomere	*vomit up*
pectore: pectus	*chest*
Menoetēn	*Greek accusative of* Menoetēs
Teucrī	*Trojans*

1 Who is the "iuvenis" (line 1)? What does he do to Menoetes in lines 2–3?

2 Who replaces Menoetes as helmsman? What are his first actions on taking over?

3 Which words and phrases in line 6 indicate that Menoetes (*a*) went a long way down, (*b*) did not resurface for some time, (*c*) could do nothing about getting to the surface himself but could only wait for the sea to buoy him up?

4 Why do you think Vergil includes the phrase "iam senior" (line 7) in his description of Menoetes? Which word in line 6 is partly explained by the phrase "madidāque fluēns in veste" in line 7?

5 What did Menoetes do as soon as he had resurfaced?

6 What three actions of Menoetes are described in lines 9–10? Do the Trojans show any sympathy for him? Does Vergil?

Relief from Athens, A.D. 165, showing competitors in a boat-race.

Sergestus et Mnēstheus

I

And now the two tail-enders, Mnestheus and Sergestus,
Are fired with a joyful hope of catching Gyas.
As they reach the rock, Sergestus is in the lead,
Though not by as much as a boat-length; his bows are in front,
But his stern is overlapped by the eager *Pristis*.
And Mnestheus, pacing between his lines of rowers,
Is driving them on: "Now pull with your oars;
Once you were comrades of Hector, and when Troy fell
You became my chosen companions; now summon your strength,
Now summon the courage you showed on the African sandbanks,
The Ionian sea, the racing waves of Greece.
I can hope no longer now to finish first
(Though perhaps . . . but victory lies in the hands of Neptune) –
Yet to come in last, my friends, would be shameful;
Prevent the disgrace!" And his men, with a mighty heave,
Pulled hard on their oars; the whole ship shook with their efforts;
The sea raced by beneath them, their throats and limbs
Were gripped by breathless exertion, they streamed with sweat.

II

attulit ipse virīs optātum cāsus honōrem.
namque <u>furēns animī</u> dum prōram ad saxa suburget
interior spatiōque subit <u>Sergestus</u> inīquō,
īnfēlīx saxīs in prōcurrentibus haesit.
cōnsurgunt nautae et magnō clāmōre morantur   5
ferrātāsque trudēs et acūtā cuspide contōs
expediunt frāctōsque legunt in gurgite rēmōs.

cāsus	*chance*
furēns animī	*furiously determined, with furious eagerness*
prōram: prōra	*prow*
suburget: suburgēre	*drive . . . up close*
interior	*on the inside*
subit: subīre	*approach*
inīquō: inīquus	*narrow, dangerous*
prōcurrentibus: prōcurrere	*project*

cōnsurgunt: cōnsurgere	*jump up*
morantur: morārī	*hold (the ship) steady*
ferrātās: ferrātus	*tipped with iron*
trudēs: trudis	*pole*
acūtā: acūtus	*sharp*
cuspide: cuspis	*point*
contōs: contus	*pole, rod*
expediunt: expedīre	*bring out, get out*
legunt: legere	*gather up*

About the Language

1 From Unit 1 onwards, you have met sentences like these:

sacerdōs **ā templō** discessit.
*The priest departed **from the temple**.*

servī **in agrīs** labōrābant.
*The slaves were working **in the fields**.*

In these sentences, *from* is expressed by one of the prepositions **ā**, **ab**, **ē** or **ex**, while *in* is expressed by the preposition **in**. Each preposition is followed by a noun in the ablative case.

2 In poetry, however, the idea of *in* or *from* is often expressed by the ablative case alone, without any preposition:

ipse diem noctemque negat discernere **caelō** . . . Palinūrus.
*Palinurus himself says he cannot distinguish day and night **in the sky**.*

fīnibus omnēs . . . prōsiluēre **suīs**.
*They all leapt forward **from their starting-places**.*

. . . **immōtā**que attollitur **undā**.
*. . . and it rises up **from the still water**.*

Further examples:

1 nōbīs tempus erat patriā discēdere cārā.
2 flūmine nant piscēs, arbore cantat avis.
3 iamque senex laetus nostrā proficīscitur urbe.
4 dīcitur immēnsā Cyclōps habitāre cavernā.

victor

I

at laetus Mnēstheus successūque ācrior ipsō
prōna petit maria et pelagō dēcurrit apertō.
et prīmum in scopulō <u>lūctantem</u> dēserit altō
<u>Sergestum</u> brevibusque vadīs frūstrāque vocantem
auxilia et frāctīs discentem currere rēmīs.   5
inde Gyān ipsamque ingentī mōle Chimaeram
cōnsequitur; cēdit, quoniam spoliāta magistrō est.

successū: successus	*success*	currere	*race, row*
ācrior: ācer	*eager, excited*	mōle: mōlēs	*bulk*
prōna: prōnus	*easy*	quoniam	*since*
dēcurrit: dēcurrere	*speed, race*	spoliāta . . . est: spoliāre	*deprive*
dēserit: dēserere	*leave behind*	Gyān:	*Greek accusative of Gyās*
brevibus: brevis	*shallow*		

1 Why does Mnestheus feel encouraged at this point?
2 Who is the first competitor to be overtaken by Mnestheus? What is he doing, and trying to do?
3 Whom does Mnestheus overtake next? Why is he able to do so?

II

sōlus iamque <u>ipsō</u> superest in <u>fīne</u> Cloanthus:
quem petit et summīs adnīxus vīribus urget.
tum vērō ingeminat clāmor cūnctīque sequentem
īnstīgant studiīs, resonatque fragōribus aethēr.
hī proprium decus et partum indignantur honōrem   5

adnīxus: adnītī	*strain, exert oneself*
urget: urgēre	*pursue, press upon*
cūnctī: cūnctus	*all*
īnstīgant: īnstīgāre	*urge on*
studiīs: studium	*shout of support, cheer*
resonat: resonāre	*resound*
fragōribus: fragor	*shout*
proprium: proprius	*one's own, that belongs to one*
decus	*glory*
partum: parere	*gain, win*
indignantur: indignārī	*feel shame, think it shameful*

Sea nymphs (Nereids). Painting by William Etty.

nī teneant, vītamque volunt prō laude pacīscī;
hōs successus alit: possunt, quia posse videntur.
et fors aequātīs cēpissent praemia rōstrīs,
nī palmās pontō tendēns utrāsque Cloanthus
fūdissetque precēs dīvōsque in vōta vocāsset: 10
"dī, quibus imperium est pelagī, quōrum aequora currō,
vōbīs laetus ego hōc candentem in lītore taurum
cōnstituam ante ārās vōtī reus, extaque salsōs
prōiciam in flūctūs et vīna liquentia fundam."
dīxit, eumque īmīs sub flūctibus audiit omnis   15
Nēreidum Phorcīque chorus Panopēaque virgō,
et pater ipse manū magnā Portūnus euntem
impulit; illa Notō citius volucrīque sagittā
ad terram fugit et portū sē condidit altō.

vōtī reus	bound by one's vow, in payment of one's vow
prōiciam: prōicere	cast (as an offering)
liquentia: liquēre	flow
citius: citō	quickly
volucrī: volucer	winged, swift
sagittā: sagitta	arrow
sē condidit: sē condere	bring oneself to rest

Nēreidum: Nēreis	*sea-nymph*
Phorcī: Phorcus	*Phorcus (a sea-god)*
Panopēa	*Panopea (one of the sea-nymphs)*
Portūnus	*Portunus (god of harbors)*
nī = nisi	
indignantur . . . nī teneant	*think it shameful if they do not hold on to*
pacīscī	*exchange, bargain*
alit: alere	*encourage*
fors	*perhaps*
aequātīs: aequātus	*level, side by side*
rōstrīs: rōstrum	*prow*
palmās: palma	*hand (literally "palm")*
tendēns: tendere	*stretch out*
fūdisset: fundere	*pour out*
in vōta	*to (hear) his vow*
vocāsset = vocāvisset	
candentem: candēns	*gleaming white*

A1 Which two captains are involved in the final dash for victory? Which of them has the better chance, and which phrase in line 1 emphasizes this?

2 What happens in line 3 to the noise-level? Suggest a reason for this. Which contestant do the spectators support?

3 Why are Cloanthus' men especially anxious not to be beaten? How deeply (according to Vergil) do they care about winning?

4 What psychological advantages do Mnestheus and his men have?

5 What would the result have been, but for Cloanthus' prayer?

6 Which gods does Cloanthus address? What three promises does he make? Does his prayer imply a request as well as a promise?

7 Who heard the prayer? What help did Cloanthus receive?

8 Which word in lines 17–18 has Vergil placed in an especially emphatic position, and why?

9 What is the speed of Cloanthus' boat compared to? What is the result of Portunus' action?

B1 To what extent (if any) do the *personalities* of the four captains influence the action and result of the race?

2 Consider how Part II of "victor" should be read aloud. At which point or points should the reading be liveliest? How should Cloanthus' prayer be read? Are there any points where the reading should be calm or quiet?

About the Language

1 Study the following quotations from Latin verse:

ōraque caeruleā patrium clāmantia nōmen
excipiuntur aquā. (*Ovid*)

*And **his mouth**, shouting the name of his father, was received
by the dark blue water.*

per amīca **silentia** lūnae (*Vergil*)
*through **the** friendly **silence** of the moonlight.*

cōnscendit furibunda **rogōs**. (*Vergil*)
*She climbed **the funeral pyre** in a mad frenzy.*

In each of these phrases or sentences, the poet uses a *plural* noun (**ōra**, **silentia**, **rogōs**) with a singular meaning (*mouth, silence, pyre*). A similar use of the plural is sometimes found in English verse:

And it is clear to my long-searching eyes
That love at last has might upon the **skies**.

While Shasta signals to Alaskan **seas**
That watch old sluggish glaciers downwards creep.

(*William Vaughan Moody*)

2 From each of the following lines in Stage 47, pick out one example of a plural noun used with a singular meaning:

1 "victor" Part I (p.244), line 5.
2 "victor" Part II (p.246), line 14.

Practicing the Language

1 Match each word in the left-hand column with a word of similar meaning taken from the right-hand column.

castīgāre	suāvis
dēcipere	quod
dīvitiae	culpāre
dulcis	laedere
ignis	quidem
nocēre	vincere
nōn	fallere

ōlim	contemnere
quia	haud
scelus	opēs
spernere	verērī
superāre	incolumis
timēre	facinus
tūtus	quondam
vērō	incendium

2 Complete each sentence with the right word and then translate.

1 sī mē rogāvissēs, ... (dūxissem, respondissem)
2 sī Īcarus mandātīs patris pāruisset, nōn in mare . . . . . . (cecidisset, crēdidisset)
3 sī exercituī nostrō subvēnissētis, vōbīs magnum praemium . . . . . . (dedissēmus, exstrūxissēmus)
4 sī in Circō herī adfuissēs, spectāculō . . . . . . (dēlectātus essēs, dēpositus essēs)
5 nisi senex ā lībertīs dēfēnsus esset, latrōnēs eum . . . . . . (exiissent, occīdissent)

3 Translate each sentence, then replace the verb in boldface with the correct form of the verb in parentheses, keeping the same person, tense, etc. Refer if necessary to the vocabulary at the end of the book, and to the tables of deponent verbs on pp.303–06.

For example: cōnsul pauca verba **dīxit**. (loquī)
This becomes: cōnsul pauca verba **locūtus est**.
               *The consul **said** a few words.*

1 dux nautās **incitābat**. (hortārī)
2 captīvus quidem sum; sed effugere **temptābō**. (cōnārī)
3 crās ab hōc oppidō **discēdēmus**. (proficīscī)
4 **prōmīsī** mē pecūniam mox redditūrum esse. (pollicērī)
5 mīlitēs arma nova **comparāvērunt**. (adipīscī)
6 cognōscere volēbam num omnēs nūntiī **revēnissent**. (regredī)

4 Complete each sentence with the most suitable word from the list below, and then translate. Refer to the story on pages 236–46 where necessary.

ēiceret, taurum, ~~tuba~~, relictō, parum

(handwritten annotations above words: "throw out" over ēiceret, "bull" over taurum, "trumpet" over tuba, "leave" over relictō, "too little" over parum)

1 simulatque . . . . . sonuit, omnēs nāvēs prōsiluērunt.
2 iuvenis adeō īrātus erat ut senem ē nāve . . . . . . *(handwritten: "the young sp. – angry was to")*
3 Sergestus, quī . . . . . cautē nāvigābat, in scopulum incurrit.
4 saxō . . . . ., nautae cursum ad lītus dīrigēbant.
5 Cloanthus pollicitus est sē . . . . . deīs sacrificātūrum esse.

The Chariot-race in Homer's *Iliad*

When Vergil wrote the *Aeneid*, part of his inspiration came from two famous epic poems of ancient Greece, the *Iliad* and *Odyssey* of Homer. Throughout his poem, Vergil uses ideas, incidents, and phrases from Homer, but reshapes them, combines them with his own subject-matter, and handles them in his own style, to produce a poem which in some ways is very similar to the *Iliad* and *Odyssey*, but in other ways is utterly different.

The following extracts from Book Twenty-three of Homer's *Iliad* describe the chariot-race which took place during the funeral games held by the Achaians (Greeks) outside the walls of Troy during the Trojan War. Homer's account provided Vergil with some of the raw material for his description of the boat-race. The chief characters involved are:

ACHILLEUS (often known as Achilles), who has organized the games in honor of his dead friend Patroklos;

ANTILOCHOS son of Nestor and grandson of Neleus;

DIOMEDES son of Tydeus, hated by the god Phoibos Apollo but befriended and supported by the goddess Athene; he drives a team of horses which he has captured from the Trojans, and his companion is named Sthenelos;

EUMELOS son of Admetos (sometimes described as son of Pheres);

MENELAOS son of Atreus (Atreides), brother of the great king Agamemnon, whose mare Aithe he has borrowed for the chariot-race.

The winner of the race is to receive as his prize a skilled slave-woman and a huge tripod with ear-shaped handles.

They stood in line for the start, and Achilleus showed them the turn-post
far away on the level plain, and beside it he stationed
a judge, Phoinix the godlike, the follower of his father . . .

Then all held their whips high-lifted above their horses,
then struck with the whip thongs and in words urged their horses
        onward
into speed. Rapidly they made their way over the flat land
and presently were far away from the ships. The dust lifting
clung beneath the horses' chests like cloud or a stormwhirl.
Their manes streamed along the blast of the wind, . . .

                                 . . . the drivers
stood in the chariots, with the spirit beating in each man
with the strain to win, and each was calling aloud upon his own
horses, and the horses flew through the dust of the flat land.
But as the rapid horses were running the last of the race-course
back, and toward the grey sea, then the mettle of each began to
show itself, and the field of horses strung out, and before long
out in front was the swift-stepping team of the son of Pheres,
Eumelos, and after him the stallions of Diomedes,
the Trojan horses, not far behind at all, but close on him,
for they seemed forever on the point of climbing his chariot
and the wind of them was hot on the back and on the broad shoulders
of Eumelos. They lowered their heads and flew close after him.
    And now he might have passed him or run to a doubtful decision,
had not Phoibos Apollo been angry with Diomedes,
Tydeus' son, and dashed the shining whip from his hands, so
that the tears began to stream from his eyes, for his anger
as he watched how the mares of Eumelos drew far ahead of him
while his own horses ran without the whip and were slowed. Yet
Athene did not fail to see the foul play of Apollo
on Tydeus' son. She swept in speed to the shepherd of the people
and gave him back his whip, and inspired strength into his horses.
Then in her wrath she went on after the son of Admetos
and she, a goddess, smashed his chariot yoke, and his horses
ran on either side of the way, the pole dragged and Eumelos
himself was sent spinning out beside the wheel of the chariot
so that his elbows were all torn, and his mouth, and his nostrils,
and his forehead was lacerated about the brows, and his eyes
filled with tears, and the springing voice was held fast within him.
    Then the son of Tydeus, turning his single-foot horses to pass him,
went far out in front of the others, seeing that Athene
had inspired strength in his horses and to himself gave the glory.

The Plain of Troy.

After him came the son of Atreus, fair-haired Menelaos.
But Antilochos cried out aloud to his father's horses:
"Come on, you two. Pull, as fast as you can! I am not
trying to make you match your speed with the speed of those others,
the horses of Tydeus' valiant son, to whom now Athene
has granted speed and to their rider has given the glory.
But make your burst to catch the horses of the son of Atreus
nor let them leave you behind, for fear Aithe who is female
may shower you in mockery. Are you falling back, my brave horses?
For I will tell you this, and it will be a thing accomplished.
There will be no more care for you from the shepherd of the people,
Nestor, but he will slaughter you out of hand with the edge
of bronze, if we win the meaner prize because you are unwilling.
Keep on close after him and make all the speed you are able.
I myself shall know what to do and contrive it, so that
we get by in the narrow place of the way. He will not escape me."
    So he spoke, and they fearing the angry voice of their master
ran harder for a little while, and presently after this
battle-stubborn Antilochos saw where the hollow way narrowed.
There was a break in the ground where winter water had gathered
and broken out of the road, and made a sunken place all about.
Menelaos shrinking from a collision of chariots steered there,
but Antilochos also turned out his single-foot horses
from the road, and bore a little way aside, and went after him;

and the son of Atreus was frightened and called out aloud to Antilochos:
"Antilochos, this is reckless horsemanship. Hold in your horses.
The way is narrow here, it will soon be wider for passing.
Be careful not to crash your chariot and wreck both of us."
    So he spoke, but Antilochos drove on all the harder
with a whiplash for greater speed, as if he had never heard him.
As far as is the range of a discus swung from the shoulder
and thrown by a stripling who tries out the strength of his young
        manhood,
so far they ran even, but then the mares of Atreides gave way
and fell back, for he of his own will slackened his driving
for fear that in the road the single-foot horses might crash
and overturn the strong-fabricated chariots, and the men
themselves go down in the dust through their hard striving for victory.
But Menelaos of the fair hair called to him in anger:
"Antilochos, there is no other man more cursed than you are.
Damn you. We Achaians lied when we said you had good sense.
Even so, you will not get this prize without having to take oath."

•

A Greek two-horse chariot.

Fragment of Greek painted vase showing spectators watching a chariot-race.

(*The finish:*)
   . . . and now Tydeus' son in his rapid course was close on them
and he lashed them always with the whipstroke from the shoulder. His
      horses
still lifted their feet light and high as they made their swift passage.
Dust flying splashed always the charioteer, and the chariot
that was overlaid with gold and tin still rolled hard after
the flying feet of the horses, and in their wake there was not much
trace from the running rims of the wheels left in the thin dust.
The horses came in running hard. Diomedes stopped them
in the middle of where the men were assembled, with the dense sweat
      starting
and dripping to the ground from neck and chest of his horses.
He himself vaulted down to the ground from his shining chariot
and leaned his whip against the yoke. Nor did strong Sthenelos
delay, but made haste to take up the prizes, and gave the woman
to his high-hearted companions to lead away and the tripod
with ears to carry, while Diomedes set free the horses.

After him Neleian Antilochos drove in his horses,
having passed Menelaos, not by speed but by taking advantage.
But even so Menelaos held his fast horses close on him . . .
. . . At first he was left behind the length of a discus
thrown, but was overhauling him fast, with Aithe
of the fair mane, Agamemnon's mare, putting on a strong burst.
If both of them had had to run the course any further,
Menelaos would have passed him, and there could have been no
    argument . . .

Last and behind them all came in the son of Admetos
dragging his fine chariot and driving his horses before him.

(translation by Richmond Lattimore)

1 What part do the gods play in Homer's chariot-race? In what way does
   it differ from the part they play in Vergil's boat-race?
2 Compare the incident at the "narrow place" (lines 43–82) with the
   incident at the rock in "Sergestus et Mnēstheus," Parts I and II, p.242,
   and "victor," Part I, p.244. What are the similarities and differences
   between the two incidents?
3 What other points of similarity do you notice between Vergil's account
   of the boat-race and Homer's account of the chariot-race?

Words and Phrases Checklist

aequor, aequoris	*sea*
careō, carēre, caruī	*lack, be without*
flūctus, flūctūs	*wave*
lābor, lābī, lāpsus sum	*(1) fall, glide, (2) pass by*
laus, laudis	*praise*
mora, morae	*delay*
optō, optāre, optāvī, optātus	*pray for, long for*
parum	*too little*
pondus, ponderis	*weight*
quoniam	*since*
sagitta, sagittae	*arrow*
spatium, spatiī	*space, distance*
vīrēs, vīrium	*strength*

Give the meaning of each of the following:

fluere, morārī, ponderōsus, sagittārius.

Synonym Search

glōria (41), mare (17), ōrāre (31), precārī (34), quia (32), unda (15).

Nerō et Agrippīna

The two chief characters in this Stage are the Emperor Nero, who ruled from A.D.54 to A.D.68, and his mother Agrippina. The Latin text is based on the account written by Tacitus in his *Annals* (a history of Rome from the accession of the Emperor Tiberius to the death of Nero).

Agrippina was an able, ambitious, and unscrupulous woman. In A.D. 54 she arranged the murder of her husband, the Emperor Claudius, by poison. Then with the help of Burrus, the commander of the praetorian guard, she had Nero proclaimed Emperor, although he was still only a youth of sixteen.

At first Agrippina enjoyed not only great prestige as the emperor's mother but also considerable power. Possible rivals to the young emperor were removed quickly, efficiently, and ruthlessly. But before long, Agrippina's power and influence were considerably weakened by Burrus and by Nero's tutor Seneca, who established themselves as Nero's chief advisers. They handled Nero skillfully, mixing their advice with flattery, and in this way they controlled most of the major decisions about the government of Rome and the empire.

As time went on, however, Nero became more and more interested in getting his own way. He also increasingly hated his mother, partly because he had fallen violently in love with the beautiful Poppaea Sabina, and was determined to marry her, while his mother was equally determined that he should not. In the following pages, the outcome of their struggle is described.

īnsidiae

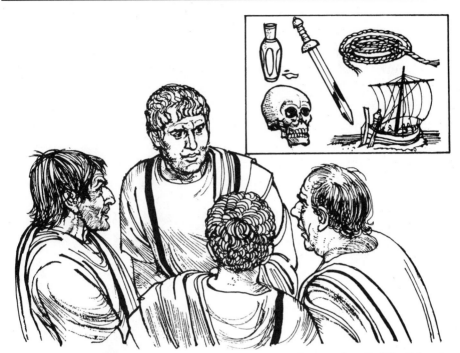

ministrōs convocātōs cōnsuluit utrum venēnō an ferrō vel quā aliā vī ūterētur. (lines 3–4)

at Nerō, quī vetustāte imperiī fīēbat iam audācior, amōre Poppaeae magis magisque accēnsus, postrēmō mātrem interficere cōnstituit; ministrōs convocātōs cōnsuluit utrum venēnō an ferrō vel quā aliā vī ūterētur. placuit prīmō venēnum. sī tamen inter epulās prīncipis venēnum darētur, mors cāsuī assignārī nōn poterat, nam similī   5 exitiō Britannicus anteā perierat; atque Agrippīna ipsa

vetustāte: vetustās	*length, duration*
imperiī: imperium	*rule, reign*
accēnsus	*inflamed, on fire*
quā: quī	*some*
epulās: epulae	*feast, banquet*
assignārī: assignāre	*attribute,*
	put down to
Britannicus	*Britannicus (the Emperor Claudius' son, poisoned on Nero's orders)*

praesūmendō remēdia mūnierat corpus. quō modō vīs et caedēs
cēlārentur nēmō excōgitāre poterat; et metuēbat Nerō nē quis tantō
facinorī dēlēctus iussa sperneret.

tandem Anicētus lībertus, cui Agrippīna odiō erat, cōnsilium   10
callidum prōposuit: nāvem posse compōnī cuius pars, in ipsō marī
per artem solūta, Agrippīnam ēiceret ignāram. subrīdēns Anicētus
"nihil" inquit, "tam capāx fortuitōrum quam mare; et sī naufragiō
Agrippīna perierit, quis adeō suspīciōsus erit ut scelerī id assignet
quod ventī et flūctūs fēcerint? mātre dēfūnctā, facile erit prīncipī   15
pietātem ostendere templō exstruendō vel ad ārās sacrificandō."

praesūmendō:
   praesūmere   *take in advance*
caedēs   *murder*
metuēbat: metuere   *be afraid, fear*
nē quis   *lest anyone, that anyone*
dēlēctus: dēligere   *choose, select*
sperneret: spernere *disobey, disregard*
compōnī: compōnere *construct*
per artem   *deliberately, by design*
ignāram: ignārus   *unsuspecting*
subrīdēns: subrīdēre *smile, smirk*
capāx   *liable to, full of*
fortuitōrum: fortuita *accidents*
dēfūnctā: dēfūnctus *dead*

**Coin showing Nero and
Agrippina.**

1 What two reasons, according to Tacitus, led Nero to make up his mind
   to kill his mother?
2 Whose advice did Nero seek? What question did he put to them?
3 What were the two disadvantages of poison? What were the two
   disadvantages of violence?
4 Who offered a solution to the problem? What plan did he suggest?
5 Why (according to Anicetus) would his plan be unlikely to arouse
   suspicion? What further steps did he suggest to convince people of
   Nero's innocence?

The gulf of Baiae.

II

placuit Nerōnī calliditās Anicētī; praetereā occāsiō optima reī
temptandae aderat, nam Nerō illō tempore Bāiās ad diem festum
celebrandum vīsitābat. illūc mātrem ēlicuit; advenientī in itinere
obviam iit; excēpit manū et complexū; ad vīllam eius maritīmam,
Baulōs nōmine, dūxit. stābat prope vīllam nāvis ōrnātissima, quasi   5
ad mātrem prīncipis honōrandam; invītāta est Agrippīna ad epulās
Bāiīs parātās, ut facinus nocte ac tenebrīs cēlārētur. rūmōre tamen
īnsidiārum per aliquem prōditōrem audītō, Agrippīna incerta
prīmō num crēderet, tandem Bāiās lectīcā vecta est. ibi blanditiae
sublevāvēre metum: cōmiter excepta, iuxtā Nerōnem ipsum ad   10
cēnam collocāta est. Nerō modo familiāritāte iuvenīlī sē gerēbat,

complexū:
   complexus   *embrace*
maritīmam:
   maritīmus   *seaside, by the sea*
prōditōrem: prōditor *betrayer, informer*
sublevāvēre:
   sublevāre   *remove, relieve*
familiāritāte:
   familiāritās   *friendliness*
iuvenīlī: iuvenīlis   *youthful*

modo graviter loquēbātur. tandem, cēnā multīs sermōnibus diū
prōductā, prōsequitur Agrippīnam abeuntem, artius oculīs et
pectorī haerēns, vel ad simulātiōnem explendam vel quod peritūrae
mātris suprēmus aspectus saevum animum eius retinēbat.   15

prōductā:		aspectus	*sight*
prōdūcere	*prolong, continue*	retinēbat: retinēre	*restrain, check*
artius	*particularly closely*	Bāiās: Bāiae	*Baiae (seaside resort)*
haerēns: haerēre	*linger, cling*	Baulōs: Baulī	*Bauli (villa owned by*
simulātiōnem:			*Agrippina)*
simulātiō	*pretense, play-acting*	Bāiīs	*at Baiae*
explendam: explēre	*complete, put the*	Bāiās (*line 0*)	*to Baiae*
	final touch to		
suprēmus	*last*		

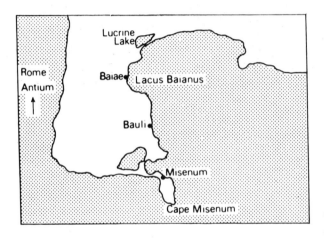

The coast near Baiae.

1 What did Nero think of Anicetus' suggestion? Why did he have a good
   opportunity to put the plan into operation?
2 What did Nero do when Agrippina arrived? Suggest a reason for his
   behavior.
3 What method of travel was available to Agrippina at Bauli? What did
   Nero invite her to do? Why was it important to Nero that his mother's
   journey to Baiae should take place in the evening?
4 What happened at this point to upset Nero's plan? What was
   Agrippina's first reaction to the information? How did she eventually
   travel to Baiae?
5 In what way did her feelings change at Baiae? How was she treated
   there? How did Nero vary his manner during the feast?
6 How did Nero behave on his mother's departure? What two
   explanations does Tacitus give for this?

About the Language

1 From Stage 38 onwards, you have met sentences like these:

quid **faciam**?   quā tē regiōne **requīram**?
*What **am I to do**?*   *In what region **am I to search** for you?*

utrum captīvōs **līberēmus** an **interficiāmus**?
***Should we free** the prisoners or **kill** them?*

Questions like these are usually known as *deliberative questions* (or sometimes as *direct deliberative* questions), because the speaker is "deliberating," or wondering what to do.

Further examples:

1   quid dīcam?   3   quō mē vertam?
2   unde auxilium petāmus?   4   utrum abeāmus an maneāmus?

2 You have also met sentences like these:

prīnceps amīcōs rogāvit quid **faceret**.
*The emperor asked his friends what **he should do**.*

pater nesciēbat quā regiōne fīlium **requīreret**.
*The father did not know in what region **he was to search** for his son.*

incertus eram utrum vī an venēnō **ūterer**.
*I was uncertain whether **I should use** violence or poison.*
Or, in more natural English:
I was uncertain whether to use violence or poison.

In each of these examples, a deliberative question is being *reported* or *mentioned*. Examples like these are known as *indirect deliberative questions*.

Further examples of indirect deliberative questions:

1   difficile erat Nerōnī scīre quid respondēret.
2   lībertum rogābō quō modō rem administrem.
3   mīlitēs incertī erant utrum cēderent an resisterent.
4   in animō volvēbāmus quāle dōnum rēgī darēmus.

3 Notice that the verb in a deliberative question, whether direct or indirect, is always subjunctive.

---

naufragium

deī noctem sīderibus illūstrem et placidō marī quiētam praebuēre,
quasi ad scelus patefaciendum. nec multum erat prōgressa nāvis,
duōbus amīcīs Agrippīnam comitantibus ex quibus Crepereius
Gallus haud procul gubernāculō. adstābat, Acerrōnia ad pedēs
Agrippīnae cubitantis recumbens paenitentiam fīliī per gaudium   5
commemorābat, cum datō signō ruere tēctum multō plumbō grave.
pressus Crepereius statim periit; Agrippīna et Acerrōnia
ēminentibus lectī parietibus prōtēctae sunt. nec dissolūtiō nāvis
sequēbātur, turbātīs omnibus et quod plērīque nautae, sceleris
ignārī, eōs impediēbant quī cōnsciī erant. hī igitur cōnātī sunt ūnum   10
in latus inclīnāre atque ita nāvem summergere; nōn tamen eīs erat
prōmptus in rem subitam cōnsēnsus, et aliī contrā nītentēs dedēre
Agrippīnae facultātem lēniter in mare dēscendendī.

illūstrem: illūstris	bright	dissolūtiō	disintegration, break-up
cubitantis: cubitāre	lie down, rest	turbātīs: turbātus	confused
paenitentiam:		inclīnāre	lean
paenitentia	repentance, change	prōmptus	quick
	of heart	in rem subitam	to meet the sudden crisis
per gaudium	joyfully	cōnsēnsus	agreement
ruere = ruit: ruere	collapse	contrā	in the opposite direction
plumbō: plumbum	lead	nītentēs: nītī	lean
pressus: premere	crush	facultātem:	
ēminentibus: ēminēre	project	facultās	opportunity
parietibus: pariēs	side		
prōtēctae sunt:			
prōtegere	protect		

Acerrōnia autem, dum sē Agrippīnam esse imprūdenter clāmat
utque subvenīrētur mātrī prīncipis, contīs et rēmīs cōnficitur.   15
Agrippīna silēns eōque minus agnita (ūnum tamen vulnus umerō
excēpit) ad lēnunculōs quōsdam nandō pervenit quī haud procul
erant; deinde in Lucrīnum lacum vecta, ad vīllam suam dūcitur.
   ibi cōgitābat quid faceret; animadverterat enim nāvem neque
ventīs ad lītus āctam, neque saxīs impulsam esse, sed summā suī   20
parte velut terrestre māchināmentum concidisse. observāns etiam
Acerrōniae caedem, simul suum vulnus aspiciēns, sōlum

Agrippine the Younger.

īnsidiārum remēdium esse putāvit, sī nōn intellegere vidērētur. mīsit igitur lībertum quī nūntiāret fīliō sē benignitāte deōrum et fortūnā eius ēvāsisse gravem cāsum; ōrāre ut Nerō, quamvīs 25 perīculō mātris perterritus, vīsendī cūram differret; sibi ad praesēns

imprūdenter	*stupidly, folishly*
subvenīrētur	*help would be brought*
cōnficitur: cōnficere	*finish off, murder*
eō	*therefore, for this reason*
agnita: agnōscere	*recognize*
lēnunculōs: lēnunculus	*small boat*
āctam: agere	*drive*
summā suī parte	*from the top downwards (literally "from its highest part")*
terrestre: terrestris	*on land*
māchināmentum	*machine, contraption*
concidisse: concidere	*collapse*
observāns: observāre	*notice, observe*
ēvāsisse: ēvādere	*escape*
quamvīs	*although*
vīsendī: vīsere	*come to visit*
cūram: cūra	*trouble, bother*
ad praesēns	*for the present, for the moment*
Lucrīnum lacum: Lucrīnus lacus	*the Lucrine lake (a lagoon near Baiae)*

quiēte opus esse. atque interim medicāmenta vulnerī adhibet; imperat quoque ut testāmentum Acerrōniae requīrātur – hoc sōlum nōn per simulātiōnem.

1 In what way, according to Tacitus, did the gods take sides (or seem to take sides) in the murder attempt?
2 What was Acerronia doing when the roof fell in? Why does Tacitus mention this?
3 What did the conspirators try to do after the original plan misfired? Why were they again unsuccessful?
4 Why do you think Acerronia shouted out that she was Agrippina? Is there more than one possible explanation for her action?
5 What reasons led Agrippina to realize that the shipwreck had been a deliberate attempt on her life? What did she decide was her only hope of safety?
6 In her message, Agrippina described Nero as "perīculō mātris perterritus." Is this likely to be true? If not, why did Agrippina describe him in this way?
7 What order did Agrippina give? What do you think her reason was?
8 What impression do you gain from this passage of Agrippina's ability and character?

II

at Nerōnī, nūntiōs patrātī facinoris exspectantī, affertur Agrippīnam ēvāsisse ictū levī vulnerātam. tum pavōre exanimis et affirmāns iam iamque adfore mātrem ultiōnis avidam, Burrum et Senecam statim arcessīvit. longum utrīusque silentium; tandem Seneca respexit Burrum ac rogāvit num mīlitēs caedem Agrippīnae   5
exsequī iubērentur. ille praetōriānōs tōtī Caesarum domuī obstrictōs esse respondit: "mīlitēs" inquit, "nihil ātrōx adversus fīliam Germānicī facere audēbunt; efficiat Anicētus prōmissa." quī haudquāquam haesitat; poscit summam sceleris. ad haec verba Nerō profitētur illō diē sibi tandem darī imperium auctōremque   10
tantī mūneris esse lībertum; Anicētō imperāvit ut ad vīllam statim proficīscerētur dūceretque sēcum hominēs fidēlissimōs.

patrātī: patrāre	*accomplish, commit*	
affertur: afferre	*bring news, report*	
ictū: ictus	*blow*	
exanimis	*out of one's mind*	
iam iamque	*at any moment now*	
adfore:	*future infinitive of* adesse *be present, arrive*	

Members of the praetorian guard, the emperor's personal bodyguard (see pp.277–8).

exsequī	*carry out*
domuī: domus	*family*
obstrictōs esse: obstringere	*bind (with oath of loyalty)*
ātrōx	*violent, dreadful*
prōmissa: prōmissum	*promise*
summam: summa	*full responsibility, supreme command*
profitētur: profitērī	*declare*
Caesarum: Caesarēs	*the Caesars (family of the first Roman emperors)*
Germānicī: Germānicus	*Germanicus (Agrippina's father, a popular general and member of the imperial family)*

1 Describe Nero's reaction to the news of Agrippina's escape. Compare it with Agrippina's own reaction to the attempt on her life.
2 Why do you think Seneca and Burrus are so silent and unhelpful (lines 4–8)? Why do you think Anicetus is so eager to carry out the deed (lines 8–9)?
3 How does Nero's mood change after Anicetus has taken charge? Explain his comment "illō diē . . . esse lībertum" (lines 10–11).

About the Language

1 From Unit 1 onwards, you have met sentences like this:

Pompēiānī **rīdēbant, clāmābant, plaudēbant**.
*The Pompeians **were laughing**, **shouting**, and **applauding**.*

2 In Stage 46, you met a different way of expressing the same idea:

Pompēiānī **rīdēre clāmāre plaudere**.

Further examples:

māter **ōrāre hortārī iubēre** ut fugerem.
*My mother **begged**, **urged**, and **ordered** me to flee.*

spectāculum horribile in campīs patentibus – **sequī fugere occīdī capī**.
*There was a hideous sight on the open plains – men **were chasing**, **were fleeing**, **were being killed**, and **were being captured**.*

Notice how the *infinitive* of the verb is used in these examples, instead of an indicative tense such as an imperfect, to describe events happening in the past. This is known as the *historical* use of the infinitive ("*historical infinitive*" for short). It occurs most often in descriptions of lively and rapid action.

3 Further examples:
1 omnēs amīcī bibere cantāre saltāre.
2 in urbe maximus pavor; aliī ad portās fugere; aliī bona sua in plaustra impōnere; aliī uxōrēs līberōsque quaerere; omnēs viae multitūdine complērī. (*from the historian Sallust*)

percussōrēs

interim vulgātō Agrippīnae perīculō, omnēs, ut quisque audīverat, dēcurrere ad lītus. hī mōlēs, hī proximās scaphās cōnscendere; aliī, quantum corpus sinēbat, prōcēdere in mare; nōnnūllī manūs extendere; omnis ōra complērī questibus, precibus, clāmōre hominum dīversa rogantium aut incerta respondentium; affluere ingēns multitūdō cum lūminibus, atque ubi incolumem esse Agrippīnam vulgātum est, ad grātulandum sēsē expedīre, dōnec

5

percussōrēs: percussor	*assassin*
vulgātō: vulgāre	*make known*
ut quisque	*as soon as each one*
hī . . . hī	*some . . . others*
mōlēs: mōlēs	*embankment, sea-wall*
quantum	*as far as*
sinēbat: sinere	*allow*
questibus: questus	*lamentation, cry of grief*
affluere	*flock to the spot*
sēsē expedīre	*prepare oneself, get ready*

"dīcite mihi quārē hūc missī sītis." (line 16)

ancillā, Agrippīna "tū quoque mē dēseris" inquit; tum respicit
Anicētum triērarchō et centuriōne comitātum. "quī estis?" inquit.
abripit quī obstant, dōnec ad forēs cubiculī venīret; ibi paucī 10
adstābant, cēterīs terrōre irrumpentium exterritīs. cubiculō
modicum lūmen inerat et ancillārum ūna; magis ac magis anxia
fīēbat Agrippīna quod nēmō ā fīliō vēnisset. abeunte dēnique
ancillā, Agrippīna "tū quoque mē dēseris" inquit; tum respicit
Anicētum triērarchō et centuriōne comitātum. "quī estis?" inquit. 15
"dīcite mihi quārē hūc missī sītis." nūllum respōnsum;
circumsistunt lectum percussōrēs et prior triērarchus fūstī caput
eius afflīxit. deinde centuriōnī gladium ad occīdendum dēstringentī
Agrippīna prōtendēns uterum "ventrem ferī" exclāmāvit multīsque
vulneribus cōnfecta est. 20

cremāta est eādem nocte convīvālī lectō et exequiīs vīlibus; num
īnspexerit mātrem mortuam Nerō (ut multī affirmant) et fōrmam
corporis eius admīrātus sit, incertum est. hunc fore suī fīnem multōs
ante annōs crēdiderat Agrippīna contempseratque. nam eī rogantī
dē fortūnā Nerōnis respondērunt astrologī illum imperātūrum 25
mātremque occīsūrum; atque Agrippīna "occīdat" inquit, "dum
imperet."

disiectī sunt: disicere	*scatter, disperse*
abripit: abripere	*remove by force*
forēs	*door*
exterritīs: exterrēre	*frighten away*
triērarchō:	
triērarchus	*naval captain*
circumsistunt:	
circumsistere	*take up position around*
fūstī	*ablative of* fūstis
afflīxit: afflīgere	*strike*
prōtendēns:	
prōtendere	*thrust forward*
uterum: uterus	*womb*
convīvālī: convīvālis	*dining*
exequiīs: exequiae	*funeral rites*
fore = futūrum esse	
contempserat:	
contemnere	*disregard*
imperātūrum (esse):	
imperāre	*be emperor*
dum	*provided that*

About the Language

1 In Stage 30, you met the perfect indicative passive:

duo cōnsulēs **creātī sunt**.   *Two consuls **have been appointed**.*

2 In Stage 48, you have met sentences like these:

ɒuer stultus nescit quot cōnsulēs **creātī sint**.
*The stupid boy does not know how many consuls **have been appointed**.*

dominus cognōscere vult quanta pecūnia **impēnsa sit**.
*The master wants to find out how much money **has been spent**.*

The Latin form of the verb in boldface is the *perfect subjunctive passive*.

Further examples:

1 incertī sumus utrum Agrippīna servāta an necāta sit.
2 dīcite mihi quot hostēs captī sint.
3 ignōrō quārē ā centuriōne ēlēctus sim.

3 Compare the indicative and subjunctive forms of the perfect passive of
portō:

PERFECT INDICATIVE PASSIVE	PERFECT SUBJUNCTIVE PASSIVE
portātus sum	**portātus sim**
portātus es	**portātus sīs**
portātus est	**portātus sit**
portātī sumus	**portātī sīmus**
portātī estis	**portātī sītis**
portātī sunt	**portātī sint**

Perfect subjunctive passive forms of **doceō**, **trahō**, **capiō**, and **audiō**
are given on page 300.

4 Study the following examples:

tam callidus est mercātor ut magnās opēs **adeptus sit**.
The merchant is so clever that **he has obtained** *great wealth.*

iūdex scīre vult num senī umquam **minātī sīmus**.
The judge wants to know whether **we have** *ever* **threatened** *the old man.*

The Latin words in boldface are *perfect subjunctive* forms of *deponent* verbs.

Further examples:

1 dīc mihi quid patrōnus tibi pollicitus sit.
2 scīre volō quārē nūntiī nōndum profectī sint.

Perfect subjunctive forms of **cōnor**, **vereor**, etc. are given on p.305.

Practicing the Language

1 Translate each sentence into Latin by selecting correctly from the list of Latin words.

1 *I gave money to the boy (who was) carrying the books.*

| puerī | librōs | portantī | pecūnia | dedī |
| puerō | līberōs | portātī | pecūniam | dederam |

2 *The same women are here again, master.*

| eadem | fēminae | simul | adsunt | dominus |
| eaedem | fēminam | rūrsus | absunt | domine |

3 *By running, he arrived at the prison more quickly.*

| currendō | ad carcerem | celeriter | advēnit |
| currentī | ā carcere | celerius | advēnī |

4 *If you do not obey the laws, you will be punished.*

| sī | lēgibus | pārueritis | pūnīminī |
| nisi | lēgī | pārēbātis | pūniēminī |

5 *Let us force the chiefs of the barbarians to turn back.*

| prīncipēs | barbarīs | revertor | cōgimus |
| prīncipem | barbarōrum | revertī | cōgāmus |

6 *Men of this kind ought not to be made consuls.*

| hominibus | huius | generis | cōnsulem | facere | nōnne | dēbet |
| hominēs | huic | generī | cōnsulēs | fierī | nōn | dēbent |

2 In each pair of sentences, translate sentence (a); then, with the help of pages 284–5 and 299, express the same idea in a passive form by correctly completing the nouns and verbs in sentence (b), and translate again. For example:

(a) timēbam nē mīlitēs mē caperent.
(b) timēbam nē ā mīl. . . caper. . . .
Translated and completed, this becomes:
(a) timēbam nē **mīlitēs mē caperent**.
 I was afraid that **the soldiers would catch me**.
(b) timēbam nē ā *mīlitibus caperer*.
 I was afraid that **I would be caught** *by the soldiers*.

(a) dīc mihi quārē domina numquam ancillās laudet.
(b) dīc mihi quārē ancill. . . numquam ā domin. . . laud. . . .
Translated and completed, this becomes:
(a) dīc mihi quārē **domina** numquam **ancillās laudet**.
 Tell me why **the mistress** *never* **praises the slave-girls**.
(b) dīc mihi quārē **ancillae** numquam ā **dominā laudentur**.
 Tell me why **the slave-girls are** *never* **praised** *by the mistress*.

1a dominus cognōscere vult num servī cēnam parent.
1b dominus cognōscere vult num cēn. . . ā serv. . . par. . . .
2a tantum erat incendium ut flammae aulam dēlērent.
2b tantum erat incendium ut aul. . . flamm. . . dēlēr. . . .
3a barbarī frūmentum incendērunt ut inopia cibī nōs impedīret.
3b barbarī frūmentum incendērunt ut inop. . . cibī imped. . . .
4a in silvā tibi latendum est nē hostēs tē videant.
4b in silvā tibi latendum est nē ab host. . . vid. . . .
5a nisi vōs adiūvissem, barbarī vōs circumvēnissent.
5b nisi vōs adiūvissem, ā barbar. . . circumven. . . . .
6a nescio quārē prīnceps mē relēgāverit.
6b nescio quārē ā prīncip. . . relēg. . . . .

The Emperor

By A.D. 59, when the events described in Stage 48 took place, Rome had been ruled by emperors for nearly a century. The Republican system of government (in which two consuls were elected annually as joint heads of state, assisted by other magistrates and the senate) had collapsed in violence and bloodshed at the end of the first century B.C. Supreme power in the Roman world was in the hands of a single ruler: the emperor.

To the senate and people of Rome, the emperor was often known as the **prīnceps** (*chief citizen*); to the soldiers, he was **imperātor** (*commander*). But the word **rēx** (*king*), which might seem a very appropriate title in view of the emperor's great personal power, was deliberately avoided, because the Romans had a long tradition of hatred towards the idea of kings. Kings had ruled Rome in the distant past, and the last one had been so unpopular that he was driven out; four-and-a-half centuries later, when Julius Caesar was suspected of intending to make himself a king, he was assassinated.

The first emperor (Augustus) and most of his successors tried to encourage the belief that in many ways the business of government was being carried on much as before. For example, consuls and other magistrates continued to be appointed, and the senate continued to meet, just as in the days of the Republic. However, the senate, consuls and magistrates were now much less powerful than before; and they were no longer elected by the people of Rome, but were in many cases appointed directly by the emperor.

The lives and reigns of the emperors in the first century A.D. are narrated by Tacitus in his *Annals* and *Histories*, and by Suetonius in his *Lives of the Emperors*. They give a vivid and sometimes appalling description of the emperors' immense personal power, the stupidity, greed, lust, extravagance, and cruelty of individual emperors, the frequent plottings and struggles for power that went on among the emperors' advisers and associates, and the savagery and ruthlessness with which emperors treated possible rivals or conspirators.

But even when the emperor was vicious, eccentric, or tyrannical, government of the empire still carried on, and the emperor himself crucial part to play; otherwise he risked losing popularity and power. Some emperors behaved sadistically or arrogantly to individuals and still carried out humane and efficient policies in government. For example, Domitian treated the senate with insolence and contempt, and put several of its members to death with little or no excuse, but Suetonius says of him that "he took such great care in supervising the city magistrates and provincial governors that they were more honest and just during his reign than at any other time."

If an emperor was conscientious, his workload was heavy. He took an important and ever-increasing part in administering the law; he chose men for provincial governorships, legionary commands, consulships, the senate, and numerous other positions and privileges; he acted as the commander-in-chief of the Roman army, determining the soldiers' pay, selecting the officers, allocating the legions and auxiliaries to particular parts of the empire, and (in the case of some emperors) leading troops on military campaigns; he received ambassadors from provinces and foreign states who brought him greetings, petitions, complaints, or accusations, to which he would be expected to make an eloquent speech in reply (one of the causes of Nero's dispute with his mother was her attempt to sit at his side, as if she were joint ruler with him, when foreign

Roman bridge built by Trajan at Alcantara, Spain.

ambassadors came to see him); he dealt with the problems referred to him by provincial governors (the Bithynia correspondence of Pliny and Trajan provides a good example of this); he often had to care for the **plēbs** or ordinary people of Rome, by providing regular distributions of grain or money to the citizens, putting on splendid and costly shows in the circus and amphitheater, and undertaking large programs of public building to beautify the city and relieve unemployment; he had the power to make law by bringing proposals before the senate; and by holding the post of Pontifex Maximus he was the official head of the state religion.

The Emperor at Work

For much of his time, the emperor carried out his responsibilities by receiving and replying to requests, and by hearing and judging disputes. The following examples (based on actual situations and incidents) give some indication of the variety of pleas and problems which he dealt with:

"The inhabitants of a neighboring town have made a violent attack on us, killing and injuring many innocent people."

"Please, will you give Roman citizenship to a doctor who cured me of a dangerous illness."

"Several towns in this province have been badly damaged by an earthquake; please, can troops and money be sent."

"My husband has been in exile for many years and is now old and ill; I appeal to you to allow him to come back."

"There is a serious danger of revolt by the local tribes, and our soldiers urgently need reinforcements."

"Please grant our city the privilege of building a temple in honor of your late father."

"My neighbor claims this slave is his, but he's a liar; the slave is mine."

"Please, will you grant me the honor of the 'lātus clāvus' (broad purple stripe on tunic and toga, indicating membership in the senate)."

"The governor of our province has illegally tortured and executed Roman citizens; we ask that he be tried and punished."

Some of these requests and disputes were handled in writing; a constant stream of letters, petitions, appeals, accusations, and other documents poured onto the emperor's desk. He was expected to deal with each one personally, deciding the substance of the reply and in many cases dictating its actual words, occasionally adding a sentence or two in his own handwriting. This correspondence was sometimes carried on in Latin, but often in Greek, especially when dealing with the eastern part of the empire. Other requests and disputes were presented verbally to the emperor in person by the people concerned, some of whom traveled vast distances to do so. An anecdote told by the Greek writer Dio about the Emperor Hadrian illustrates the way in which a Roman emperor was expected to make himself available to his subjects:

> "When Hadrian was on a journey, he was stopped by a woman who wished to put a request to him. Being in a hurry, he moved on, saying 'I'm too busy,' whereupon the woman shouted after him 'Then stop being emperor!' On hearing this, Hadrian turned around, came back, and listened to her request."

The Emperor's Helpers

It was impossible, of course, for one man to govern an empire of fifty million inhabitants single-handed, and although the emperors were reluctant to share power with other people, they needed reliable assistants of various sorts. For military tasks, the emperor could turn to the praetorian guard, who acted as his personal bodyguard and could be immensely important at times of crisis. In Tacitus' account of Nero's attempt to murder Agrippina, one of the first people the emperor sends for when the plot goes wrong is Burrus, the praetorian guard's commander (see p.266, line 3). When the emperor was administering the law or making a decision on which he wanted advice, he could summon his **cōnsilium** (*council*) and ask for the opinions of his **amīcī** (*friends*). For assistance in the day-to-day running of government, the emperor could make use of his slaves and (more particularly) his freedmen. These were not official employees of the state, but were members of the emperor's personal household. Some of the freedmen possessed great power and influence; for instance, in the events related in Stage 48, a crucial part was played by the freedman Anicetus, who not only invented a method for carrying out Agrippina's murder (p.260, lines 10–16), but also took control of the situation when the plot misfired (p.266, lines 8–12).

The Emperor Augustus as Pontifex Maximus presiding at a sacrifice.

The Succession

One of the most important questions facing an emperor was to decide who should succeed him. Sometimes the position of emperor was inherited by a son from his father; sometimes an emperor with no sons of his own adopted another member of the family as his heir and successor. Some emperors deliberately looked outside their family in an effort to find the most suitable person; the Emperor Nerva chose an experienced and popular general (Trajan) to succeed him, and adopted him as his heir in preference to any of his own relatives. But on many occasions, the question was settled by force and violence. For example, in A.D. 41 the soldiers of the praetorian guard, having murdered the Emperor Caligula, found Caligula's uncle Claudius hiding in the palace and proclaimed him as the new emperor; nobody was in a position to stop them, because they could get their way by physical force. And in A.D. 69, which became known as the "year of the four emperors," there was a savage civil war, in which each of several rival candidates, supported by different sections of the Roman army, tried to make himself emperor.

Emperor-Worship

At his death, an emperor was normally deified. He received the title **dīvus** (*god*) and was honored with prayers and sacrifices; altars and (sometimes) temples were dedicated to him. Some emperors were worshiped as gods even during their lifetime, especially in the eastern provinces, which had long been accustomed to paying divine honors to their own rulers. For many inhabitants of the empire, worship of this kind was a natural response to the immense power possessed by a Roman emperor.

Carved gem showing the deification of the Emperor Augustus.

Words and Phrases Checklist

caedēs, caedis	*murder, slaughter*
dōnec	*until*
ēvādō, ēvādere, ēvāsī	*escape*
incolumis, incolume	*safe*
latus, lateris	*side*
metuō, metuere, metuī	*be afraid, fear*
mūnus, mūneris	*gift*
nē quis	*in case anyone*
nē quid	*in case anything*
pectus, pectoris	*breast, heart*
pietās, pietātis	*duty, piety (respect for (1) the gods, (2) homeland, (3) family)*
premō, premere, pressī,	
pressus	*press, crush*
quisque	*each*
vel. . . vel	*either. . . or*
velut	*as if, like*
vīs	*force, violence*

Give the meaning of each of the following:

caedere, incolumitās, invādere, metus, pius.

Synonym Search

dōnum (14), dum (+*subj.*) (34), effugere (16), timēre (12), tūtus (22), verērī (38).

Numbers

CARDINAL			ORDINAL	
ūnus	one		prīmus	*first*
duo	*two*		secundus	*second*
trēs	*three*		tertius	*third*
quattuor	*four*		quārtus	*fourth*
quīnque	*five*		quīntus	*fifth*
sex	*six*		sextus	*sixth*
septem	*seven*		septimus	*seventh*
octō	*eight*		octāvus	*eighth*
novem	*nine*		nōnus	*ninth*
decem	*ten*		decimus	*tenth*

ūndecim	*eleven*
duodecim	*twelve*
trēdecim	*thirteen*
quattuordecim	*fourteen*
quīndecim	*fifteen*
sēdecim	*sixteen*
septendecim	*seventeen*
duodēvīgintī	*eighteen*
ūndēvīgintī	*nineteen*
vīgintī	*twenty*

trīgintā	*thirty*
quadrāgintā	*forty*
quīnquāgintā	*fifty*
sexāgintā	*sixty*
septuāgintā	*seventy*
octōgintā	*eighty*
nōnāgintā	*ninety*
centum	*a hundred*

ducentī	*two hundred*
trecentī	*three hundred*
quadringentī	*four hundred*
quīngentī	*five hundred*
sescentī	*six hundred*
septingentī	*seven hundred*
octingentī	*eight hundred*
nōngentī	*nine hundred*
mīlle	*a thousand*
duo mīlia	*two thousand*

Language
Information
Section

PART ONE: Review Grammar

Nouns

1

	first declension	*second declension*			*third declension*	
	f.	*m.*	*m.*	*n.*	*m.*	*m.*
SINGULAR						
nominative and vocative	puella	servus (*voc.* serve)	puer	templum	mercātor	leō
genitive	puellae	servī	puerī	templī	mercātōris	leōnis
dative	puellae	servō	puerō	templō	mercātōrī	leōnī
accusative	puellam	servum	puerum	templum	mercātōrem	leōnem
ablative	puellā	servō	puerō	templō	mercātōre	leōne
PLURAL						
nominative and vocative	puellae	servī	puerī	templa	mercātōrēs	leōnēs
genitive	puellārum	servōrum	puerōrum	templōrum	mercātōrum	leōnum
dative	puellīs	servīs	puerīs	templīs	mercātōribus	leōnibus
accusative	puellās	servōs	puerōs	templa	mercātōrēs	leōnēs
ablative	puellīs	servīs	puerīs	templīs	mercātōribus	leōnibus

	fourth declension		*fifth declension*	
	f.	*n.*	*m.*	*f.*
SINGULAR				
nominative and vocative	manus	genū	diēs	rēs
genitive	manūs	genūs	diēī	reī
dative	manuī	genū	diēī	reī
accusative	manum	genū	diem	rem
ablative	manū	genū	diē	rē
PLURAL				
nominative and vocative	manūs	genua	diēs	rēs
genitive	manuum	genuum	diērum	rērum
dative	manibus	genibus	diēbus	rēbus
accusative	manūs	genua	diēs	rēs
ablative	manibus	genibus	diēbus	rēbus

m.	m.	f.	n.	n.	n.	
						SINGULAR
cīvis	rēx	urbs	nōmen	tempus	mare	*nominative and vocative*
cīvis	rēgis	urbis	nōminis	temporis	maris	*genitive*
cīvī	rēgī	urbī	nōminī	temporī	marī	*dative*
cīvem	rēgem	urbem	nōmen	tempus	mare	*accusative*
cīve	rēge	urbe	nōmine	tempore	marī	*ablative*
						PLURAL
cīvēs	rēgēs	urbēs	nōmina	tempora	maria	*nominative and vocative*
cīvium	rēgum	urbium	nōminum	temporum	marium	*genitive*
cīvibus	rēgibus	urbibus	nōminibus	temporibus	maribus	*dative*
cīvēs	rēgēs	urbēs	nōmina	tempora	maria	*accusative*
cīvibus	rēgibus	urbibus	nōminibus	temporibus	maribus	*ablative*

2   Compare the genitive (and dative) singular **diēī** with **reī**. Have you noticed that the **-ē-** of **diēī** has a long mark, but the **-e-** of **reī** does not?

3   Compare the endings of **mare** with those of **nōmen** and **tempus**. Notice that in the ablative singular **mare** has an **-ī** instead of **-e**. Other third declension neuter nouns whose nominative singular ends in **-e**, such as **conclāve** (*room*) and **cubīle** (*bed*), form their cases in the same way as **mare**.

4   For examples of the locative case, see p.314.

5   For the ways in which the different cases are used, see pp.311–13.

6   In some of the Latin poems in Unit 4, you have met phrases and sentences in which the plural of a noun is used with a singular meaning:

ignārus sua sē tractāre **perīcla**.
*unaware that he was handling **a cause of danger** to himself.*

Adjectives

1 first and second declension:

	masculine	feminine	neuter
SINGULAR			
nominative and vocative	**bonus** (*voc.* **bone**)	**bona**	**bonum**
genitive	**bonī**	**bonae**	**bonī**
dative	**bonō**	**bonae**	**bonō**
accusative	**bonum**	**bonam**	**bonum**
ablative	**bonō**	**bonā**	**bonō**
PLURAL			
nominative and vocative	**bonī**	**bonae**	**bona**
genitive	**bonōrum**	**bonārum**	**bonōrum**
dative	**bonīs**	**bonīs**	**bonīs**
accusative	**bonōs**	**bonās**	**bona**
ablative	**bonīs**	**bonīs**	**bonīs**

	masculine	feminine	neuter
SINGULAR			
nominative and vocative	**pulcher**	**pulchra**	**pulchrum**
genitive	**pulchrī**	**pulchrae**	**pulchrī**
dative	**pulchrō**	**pulchrae**	**pulchrō**
accusative	**pulchrum**	**pulchram**	**pulchrum**
ablative	**pulchrō**	**pulchrā**	**pulchrō**
PLURAL			
nominative and vocative	**pulchrī**	**pulchrae**	**pulchra**
genitive	**pulchrōrum**	**pulchrārum**	**pulchrōrum**
dative	**pulchrīs**	**pulchrīs**	**pulchrīs**
accusative	**pulchrōs**	**pulchrās**	**pulchra**
ablative	**pulchrīs**	**pulchrīs**	**pulchrīs**

2 third declension:

	masc. and fem.	*neuter*	*masc. and fem.*	*neuter*
SINGULAR				
nominative and vocative	fortis	forte	fēlīx	fēlīx
genitive	fortis	fortis	fēlīcis	fēlīcis
dative	fortī	fortī	fēlīcī	fēlīcī
accusative	fortem	forte	fēlīcem	fēlīx
ablative	fortī	fortī	fēlīcī	fēlīcī
PLURAL				
nominative and vocative	fortēs	fortia	fēlīcēs	fēlīcia
genitive	fortium	fortium	fēlīcium	fēlīcium
dative	fortibus	fortibus	fēlīcibus	fēlīcibus
accusative	fortēs	fortia	fēlīcēs	fēlīcia
ablative	fortibus	fortibus	fēlīcibus	fēlīcibus

	masc. and fem.	*neuter*	*masc. and fem.*	*neuter*
SINGULAR				
nominative and vocative	ingēns	ingēns	longior	longius
genitive	ingentis	ingentis	longiōris	longiōris
dative	ingentī	ingentī	longiōrī	longiōrī
accusative	ingentem	ingēns	longiōrem	longius
ablative	ingentī	ingentī	longiōre	longiōre
PLURAL				
nominative and vocative	ingentēs	ingentia	longiōrēs	longiōra
genitive	ingentium	ingentium	longiōrum	longiōrum
dative	ingentibus	ingentibus	longiōribus	longiōribus
accusative	ingentēs	ingentia	longiōrēs	longiōra
ablative	ingentibus	ingentibus	longiōribus	longiōribus

NOTE: The ablative singular **-ī** ending is generally used when the adjective modifies a stated noun, e.g. **ā servō ingentī** (*by the huge slave*). The **-e** ending is generally used when the adjective describes a noun not stated, but understood, e.g. **ab ingente** (*by the huge (person)*).

Comparison of Adjectives and Adverbs

Adjectives

1

	COMPARATIVE	SUPERLATIVE
longus	**longior**	**longissimus**
long	*longer*	*longest, very long*
pulcher	**pulchrior**	**pulcherrimus**
beautiful	*more beautiful*	*most beautiful, very beautiful*
fortis	**fortior**	**fortissimus**
brave	*braver*	*bravest, very brave*
fēlīx	**fēlīcior**	**fēlīcissimus**
lucky	*luckier*	*luckiest, very lucky*
prūdēns	**prūdentior**	**prūdentissimus**
shrewd	*shrewder*	*shrewdest, very shrewd*
facilis	**facilior**	**facillimus**
easy	*easier*	*easiest, very easy*

2 Irregular forms:

bonus	**melior**	**optimus**
good	*better*	*best, very good*
malus	**peior**	**pessimus**
bad	*worse*	*worst, very bad*
magnus	**maior**	**maximus**
big	*bigger*	*biggest, very big*
parvus	**minor**	**minimus**
small	*smaller*	*smallest, very small*
multus	**plūs**	**plūrimus**
much	*more*	*most, very much*
multī	**plūrēs**	**plūrimī**
many	*more*	*most, very many*

NOTE: **plūs**, the comparative form of **multus** above, is a neuter noun, e.g. **plūs pecūniae** *more (of) money*.

3 The forms of the comparative adjective **longior** are shown on p.287.

4 Superlative adjectives like **longissimus** change their endings in the same way as **bonus** (shown on p.286).

Adverbs

1

	COMPARATIVE	SUPERLATIVE
lātē	**lātius**	**lātissimē**
widely	*more widely*	*most widely, very widely*
pulchrē	**pulchrius**	**pulcherrimē**
beautifully	*more beautifully*	*most beautifully, very beautifully*
fortiter	**fortius**	**fortissimē**
bravely	*more bravely*	*most bravely, very bravely*
fēlīciter	**fēlīcius**	**fēlīcissimē**
luckily	*more luckily*	*most luckily, very luckily*
prūdenter	**prūdentius**	**prūdentissimē**
shrewdly	*more shrewdly*	*most shrewdly, very shrewdly*
facile	**facilius**	**facillimē**
easily	*more easily*	*most easily, very easily*

2 Irregular forms:

bene	**melius**	**optimē**
well	*better*	*best, very well*
male	**peius**	**pessimē**
badly	*worse*	*worst, very badly*
magnopere	**magis**	**maximē**
greatly	*more*	*most, very greatly*
paulum	**minus**	**minimē**
little	*less*	*least, very little*
multum	**plūs**	**plūrimum**
much	*more*	*most, very much*

3 Translate the following examples:

1 mīlitēs nostrī fortius pugnāvērunt quam barbarī.
2 faber mūrum facillimē refēcit.
3 ubi strepitum audīvī, magis timēbam.
4 optimē respondistī, mī fīlī.

Pronouns

1 Personal pronouns: **ego** and **tū** (*I, you*, etc.)

	singular		*plural*	
nominative	**ego**	**tū**	**nōs**	**vōs**
genitive	**meī**	**tuī**	**nostrum**	**vestrum**
dative	**mihi**	**tibi**	**nōbīs**	**vōbīs**
accusative	**mē**	**tē**	**nōs**	**vōs**
ablative	**mē**	**tē**	**nōbīs**	**vōbīs**

2 Reflexive pronoun: **sē** (*himself, herself, themselves* etc.)

	singular	*plural*
nominative (no forms)		
genitive	**suī**	**suī**
dative	**sibi**	**sibi**
accusative	**sē**	**sē**
ablative	**sē**	**sē**

3 Demonstrative pronoun: **hic** (*this, these*, etc.; also used with the meaning *he, she, they*, etc.)

	singular			*plural*		
	masculine	*feminine*	*neuter*	*masculine*	*feminine*	*neuter*
nominative	**hic**	**haec**	**hoc**	**hī**	**hae**	**haec**
genitive	**huius**	**huius**	**huius**	**hōrum**	**hārum**	**hōrum**
dative	**huic**	**huic**	**huic**	**hīs**	**hīs**	**hīs**
accusative	**hunc**	**hanc**	**hoc**	**hōs**	**hās**	**haec**
ablative	**hōc**	**hāc**	**hōc**	**hīs**	**hīs**	**hīs**

4 Demonstrative pronoun: **ille** (*that, those*, etc.; also used with the meaning *he, she, they*, etc.)

	singular			*plural*		
	masculine	*feminine*	*neuter*	*masculine*	*feminine*	*neuter*
nominative	**ille**	**illa**	**illud**	**illī**	**illae**	**illa**
genitive	**illīus**	**illīus**	**illīus**	**illōrum**	**illārum**	**illōrum**
dative	**illī**	**illī**	**illī**	**illīs**	**illīs**	**illīs**
accusative	**illum**	**illam**	**illud**	**illōs**	**illās**	**illa**
ablative	**illō**	**illā**	**illō**	**illīs**	**illīs**	**illīs**

5 *Intensive pronoun:* **ipse** (*myself, yourself, himself, etc.*)

	singular			plural		
	masculine	feminine	neuter	masculine	feminine	neuter
nominative	ipse	ipsa	ipsum	ipsī	ipsae	ipsa
genitive	ipsīus	ipsīus	ipsīus	ipsōrum	ipsārum	ipsōrum
dative	ipsī	ipsī	ipsī	ipsīs	ipsīs	ipsīs
accusative	ipsum	ipsam	ipsum	ipsōs	ipsās	ipsa
ablative	ipsō	ipsā	ipsō	ipsīs	ipsīs	ipsīs

6 *Demonstrative pronoun:* **is** (*he, she, it,* etc; also used with the meaning *that, those,* etc)

	singular			plural		
	masculine	feminine	neuter	masculine	feminine	neuter
nominative	is	ea	id	eī	eae	ea
genitive	eius	eius	eius	eōrum	eārum	eōrum
dative	eī	eī	eī	eīs	eīs	eīs
accusative	eum	eam	id	eōs	eās	ea
ablative	eō	eā	eō	eīs	eīs	eīs

For examples in which forms of **is** are used with the relative pronoun **qui**, see paragraph 9, p.292.

7 *Determinative pronoun:* **īdem** (*the same*)

	singular			plural		
	masculine	feminine	neuter	masculine	feminine	neuter
nominative	īdem	eadem	idem	eīdem	eaedem	eadem
genitive	eiusdem	eiusdem	eiusdem	eōrundem	eārundem	eōrundem
dative	eīdem	eīdem	eīdem	eīsdem	eīsdem	eīsdem
accusative	eundem	eandem	idem	eōsdem	eāsdem	eadem
ablative	eōdem	eādem	eōdem	eīsdem	eīsdem	eīsdem

8 *Relative pronoun:* **quī** (*who, which,* etc.; also used as a *connecting relative* with the meaning *he, this,* etc.)

	singular			plural		
	masculine	feminine	neuter	masculine	feminine	neuter
nominative	quī	quae	quod	quī	quae	quae
genitive	cuius	cuius	cuius	quōrum	quārum	quōrum
dative	cui	cui	cui	quibus	quibus	quibus
accusative	quem	quam	quod	quōs	quās	quae
ablative	quō	quā	quō	quibus	quibus	quibus

Notice again the use of the *connecting relative:*

tertiā hōrā dux advēnit. **quem** cum cōnspexissent, mīlitēs magnum clāmōrem sustulērunt.
At the third hour the leader arrived. When they caught sight of **him**, *the soldiers raised a great shout.*

deinde nūntiī locūtī sunt. **quōrum** verbīs obstupefactus, rēx diū tacēbat.
Then the messengers spoke. Stunned by **their** *words, the king was silent for a long time.*

9 Notice again how forms of the demonstrative pronoun **is** can be used as antecedents of the relative pronoun **quī**:

1 **is quī** illam fābulam nārrāvit mentiēbātur.
   He who *told that story was lying.*
   Or, ***The man who*** *told that story was lying.*

2 **eī quī** fūgērunt mox capientur.
   Those who *ran away will soon be caught.*

3 **id quod** nūntius dīxit nōs maximē perturbāvit.
   That which *the messenger said alarmed us very much.*
   Or, ***What*** *the messenger said alarmed us very much.*

4 **eās** vīllās vēndidī **quae** mē minimē dēlectābant.
   I sold ***those*** *villas* ***which*** *least appealed to me.*

Pick out the antecedent, relative pronoun, and relative clause in each example.

In Stage 45, you met sentences in which the antecedent comes after the relative clause, or is omitted altogether:

5 **quī** tē heri culpābat, **is** tē hodiē laudat.
   The person who *was blaming you yesterday is praising you today.*

6 **quae** dominus iussit, **ea** servōs efficere oportet.
   What *the master has ordered, the slaves must carry out.*
   Or, *The slaves must carry out* **what** *the master has ordered.*

7 **quod** potuī, fēcī.
   I have done **what** *I could.*

Pick out the relative pronoun, relative clause, and antecedent (if there is one) in each example.

10 *Indefinite adjective:* **quīdam** (*one, a certain*)

	singular			plural		
	masculine	*feminine*	*neuter*	*masculine*	*feminine*	*neuter*
nominative	quīdam	quaedam	quoddam	quīdam	quaedam	quaedam
genitive	cuiusdam	cuiusdam	cuiusdam	quōrundam	quārundam	quōrundam
dative	cuidam	cuidam	cuidam	quibusdam	quibusdam	quibusdam
accusative	quendam	quandam	quoddam	quōsdam	quāsdam	quaedam
ablative	quōdam	quādam	quōdam	quibusdam	quibusdam	quibusdam

quōsdam hominēs nōvī, quī tē adiuvāre poterunt.
I know **certain** *men, who will be able to help you.*

subitō senātor **quīdam**, celeriter prōgressus, silentium poposcit.
Suddenly **one** *senator stepped forward quickly and demanded silence.*

Compare the forms of **quīdam** with those of **quī** in paragraph 8.

With the help of the table above, find the Latin for the words in boldface in the following sentences:

1 **Certain** ladies were standing outside the senate-house.
2 We saw **one** soldier trying to escape.
3 I was staying at the house of **a certain** friend.

Regular Verbs

Indicative Active

1

first conjugation	*second conjugation*	*third conjugation*	*third "-iō" conjugation*	*fourth conjugation*
PRESENT *("I carry," "I am carrying," etc.)*				
portō	doceō	trahō	capiō	audiō
portās	docēs	trahis	capis	audīs
portat	docet	trahit	capit	audit
portāmus	docēmus	trahimus	capimus	audīmus
portātis	docētis	trahitis	capitis	audītis
portant	docent	trahunt	capiunt	audiunt
FUTURE *("I shall/will carry," etc.)*				
portābō	docēbō	traham	capiam	audiam
portābis	docēbis	trahēs	capiēs	audiēs
portābit	docēbit	trahet	capiet	audiet
portābimus	docēbimus	trahēmus	capiēmus	audiēmus
portābitis	docēbitis	trahētis	capiētis	audiētis
portābunt	docēbunt	trahent	capient	audient
IMPERFECT *("I was carrying," etc.)*				
portābam	docēbam	trahēbam	capiēbam	audiēbam
portābās	docēbās	trahēbās	capiēbās	audiēbās
portābat	docēbat	trahēbat	capiēbat	audiēbat
portābāmus	docēbāmus	trahēbāmus	capiēbāmus	audiēbāmus
portābātis	docēbātis	trahēbātis	capiēbātis	audiēbātis
portābant	docēbant	trahēbant	capiēbant	audiēbant

2 Translate each word, then change it from the singular to the plural, so that it means *we shall . . .* or *they will . . .* instead of *I shall . . .* or *he will . . .* , and translate again:

1 portābit; traham; audiet; docēbō; capiam.
2 nāvigābō; mittet; faciam; persuādēbit; impediet.

3 For ways of checking whether a verb ending in **-ēs**, **-et**, etc. belongs to the *present* tense of a *second* conjugation verb or the *future* tense of a *third* or *fourth* conjugation verb, see paragraph 1 on p.294.

4 In Stage 44, you met the *historical present* tense, in which the present tense is used to describe events which happened in the past:

tābuerant cērae; nūdōs **quatit** ille lacertōs,
rēmigiōque carēns nōn ūllās **percipit** aurās.
*The wax had melted; he **flaps** his bare arms, and being without wings he **fails** to get any grip on the air.*

The historical present can be translated *either* by an English present tense (as in the example above), *or* by a past tense.

Notice again the use of the historical present tense in sentences containing **dum** (*while . . .* , *at the moment when . . .*):

dum cēterī **labōrant**, duo servī effūgērunt.
*While the rest **were working**, two slaves escaped.*

5

first *conjugation*	*second* *conjugation*	*third* *conjugation*	*third "-iō"* *conjugation*	*fourth* *conjugation*
PERFECT ("I have carried," "I carried," etc.)				
portāvī	docuī	trāxī	cēpī	audīvī
portāvistī	docuistī	trāxistī	cēpistī	audīvistī
portāvit	docuit	trāxit	cēpit	audīvit
portāvimus	docuimus	trāximus	cēpimus	audīvimus
portāvistis	docuistis	trāxistis	cēpistis	audīvistis
portāvērunt	docuērunt	trāxērunt	cēpērunt	audīvērunt
FUTURE PERFECT ("I shall/will have carried," etc.; but often translated by an English present tense: "I carry," etc.)				
portāverō	docuerō	trāxerō	cēperō	audīverō
portāveris	docueris	trāxeris	cēperis	audīveris
portāverit	docuerit	trāxerit	cēperit	audīverit
portāverimus	docuerimus	trāxerimus	cēperimus	audīverimus
portāveritis	docueritis	trāxeritis	cēperitis	audīveritis
portāverint	docuerint	trāxerint	cēperint	audīverint
PLUPERFECT ("I had carried," etc.)				
portāveram	docueram	trāxeram	cēperam	audīveram
portāverās	docuerās	trāxerās	cēperās	audīverās
portāverat	docuerat	trāxerat	cēperat	audīverat
portāverāmus	docuerāmus	trāxerāmus	cēperāmus	audīverāmus
portāverātis	docuerātis	trāxerātis	cēperātis	audīverātis
portāverant	docuerant	trāxerant	cēperant	audīverant

6 In Stages 41–48, you met a new form of the 3rd person plural of the perfect tense:

portāvēre = **portāvērunt**   *they (have) carried*
trāxēre   = **trāxērunt**   *they (have) dragged*

Further examples:

audīvēre; recitāvēre; scrīpsēre; praebuēre.

Indicative Passive

1 In Stages 29–34, you met the 3rd person forms of the present, future and imperfect passive tenses. The other forms of these tenses are introduced in Stage 35 (1st and 2nd persons singular) and Stage 39 (1st and 2nd persons plural). The complete tenses are as follows:

PRESENT *("I am carried," "I am being carried," etc.)*				
portor	doceor	trahor	capior	audior
portāris	docēris	traheris	caperis	audīris
portātur	docētur	trahitur	capitur	audītur
portāmur	docēmur	trahimur	capimur	audīmur
portāminī	docēminī	trahiminī	capiminī	audīminī
portantur	docentur	trahuntur	capiuntur	audiuntur

FUTURE *("I shall/will be carried," etc.)*				
portābor	docēbor	trahar	capiar	audiar
portāberis	docēberis	trahēris	capiēris	audiēris
portābitur	docēbitur	trahētur	capiētur	audiētur
portābimur	docēbimur	trahēmur	capiēmur	audiēmur
portābiminī	docēbiminī	trahēminī	capiēminī	audiēminī
portābuntur	docēbuntur	trahentur	capientur	audientur

IMPERFECT *("I was being carried," etc.)*				
portābar	docēbar	trahēbar	capiēbar	audiēbar
portābāris	docēbāris	trahēbāris	capiēbāris	audiēbāris
portābātur	docēbātur	trahēbātur	capiēbātur	audiēbātur
portābāmur	docēbāmur	trahēbāmur	capiēbāmur	audiēbāmur
portābāminī	docēbāminī	trahēbāminī	capiēbāminī	audiebāminī
portābantur	docēbantur	trahēbantur	capiēbantur	audiēbantur

2 In paragraph 1 above, find the Latin for:

1 I am heard; I shall be taught; I was being dragged.
2 you (sg.) will be carried; you (sg.) were being heard; you (sg.) are taught.
3 we are taught; we were being carried.
4 you (pl.) are taken; you (pl.) will be dragged; you (pl.) are heard.

3 Translate each word, then change it from the singular to the plural, so that it means *we shall be . . .* instead of *I shall be . . .* :

1 portābor; laudābor; docēbor; monēbor.
2 trahar; cōgar; audiar; impediar.

Translate each word, then change it from the singular to the plural, so that it means *you* (pl.) *will be . . .* instead of *you* (sg.) *will be . . .*:

1 portāberis; cūrāberis; docēberis; movēberis.
2 trahēris; mittēris; audiēris; custōdiēris.

4

PERFECT *("I have been carried," "I was carried," etc.)*

portātus sum	doctus sum	tractus sum	captus sum	audītus sum
portātus es	doctus es	tractus es	captus es	audītus es
portātus est	doctus est	tractus est	captus est	audītus est
portātī sumus	doctī sumus	tractī sumus	captī sumus	audītī sumus
portātī estis	doctī estis	tractī estis	captī estis	audītī estis
portātī sunt	doctī sunt	tractī sunt	captī sunt	audītī sunt

FUTURE PERFECT *("I shall/will have been carried," etc.; but often translated as an English present tense: "I am carried," etc.)*

portātus erō	doctus erō	tractus erō	captus erō	audītus erō
portātus eris	doctus eris	tractus eris	captus eris	audītus eris
portātus erit	doctus erit	tractus erit	captus erit	audītus erit
portātī erimus	doctī erimus	tractī erimus	captī erimus	audītī erimus
portātī eritis	doctī eritis	tractī eritis	captī eritis	audītī eritis
portātī erunt	doctī erunt	tractī erunt	captī erunt	audītī erunt

PLUPERFECT *("I had been carried," etc.)*

portātus eram	doctus eram	tractus eram	captus eram	audītus eram
portātus erās	doctus erās	tractus erās	captus erās	audītus erās
portātus erat	doctus erat	tractus erat	captus erat	audītus erat
portātī erāmus	doctī erāmus	tractī erāmus	captī erāmus	audītī erāmus
portātī erātis	doctī erātis	tractī erātis	captī erātis	audītī erātis
portātī erant	doctī erant	tractī erant	captī erant	audītī erant

NOTE: The gender may be changed in the forms above, e.g. **docta est** (*she has been taught*) or **portātum est** (*it has been carried*).

Notice again that the future perfect passive, like the future perfect active, is often translated by an English present tense:

sī exercitus noster crās **victus erit**, hostēs oppidum capere poterunt.
*If our army **is defeated** tomorrow, the enemy will be able to capture the town.*

5 Translate each example, then change it from the pluperfect to the perfect tense, keeping the same person and number (i.e. 1st person singular, etc.), and translate again. For example, **portātī erāmus** (*we had been carried*) would become **portātī sumus** (*we have been carried, we were carried*).

doctus eram; portātī erant; captus erās; tractus erat; audītī erātis; damnātī erāmus; coāctus erās; factī erant.

6 Translate each example; then, with the help of paragraph 1, change it from the perfect to the present tense, keeping the same person and number (i.e. 1st person singular, etc.), and translate again. For example, **audītus sum** (*I have been heard, I was heard*) would become **audior** (*I am heard, I am being heard*).

portātī sunt; audītus es; tractus est; doctī sumus; mūtātī estis; impedītus sum.

Subjunctive Active

1 In Stage 36, you met the PRESENT tense of the subjunctive:

first conjugation	*second conjugation*	*third conjugation*	*third "-iō" conjugation*	*fourth conjugation*
portem	doceam	traham	capiam	audiam
portēs	doceās	trahās	capiās	audiās
portet	doceat	trahat	capiat	audiat
portēmus	doceāmus	trahāmus	capiāmus	audiāmus
portētis	doceātis	trahātis	capiātis	audiātis
portent	doceant	trahant	capiant	audiant

2 IMPERFECT SUBJUNCTIVE

portārem	docērem	traherem	caperem	audīrem
portārēs	docērēs	traherēs	caperēs	audīrēs
portāret	docēret	traheret	caperet	audīret
portārēmus	docērēmus	traherēmus	caperēmus	audīrēmus
portārētis	docērētis	traherētis	caperētis	audīrētis
portārent	docērent	traherent	caperent	audīrent

3   In Stage 38, you met the PERFECT tense of the subjunctive:

PERFECT SUBJUNCTIVE				
portāverim	docuerim	trāxerim	cēperim	audīverim
portāverīs	docueris	trāxerīs	cēperis	audīverīs
portāverit	docuerit	trāxerit	cēperit	audīverit
portāverīmus	docuerīmus	trāxerīmus	cēperīmus	audīverīmus
portāverītis	docuerītis	trāxerītis	cēperītis	audīverītis
portāverint	docuerint	trāxerint	cēperint	audīverint

4   PLUPERFECT SUBJUNCTIVE

portāvissem	docuissem	trāxissem	cēpissem	audīvissem
portāvissēs	docuissēs	trāxissēs	cēpissēs	audīvissēs
portāvisset	docuisset	trāxisset	cēpisset	audīvisset
portāvissēmus	docuissēmus	trāxissēmus	cēpissēmus	audīvissēmus
portāvissētis	docuissētis	trāxissētis	cēpissētis	audīvissētis
portāvissent	docuissent	trāxissent	cēpissent	audīvissent

5   For ways in which the subjunctive is used, see pp.316–7.

Subjunctive Passive

1   The forms of the PRESENT tense of the subjunctive passive (introduced in Stage 41) are as follows:

porter	docear	trahar	capiar	audiar
portēris	doceāris	trahāris	capiāris	audiāris
portētur	doceātur	trahātur	capiātur	audiātur
portēmur	doceāmur	trahāmur	capiāmur	audiāmur
portēminī	doceāminī	trahāminī	capiāminī	audiāminī
portentur	doceantur	trahantur	capiantur	audiantur

2   The IMPERFECT tense of the subjunctive passive (introduced in Stage 43):

portārer	docērer	traherer	caperer	audīrer
portārēris	docērēris	traherēris	caperēris	audīrēris
portārētur	docērētur	traherētur	caperētur	audīrētur
portārēmur	docērēmur	traherēmur	caperēmur	audīrēmur
portārēminī	docērēminī	traherēminī	caperēminī	audīrēminī
portārentur	docērentur	traherentur	caperentur	audīrentur

3 The PERFECT tense of the subjunctive passive (introduced in Stage 48):

portātus sim	doctus sim	tractus sim	captus sim	audītus sim
portātus sīs	doctus sīs	tractus sīs	captus sīs	audītus sīs
portātus sit	doctus sit	tractus sit	captus sit	audītus sit
portātī sīmus	doctī sīmus	tractī sīmus	captī sīmus	audītī sīmus
portātī sītis	doctī sītis	tractī sītis	captī sītis	audītī sītis
portātī sint	doctī sint	tractī sint	captī sint	audītī sint

4 The PLUPERFECT tense of the subjunctive passive (introduced in Stage 46):

portātus essem	doctus essem	tractus essem	captus essem	audītus essem
portātus essēs	doctus essēs	tractus essēs	captus essēs	audītus essēs
portātus esset	doctus esset	tractus esset	captus esset	audītus esset
portātī essēmus	doctī essēmus	tractī essēmus	captī essēmus	audītī essēmus
portātī essētis	doctī essētis	tractī essētis	captī essētis	audītī essētis
portātī essent	doctī essent	tractī essent	captī essent	audītī essent

Other Forms

1 IMPERATIVE SINGULAR AND PLURAL (*"carry!" etc.*)

portā, portāte   docē, docēte   trahe, trahite   cape, capite   audī, audīte

NOTE: Negative commands are formed by using the imperative of **nōlō** with the infinitive, e.g. **nōlī/nōlīte portare** "Don't carry!".

2 PRESENT PARTICIPLE (*"carrying," etc.*)

portāns   docēns   trahēns   capiēns   audiēns

NOTE: Present participles change their endings in the same way as **ingēns** (shown on p.287).

Study the forms of the present participle **portāns**:

	singular		plural	
	masc. and fem.	*neuter*	*masc. and fem.*	*neuter*
nominative and vocative	portāns	portāns	portantēs	portantia
genitive	portantis	portantis	portantium	portantium
dative	portantī	portantī	portantibus	portantibus
accusative	portantem	portāns	portantēs	portantia
ablative	portant-ī/-e	portant-ī/-e	portantibus	portantibus

3 PERFECT PASSIVE PARTICIPLE (*"having been carried," etc.*)

portātus   **doctus**   **tractus**   **captus**   **audītus**

For perfect *active* participles, see Deponent Verbs, p.303.

4 FUTURE PARTICIPLE (*"about to carry," etc.*)

portātūrus   **doctūrus**   **tractūrus**   **captūrus**   **audītūrus**

Perfect passive and future participles change their endings in the same way as **bonus** (p.286).

For examples of ways in which participles are used, see p.315.

5 PRESENT ACTIVE INFINITIVE (*"to carry," etc.*)

portāre   **docēre**   **trahere**   **capere**   **audīre**

6 PRESENT PASSIVE INFINITIVE (*"to be carried," etc.*)

portārī   **docērī**   **trahī**   **capī**   **audīrī**

Another way of using the present active and passive infinitives is described on p.268, Stage 48.

7 PERFECT ACTIVE INFINITIVE (*"to have carried," etc.*)

portāvisse   **docuisse**   **trāxisse**   **cēpisse**   **audīvisse**

8 PERFECT PASSIVE INFINITIVE (*"to have been carried," etc.*)

portātus esse   **doctus esse**   **tractus esse**   **captus esse**   **audītus esse**

9 FUTURE ACTIVE INFINITIVE (*"to be about to carry," etc.*)

portātūrus esse   **doctūrus esse**   **tractūrus esse**   **captūrus esse**   **audītūrus esse**

For examples of ways in which infinitives are used to express indirect statements, see pp.319–21.

10   GERUND (*"carrying," etc.*)

The cases of the gerund are formed in the following way:

nominative (no forms)					
genitive	**portandī**	**docendī**	**trahendī**	**capiendī**	**audiendī**
dative	**portandō**	**docendō**	**trahendō**	**capiendō**	**audiendō**
accusative	**portandum**	**docendum**	**trahendum**	**capiendum**	**audiendum**
ablative	**portandō**	**docendō**	**trahendō**	**capiendō**	**audiendō**

Notice that the gerund changes its endings in the same way as second declension nouns such as **templum**; but it has no nominative case and no plural.

For ways in which the gerund is used, see p.324.

11   GERUNDIVE (*"being carried," "needing to be carried," etc.*)

portandus   **docendus**   **trahendus**   **capiendus**   **audiendus**

NOTE: Gerundives change their endings in the same way as **bonus** (p.286). For ways in which the gerundive is used, see pp.324–25.

Deponent Verbs

Indicative

1 Study the forms of the deponent verbs **cōnor** (*I try*), **vereor** (*I fear*), **loquor** (*I speak*), **ēgredior** (*I go out*), and **mentior** (*I lie, I tell a lie*):

first conjugation	*second conjugation*	*third conjugation*	*third "-iō" conjugation*	*fourth conjugation*
PRESENT ("*I try*," *etc.*)				
cōnor	**vereor**	**loquor**	**ēgredior**	**mentior**
cōnāris	**verēris**	**loqueris**	**ēgrederis**	**mentīris**
cōnātur	**verētur**	**loquitur**	**ēgreditur**	**mentītur**
cōnāmur	**verēmur**	**loquimur**	**ēgredimur**	**mentīmur**
cōnāminī	**verēminī**	**loquiminī**	**ēgrediminī**	**mentīminī**
cōnantur	**verentur**	**loquuntur**	**ēgrediuntur**	**mentiuntur**
FUTURE ("*I shall/will try*," *etc.*)				
cōnābor	**verēbor**	**loquar**	**ēgrediar**	**mentiar**
cōnāberis	**verēberis**	**loquēris**	**ēgrediēris**	**mentiēris**
cōnābitur	**verēbitur**	**loquētur**	**ēgrediētur**	**mentiētur**
cōnābimur	**verēbimur**	**loquēmur**	**ēgrediēmur**	**mentiēmur**
cōnābiminī	**verēbiminī**	**loquēminī**	**ēgrediēminī**	**mentiēminī**
cōnābuntur	**verēbuntur**	**loquentur**	**ēgredientur**	**mentientur**
IMPERFECT ("*I was trying*," *etc.*)				
cōnābar	**verēbar**	**loquēbar**	**ēgrediēbar**	**mentiēbar**
cōnābāris	**verēbāris**	**loquēbāris**	**ēgrediēbāris**	**mentiēbāris**
cōnābātur	**verēbātur**	**loquēbātur**	**ēgrediēbātur**	**mentiēbātur**
cōnābāmur	**verēbāmur**	**loquēbāmur**	**ēgrediēbāmur**	**mentiēbāmur**
cōnābāminī	**verēbāminī**	**loquēbāminī**	**ēgrediēbāminī**	**mentiēbāminī**
cōnābantur	**verēbantur**	**loquēbantur**	**ēgrediēbantur**	**mentiēbantur**

2 In paragraph 1, find the Latin for:

he tries; you (pl.) speak; we fear; I lie; I shall fear; she will go out; we shall speak; they were trying; you (sg.) were lying.

3 Give the meaning of:

1 loquitur; verēris; ēgrediuntur; mentīmur; cōnāminī.
2 cōnābor; ēgrediētur; verēbimur; loquar; mentientur.
3 loquēbāris; cōnābāmur; ēgrediēbāminī; verēbar; mentiēbantur.

4 PERFECT *("I have tried," "I tried," etc.)*

cōnātus sum	veritus sum	locūtus sum	ēgressus sum	mentītus sum
cōnātus es	veritus es	locūtus es	ēgressus es	mentītus es
cōnātus est	veritus est	locūtus est	ēgressus est	mentītus est
cōnātī sumus	veritī sumus	locūtī sumus	ēgressī sumus	mentītī sumus
cōnātī estis	veritī estis	locūtī estis	ēgressī estis	mentītī estis
cōnātī sunt	veritī sunt	locūtī sunt	ēgressī sunt	mentītī sunt

FUTURE PERFECT *("I shall/will have tried," etc.; but often translated by an English present tense: "I try," etc.)*

cōnātus erō	veritus erō	locūtus erō	ēgressus erō	mentītus erō
cōnātus eris	veritus eris	locūtus eris	ēgressus eris	mentītus eris
cōnātus erit	veritus erit	locūtus erit	ēgressus erit	mentītus erit
cōnātī erimus	veritī erimus	locūtī erimus	ēgressī erimus	mentītī erimus
cōnātī eritis	veritī eritis	locūtī eritis	ēgressī eritis	mentītī eritis
cōnātī erunt	veritī erunt	locūtī erunt	ēgressī erunt	mentītī erunt

PLUPERFECT *("I had tried," etc.)*

cōnātus eram	veritus eram	locūtus eram	ēgressus eram	mentītus eram
cōnātus erās	veritus erās	locūtus erās	ēgressus erās	mentītus erās
cōnātus erat	veritus erat	locūtus erat	ēgressus erat	mentītus erat
cōnātī erāmus	veritī erāmus	locūtī erāmus	ēgressī erāmus	mentītī erāmus
cōnātī erātis	veritī erātis	locūtī erātis	ēgressī erātis	mentītī erātis
cōnātī erant	veritī erant	locūtī erant	ēgressī erant	mentītī erant

NOTE: The gender may be changed in the forms above, e.g. **cōnāta est** *(she (has) tried)* or **locūtae sunt** *(they* (females) *spoke or have spoken).*

5 Translate each example, then change it from the pluperfect to the perfect tense, keeping the same person and number (i.e. 1st person singular, etc.) and translate again. For example, **cōnātus erās** *(you (sg.) had tried)* would become **cōnātus es** *(you have tried, you tried).*

locūtī erant; cōnātus eram; cōnātī erāmus; locūta erat; secūtī erant; adeptae erant; cōnāta eram.

Translate each example; then, with the help of paragraph 1, change it from the perfect to the present tense, keeping the same person and number (i.e. 1st person singular, etc.), and translate again. For example, **mentītus sum** (*I have lied, I lied*) would become **mentior** (*I lie*).

cōnātus es; locūtus sum; veritī sumus; ēgressus est; mentītī estis; precātī sunt; secūtus est.

Subjunctive

Deponent verbs form their subjunctive in the following way. Compare these forms with those of the subjunctive passive, shown on p.299.

PRESENT SUBJUNCTIVE *(introduced in Stage 41)*				
cōner	verear	loquar	ēgrediar	mentiar
cōnēris	vereāris	loquāris	ēgrediāris	mentiāris
cōnētur	vereātur	loquātur	ēgrediātur	mentiātur
cōnēmur	vereāmur	loquāmur	ēgrediāmur	mentiāmur
cōnēminī	vereāminī	loquāminī	ēgrediāminī	mentiāminī
cōnentur	vereantur	loquantur	ēgrediantur	mentiantur

IMPERFECT SUBJUNCTIVE *(introduced in Stage 43)*				
cōnārer	verērer	loquerer	ēgrederer	mentīrer
cōnārēris	verērēris	loquerēris	ēgrederēris	mentīrēris
cōnārētur	verērētur	loquerētur	ēgrederētur	mentīrētur
cōnārēmur	verērēmur	loquerēmur	ēgrederēmur	mentīrēmur
cōnārēminī	verērēminī	loquerēminī	ēgrederēminī	mentīrēminī
cōnārentur	verērentur	loquerentur	ēgrederentur	mentīrentur

PERFECT SUBJUNCTIVE *(introduced in Stage 48)*				
cōnātus sim	veritus sim	locūtus sim	ēgressus sim	mentītus sim
cōnātus sīs	veritus sīs	locūtus sīs	ēgressus sīs	mentītus sīs
cōnātus sit	veritus sit	locūtus sit	ēgressus sit	mentītus sit
cōnātī sīmus	veritī sīmus	locūtī sīmus	ēgressī sīmus	mentītī sīmus
cōnātī sītis	veritī sītis	locūtī sītis	ēgressī sītis	mentītī sītis
cōnātī sint	veritī sint	locūtī sint	ēgressī sint	mentītī sint

PLUPERFECT SUBJUNCTIVE *(introduced in Stage 46)*				
cōnātus essem	veritus essem	locūtus essem	ēgressus essem	mentītus essem
cōnātus essēs	veritus essēs	locūtus essēs	ēgressus essēs	mentītus essēs
cōnātus esset	veritus esset	locūtus esset	ēgressus esset	mentītus esset
cōnātī essēmus	veritī essēmus	locūtī essēmus	ēgressī essēmus	mentītī essēmus
cōnātī essētis	veritī essētis	locūtī essētis	ēgressī essētis	mentītī essētis
cōnātī essent	veritī essent	locūtī essent	ēgressī essent	mentītī essent

Other forms

1 PRESENT PARTICIPLE *("trying," etc.)*

cōnāns   verēns   loquēns   ēgrediēns   mentiēns

NOTE: **verēns** is rarely used; **veritus** is more commonly used to mean *'fearing.'*

2 PERFECT ACTIVE PARTICIPLE *("having tried," etc.)*

cōnātus   veritus   locūtus   ēgressus   mentītus

3 FUTURE PARTICIPLE *("about to try," etc.)*

cōnātūrus   veritūrus   locūtūrus   ēgressūrus   mentītūrus

NOTE: Perfect active and future participles change their endings in the same way as '**bonus**,' shown on p.000.

4 PRESENT INFINITIVE *("to try," etc.)*

cōnārī   verērī   loquī   ēgredī   mentīrī

5 PERFECT INFINITIVE *("to have tried," etc.)*

cōnātus esse   veritus esse   locūtus esse   ēgressus esse   mentītus esse

NOTE: The participle in the perfect infinitive changes its ending like **bonus** (shown on p.286).

6 FUTURE INFINITIVE *("to be about to try," etc.)*

cōnātūrus esse   veritūrus esse   locūtūrus esse   ēgressūrus esse   mentītūrus esse

NOTE: The participle in the future infinitive changes its endings like **bonus** (shown on p.286).

Irregular Verbs

1 *Indicative*

PRESENT *("I am," "you are," etc.)*

sum	possum	eō	volō	nōlō	mālō	ferō
es	potes	īs	vīs	nōn vīs	māvīs	fers
est	potest	it	vult	nōn vult	māvult	fert
sumus	possumus	īmus	volumus	nōlumus	mālumus	ferimus
estis	potestis	ītis	vultis	nōn vultis	māvultis	fertis
sunt	possunt	eunt	volunt	nōlunt	mālunt	ferunt

FUTURE *("I shall/will be," etc.)*

erō	poterō	ībō	volam	nōlam	mālam	feram
eris	poteris	ībis	volēs	nōlēs	mālēs	ferēs
erit	poterit	ībit	volet	nōlet	mālet	feret
erimus	poterimus	ībimus	volēmus	nōlēmus	mālēmus	ferēmus
eritis	poteritis	ībitis	volētis	nōlētis	mālētis	ferētis
erunt	poterunt	ībunt	volent	nōlent	mālent	ferent

IMPERFECT *("I was," "I could," "I was going," etc.)*

eram	poteram	ībam	volēbam	nōlēbam	mālēbam	ferēbam
erās	poterās	ībās	volēbās	nōlēbās	mālēbās	ferēbās
erat	poterat	ībat	volēbat	nōlēbat	mālēbat	ferēbat
erāmus	poterāmus	ībāmus	volēbāmus	nōlēbāmus	mālēbāmus	ferēbāmus
erātis	poterātis	ībātis	volēbātis	nōlēbātis	mālēbātis	ferēbātis
erant	poterant	ībant	volēbant	nōlēbant	mālēbant	ferēbant

PERFECT *("I have been," or "I was," etc.)*

fuī	potuī	iī	voluī	nōluī	māluī	tulī
fuistī	potuistī	iistī	voluistī	nōluistī	māluistī	tulistī
fuit	potuit	iit	voluit	nōluit	māluit	tulit
fuimus	potuimus	iimus	voluimus	nōluimus	māluimus	tulimus
fuistis	potuistis	iistis	voluistis	nōluistis	māluistis	tulistis
fuērunt	potuērunt	iērunt	voluērunt	nōluērunt	māluērunt	tulērunt

FUTURE PERFECT *("I shall/will have been," also often translated as "I am," etc.)*

fuerō	potuerō	ierō	voluerō	nōluerō	māluerō	tulerō
fueris	potueris	ieris	volueris	nōlueris	mālueris	tuleris
fuerit	potuerit	ierit	voluerit	nōluerit	māluerit	tulerit
fuerimus	potuerimus	ierimus	voluerimus	nōluerimus	māluerimus	tulerimus
fueritis	potueritis	ieritis	volueritis	nōlueritis	mālueritis	tuleritis
fuerint	potuerint	ierint	voluerint	nōluerint	māluerint	tulerint

PLUPERFECT *("I had been," etc.)*

fueram	potueram	ieram	volueram	nōlueram	mālueram	tuleram
fuerās	potuerās	ierās	voluerās	nōluerās	māluerās	tulerās
fuerat	potuerat	ierat	voluerat	nōluerat	māluerat	tulerat
fuerāmus	potuerāmus	ierāmus	voluerāmus	nōluerāmus	māluerāmus	tulerāmus
fuerātis	potuerātis	ierātis	voluerātis	nōluerātis	māluerātis	tulerātis
fuerant	potuerant	ierant	voluerant	nōluerant	māluerant	tulerant

2 In stage 46, you met sentences in which forms of **sum** (e.g. **est, erat**, etc.) were omitted:

iam horā diēī prīma.   *Now it **was** the first hour of the day.*

3 *Subjunctive*

PRESENT SUBJUNCTIVE

sim	possim	eam	velim	nōlim	mālim	feram
sīs	possīs	eās	velīs	nōlīs	mālīs	ferās
sit	possit	eat	velit	nōlit	mālit	ferat
sīmus	possīmus	eāmus	velīmus	nōlīmus	mālīmus	ferāmus
sītis	possītis	eātis	velītis	nōlītis	mālītis	ferātis
sint	possint	eant	velint	nōlint	mālint	ferant

IMPERFECT SUBJUNCTIVE

essem	possem	īrem	vellem	nōllem	māllem	ferrem
essēs	possēs	īrēs	vellēs	nōllēs	māllēs	ferrēs
esset	posset	īret	vellet	nōllet	māllet	ferret
essēmus	possēmus	īrēmus	vellēmus	nōllēmus	māllēmus	ferrēmus
essētis	possētis	īrētis	vellētis	nōllētis	māllētis	ferrētis
essent	possent	īrent	vellent	nōllent	māllent	ferrent

PERFECT SUBJUNCTIVE

fuerim	potuerim	ierim	voluerim	nōluerim	māluerim	tulerim
fuerīs	potuerīs	ierīs	voluerīs	nōluerīs	māluerīs	tulerīs
fuerit	potuerit	ierit	voluerit	nōluerit	māluerit	tulerit
fuerīmus	potuerīmus	ierīmus	voluerīmus	nōluerīmus	māluerīmus	tulerīmus
fuerītis	potuerītis	ierītis	voluerītis	nōluerītis	māluerītis	tulerītis
fuerint	potuerint	ierint	voluerint	nōluerint	māluerint	tulerint

PLUPERFECT SUBJUNCTIVE

fuissem	potuissem	iissem	voluissem	nōluissem	māluissem	tulissem
fuissēs	potuissēs	iissēs	voluissēs	nōluissēs	māluissēs	tulissēs
fuisset	potuisset	iisset	voluisset	nōluisset	māluisset	tulisset
fuissēmus	potuissēmus	iissēmus	voluissēmus	nōluissēmus	māluissēmus	tulissēmus
fuissētis	potuissētis	iissētis	voluissētis	nōluissētis	māluissētis	tulissētis
fuissent	potuissent	iissent	voluissent	nōluissent	māluissent	tulissent

4 *Infinitives*

PRESENT INFINITIVE (*"to be," "to be able," "to go," etc.*)

esse	posse	īre	velle	nōlle	mālle	ferre

PERFECT INFINITIVE (*"to have been," "to have been able," "to have gone," etc.*)

fuisse	potuisse	iisse	voluisse	nōluisse	māluisse	tulisse

FUTURE INFINITIVE (*"to be about to be," "to be about to go," etc.*)

futūrus esse	–	itūrus esse	–	–	–	lātūrus esse

(*sometimes* **fore**)

5   The *passive* forms of **ferō** and the *irregular* forms of **fīō**:

PRESENT INDICATIVE			
feror	*I am (being) brought*	**fīō**	*I become (= I am being made)*
ferris	*you are (being) brought*	**fīs**	*you become*
fertur	*s/he, it is (being) brought*	**fit**	*s/he, it becomes*
ferimur	*we are (being) brought*	—	
feriminī	*you are (being) brought*	—	
feruntur	*they are (being) brought*	**fīunt**	*they become*

FUTURE INDICATIVE			
ferar	*I shall/will be brought*	**fīam**	*I shall/will become (= I shall be made)*
ferēris	*you will be brought*	**fīēs**	*you will become*
ferētur	*s/he, it will be brought*	**fīet**	*s/he, it will become*
ferēmur	*we shall/will be brought*	**fīēmus**	*we shall/will become*
ferēminī	*you will be brought*	**fīētis**	*you will become*
ferentur	*they will be brought*	**fīent**	*they will become*

IMPERFECT INDICATIVE			
ferēbar	*I was being brought*	**fīēbam**	*I was becoming (= I was being made)*
ferēbāris	*you were being brought*	**fīēbās**	*you were becoming*
ferēbātur	*s/he, it was being brought*	**fīēbat**	*s/he, it was becoming*
ferēbāmur	*we were being brought*	**fīēbāmus**	*we were becoming*
ferēbāminī	*you were being brought*	**fīēbātis**	*you were becoming*
ferēbantur	*they were being brought*	**fīēbant**	*they were becoming*

PERFECT INDICATIVE			
lātus sum	*I have been/was brought*	**factus sum**	*I have become, I became (= I was made)*
lātus es	*you have been/were brought*	**factus es**	*you have become, you became*
lātus est	*he has been/was brought*	**factus est**	*he has become, he became*
lātī sumus	*we have been/were brought*	**factī sumus**	*we have become, we became*
lātī estis	*you have been/were brought*	**factī estis**	*you have become, you became*
lātī sunt	*they have been/were brought*	**factī sunt**	*they have become, they became*

FUTURE PERFECT INDICATIVE			
lātus erō	*I shall/will have been brought*	**factus erō**	*I shall/will have become*
lātus eris	*you will have been brought*	**factus eris**	*you will have become*
lātus erit	*he will have been brought*	**factus erit**	*he will have become*
lātī erimus	*we shall/will have been brought*	**factī erimus**	*we shall/will have become*
lātī eritis	*you will have been brought*	**factī eritis**	*you will have become*
lātī erunt	*they will have been brought*	**factī erunt**	*they will have become*

PLUPERFECT INDICATIVE			
lātus eram	*I had been brought*	**factus eram**	*I had become (= I had been made)*
lātus erās	*you had been brought*	**factus erās**	*you had become*
lātus erat	*he had been brought*	**factus erat**	*he had become*
lātī erāmus	*we had been brought*	**factī erāmus**	*we had become*
lātī erātis	*you had been brought*	**factī erātis**	*you had become*
lātī erant	*they had been brought*	**factī erant**	*they had become*

PRESENT SUBJUNCTIVE

ferar	*(The translation of*	**fīam**
ferāris	*the subjunctive*	**fīās**
ferātur	*varies according to*	**fīat**
ferāmur	*context.)*	**fīāmus**
ferāminī		**fīātis**
ferantur		**fīant**

IMPERFECT SUBJUNCTIVE

ferrer	**fierem**
ferrēris	**fierēs**
ferrētur	**fieret**
ferrēmur	**fierēmus**
ferrēminī	**fierētis**
ferrentur	**fierent**

PERFECT SUBJUNCTIVE

lātus sim	**factus sim**
lātus sīs	**factus sīs**
lātus sit	**factus sit**
lātī sīmus	**factī sīmus**
lātī sītis	**factī sītis**
lātī sint	**factī sint**

PLUPERFECT SUBJUNCTIVE

lātus essem	**factus essem**
lātus essēs	**factus essēs**
lātus esset	**factus esset**
lātī essēmus	**factī essēmus**
lātī essētis	**factī essētis**
lātī essent	**factī essent**

PERFECT PASSIVE PARTICIPLE

lātus	*having been brought*	**factus**	*having become, having been made*

PRESENT PASSIVE INFINITIVE

ferrī	*to be brought*	**fierī**	*to become, to be made*

PERFECT PASSIVE INFINITIVE

lātus esse	*to have been brought*	**factus esse**	*to have become, to have been made*

6   The forms of **fīō** are used as present, future, and imperfect tenses of the passive of **faciō** (*I make, I do*, etc.):

servī nihil faciunt.   nihil **fit**.
The slaves are doing nothing.   *Nothing **is being done**.*
      Or, *Nothing **is happening**.*

populus mē rēgem faciet.   rēx **fīam**.
The people will make me king.   ***I shall be made** king.*
      Or, ***I shall become** king.*

The other tenses of the passive of **faciō** are formed as usual:

impetus ab equitibus **factus est**. *An attack **was made** by the cavalry.*

Uses of the Cases

1 *nominative*
    poēta recitābat.   *The poet was reciting.*

2 *vocative*
    cavē, **domine**!   *Be careful,* **master***!*

3 *genitive*
    3a fidēs **sociōrum meōrum**   *the loyalty **of my companions***
    3b parum **cibī**   *not enough **food***
    3c eques **summae audāciae**   *a horseman **of extreme boldness***
                               (Compare 6b)

4 *dative*
    4a **coniugī** pecūniam reddidī. *I returned the money **to my wife**.*
    4b **lēgibus** pārēmus.   *We obey **the laws**.*
    4c Notice how the dative of **auxilium**, **cūra**, and **odium** is used in
        the following examples:

        rēx nōbīs **magnō auxiliō**   *The king was **a great help** to us.*
           erat.

        dignitās tua mihi **cūrae** est. *Your dignity is a matter **of***
                                 concern *to me.*

        Epaphrodītus omnibus   *Epaphroditus is **hateful** to*
           odiō est.   *everyone.*
                            Or, *Everyone hates Epaphroditus.*

    4d In Stage 45, you met the dative used in sentences like this:
        fūrēs **mihi** omnia   *The thieves stole everything*
           abstulērunt.   **from me**.

    4e Notice the following use of the dative:
        est **nōbīs** nūlla spēs.   ***We** have no hope.*

        Further examples:
        1 est mihi vīlla.
        2 erant nōbīs multae gemmae.
        3 cōnsulēs, quibus est summa potestās, tē adiuvābunt.

5 *accusative*

5a **amīcōs** prōdidistī.	*You betrayed **your friends**.*
5b **multās hōrās** iter faciēbam.	*I was traveling **for many hours**.* (Compare 6d)
5c per **aquam**; in **urbem**	*through **the water**; into **the city*** (Compare 6e)

For examples of the accusative used in indirect statements, see pp.319–320.

6 *ablative*

6a **vulneribus** cōnfectus	*overcome **by wounds***
6b homō **vultū sevērō**	*a man **with a stern expression*** (Compare 3c)
6c **clārā gente** nātus	*born **from a famous family***
6d **tertiō mēnse** revēnit.	*He returned **in the third month**.* (Compare 5b)
6e ex **hortīs**; in **Britanniā**	*from **the gardens**; in **Britain*** (Compare 5c)

6f Notice the following use of the ablative:

senex erat languidior **fīliō**, ignāvior **uxōre**.

*The old man was feebler **than his son** and lazier **than his wife**.*

Compare this with another way of expressing the same idea:

senex erat languidior **quam fīlius**, ignāvior **quam uxor**.

This use of the ablative is known as the *ablative of comparison.*

6g You have also met the ablative used with adjectives such as **dignus** (*worthy*) and **plēnus** (*full*), and verbs such as **ūtor** (*I use*), **fruor** (*I enjoy*), and **careō** (*I lack*):

frūmentō plēnus	*full **of grain**.*
dignus **suppliciō**	*worthy **of punishment**.*
vītā quiētā fruēbar.	*I was enjoying **a quiet life**.*
nāvibus ūtēbātur.	*He was using **ships**.*
vīnō carēbant.	*They lacked **wine**.*

6h From Stage 29 onwards, you met *ablative absolute* phrases:

senex, **ratiōnibus subductīs**, filiōs arcessīvit.
After drawing up his accounts, *the old man sent for his sons.*

Epaphrodītō loquente, nūntius accurrit.
While Epaphroditus was speaking, *a messenger came dashing up.*

6i In some of the Latin poems in Stages 42, 44–45, and 47, you have
met additional ways of using the ablative. For example, in Stage
47 you met sentences like these:

exarsit dolor **ossibus**.   *Indignation blazed **in his bones**.*
pelagō dēcurrit **apertō**.   *He races **over the open sea**.*

7 Further examples of some of the uses listed above:

1 satis pecūniae habētis?
2 theātrum spectātōribus plēnum erat.
3 septem hōrās dormiēbam.
4 es stultior asinō!
5 mīlitēs gladiīs et pugiōnibus ūtēbantur.
6 Myropnous vōbīs auxiliō erit.
7 sextō diē discessērunt.
8 tōtam noctem nāvigābāmus.
9 perītior frātre sum.
10 centuriōnī crēdēbam.
11 faber sacerdōtī minimō auxiliō erat.
12 puella capillīs longīs nōbilī gente nāta est.

8 Study the following examples:

1 **Rōmae** manēbam.
   I was staying in Rome.
2 **Londiniī** habitāmus.
   We live in London.
3 **Neāpolī** mortuus est.
   He died in Naples.
4 quid **Pompēiīs** accidit?
   What happened in Pompeii?

The words in boldface are in the *locative* case.

The locative case is used only in names of towns and small islands and a small number of other words; it is therefore not normally included in lists of cases such as the table on pp.284–85. In first and second declension singular nouns, the locative case has the same form as the genitive; in third declension singular nouns, it is the same as the dative; in plural nouns of all declensions, it is the same as the ablative.

Notice the locative case of **domus** (*home*) and **rūs** (*country*):

5 **domī** dormiēbat.
   He was sleeping at home.
6 **rūrī** numquam labōrō.
   I never work in the country.

Further examples:

7 hanc epistulam Ephesī scrībō.
8 Athēnīs manēbimus.
9 mīlitēs in castrīs Dēvae erant.
10 rūrī ōtiōsus sum.

Uses of the Participle

1   From Stage 21 onwards, you have seen how participles are used to describe nouns or pronouns:

clientēs, sportulam **adeptī**, discessērunt.
*The clients, **having obtained** their handout, departed.*

centuriō tē in umbrā **latentem** vīdit.
*The centurion saw you **hiding** in the shadow.*

In the first example, the perfect active participle **adeptī** describes **clientēs**; in the second example, the present participle **latentem** describes **tē**.

2   Notice again how a noun and participle in the dative case may be placed at the beginning of the sentence:

Salviō dē fortūnā **querentī** nūllum respōnsum dedī.
***To Salvius complaining** about his luck I gave no reply.*
   Or, in more natural English:
When Salvius complained about his luck, I gave him no reply.

3   Sometimes the noun or pronoun described by a participle is omitted:

valdē **perturbātus**, ex urbe fūgit.
***Having been** thoroughly **alarmed**, **he** fled from the city.*

moritūrī tē salūtāmus.
***We, (who are) about to die**, salute you.*

In examples like these, the ending of the verb (**fūg*it*, salūt*ā*mus**, etc.) makes it clear that the participle refers to *he, we*, etc.

4   Sometimes the participle refers not to a particular person or thing but more vaguely to *somebody* or *some people*:

tū faciem sub aquā, Sexte, **natantis** habēs.
*You have the face, Sextus, **of (someone) swimming** under water.*

ārea plēna strepitū **labōrantium** erat.
*The courtyard was full of the noise **of (people) working**.*

5   Further examples:

1 flammīs exstīnctīs, dominus ruīnam īnspexit.
2 ubīque vōcēs poētam laudantium audiēbantur.
3 ā iūdice damnātus, in exilium iit.
4 līberī, plūrimōs cāsūs passī, auxilium nostrum petēbant.
5 servō haesitantī lībertātem pecūniamque obtulī.
6 sōle oriente, lux fiēbat.

Uses of the Subjunctive

1   *with* **cum** *(meaning "when")*
cum prōvinciam circumīrem, incendium Nīcomēdīae coortum est.
When I was going around the province, *a fire broke out in Nicomedia.*

2   *indirect question*
mīlitēs cognōscere volunt **ubi senex gemmās cēlāverit**.
The soldiers want to find out **where the old man has hidden the jewels**.

Sometimes the verb of asking, etc. (e.g. **rogō**, **scio**) is placed *after* the indirect question:

utrum custōs esset an carnifex, nēmō **sciēbat**.
Whether he was a guard or an executioner, no one **knew**.

3   *purpose clause*
hīc manēbō, **ut vīllam dēfendam**.
I shall stay here, **to defend the villa**.

prīnceps Plīnium ēmīsit **quī Bīthȳnōs regeret**.
The Emperor sent Pliny out **to rule the Bithynians**.

tacēbāmus, **nē ā centuriōne audīrēmur**.
We kept quiet, **in order not to be heard by the centurion**.

4 *indirect command*
tē moneō **ut lēgibus pāreās.**
*I advise you **to obey the laws.***

medicus nōbīs imperāvit **nē ingrederēmur.**
*The doctor told us **not to go in.***

5 *result clause*
barbarī tot hastās coniēcērunt **ut plūrimī equitēs vulnerārentur.**
*The barbarians threw **so** many spears **that most horsemen were wounded.***

6 *with* **priusquam** *"before" and* **dum** *"until".*
nōbīs fugiendum est, **priusquam custōdēs nōs cōnspiciant.**
*We must run away **before the guards catch sight of us.***

exspectābant **dum centuriō signum daret.**
*They were waiting **until the centurion should give the signal.***
    Or, in more natural English:
*They were waiting **for the centurion to give the signal.***

abībō, **priusquam ā dominō agnōscar.**
*I shall go away, **before I am recognized by the master.***

7 The following examples include all the six uses of the subjunctive listed above, and all the four subjunctive tenses (present, imperfect, perfect, and pluperfect, listed on p.298):

1 senex, cum verba medicī audīvisset, testāmentum fēcit.
2 mīlitibus persuādēbō ut marītō tuō parcant.
3 latrōnēs mercātōrem occīdērunt priusquam ad salūtem pervenīret.
4 tam benignus est rēx ut omnēs eum ament.
5 scīre volō quis fenestram frēgerit.
6 dominus ad iānuam festīnāvit ut hospitēs exciperet.
7 Domitiānus ipse adest ut fābulam spectet.
8 Agricola Britannōs hortātus est ut mōrēs Rōmānōs discerent.
9 mīlitēs ēmīsit quī turbam dēpellerent.
10 haruspicēs cognōscere cōnābuntur num ōmina bona sint.
11 tantās dīvitiās adeptus est ut vīllam splendidam iam possideat.
12 ducem ōrābimus nē captīvōs interficiat.

8 From Stage 37 onwards, you have met the subjunctive used in sentences like these:

avārus timēbat **nē fūr aurum invenīret**.
*The miser was afraid **that a thief would find his gold**.*

vereor **nē inimīcī nostrī tibi noceant**.
*I am afraid **that our enemies may harm you**.*

The groups of words in bold face are known as *fearing clauses*.

Further examples:

1 timeō nē Britannī urbem mox capiant.
2 dominus verēbātur nē servī effugerent.
3 perīculum est nē occīdāris.
4 verēbāmur nē omnēs nāvēs dēlētae essent.

9 In Stage 45, you met the *jussive* subjunctive:

lūdōs **spectēmus**!   epistulam statim **recitet**.
Let us watch *the games!*   **Let him read out** *the letter at once.*

10 Translate the following examples, referring if necessary to the tables of subjunctive forms on pp.298–99 and 305:

1 senex mīlitibus persuāsit ut arma dēpōnerent.
2 fugite, priusquam ā custōdibus capiāminī.
3 amīcī tuī timēbant nē interfectus essēs.
4 proficīscāmur!
5 cum pecūniam repperissem, revēnī.
6 rēx captīvīs pepercit nē crūdēlis vidērētur.
7 tantus erat strepitus ut omnēs terrērēmur.
8 quārē Imperātor Agricolam revocāverit, nescio.
9 aquam ferte, quā flammās exstinguam!
10 Salvius nunc respondeat.

In each sentence, find the reason why a subjunctive is being used.

11 For examples of the subjunctive in conditional sentences, see pp.322–23.

12 For examples of the subjunctive used with the accusative and infinitive in indirect statements, see paragraphs 4 and 5 on p.327.

---

13 For examples of the subjunctive in direct and indirect deliberative questions, see p.263, Stage 48.

Indirect Statement

1 From Stage 35 onwards, you have met indirect statements, expressed by a noun or pronoun in the *accusative* case and one of the following *infinitive* forms of the verb. Some indirect statements are introduced by a verb in the *present* tense (e.g. **dīcō**, **crēdunt**), while others are introduced by a verb in the *perfect* or *imperfect* tense (e.g. **dīxī**, **crēdēbant**); notice again how this makes a difference to the translation of the infinitive.

1 *present active infinitive*
   crēdō prīncipem Agricolae **invidēre**.
   I believe that *the Emperor **is jealous** of Agricola.*

   crēdēbam prīncipem Agricolae **invidēre**.
   I believed that the Emperor **was jealous** of Agricola.

   (Compare this with the direct statement:
   "prīnceps Agricolae invidet.")

2 *present passive infinitive*
   scit multās prōvinciās ā latrōnibus **vexārī**.
   He knows that *many provinces **are troubled** by bandits.*

   sciēbat *multās prōvinciās ā latrōnibus* **vexārī**.
   He knew that *many provinces **were troubled** by bandits.*

   (Compare: "multae prōvinciae ā latrōnibus vexantur.")

3 *perfect active infinitive*
   centuriō hostēs **dīcit cōnstitisse**.
   *The centurion **says that** the enemy **have halted**.*

   centuriō hostēs **dīxit cōnstitisse**.
   *The centurion **said that** the enemy **had halted**.*

   (Compare: "hostēs cōnstitērunt.")

---

4 *perfect passive infinitive*

vir uxōrem **servātam esse putat**.
*The man **thinks that** his wife **has been saved**.*

vir uxōrem **servātam esse putāvit**.
*The man **thought that** his wife **had been saved**.*

(Compare: "uxor servāta est.")

5 *future active infinitive*

senātōrēs **prō certō habent** cīvēs numquam **cessūrōs esse**.
*The senators **are sure that** the citizens **will** never **give in**.*

senātōrēs **prō certō habēbant** cīvēs numquam **cessūrōs esse**.
*The senators **were sure that** the citizens **would** never **give in**.*

(Compare: "cīvēs numquam cēdent.")

The verb of speaking, etc. (e.g. **crēdō**, **dīcit**, **putat**) can be placed either at the beginning of the sentence (as in example 1 above) or in the middle of the indirect statement (as in example 3) or at the end of the sentence (example 4).

2   Notice how the verb **negō** is used with indirect statements:

iuvenis **negāvit** sē pecūniam perdidisse.
The young man **denied that** he had wasted the money.
Or, The young man **said that** he had **not** wasted the money.

3   Further examples:

1 audiō trēs Virginēs Vestālēs damnātās esse.
2 illum poētam putō optimē recitāre.
3 ancilla dīcit dominum in hortō ambulāre.
4 fāma vagātur multa oppida dēlēta esse.
5 ducem auxilium mox missūrum esse spērāvimus.
6 nūntius negāvit Agricolam ad ultimās partēs Britanniae pervēnisse.
7 cūr suspicātus es Salvium testāmentum finxisse?
8 fēmina marītum illō carcere tenērī putat.
9 crēdō mīlitēs fidem servātūrōs esse.
10 servus crēdēbat multōs hospitēs invītārī.

4 Compare the following examples:

    1 Salvius dīcit **sē** in Ītaliā habitāre.
      (Direct statement: "in Ītaliā habit**ō**.")
    2 Salvius dīcit **eum** in forō ambulāre.
      (Direct statement: "in forō ambul**at**.")

5 Further examples:

    1 nauta dīcit sē nāvem mox refectūrum esse.
    2 nauta dīxit sē nāvem mox refectūrum esse.
    3 sciō magnum perīculum nōbīs imminēre.
    4 sciēbam magnum perīculum nōbīs imminēre.
    5 dux eum discessisse crēdit.
    6 dux eum discessisse crēdēbat.
    7 nūntiī vīllās negant dēlētās esse.
    8 nūntiī vīllās negāvērunt dēlētās esse.
    9 audiō multōs captīvōs ad mortem cotīdiē dūcī.
   10 audīvī multōs captīvōs ad mortem cotīdiē dūcī.

6 Sometimes one indirect statement is followed immediately by another:

rēx dīxit Rōmānōs exercitum parāvisse; mox prīmōs mīlitēs adventūrōs esse.
*The king said that the Romans had prepared an army; (**he said that**) the first soldiers would soon arrive.*

Notice that the verb **dīxit** is not repeated in the second half of the sentence; the use of the accusative (**prīmōs mīlitēs**) and the infinitive (**adventūrōs esse**) makes it clear that the sentence is still reporting what the king said.

Further examples:

    1 servus nūntiāvit cōnsulem morbō gravī afflīgī; medicōs dē vītā eius dēspērāre.
    2 fāma vagābātur decem captīvōs ē carcere līberātōs esse; Imperātōrem enim eīs ignōvisse.

7 For examples of the subjunctive used with the infinitive in indirect statements, see paragraphs 4 and 5 on pp.327–28.

Conditional Sentences

1   In Stage 42, you met conditional sentences in which *indicative* forms of the verb were used:

sī valēs, gaudeō.   *If you are well, I am pleased.*

Notice again that a Latin future perfect (or future) tense in a conditional clause is usually translated by an English present tense:

sī illud iterum **fēceris**, tē pūniam.

*If you **do** that again, I shall punish you.*

2   In Stage 46, you met conditional sentences in which *pluperfect subjunctive* forms of the verb were used:

sī dīligentius **labōrāvissem**, dominus mē **līberāvisset**.
*If **I had worked** harder, the master **would have freed** me.*

sī in eōdem locō **mānsissēs**, perīculum **vītāvissēs**.
*If **you had stayed** in the same place, **you would have avoided** the danger.*

3   Notice again how the word **nisi** is used in conditional sentences:

nisi Imperātor novās cōpiās mīserit, opprimēmur.
If *the Emperor does **not** send reinforcements, we shall be overwhelmed.*
Or, **Unless the Emperor sends reinforcements, we shall be overwhelmed.**

4   Further examples of conditional sentences containing indicative and pluperfect subjunctive forms of the verb:

1   sī illud putās, longē errās.
2   sī Milō cēterōs āthlētās superāvisset, cīvēs statuam eī posuissent.
3   nisi amīcī nōbīs subvēnerint, in carcerem coniciēmur.
4   nisi cliēns vehementer exclāmāvisset, patrōnus eum nōn animadvertisset.
5   sī diūtius in urbe morātī essētis, numquam effūgissētis.

5 You have also met the *imperfect* tense of the *subjunctive* in conditional sentences. For example:

sī Rōmae nunc **habitārem**, clientēs mē assiduē **vexārent**.
*If **I were living** in Rome now, my clients **would be** continually **pestering** me.*

sī Domitiānus nōs adhūc **regeret**, miserrimī essēmus.
*If Domitian **were** still **ruling** us, we **would be** very unhappy.*

Notice that the imperfect subjunctive in conditional sentences is usually translated by *were . . .* followed by *would be . . .* or *should be . . ..*

Further examples:

1 sī Marcus hodiē vīveret, cum Imperātōre cēnāret.
2 sī rēx essem, nōn in hāc vīllā labōrārem.
3 sī ego tuum fundum administrārem, tū dīvitissimus essēs.

6 In the following conditional sentences, the *present subjunctive* is being used:

sī hanc medicīnam **bibās**, statim **convalēscās**.
*If **you were to drink** this medicine, **you would get better** at once.*

sī piscēs per āera **volent**, omnēs **mīrentur**.
*If fish **were to fly** through the air, everybody **would be amazed**.*

The present subjunctive in conditional sentences can usually be translated by *were to . . .* followed by *would . . .* or *should . . ..*

Further examples:

1 sī Iuppiter ipse Lesbiam petat, illa eum spernat.
2 sī forte aurum in Britanniā inveniāmus, dīvitēs fīāmus.
3 sī mīlitēs urbem oppugnent, facile eam capiant.

Gerund and Gerundive

1 Since Stage 41, you have met the *gerund*, e.g. **portandum** (*carrying*), **docendum** (*teaching*), etc. Notice again how the various cases of the gerund are used:

genitive
optimam habeō occāsiōnem **cognōscendī** quid acciderit.
*I have an excellent opportunity **of finding out** what has happened.*

accusative (with **ad**, meaning *for the purpose of*)
multī hominēs **ad audiendum** aderant.
*Many men were there **for the purpose of listening**.*
    Or, in more natural English:
*Many men were there **to listen**.*

ablative
prūdenter **emendō** et **vēndendō**, pater meus dīvitissimus fit.
***By buying** and **selling** sensibly, my father is becoming very rich.*

The cases of the gerund are listed in full on p.302.

Further examples:

1 senātor ad dīcendum surrēxit.
2 puer artem cantandī discere cōnābātur.
3 decem gladiātōrēs ad pugnandum ēlēctī sunt.
4 diū labōrandō, lībertātem adeptus sum.
5 senex nūllam spem convalēscendī habēbat.

2 You have also met sentences in which **ad** (*for the purpose of*) is used with the *gerundive*, e.g. **portandus** (*being carried*), **docendus** (*being taught*), etc.:

iuvenis **ad epistulam legendam** cōnsēdit.
*The young man sat down **for the purpose of the letter being read**.*
    Or, in more natural English:
*The young man sat down **to read the letter**..*

Further examples:

1 multī clientēs advēnērunt ad nōs salūtandōs.
2 cīvēs in theātrum ad fābulam spectandam conveniēbant.
3 servus aquam ad flammās exstinguendās quaerēbat.

3 Notice again a rather different type of sentence, which you have met from Stage 24 onwards, in which the gerundive (**portandus**, **docendus**, etc.) has the meaning *needing to be carried, needing to be taught*, etc., and is used with some form of the verb **esse** (e.g. **est, sunt, erit, erat**) to indicate that something *ought* to be done:

1 nōbīs vīlla **aedificanda est**.
   *We **must build** a house.*
   (Compare this with another way of expressing the same idea: necesse est nōbīs vīllam aedificāre.)
2 mīlitibus **cōnsistendum erit**.
   *The soldiers **will have to halt**.*
   (Compare: necesse erit mīlitibus cōnsistere.)
3 mihi longum iter **faciendum erat**.
   *I **had to make** a long journey.*
4 fūrēs **pūniendī sunt**.
   *The thieves **must be punished**.*

When the gerundive is used in this way, it is known as a *gerundive of obligation*.

Further examples:

5 tibi novae vestēs emendae sunt.
   (Compare: necesse est tibi novās vestēs emere.)
6 servīs currendum erat.
   (Compare: necesse erat servīs currere.)
7 mihi fundus īnspiciendus erit.
8 pecūnia reddenda est.
9 nōbīs in hāc vīllā dormiendum erit.
10 mihi multae epistulae scrībendae sunt.
11 exīstimō captīvōs līberandōs esse.

[handwritten annotations:]
ad pacem portandam
to, acc. acc.
principēs Romam
nom.
venire contendebant
to come
The chiefs were hurrying to come towards Rome to bring the peace.

Sentences with dum (meaning "while")

1   From Stage 29 onwards, you have met **dum** used with the meaning "while":

dum cīvēs sacrificium **spectant**, iuvenis subitō prōsiluit.
*While the citizens **were watching** the sacrifice, a young man suddenly leapt forward.*

dum bellum in Britanniā **geritur**, rēs dīra Rōmae accidit.
*While the war **was being waged** in Britain, a terrible disaster happened at Rome.*

Notice that in sentences like these **dum** is used with the indicative *present* tense, even when the statement refers to the past.

Further examples:
1 dum custōdēs dormiunt, captīvī effūgērunt.
2 dum nūntius in līmine haesitat, Imperātor "intrā!" clāmāvit.

2   For examples of **dum** used with the meaning "until," see paragraph 6 on p.317.

Longer Sentences

1   From Unit 1 onwards, you have met sentences like these:

1 coquus numquam labōrat, **quod semper dormit**.
*The cook never works, **because he is always asleep**.*
2 fūrēs, **postquam canem excitāvērunt**, fūgērunt.
*The thieves, **after they woke the dog up**, ran away.*
Or, *The thieves ran away **after they woke the dog up**.*

Each of these sentences is made up of:

(i)   a group of words which would make a complete sentence on its own, e.g. **coquus numquam labōrat** in example 1, and **fūrēs fūgērunt** in example 2. Groups of words like these are known as *main clauses*.

(ii)   a group of words introduced by a word like **quod** or **postquam**, e.g. **quod semper dormit** in example 1, and **postquam canem excitāvērunt** in example 2. Groups of words like these are known as *subordinate clauses*. Notice that a subordinate clause on its own would not make a complete sentence.

2 There are many different kinds of subordinate clause. The commonest kind is the *relative* clause, which you have met from Unit 2 onwards in sentences like this:

servī **quī vīnum effundunt** magnō pretiō ēmptī sunt.
*The slaves **who are pouring out the wine** were bought at a high price.*

In this example, the *main clause* is **servī magnō pretiō ēmptī sunt**, and the *subordinate clause* is a relative clause: **quī vīnum effundunt**.

3 Translate the following examples:

1 togae, quās ille senex vēndit, sunt sordidae.
2 amīcus meus currere nōn potest, quod pēs dolet.
3 hospitēs, postquam cibum gustāvērunt, vehementer plausērunt.
4 virgō quae senātōrī nūpsit trēdecim annōs nāta est.

Pick out the main clause and subordinate clause in each sentence.

4 Compare the Latin sentences in paragraphs 1 and 2, which were all *direct* statements, with the following examples, which are all *indirect* statements:

1 audiō coquum numquam labōrāre, **quod semper dormiat.**
*I hear that the cook never works, **because he is always asleep**.*
2 puer affirmāvit fūrēs, **postquam canem excitāvissent**, fūgisse.
*The boy declared that the thieves, **after they had waked the dog**, had run away.*
3 mercātor respondit servōs **quī vīnum effunderent** magnō pretiō ēmptōs esse.
*The merchant replied that the slaves **who were pouring out the wine** had been bought at a high price.*

Notice in particular that when an indirect statement contains a subordinate clause, the verb in the subordinate clause is normally *subjunctive* (e.g. **dormiat, excitāvissent, effunderent**).

5 Translate the following examples:

1 servus dīcit togās, quās ille senex vēndat, sordidās esse.
2 praecō spērābat clientēs, simulac patrōnum salūtāvissent, abitūrōs esse.
3 iuvenis nūntiāvit patrem, quod morbō afflīgerētur, domī manēre.
4 cīvēs exīstimābant Agricolam, postquam Calēdoniōs vīcisset, iniūstē revocātum esse.

Pick out the subordinate clause in each sentence.

PART TWO: Reference Grammar

I Nouns

See Review Grammar, pp.284–85, for complete tables of nouns of all five declensions.

II Adjectives

See Review Grammar, pp.286–87, for tables of adjectives, adverbs, and their comparative forms.

III Pronouns

See Review Grammar, pp.290–93, for tables of personal and reflexive pronouns, and also **hic, ille, ipse, is, īdem, quī,** and **quīdam**.

IV Regular Verbs

See Review Grammar, pp.294–302, for complete tables of active and passive forms of regular verbs, including imperatives, participles, infinitives, gerunds, and gerundives.

V Deponent Verbs

See Review Grammar, pp. 303–6, for complete tables of deponent verbs, including participles and infinitives.

VI Irregular Verbs

See Review Grammar, pp. 307–10, for complete tables of the irregular verbs **sum, possum, eō, volō, nōlō, mālō, ferō,** and **fīō**, including infinitives.

VII Fearing Clauses

Verbs of fearing like **timeō, metuō, vereor** (*I fear that*. . .), or expressions of fearing like **perīculum est** (*there is a danger that* . . .) are often followed by clauses, introduced by **nē**, which express what is feared. (See Review Grammar, "Uses of the Subjunctive," p.318, ¶8.)

Fears about the present or future are expressed in **nē**-clauses with the verb in the *present subjunctive* if the main verb of the entire sentence is present, present-perfect, or future tense; with the *imperfect subjunctive* if the main verb is imperfect, perfect, or pluperfect tense. Study and compare, for example, the following pairs of sentences:

vereor nē paulātim **fīam** pauperior.
*I am afraid that I **may** gradually **become** poorer.*
verebar nē paulātim **fierem** pauperior.
*I was afraid that I **might** gradually **become** poorer.*

saepe timuī nē Imperātōrem **offendam**.
*I have often feared that **I may offend** the Emperor.*
saepe timueram nē Imperātōrem **offenderem.**
*I had often feared that **I might offend** the Emperor.*

metuērunt nē Agrippīna e nāve **ēlābātur**.
*They have been afraid that Agrippina **will escape** from the ship.*
metuērunt nē Agrippīna e nāve **ēlāberētur**.
*They feared that Agrippina **would escape** from the ship.*

Fears about the past are expressed in **nē**-clauses with the verb in the *perfect subjunctive* if the main verb of the entire sentence is present, present-perfect, or future tense; with the *pluperfect subjunctive* if the leading verb is imperfect, perfect, or pluperfect tense. Study and compare, for example, the following pairs of sentences:

Nerō verētur nē māter e nāve **ēlāpsa sit**.
*Nero fears that his mother **has escaped** from the ship.*
Nerō verēbātur nē māter e nāve **ēlāpsa esset**.
*Nero was afraid that his mother **had escaped** from the ship.*

metuēmus nē inimīcī **convēnerint?**
*Will we be afraid that our enemies **have come together?***
metuerāmus nē inimīcī **convēnissent?**
*Had we been afraid that our enemies **had come together?***

Nīcerōs timuit nē mīles **factus sit** versipellis.
*Niceros has been afraid that the soldier **has become** a werewolf.*
Nīcerōs timuit nē mīles **factus esset** versipellis.
*Niceros feared that the soldier **had become** a werewolf.*

VIII Jussive Subjunctive

When a subjunctive verb is used independently, outside a subordinate clause, it is often a *jussive subjunctive*, expressing what is to be done. In the first person, it expresses self-encouragement or intention; in the second or third person, a command or, with **nē** in front, a prohibition. (See Stage 45, p.204, and Review Grammar, p.318, **¶9**.) Examples:

nē **vereāmur**, fortēs **sīmus**!
***Let's** not **be afraid, let's be** brave!*

ignōscās mihi!   **Forgive** *me!*
*nē arrogāns **sīs**!*   **Don't be** *arrogant!*

vīlicus nē **sit** ignāvus, officium **agat** semper!
*The overseer **should** not **be** lazy, he **should** always **do** his duty!*

IX Indirect Statement

When statement with an indicative verb is reported after a verb of saying, whether expressed or implied, it becomes a noun clause in which the subject is changed to an accusative and the indicative verb to an infinitive. (See Stage 35, pp.11–2; Stage 37, p.38 and p.43; Stage 38, pp.65–6 and p.57; Stage 40, pp.99–100; and Review Grammar, "Indirect Statement," pp.319–21.) Examples:

Indicative Statement:
Portūnus nāvem Cloanthī ad terram impulit.
Portunus pushed Cloanthus' ship towards land.

Noun clause after, e.g. **dīxērunt:**

dīxērunt Portūnum nāvem Cloanthī ad terram impulisse.
They said that Portunus (had) pushed Cloanthus' ship towards land.

1 Negative Statements
When a negative direct statement, e.g. **Portūnus nāvem Cloanthī ad terram nōn impulit**, is changed into a noun clause, the **nōn** is removed and the verb of saying changed into a form of **negō**. For example:

Portūnus nāvem Cloanthī ad terram **nōn** impulit.
*Portunus did **not** push Cloanthus' ship towards land.*

negāvērunt Portūnum nāvem Cloanthī ad terram impulisse.
*They **denied** that Portunus pushed Cloanthus' ship towards land.*
Or, *They **said** that Portunus did **not** push Cloanthus' ship towards land.*

See also Review Grammar, "Indirect Statement," p.319, **¶2.**

2 Subordinate Clauses in Indirect Statement
The verb of a subordinate clause within an indirect statement is nearly always subjunctive. Its tense depends on the tense of the main verb of speaking:

A   If the verb of speaking is in the present, present-perfect, or future tense, the verb in the subordinate clause is either present or perfect subjunctive. Examples:

1   Direct Statement:
Vespillō dolōre afflīctus est, quod Tūria **moritur.**
*Vespillo is stricken with grief, because Turia **is dying**.*

2   Noun Clause, with subordinate clause:
2a   dīcunt Vespillōnem dolōre afflīctum esse, quod Tūria **moriātur.**
*They say that Vespillo is stricken with grief because Turia **is dying**.*
2b   dīcēbant Vespillōnem dolōre afflīctum esse, quod Tūria **morerētur.**
*They kept saying that Vespillo was stricken with grief because Turia **was dying**.*
2c   dīxērunt Vespillōnem dolōre afflīctum esse, quod Tūria **moriātur.**
*They have said that Vespillo is stricken with grief, because Turia **is dying**.*
2d   dīxērunt Vespillōnem dolōre afflīctum esse, quod Tūria **morerētur.**
*They said that Vespillo was stricken with grief, because Turia **was dying**.*

B   If the verb of speaking is in the imperfect, perfect, or pluperfect tense, the verb in the subordinate clause is either imperfect or pluperfect subjunctive. Examples:

3   Direct Statement:
Lesbia, quae Catullum **dīligēbat**, nunc alium virum bāsiāre māvult.
*Lesbia, who **used to be fond of** Catullus, now prefers to kiss another man.*

4   Noun Clause, with subordinate clause:
4a   affirmant Lesbiam, quae Catullum **dīlēxerit**, nunc alium virum bāsiāre mālle.
*They declare that Lesbia, who once **was fond of** Catullus, now prefers to kiss another man.*
4b   affirmāvērunt Lesbiam, quae Catullum **dīlēxisset**, nunc alium virum bāsiāre mālle.
*They declared that Lesbia, who once **had been fond of** Catullus, now preferred to kiss another man.*

X Conditional Sentences with the Subjunctive

Conditional sentences with the indicative are straightforward and fairly easy to understand. Examples:

sī hoc facis, peccās.	*If you are doing this, you are doing wrong.*
sī hoc faciēbās, peccābās.	*If you were doing this, you were doing wrong.*
sī hoc fēcistī, peccāvistī.	*If you did this, you did wrong.*

1 Present and Past Unfulfilled (= Contrary-to-Fact) Sentences
Conditional sentences with the *imperfect* subjunctive describe action that is not happening; with the *pluperfect* subjunctive, action that did not happen. (See Stage 42, p.147, ¶5; Stage 46, p.228; and Review Grammar, "Conditional Sentences," ¶¶2 and 5.) Examples:

Present Unfulfilled, or Contrary-to-Fact, Conditional:
sī mē **iuvārēs**, effugere **possem**.
*If you **helped** me, I **would be able** to escape.* (But you are not helping me, and I am not able to escape.)

Past Unfulfilled, or Contrary-to-Fact, Conditional:
sī Īcarus īnferius **volāvisset**, e caelō nōn **cecidisset**.
*If Icarus **had flown** lower, he **would** not **have fallen** from the sky.* (But he flew too high, and he fell.)

2 Future Remote (= Ideal) Conditional Sentences
Conditional sentences with the present subjunctive describe action which may occur, perhaps, at a future time. (See Review Grammar, "Conditional Sentences," ¶6.) Example:

Future Remote, or Ideal, Conditional:
sī porta **aperiātur,** exeāmus.
*If the gate **were to be opened,** we **would go out.***
(But we are not sure whether the gate will be opened.)

XI Gerund; Gerundive with *ad*
Although the gerund and the gerundive often look the same because of their **-nd-** infix, a gerund is a verbal noun, and a gerundive, a verbal adjective. (See Stage 40, p.104; Stage 41, pp.118–19; Stage 43, p.170; Review Grammar, "Gerund and Gerundive," pp.324–25.)

1 A gerund is always active in meaning and may take a direct object. After **ad**, the accusative gerund expresses purpose. Examples:

genitive case:	spēs **inveniendī** pecūniam
	*the hope **of finding** money*
accusative case:	puella exiit **ad lūdendum.**
	*The girl went out for **the purpose of playing/to play.***
ablative case:	āthlēta **vincendō** certāmen dēlectātur.
	*An athlete is pleased **by winning** a contest.*

2 A gerundive after **ad** and a noun in the accusative expresses purpose. Example:

Rōmānī ad **necandōs** hostēs profectī sunt.
*They set out **for the purpose of the enemy being killed.***
   for the purpose of killing the enemy.
   to kill the enemy.

Compare **ad** with the gerund of an *intransitive* verb and **ad** with a noun and gerundive of a *transitive* verb:

dominus hortum ad **ambulandum** intrāvit.
*The master entered his garden **to take a walk.***
dominus tablīnum ad **numerandam** pecūniam intrāvit.
*The master entered his study **to count** his money.*

XII Sentence Patterns

Below are some of the most important sentence patterns in the prose which you have studied in Unit 4. The patterns are shown on the left, with examples on the right.
Key: NOM = nominative; ACC = accusative; V = verb; INF = infinitive.

PATTERNS		EXAMPLES
XII.1	V of speaking, etc. + ACC and INF	dīcunt Daedalum fīlium docēre.
		They say that Daedalus is teaching his son.
XII.2	ACC and INF + V of speaking, etc.	Īcarum cadere vident.
		They see that Icarus is falling.
XII.3	NOM + *est* + gerundive of obligation	Tūria est laudanda.
		Turia should be praised.
XII.4	V of asking/knowing, etc. + indirect question	rogō Imperātōrem quid faciam.
		I ask the Emperor what I should do.
XII.5	*mālō* + INF + *quam* + INF	mālō imperāre quam pārēre.
		I prefer to command rather than (to) obey.
XII.6	subordinate clauses in indirect statement	mīlitem, quī mātrōnam Ephesiam animadvertisset, multās hōrās cum eā in sepulcrō manēre affirmāvērunt.
		They declared that the soldier, who had noticed the Ephesian lady, spent many hours with her in the tomb.

PART THREE: Supplementary Reading

1 mīles versipellis

"I (Niceros) set out for Melissa's with a soldier as companion. The soldier stopped at some tombs by the road, did weird things, and turned into a . . . wolf! I was frightened when I arrived alone at Melissa's. She told me about a wolf. He had just attacked her sheep, been wounded by a slave, but ran away. I rushed home, where I made an amazing discovery."

"nactus ego occāsiōnem, cum forte dominus meus exiisset, persuādeō hospitī nostrō, ut mēcum ad quīntum mīliārium veniat. erat autem mīles, fortis tamquam Orcus. proficīscimur nōs circā gallicinia; lūna lūcēbat tamquam merīdiē. vēnimus inter monumenta: homō meus coepit ad stēlās facere; sedeō ego cantāns   5
et stēlās numerō. deinde ut respexī ad comitem, ille exuit sē et omnia vestīmenta iuxtā viam posuit. mihi anima in nāsō erat; stābam tamquam mortuus. at ille circummīnxit vestīmenta sua, et subitō lupus factus est. nōlīte mē iocārī putāre; nūllīus patrimōnium tantī faciō ut mentiar. sed, quod coeperam dīcere, postquam lupus factus   10
est, ululāre coepit et in silvās fūgit. ego prīmō nesciēbam ubi essem; deinde accessī, ut vestīmenta eius tollerem: illa autem lapidea facta sunt. quī 'morī timōre' nisi ego? gladium tamen strīnxī et umbrās cecīdī, dōnec ad vīllam amīcae meae pervenīrem. ut lārva intrāvī, paene exspīrāvī, sūdor mihi per bifurcum volābat, oculī mortuī; vix   15
refectus sum. Melissa mea mīrārī coepit, quod tam sērō ambulārem, et: 'sī ante,' inquit, 'vēnissēs, saltem nōs adiūvissēs; lupus enim vīllam intrāvit et omnia pecora tamquam lanius lacerāvit. nec tamen dērīsit, etiamsī fūgit; servus enim noster hastā collum eius trāiēcit.' haec ut audīvī, operīre oculōs amplius nōn   20
potuī, sed lūce clārā domum fūgī tamquam caupō compīlātus; et postquam vēnī in illum locum in quō lapidea vestīmenta erant facta, nihil invēnī nisi sanguinem. ut vērō domum vēnī, iacēbat mīles meus in lectō tamquam bōs, et collum illīus medicus cūrābat. intellēxī illum versipellem esse, nec posteā cum illō pānem gustāre   25
potuī, nōn sī mē occīdissēs."

You may have to consult the Vocabulary at the end of the book to understand some of the words in these passages.

1　The Werewolf Soldier

Niceros, a former slave, is a guest at a dinner-party thrown by a rough-and-ready millionaire named Trimalchio. After dinner he tells what happened when he went to visit Melissa, a former girlfriend. The story is taken from Petronius, *Satyrica*, LXII.

nactus ego occāsiōnem (i.e. the opportunity to visit Melissa)

mīliārium *milestone* (Milestones by a road marked distances from the Golden Milestone in the forum of Rome; see *Unit 3*, Stage 29, p.166, and map, p.168.)

gallicinia: gallicinium *cockcrow, dawn*

merīdiē: merīdiēs *noon*

5 inter monumenta (Roman tombs were built by the side of a road; see *Unit 1*, Stage 7, p.112.)

stēlās: stēla *stone slab, tombstone*

facere (here =) *make (water), urinate*

exuit: exuere *strip*

mihi anima in nāsō erat *my spirit was in my nose*, i.e. *my heart was in my mouth*

circummīnxit: circummingere *urinate around*

iocārī *joke*

nūllīus (here used as genitive of *nēmō*) *of nobody*

patrimōnium *fortune, inheritance*

10 tantī faciō ut *I rate (nobody's fortune) so high that (I'd tell a lie)*

accessī: accēdere *go up, approach*

quī? = quis?

'morī timōre' *'to die from fear'* (proverb. The infinitive is used here instead of the perfect tense, see p.268.)

ut lārva *like a ghost, white as a ghost*

sūdor *sweat*

bifurcum *fork of the thighs, crotch*

volābat: volāre *fly*, (here =) *pour down*

refectus sum *I got over it, I recovered*

saltem *at least*

pecora: pecus *sheep*

lanius *butcher*

dērīsit: dērīdēre *be able to laugh*, (here =) *get off scot-free*

etiamsī *even if, although*

20 collum *neck*

trāiēcit: trāicere *stab*

operīre *shut*

compīlātus: compīlāre *rob*

ut . . . vēnī = cum . . . vēnissem

bōs *ox, bull*

2a mōrēs avunculī Plīniī

When Pliny's uncle was sunbathing in the morning, he took notes while a slave read aloud to him. After lunch and a nap, he studied until dinnertime. During the dinner, he listened to a book being read aloud and took notes. When he was staying in the country, he studied all the time except when bathing. He never traveled without a secretary accompanying him. He left his nephew 160 notebooks, some of which he could once have sold for as much as 400,000 sesterces.

post cibum saepe, quem interdiū levem et facilem veterum mōre
sūmēbat, aestāte, sī quid ōtiī, iacēbat in sōle, liber legēbātur,
adnotābat excerpēbatque. nihil enim lēgit, quod nōn excerperet;
dīcere etiam solēbat nūllum esse librum tam malum, ut nōn aliquā
parte prōdesset. post sōlem plērumque frīgidā lavābātur, deinde   5
gustābat dormiēbatque minimum; mox quasi aliō diē studēbat in
cēnae tempus. super hanc liber legēbātur, adnotābātur et quidem
cursim. meminī quendam ex amīcīs, cum lēctor quaedam perperam
prōnūntiāvisset, revocāvisse et repetī coēgisse; huic avunculum
meum dīxisse: "intellēxerās nempe?" cum ille adnuisset, "cūr ergō   10
revocābās? decem amplius versūs hāc tuā interpellātiōne
perdidimus." tanta erat parsimōnia temporis. surgēbat aestāte ā
cēnā lūce, hieme intrā prīmam noctis et tamquam aliquā lēge
cōgente. haec inter mediōs labōrēs urbisque fremitum; in sēcessū
sōlum balneī tempus studiīs eximēbātur: cum dīcō "balneī," dē   15
interiōribus loquor; nam dum dēstringitur tergiturque, audiēbat
aliquid aut dictābat. in itinere quasi solūtus cēterīs cūrīs huic ūnī
vacābat: ad latus notārius cum librō et pugillāribus, cuius manūs
hieme manicīs mūniēbantur, ut nē caelī quidem asperitās ūllum
studiīs tempus ēriperet; quā ex causā Rōmae quoque sellā   20
vehēbātur. repetō mē correptum esse ab eō, cūr ambulārem:
"poterās," inquit, "hās hōrās nōn perdere"; nam perīre omne
tempus arbitrābātur, quod studiīs nōn impenderētur. hāc
intentiōne tot ista volūmina perēgit ēlectōrumque commentāriōs
centum sexāgintā mihi relīquit, opisthographōs quidem et   25
minūtissimīs scrīptōs; quā ratiōne multiplicātur hic numerus.
referēbat ipse potuisse sē, cum prōcūrāret in Hispāniā, vēndere hōs
commentāriōs Larciō Licinō quadringentīs mīlibus nummōrum, et
tunc aliquantō pauciōrēs erant.

2a   The Lifestyle of Pliny's Uncle

Pliny the nephew shared with his uncle Pliny an enthusiasm for writing. Both managed to balance the demands of public life with those of literature by devoting almost all their spare time to research and writing. Not surprisingly, the Younger Pliny described with admiration the literary discipline of his uncle which resulted in (among other works) a sort of encyclopedia in thirty-seven books, called the *Natural History*. The description of the Elder Pliny's literary habits is taken from the Younger Pliny's *Letters*, III.5. 10–17.

post cibum (here =) *after a mid-morning meal*
veterum mōre *in accordance with the custom of the old-timers*
excerpēbat: excerpere *make excerpts* (Making collections of specially good or interesting passages was a common literary activity in Roman times.)
5 post sōlem *after his sunbath*
frīgidā (aquā) lavābātur *bathed in cold water*
gustābat: gustāre (here =) *have a snack*
quasi aliō diē *as if on another day* (He got up from his afternoon nap as if he were starting another day.)
in cēnae tempus *until dinner time*
super hanc (cēnam) *during dinner*
quaedam (verba)
revocāvisse et repetī coēgisse *he made (the reader) go back and compelled (the words) to be repeated*
11 decem amplius versūs *more than ten lines*
intrā prīmam (hōram) noctis *during the first hour of darkness* (Many other rich Romans would have dawdled over their wine-cups until the early hours of the morning.)
in sēcessū *in retreat* (at a country estate)
15 dē interiōribus (partibus) *about the inner rooms (of the bath)* (The "inner rooms," or the caldārium and frīgidārium, had a hot and cold tub or pool respectively (see *Unit 1*, Stage 9, pp. 146–47.))
dēstringitur: dēstringere (here =) *scrape with a strigil*
huic ūnī (cūrae) *for this one concern* (i.e. literary study)
20 sellā: sella (here =) *sedan-chair*
repetō: repetere *recall*
25 relīquit: relinquere *leave (as inheritance)* (The Younger Pliny was his uncle's heir.)
minūtissimīs (litterīs) *in very small handwriting* (literally "letters")
cm prōcūrāret in Hispāniā *when he was serving as procurator* (i.e. *governor*) *of Spain* (in about A.D. 73) (He died six years later.)
Larciō Licinō: Larcius Licinus (Larcius Licinus was evidently very rich.)
quadringentīs mīlibus *for 400,000 (sesterces)* (400,000 sesterces was no small sum; it was exactly the price of membership in the equestrian class (see *Stage 32*, p.219) to which the Elder Pliny belonged.)
pauciōrēs erant (commentāriī)

2b animālia mīrābilia

*1 A Greek traveler, when treed by a lion, discovered the lion was mutely asking
him for a favor. The traveler obliged, and the lion rewarded him.*
*2 A panther waylaid an old man. When he started to step back, she rolled over
and looked sad. The old man, realizing something was wrong, allowed her to
lead him to a pit where he made an interesting discovery.*
*3 The hippopotamus, when it has overeaten, walks ashore looking for a sharp
reed-stalk. When it finds a very sharp one, it gives itself a curious medical
treatment.*
*4 The Tentyritae are a tribe of pygmies who live on an island in the Nile. They
are not frightened of crocodiles, but ride their backs as if they were horses. When
the crocodiles rear back to bite them, the Tentyritae save themselves and their
less fortunate comrades in an unusual way.*

1 vir Graecus in Āfricam dēlātus nāve iuxtā lītus cōnspectō leōne
hiātū minācī arborem fugā petit. neque fugientī, cum potuisset, fera
īnstiterat, et prōcumbēns ad arborem hiātū quō terruerat
miserātiōnem quaerēbat. (os morsū avidiōre inhaeserat dentibus
cruciābatque inediā.) dēgressus tandem vir ē dentibus leōnis os   5
ēvellit; trāduntque quamdiū nāvis ea in lītore steterit leōnem
rettulisse grātiam vēnātūs adgerendō.

2 panthēram, quae in mediā viā iacēbat hominem exspectāns,
repente cōnspexit senex. ille pavōre coepit regredī, fera vērō
circumvolūtārī nōn dubiē blandiēns sēque cōnflīctāns dolōre quī   10
etiam in panthērā intellegī possit: fēta erat catulīs procul in foveam
dēlāpsīs. prīmum ergō miserātiōnis fuit nōn expavēscere, deinde
cūram praestāre; secūtusque quā trahēbat vestem unguium levī
iniectū, ut causam dolōris intellēxit, exēmit catulōs. deinde
panthēra, catulīs mātrem sequentibus, extrā sōlitūdinēs senem   15
dēdūxit laeta ac ita gestiēns ut facile appārēret grātiam referre.

3 hippopotamus in quādam medicīnae parte etiam magister
exsistit; nam assiduā satietāte obēsus exit in lītus ut recentēs
harundinum caesūrās speculētur atque ubi acūtissimam vīdit
stirpem imprimēns corpus vēnam quandam in crūre vulnerat.   20
itaque hippopotamus prōfluviō sanguinis morbidum aliās corpus
exonerat et vulnus līmō rūrsus obdūcit.

2b   Marvelous Animals

Perhaps the excerpts below were among those which the Elder Pliny heard and noted down while sunbathing or being scraped with a strigil. They are taken from the Elder Pliny's encyclopedic collection, called the *Natural History*, VIII.21. 57–60; 38. 92–93; 40. 96.

1   hiātū: hiātus *open jaws*
        minācī: minax *threatening*
        neque fugientī, cum potuisset, fera īnstiterat *nor had the beast harassed him when he was running away, although it could have*
        miserātiōnem: miserātiō *pity, compassion*
        morsū *because of a bite*
    5 cruciābat: cruciāre *torture, torment*
        dēgressus: dēgredī *come down*
        ēvellit: ēvellere *pull out*
        trādunt *they say, people say*
        quamdiū *as long as*
        rettulisse grātiam: referre grātiam *show gratitude, thank*
        vēnātūs: vēnātus *catch (from the hunt)*
        adgerendō *by bringing up*

2 10 circumvolūtārī (deponent) *roll over*
        nōn dubiē *undoubtedly, clearly*
        blandiēns: blandīrī *coax*
        sē . . . cōnflīctāns: sē cōnflīctāre *torment oneself*
        fēta erat *she had recently given birth*
        catulīs: catulus *cub*
        foveam: forea *pit*
        dēlāpsīs: dēlābī *fall into*
        miserātiōnis fuit *the result of his pity was*
        expavēscere *panic*
        quā *where*
        iniectū: iniectus *placing, touch*
        exēmit: eximere *get out*
    16 gestiēns: gestīre *leap for joy, gambol*

3   etiam magister exsistit *even stands out as a master, is actually a master*
        satietāte: satietās *gorging, eating one's fill*
        recentēs . . . caesūrās *recent cuttings*
        speculētur: speculārī *spy out*
    20 stirpem: stirps *stem*
        crūre: crūs *leg*
        prōfluviō: prōfluvium *flow*
        morbidum aliās corpus *body otherwise liable to disease*
        exonerat: exonerāre *unburden, relieve*
        obdūcit: obdūcere *cover over, close up*

---

4 gēns hominum est crocodīlō adversa quae in īnsulā flūminis Nīlī
habitat. (hī hominēs appellantur Tentyrītae.) mēnsūra eōrum
parva est, sed praesentia animī in hōc tantum ūsū mīra. terribilis   25
contrā fugācēs crocodīlus est, fugāx contrā sequentēs. sed
adversum īre sōlī hī audent, quī flūminī innatant, tergōque
equitantium modō impositī, hiantibus resupīnō capite ad
morsum crocodīlīs, fūstem longum in ōs īnserunt et dextrā ac
laevā tenentēs extrēma eius utrimque, fūste ut frēnīs in terram   30
agunt crocodīlōs captīvōs, ac vōce etiam sōlā perterritōs cōgunt
ēvomere recentia corpora ad sepultūram. itaque ūnī huic īnsulae
crocodīlī nōn adnatant, olfactūque Tentyrītārum fugantur.

2c   mors avunculī Plīniī

*Mount Vesuvius had begun erupting on August 24, A.D. 79. On the following
day, Pliny's uncle sailed to Stabiae to help his friend, Pomponianus. There he
calmly went to sleep while the volcano belched fire and pumice. As the danger
increased, he was awakened by his friends and walked out with them into the
hail of falling stones, but eventually was asphyxiated by the increasingly thick
fumes. His body was found on the next day (August 26).*

tunc avunculus meus ventō secundissimō invectus complectitur
trepidantem, cōnsōlātur, hortātur, utque timōrem eius suā
sēcūritāte lēnīret, dēferrī in balneum iubet: lautus accubat, cēnat
aut hilaris aut, quod est aequē magnum, similis hilarī. interim ē
Vesūviō monte plūribus locīs lātissimae flammae altaque incendia   5
relūcēbant, quōrum fulgor et clāritās tenebrīs noctis excitābātur.
ille agrestium trepidātiōne ignēs relictōs dēsertāsque vīllās per
sōlitūdinem ardēre in remedium formīdinis dictitābat. tum sē quiētī
dedit et quiēvit vērissimō quidem somnō. nam meātus animae, quī
illī propter amplitūdinem corporis gravior et sonantior erat, ab eīs,   10
quī līminī obversābantur, audiēbātur. sed ārea, ē quā diaeta
adībātur, ita iam cinere mixtīsque pūmicibus opplēta surrēxerat,
ut, sī longior in cubiculō mora, exitus negārētur. excitātus prōcēdit,
sēque Pompōniānō cēterīsque, quī pervigilāverant, reddit. in
commūne cōnsulunt, intrā tēcta subsistant an in apertō vagentur.   15
nam crēbrīs vāstīsque tremōribus tēcta nūtābant et quasi ēmōta

---

4 25 praesentia *presence*
fugācēs: fugāx *running away, fleeing*
adversum *against*
innatant: innatāre *dive in*
equitantium modō *in the manner of (persons) riding horses*
hiantibus: hiāre *open the jaws*
resupīnō: resupīnus *thrown back*
īnserunt: īnserere *insert*
extrēma eius utrimque *the ends of it* (fūstis) *on each side*
30 fūste ut frēnīs *with the stick like reins*
recentia corpora *recent bodies* (i.e. human bodies recently eaten by crocodiles)
adnatant: adnatāre *swim to*
olfactū: olfactus *smell*
fugantur: fugāre *put to flight*

2c   The Death of Pliny's Uncle

As well as describing his own experiences during the eruption of Mount
Vesuvius (see Stage 46), Pliny the nephew described his uncle Pliny's
death at Stabiae. The town of Stabiae was four miles south of Pompeii on
the Bay of Naples. At the time Pliny's uncle died, he was the commander
of the Roman naval fleet at Misenum (across the bay from Stabiae). The
account of the Elder Pliny's death is taken from the Younger Pliny's
Letters, VI. 16. 12–20.

(Pompōniānum) trepidantem (Nothing else is known about Pomponianus except
that he was the Elder Pliny's friend.)
accubat: accubāre *recline at table*
hilaris *in high spirits, merry*
6 relūcēbant: relūcēre *blaze, shine out*
fulgor *glare*
excitābātur (here =) *was heightened*
agrestium: agrestis *peasant*
per sōlitūdinem (here =) *in the abandoned area*
in remedium *as a cure*
meātus animae *movement, passage of his breath*
10 sonantior: sonāns *resounding, loud*
obversābantur: obversārī *walk to and fro*
diaeta *room* (where Pliny's uncle slept)
opplēta: opplēre *fill*
sē . . . reddit: sē reddere *return, go back*
pervigilāverant: pervigilāre *sit up all night, stay awake all night*
15 in commūne *for the general advantage, for all*
subsistant an . . . vagentur *whether they should stay or wander*
nūtābant: nūtāre *sway to and fro, shake*

sēdibus suīs nunc hūc, nunc illūc abīre aut referrī vidēbantur. sub   5
diō rūrsus quamquam levium exēsōrumque pūmicum cāsus
metuēbātur; quod tamen perīculōrum collātiō ēlēgit. et apud illum
quidem ratiō ratiōnem, apud aliōs timōrem timor vīcit. cervīcālia
capitibus imposita linteīs cōnstringunt; id mūnīmentum adversus
incidentia fuit. iam diēs alibī, illīc nox omnibus noctibus nigrior   10
dēnsiorque; quam tamen facēs multae variaque lūmina sōlābantur.
placuit ēgredī in lītus et ē proximō adspicere, ecquid iam mare
admitteret; quod adhūc vāstum et adversum manēbat. ibi super
abiectum linteum recumbēns semel atque iterum frīgidam poposcit
hausitque. deinde flammae flammārumque praenūntius odor   15
sulphuris aliōs in fugam vertunt, excitant illum. innīxus servīs
duōbus surrēxit et statim concidit, ut ego colligō, crassiōre cālīgine
spīritū obstrūctō clausōque stomachō, quī illī nātūrā invalidus et
angustus et frequenter aestuāns erat. ubi diēs redditus (is ab eō,
quem novissimē vīderat, tertius), corpus inventum est integrum,   20
illaesum opertumque, ut fuerat indūtus: habitus corporis quiēscentī
quam dēfūnctō similior.

3 Rōmānī ad montem Graupium victōrēs

After initial success, the Britons panicked and thousands were massacred by the
Romans. The scene was a shambles. The victorious Roman army and navy re-
turned south, but the Emperor Domitian was embarrassed by Agricola's success.

tum vērō patentibus locīs grande et ātrōx spectāculum: sequī,
vulnerāre, capere, atque eōsdem oblātīs aliīs trucīdāre. iam hostium
prout cuique ingenium erat, catervae armātōrum pauciōribus terga
praestāre, quīdam inermēs ultrō ruere ac sē mortī offerre. passim
arma et corpora et lacerātī artūs et cruenta humus; et aliquandō   5
etiam victīs īra virtūsque. postquam silvīs appropinquāvērunt,

(in) patentibus locīs (erat) *in the open places there was*
grande: grandis *awesome*
(nostrī) sequī *(our soldiers) pursued* (This and the other infinitives in lines 2,4, and 14–18
    should be understood as regular past-tense verbs; see p.268.)
eōsdem *the same ones,* or *the prisoners*
oblātīs aliīs *when other (enemies) were offered, appeared*

Supplementary Reading

sub dīō *under the open sky*

quamquam levium exēsōrumque *however light and porous (they might be)*

quod . . . perīculōrum collātiō ēlēgit *a comparison of the dangers decided (them on) this course* (i.e. that they should walk in the open)

apud illum *with him* (i.e. the Elder Pliny)

20 ratiō ratiōnem, . . . timōrem timor vīcit *a reason (outweighed) reason, . . . a fear outweighed fear*

linteīs: linteum *linen cloth,* (here =) *towel*

incidentia *falling objects*

omnibus noctibus *(than) all (other) nights* (For another example of this use of the ablative, see p. 312, para.6 f.)

sōlābantur: sōlārī *relieve, mitigate*

placuit *it was decided*

25 ecquid iam mare admitteret *whether the sea would now allow (them to sail)*

quod (here =) et hoc (mare) (For other examples of the connecting relative, see *Unit 3,* LI Section, p.273, paragraph 10.)

frīgidam (aquam)

odor sulphuris *smell of sulphur*

cālīgine: cālīgō (here =) *fume*

stomachō: stomachus *esophagus,* (here probably =) *windpipe*

aestuāns *inflamed* (Perhaps Pliny's uncle suffered from asthma.)

redditus = redditus est

is ab eō (diē), quem novissimē vīderat, tertius *this, from the (clear day) which he had last seen, (was) the third (day)*

quiēscentī quam dēfūnctō *to a resting (person) rather than a dead one*

3   The Romans Win at Mount Graupius

In the summer of A.D. 84, the troops of the last defiant Britons gathered, at the foot of *mōns Graupius* somewhere in northern Scotland, to fight the Roman legions commanded by Agricola. This was the last and northernmost battle in Agricola's numerous campaigns to extend the boundaries of the province Britannia. The description of the battle is taken from the biography of Agricola written by his son-in-law, the historian Tacitus, *Agricola* 37.2–39.1.

prout cuique ingenium erat *according as the inclination was for each, as each was inclined* (For possessive datives, see p.311.)

catervae: caterva *band, group, squadron*

pauciōribus *to inferior numbers*

terga praestāre *showed their backs,* i.e. *ran away from*

quīdam inermēs ultrō ruere *some disarmed (soldiers) rushed, charged of their own accord*

6 etiam victīs (Britannīs erant) *even the defeated Britons possessed* (possessive dative)

(Britannī) appropinquāvērunt

---

prīmōs sequentium incautōs collēctī et locōrum gnārī circumveniēbant. cēterum ubi compositōs firmīs ōrdinibus sequī rūrsus vīdēre, in fugam versī, nōn agminibus, ut prius, nec alius alium respectantēs, rārī et vītābundī invicem longinqua atque āvia petiēre. fīnis sequendī nox et satietās fuit. caesa hostium ad decem   5
mīlia: nostrōrum trecentī sexāgintā cecidēre.

et nox quidem gaudiō praedāque laeta victōribus: Britannī errantēs mixtōque virōrum mulierumque plōrātū trahere vulnerātōs, vocāre integrōs, dēserere domōs ac per īram ultrō incendere, ēligere latebrās et statim relinquere; miscēre invicem   10
cōnsilia, deinde sēparāre; aliquandō frangī aspectū pignorum suōrum, saepius concitārī. satisque cōnstābat saevīsse quōsdam in coniugēs ac līberōs, tamquam miserērentur. proximus diēs faciem victōriae lātius aperuit: vāstum ubīque silentium, dēsertī collēs, fūmantia procul tēcta, nēmō explōrātōribus obvius. quibus in   15
omnem partem dīmissīs, Agricola in fīnēs Borestōrum exercitum dēdūcit. ibi acceptīs obsidibus, praefectō classis circumvehī Britanniam praecipit. ipse peditēs atque equitēs lentō itinere, quō novārum gentium animī ipsā trānsitūs morā terrērentur, in hībernīs locāvit. et simul classis secundā tempestāte ac fāmā Trucculēnsem   20
portum tenuit.

hunc rērum cursum, quamquam nūllā verbōrum iactantiā epistulīs Agricolae auctum, ut Domitiānō mōris erat, fronte laetus, pectore anxius excēpit. inerat cōnscientia dērīsuī fuisse nūper falsum ē Germāniā triumphum, ēmptīs per commercia, quōrum   25
habitūs et crīnēs in captīvōrum speciem fōrmārentur: at nunc vēram magnamque victōriam tot mīlitibus hostium caesīs ingentī fāmā celebrārī.

---

    sequentium: sequī *of those following, of the pursuers*
    collēctī *having been gathered, having rallied*
    gnārī: gnārus *having knowledge of, familiar with*
    cēterum *but*
    (Rōmānōs) compositōs *reunited, reorganized*
    vīdēre = vīdērunt (see p.193)
10 alius alium respectantēs *one keeping an eye on the other, keeping an eye on each other*
    rārī et vītābundī invicem *far apart and avoiding each other*
    longinqua et āvia (loca) *distant and pathless places*
    petiēre = petiērunt, *or* petīvērunt
    sequendī *of the pursuing, of the pursuit*

satietās (here =) *disgust, weariness (with killing)*
caesa (sunt)
ad *up to, about*
nostrōrum (mīlitum Rōmānōrum)
nox (erat) . . . laeta
16 miscēre invicem cōnsilia *shared plans together*
sēparāre (cōnsilia) *broke off their planning*
frangī *they were broken, their hearts were broken*
pignorum: pignus *hostage*, (or in pl. =) *children*
concitārī: concitāre *rouse to anger, enrage*
in (here =) *against*
miserērentur: miserērī *pity*
21 fūmantia: fūmāre *smoke*
nēmō explōrātōribus obvius *no one encountering spies*
fīnēs *territory*
Borestōrum: Borestī *the Boresti people* (who lived on the coast near the battlefield)
praefectō classis: praefectus classis *admiral of the fleet*
circumvehī (deponent) *sail around*
praecipit: praecipere *give instructions to* (The fleet which had been backing up Agricola's land-forces was to sail south.)
ipse *himself*, or *Agricola*
lentō: lentus *slow*
quō = ut *in order that*
25 novārum gentium *of new(-ly conquered) tribes*
trānsitūs: trānsitus *crossing*, (here =) *march*
morā: mora *slow pace*
hībernīs: hīberna (castra) *winter camp*
locāvit: locāre *place*
secundā tempestāte *with favorable weather*
fāmā: fāma *reputation*
Trucculēnsem portum: Trucculēnsis portus *Trucculensian Port* (possibly somewhere on the southeastern coast of England)
tenuit: tenēre *hold, occupy*, (here =) *reach*
iactantiā: iactantia *boasting*
auctum: augēre *increase, exaggerate*
ut Domitiānō mōris erat *as was Domitian's custom*
fronte: frōns *outward appearance*
30 (Domitiānus) excēpit
inerat cōnscientia dērīsuī fuisse *there was (in Domitian's heart) the knowledge that (recently his sham triumph over the Germans) had been a joke* (Domitian had won a campaign against the Germanic Chatti in A.D.83 and celebrated his victory in Rome the next year (see *Unit 4* "cōnsilium Domitiānī," p.42, lines 5–11).
(servīs) ēmptīs *when slaves were bought* (They were masqueraded, with their hair bleached, as blond German prisoners of war.)
fōrmārentur: fōrmāre *fashion, shape*
fāmā: fāma (here =) *success*

4a   mōrēs imperātōris Domitiānī

Domitian in his youth had been handsome, but later suffered from baldness, a paunch, and spindly legs. Although he was a skilled archer, he generally disliked exercise. Although he restocked burned-out libraries with manuscripts copied from those in Alexandria, he generally disliked reading or scholarship. He enjoyed dice, ate simple dinners, and strolled alone afterwards.

statūrā fuit prōcērā, vultū modestō rubōrisque plēnō, grandibus
oculīs, vērum aciē hebetiōre; praetereā pulcher ac decēns, maximē
in iuventā, et quidem tōtō corpore, exceptīs pedibus, quōrum
digitōs restrictiōrēs habēbat; posteā calvitiō quoque dēfōrmis et
obēsitāte ventris et crūrum gracilitāte, quae tamen eī valetūdine   5
longā remacruerant. commendārī sē verēcundiā ōris adeō sentiēbat,
ut apud senātum sīc quondam iactāverit: "usque adhūc certē et
animum meum probāvistis et vultum." calvitiō ita offendēbātur, ut
in contumēliam suam traheret, sī cui aliī iocō vel iūrgiō
obiectārētur, quamvīs libellō, quem dē cūrā capillōrum ad amīcum   10
ēdidit, haec etiam, simul illum sēque cōnsōlāns, īnseruerit: "eadem
mē manent capillōrum fāta, et fortī animō ferō comam in
adulēscentiā senēscentem." labōris impatiēns, pedibus per urbem
nōn temerē ambulāvit, in expedītiōne et agmine equō rārius, lectīcā
assiduē vectus est. armōrum nūllō, sagittārum vel praecipuō studiō   15
tenēbātur. centēnās variī generis ferās saepe in Albānō sēcessū
cōnficientem spectāvēre plērīque, atque etiam ita quārundam
capita fīgentem, ut duōbus ictibus quasi cornua efficeret.
nōnnumquam in puerī procul stantis dispānsam dextrae manūs
palmam, sagittās tantā arte dīrēxit, ut omnēs per intervalla   20
digitōrum innocuē ēvāderent.

līberālia studia imperiī initiō neglēxit, quamquam bibliothēcās
incendiō   cōnsūmptās   impēnsissimē   reficere   cūrāvisset,

prōcērā: prōcērus *tall*
rubōris: rubor *high color*
vērum *but*
aciē hebetiōre *with rather poor sight*
iuventā: iuventa *youth*
digitōs restrictiōrēs *rather pinched toes, toes which were somewhat bent in on themselves*
  (Abnormalities of the toes were quite noticeable in a society which wore open
  sandals.)

4a   The Lifestyle of the Emperor Domitian

When the Emperor Domitian began his rule in A.D.81, he was a handsome and ambitious young man. Diseases and disappointments, however, deformed both his body and spirit. His habits were described by the historian Suetonius, in his *Life of Domitian*, 18–21

calvitiō: calvitium *baldness*
dēfōrmis (erat) *he was disfigured, his looks were spoiled*
5 obēsitāte: obēsitās *corpulence, fatness*
gracilitāte: gracilitās *thinness*
valetūdine: valetūdō *ill-health, sickness*
remacruerant: remacrēscere *shrink into thinness, become spindly* (Perhaps Domitian had suffered from poliomyelitis.)
verēcundiā: verēcundia *shyness*
in contumēliam suam traheret *he took it as an insult to himself*
cui aliī *to anyone else*
obiectārētur: obiectāre *ascribe*
10 quamvīs . . . īnseruerit *although . . . he inserted*
ēdidit: ēdere *dedicate*
comam: coma *hair*
adulēscentiā: adulēscentia *youth*
senēscentem: senēscere *grow old*
nōn temerē *rarely, not without good reason*
rārius: rārō *rarely, seldom*
assiduē *normally, usually*
15 armōrum nūllō (studiō) . . . tenēbātur *was attracted* (literally *held*) *by no enthusiasm for arms*
sagittārum vel praecipuō studiō *but by a special enthusiasm for arrows*
centēnās: centēnī *a hundred at a time*
in Albānō sēcessū *in his Alban retreat* (The Alban hills were several miles southeast of Rome.)
cōnficientem (Domitiānum)
fīgentem: fīgere *pierce*
ut duōbus ictibus . . . efficeret *that with two shots he made (the arrows look) like horns*
dispānsam: dispandere *spread out*
20 in puerī . . . palmam sagittās . . . dīrēxit
innocuē *harmlessly*
līberālia studia *liberal studies* (i.e. the subjects studied by well-to-do Roman citizens, especially rhetoric and literature; see *Unit 1*, Stage 10 and *Unit 4*, Stage 39.)
bibliothēcās incendiō cōnsūmptās *libraries destroyed by fire* (Because a disastrous fire had gutted Rome the year before Domitian came to power, he had to supervise the rebuilding of many civic structures.)
impēnsissimē: impēnse *at great cost*

exemplāribus undique petītīs, missīs Alexandrīam quī dēscrīberent
ēmendārentque. numquam tamen aut historiae carminibusve
studendīs operam ūllam dedit. praeter commentāriōs et ācta Tiberiī
Caesaris nihil legēbat; epistulās ōrātiōnēsque et ēdicta aliēnō
fōrmābat ingeniō. sermōnis tamen nec inēlegantis, dictōrum   5
interdum etiam notābilium.

    quotiēns ōtium esset, aleā sē dēlectābat, etiam profēstīs diēbus
mātūtīnīsque hōrīs, ac lavābat dē diē prandēbatque ad satietātem
ut nōn temerē super cēnam praeter mālum et modicam
pōtiunculam sūmeret. ad hōram somnī nihil aliud quam sōlus   10
sēcrētō ambulābat.

> exemplāribus undique petītīs *prototypes* (manuscripts which could be copied) *were*
>   *sought everywhere*
> 25 missīs Alexandrīam quī dēscrīberent ēmendārentque *(persons) were sent to Alexandria*
>   *who could copy and correct* (On the Museum and Great Library at Alexandria, see
>   *Unit 2*, pp.154–59.)
> historiae carminibusve studendīs *to studying (books of) history or poems*

4b   mors imperātōris Domitiānī

*Domitian was worried about the likelihood of his assassination. He responded
by installing reflecting walls in his colonnades and having Epaphroditus and
Flavius Clemens executed. Omens further frightened him: lightning storms, a
bad dream about the goddess Minerva, and especially the death-prophecy of the
astrologer Ascletarion.*

    *On the fateful day, Domitian was lured to his bedroom, where, after a
struggle, he was killed by the conspirator Stephanus. The emperor's body was
then cremated by his old nurse, named Phyllis.*

tempore suspectī perīculī appropinquante, sollicitior in diēs,
porticuum, in quibus ambulāre cōnsuēverat, parietēs phengīte
lapide distīnxit, ut eius splendōre per imāginēs quidquid ā tergō
fieret prōvidēret. utque ministrīs persuādēret, nē bonō quidem
exemplō audendam esse patrōnī necem, Epaphrodītum ā libellīs   5
capitālī poenā damnāvit, quod post dēstitūtiōnem Nerō in
adipīscendā morte manū eius adiūtus esse exīstimābātur. dēnique
Flāvium Clēmentem adfīnem suum, virum contemptissimae
inertiae, cuius fīliōs etiam tum parvōs successōrēs palam

commentāriōs et ācta Tiberiī Caesaris *notebooks and (official) records of Tiberius Caesar*
(The earlier Emperor Tiberius, like Domitian, had lost popularity towards the
end of his reign and gradually withdrawn from public life.)
ēdicta: ēdictum *edict, policy statement, regulation*
aliēnō . . . ingeniō *by another's talent* (Domitian depended on secretaries and
speechwriters.)
sermōnis . . ., . . . dictōrum (fuit) *he was a man of . . ., . . .*
dictōrum: dictum *saying*
interdum *sometimes, occasionally*
notābilium: notābilis *noteworthy, memorable*
30 profēstīs: profēstus *working, not kept as a holiday*
mātūtīnīs: mātūtīnus *morning*
dē diē *before midday*
prandēbat: prandēre *lunch, have lunch*
super cēnam praeter *more for dinner than*
mālum *apple*
pōtiunculam: pōtiuncula *little drink*
nihil aliud (faciēbat) quam
sēcrētō *in solitude, in secret*

4b The Death of the Emperor Domitian

The Emperor Domitian, gradually lost what little popularity he had
once commanded. In A.D.96, he was assassinated in his palace.
Domitian's death was described by the historian Suetonius in his *Life of
Domitian*, 14–17.

suspectī: suspicere *suspect*
cōnsuēverat *he was accustomed, it was his habit to*
parietēs phengīte lapide distīnxit *set off, veneered the walls with (shiny) onyx-like stone*
splendōre: splendor *brightness, brilliance*
prōvidēret (here =) *see in front*
5 nē bonō quidem exemplō audendam esse patrōnī necem *that the murder of a patron
should not be attempted (dared) even with a good precedent* (Epaphroditus was said to
have held the sword on which the Emperor Nero threw himself on purpose and
died (see *Unit 3*, p.258).)
ā libellīs (lībertum) *his private secretary*
capitālī poenā damnāvit *he condemned to death*
dēstitūtiōnem: dēstitūtiō *deserting, abandoning*
in adipīscendā morte *in obtaining death, in taking his life*
adiūtus esse: adiuvāre *help*
successōrēs: successor *successor*
palam *openly*

dēstināverat et, abolitō priōre nōmine, alterum Vespasiānum appellārī iusserat, alterum Domitiānum, repente ex tenuissimā suspīciōne tantum nōn in ipsō eius cōnsulātū necāvit. quō maximē factō mātūrāvit sibi exitium.

continuīs octō mēnsibus tot fulgura facta nūntiātaque sunt, ut   5
exclāmāverit, "feriat iam, quem volet!" tāctum dē caelō Capitōlium templumque Flāviae gentis, item domus Palātīna et cubiculum ipsīus, atque etiam ē basī statuae triumphālis titulus excussus vī procellae in monumentum proximum dēcidit.

Minervam, quam superstitiōsē colēbat, somniāvit excēdere   10
sacrāriō negantemque ultrā sē tuērī eum posse, quod exarmāta esset ā Iove. nūllā tamen rē perinde commōtus est, quam respōnsō cāsūque Asclētāriōnis mathēmaticī. hunc dēlātum nec īnfitiantem, sē iactāvisse quae prōvīdisset ex arte, rogātus est, quis ipsum manēret exitus; et affirmantem canēs sē lacerātūrōs esse, interficī   15
quidem sine morā imperāvit Domitiānus. quod cum fieret, ēvēnit ut, repentīnā tempestāte dēiectō fūnere, sēmiustum corpus discerperent canēs.

prīdiē quam perīret Domitiānus, conversus ad proximōs, "crās," inquit, "lūna sē in Aquāriō cruentābit factumque aliquod exsistet,   20
dē quō loquentur hominēs per terrārum orbem." at circā mediam noctem ita est exterritus ut ē lectō prōsilīret. dēhinc māne haruspicem ē Germāniā missum, quī cōnsultus dē fulgure mūtātiōnem rērum praedīxerat, audīvit damnāvitque. ac dum exulcerātam in fronte verrūcam vehementius scalpit, prōfluente   25
sanguine, "utinam," inquit, "hāctenus." tunc hōrās requīrentī prō quīntā, quam metuēbat, sexta ex industriā nūntiāta est. hīs velut trānsāctō iam perīculō laetum festīnantem ad corporis cūram Parthenius cubiculō praepositus convertit, nūntiāns esse aliquem

10 dēstināverat: dēstināre *mark out as, name as*
    abolitō: abolēre *abolish*
    tantum nōn in ipsō eius cōnsulātū *only just not in his very consulship, immediately at the end of his consulship* (in A.D.95)
    maximē *in particular*
    mātūrāvit: mātūrāre *hasten*
15 "feriat iam, quem volet!" *"Now let him (Jupiter) strike whom he will!"*
    templum . . . Flāviae gentis *temple of the Flavian family* (The family of Domitian, Titus, and their father Vespasian. Domitian built this temple on the site of the house on the Quirinal where he was born.)

cubiculum ipsīus *bedroom of (the emperor) himself*
basī: basis *base, pedestal*
triumphālis *triumphal*
procellae: procella *violent wind*
in monumentum proximum *onto a tomb very close by* (The inscription's fall-place was
    ill-omened.)
superstitiōsē *superstitiously, with superstitious reverence*
colēbat: colere *worship*
somniāvit: somniāre *dream*
excēdere *come out of*
20 sacrāriō: sacrārium *shrine*
exarmāta esset: exarmāre *disarm*
perinde . . . quam *as much . . . as*
cāsū: cāsus *fate*
mathēmaticī: mathēmaticus (here =) *astrologer*
īnfitiantem: īnfitiārī (deponent) *deny*
sē iactāvisse (ea) quae prōvīdisset ex arte *that he had spoken what he had foreseen by his
    skill.*
quis . . . exitus *what death*
affirmantem (Asclētāriōnem)
26 repentīnā: repentīnus *sudden*
dēiectō fūnere *when the funeral pyre had been thrown down*
sēmiustum: sēmiustus *half-burned*
discerperent: discerpere *tear in pieces, mangle*
prīdiē quam perīret *the day before he perished*
in Aquāriō *in Aquarius* (one of the signs of the Zodiac)
cruentābit: cruentāre *stain with blood*
exsistet: exsistere *stand out, emerge*
dēhinc (here =) *accordingly*
mūtātiōnem: mūtātiō *change*
exulcerātam: exulcerātus *festering*
fronte: frōns *forehead*
verrūcam: verrūca *wart*
dum . . . scalpit *while he was scratching* (For other examples of *dum* with the present
    indicative, see p.000.)
prōfluente: prōfluere *flow, flow out*
35 "utinam . . . hāctenus" *"Would it were so much," "I hope this is all the blood I shed"*
prō quīntā (hōrā) *instead of the fifth hour*
ex industriā *on purpose*
hīs . . . laetum *happy with these things*
trānsāctō: trānsigere *end*
festīnantem ad corporis cūram . . . convertit *diverted him as he was hurrying to his siesta*
    (literally *the care of his body*)
Parthenius *Parthenius* (another highly placed ex-slave of Greek origin (cf.
    Epaphroditus above))
cubiculō praepositus *(the man) put in charge of the bedroom* (an important official with a
    large staff and in close touch with the emperor)

---

quī magnum nescio quid afferret, nec differendum. itaque summōtīs   30
omnibus in cubiculum sē recēpit atque ibi occīsus est.

dē īnsidiārum caedisque genere haec ferē dīvulgāta sunt.
cūnctantibus cōnspīrātīs, quandō et quō modō, id est lavantemne
an cēnantem aggrederentur, Stephanus, Domitillae prōcūrātor et
tunc interceptārum pecūniārum reus, cōnsilium operamque   35
obtulit. ac sinistrō bracchiō velut aegrō lānīs fasciīsque per aliquot
diēs ad āvertendam suspīciōnem obvolūtō, ad ipsam hōram
dolōnem interiēcit; professusque cōnspīrātiōnis indicium et ob hoc
admissus imperātōrī legentī trāditum ā sē libellum et attonitō
suffōdit inguina. vulnerātum ac resistentem adortī Clōdiānus   40
corniculārius et Maximus Parthenī lībertus et Satur decuriō
cubiculāriōrum et quīdam ē gladiātōriō lūdō vulneribus septem
trucīdāvērunt. puer, quī cūrae Larum cubiculī ex cōnsuētūdine
adsistēns interfuit caedī, hoc amplius nārrābat, sē iussum esse ā
Domitiānō ad prīmum statim vulnus pugiōnem sub pulvīnō   45
cēlātum porrigere ac ministrōs vocāre, neque ad caput quidquam
exceptō capulō et praetereā clausa omnia repperisse; atque illum
interim correptō dēductōque ad terram cum Stephanō lūctātum
esse diū, dum modo ferrum extorquēre, modo quamquam lacerātīs
digitīs oculōs effodere cōnātur.   50

occīsus est xiv ante Kalendās Octōbrēs, annō aetātis
quadrāgēsimō quīntō, imperiī quīntō decimō. corpus eius populārī
sandapilā per vespillōnēs exportātum Phyllis nūtrīx in suburbānō
suō Latīnā viā fūnerāvit, sed reliquiās templō Flāviae gentis clam
intulit cineribusque Iūliae Titī fīliae, quam et ipsam ēducāverat,   55
commiscuit.

nescio quid *an "I-don't-know-what," something*
nec differendum *nor could he be put off*
summōtīs: summovēre *dismiss, remove*
41 haec ferē *the following generally*
dīvulgāta sunt: dīvulgāre *make known, divulge*
cunctantibus cōnspīrātīs *while the conspirators were hesitating, debating*
. . .ne . . . aggrederentur *whether they would attack*
Stephanus *Stephanus* (another ex-slave of Greek origin)
Domitillae prōcūrātor *manager of Domitilla's household affairs* (This Domitilla was
    probably the niece of Domitian.)
interceptārum pecūniārum reus *accused of stealing money*

45 lānīs: lāna *wool*

aliquot *some, several*

sinistrō bracchiō . . . obvolūtō *with his left arm wrapped up*

ad ipsam hōram *until the precise hour* (i.e. the fifth hour of the day when Domitian was forecast to be killed)

dolōnem: dolō *dagger, stiletto*

interiēcit: intericere *insert, hide inside*

professus *declaring, claiming to have*

cōnspīrātiōnis: cōnspīrātiō *conspiracy*

imperātōrī . . . suffōdit inguina *he stabbed the groin of* (literally *for*) *the emperor*

libellum: libellus *little book* (cf. *liber*. The notebook supposedly contained evidence of a conspiracy different from the one Stephanus was implementing.)

adortī: adorīrī *assault, attack*

Clōdiānus corniculārius *Clodianus, a staff-officer*

50 Satur decuriō cubiculāriōrum *Satyr, supervisor of the emperor's bedroom-attendants* (one of the officials under Parthenius)

quīdam ē gladiātōriō lūdō *some man from a gladiators' (training) camp*

cūrae Larum cubiculī . . . adsistēns *assisting the worship* (literally *care*) *of the bedroom Lares* (The Lares were statuettes of guardian spirits; see *Unit 1 Workbook*, p.20.)

interfuit: interesse *be present at*

ad prīmum . . . vulnus *at the first wound, when he was first stabbed*

pulvīnō: pulvīnus *pillow*

55 porrigere *hand to*

ad caput *at the head (of the bed)*

exceptō capulō *except the handle* (The conspirators had removed the blade in case the emperor called for or used the dagger.)

illum = *the emperor*

extorquēre *wrest away*

effodere *gouge out*

60 xiv ante Kalendās Octōbrēs *on the 14th day before the Kalends (= 1st) of October, on 18th September*

quadrāgēsimō: quadrāgēsimus *40th*

populārī sandapilā *on an ordinary bier* (portable stand on which the bodies of the poor were taken to funerals)

per vespillōnēs *by public undertakers* (Romans as wealthy as an emperor would usually have been buried by private undertakers.)

exportātum: exportāre *carry out*

nūtrīx *nurse*

in suburbānō suō *in her own suburban home* (An emperor would normally have received a state funeral.)

fūnerāvit: fūnerāre *cremate*

Iuliae Titī filiae *of Julia, daughter of (the Emperor) Titus* (Domitian's niece; Domitian was rumored to have had an incestuous affair with her.)

ēducāverat: ēducāre *bring up, rear*

65 commiscuit: commiscēre *mingle with*

PART FOUR: Complete Vocabulary

1   Nouns, adjectives, verbs, and prepositions are listed as in the Unit 3 Language Information Section.

2   Verbs and adjectives which are often used with a noun or pronoun in the *dative* or *ablative* case are marked + *dat.* or + *abl.*

For example: careō, carēre, caruī + *abl. lack*
                 dignus, digna, dignum + *abl. worthy*
                 obstō, obstāre, obstitī + *dat. obstruct*
                 similis, simile + *dat. similar*
                 ūtor, ūtī, ūsus sum + *abl. use*

pecūniā carēbam.	*I lacked money, I had no money.*
dignus ingentī praemiō	*worthy of a huge reward*
custōdēs nōbīs obstābant.	*The guards were obstructing us.*
similis patrī meō	*similar to my father, like my father*
gladiīs brevibus ūtēbantur.	*They were using short swords.*

3   The *present* tense of *second* conjugation verbs like **doceō** has the same endings (except in the 1st person singular) as the *future* tense of *third* and *fourth* conjugation verbs like **trahō**, **capiō**, and **audiō**: **-ēs**, **-et**, etc. in the active, and **-ēris**, **-ētur**, etc. in the passive. Pages 294-95 can be used to check which conjugation a verb belongs to, and thus translate its tense properly.

For example, the conjugation and tense of **iubent** can be checked in the following way:

The verb is listed on p.376 as **iubeō**, **iubēre**, etc., so it belongs to the second conjugation like **doceō**, **docēre**, etc., and therefore **iubent** must be in the present tense: *they order.*

And the conjugation and tense of **dūcent** can be checked like this:

The verb is listed on p.367 as **dūcō**, **dūcere**, etc., so it belongs to the third conjugation like **trahō**, **trahere**, etc., and therefore **dūcent** must be in the future tense: *they will lead.*

Translate the following words, using pages 294-95 to check conjugation and tense:

1 rīdēs, intellegēs	4 convertet, ignōscet
2 pendent, venient	5 prohibentur, regentur
3 gaudēmus, monēmus	6 dūcēris, iubēris

4 Notice again the difference between the listed forms of deponent verbs and the forms of ordinary verbs:

deponent verbs
cōnor, cōnārī,
   cōnātus sum *try*
loquor, loquī,
   locūtus sum *speak*

ordinary verbs
colloco, collocāre, collocāvī,
   collocātus *place, put*
vēndō, vēndere, vēndidī,
   vēnditus *sell*

Pages 303–6 can be used to check whether a word with a passive ending (e.g. **ēgrediuntur, custōdiuntur**) comes from a deponent verb or not.

For example, **ēgrediuntur** comes from a verb which is listed as **ēgredior, ēgredī, ēgressus sum** *go out*. It is clear from the listed forms that **ēgredior** is a *deponent* verb; it therefore has an *active* meaning, and **ēgrediuntur** must mean *they go out*.

custōdiuntur, on the other hand, comes from a verb which is listed as **custōdiō, custōdīre, custōdīvī, custōdītus** *guard*. It is clear from the listed forms that **custōdiō** is *not* a deponent verb; **custōdiuntur** must therefore have a *passive* meaning, i.e. *they are being guarded*.

5 Translate the following sentences, using pages 303–6 to check whether the words in boldface are deponent verbs or not:

1 centuriō mīlitēs **hortābātur**.
2 amīcus meus ab Imperātōre **commendābātur**.
3 cūr dē fortūnā tuā semper **quereris**?
4 cūr ā dominō tuō semper **neglegeris**?
5 puer dē perīculō **monitus est**.
6 mercātor multās gemmās facile **adeptus est**.

6 All words which are given in the "Words and Phrases Checklists" for Stages 1–48 are marked with an asterisk.

a

A. = Aulus

*ā, ab +*abl.* from; by

ā libellīs *in charge of petitions to the Emperor, private secretary*

abdūcō, abdūcere, abdūxī, abductus *lead away*

*abeō, abīre, abiī *go away*

abiciō, abicere, abiēcī, abiectus *throw away, throw down*

abnuō, abnuere, abnuī *refuse*

aboleō, abolēre, abolēvī, abolitus *abolish*

abripiō, abripere, abripuī, abreptus *tear away from, remove by force*

abrumpō, abrumpere, abrūpī, abruptus *split, tear apart*

absēns, *gen.* absentis *absent*

abstineō, abstinēre, abstinuī *abstain*

abstulī *see* auferō

*absum, abesse, āfuī *be out, be absent, be away*

absurdus, absurda, absurdum *absurd*

*ac *and*

accēdō, accēdere, accessī *go up, approach*

accēnsus, accēnsa, accēnsum *inflamed, on fire*

*accidō, accidere, accidī *happen*

*accipiō, accipere, accēpī, acceptus *accept, take in, receive*

accommodō, accommodāre, accommodāvī, accommodātus *fasten*

accubō, accubāre, accubuī *recline at table*

accurrō, accurrere, accurrī *run up*

accūsātiō, accūsātiōnis, f. *accusation*

accūsātor, accūsātōris, m. *accuser, prosecutor*

*accūsō, accūsāre, accūsāvī, accūsātus *accuse*

ācer, ācris, ācre *eager, excited*

aciēs, aciēī, f. *sight, eyesight*

*ācriter *keenly, eagerly, fiercely*

ācta, āctōrum, n.pl. *official records*

āctus *see* agō

acūtus, acūta, acūtum *sharp*

*ad +*acc.* to, at, up to, about

ad convalēscendum *in order to get better*

ad praesēns *for the present, for the moment*

ad vigilandum *for keeping watch*

*addō, addere, addidī, additus *add*

addere gradum *go forward step by step*

addūcō, addūcere, addūxī, adductus *lead, lead on, encourage, pull, draw up (to the chest)*

adēmptus, adēmpta, adēmptum *taken away*

*adeō, adīre, adiī *approach, go up to*

*adeō *so much, so greatly*

trēs adeō *as many as three, three entire*

adeptus *see* adipīscor

adest, adfuī *see* adsum

adfīnis, adfīnis, m. *relative, relation by marriage*

adfīnitās, adfīnitātis, f. *relationship*

adgerō, adgerere, adgessī, adgestus *bring up*

adhibeō, adhibēre, adhibuī, adhibitus *use, apply*

precēs adhibēre *offer prayers*

*adhūc *now, still*

usque adhūc *until now, up to this time*

adībō *see* adeō

*adipīscor, adipīscī, adeptus sum *receive, obtain*

*aditus, aditūs, m. *entrance*

adiūtor, adiūtōris, m. *helper*

*adiuvō, adiuvāre, adiūvī, adiūtus *help*

adligō, adligāre, adligāvī, adligātus *tie*

*adloquor, adloquī, adlocūtus sum *speak to, address*

*administrō, administrāre, administrāvī, administrātus *manage*

rem administrāre *manage the task*

admīror, admīrārī, admīrātus sum *admire*

admittō, admittere, admīsī, admissus *admit, let in, allow*

admoneō, admonēre, admonuī, admonitus *warn, advise*

adnatō, adnatāre, adnatāvī *swim to*

adnītor, adnītī, adnīxus sum *strain, exert oneself*

adnotō, adnotāre, adnotāvī, adnotātus *make notes*

adnuō, adnuere, adnuī *nod*

adorior, adorīrī, adortus sum *assault, attack*

adsistō, adsistere, adstitī *stand by (to help)*, *assist*

adspiciō, adspicere, adspexī, adspectus *see*, *investigate*

*adstō, adstāre, adstitī *stand by*, *stand*

*adsum, adesse, adfuī *be here*, *be present*, *arrive*

adsūmō, adsūmere, adsūmpsī, adsūmptus *adopt*

adulātiō, adulātiōnis, f. *flattery*

adulēscentia, adulēscentiae, f. *youth*

adulor, adulārī, adulātus sum *flatter*

aduncus, adunca, aduncum *curved*

adūrō, adūrere, adussī, adustus *burn*

*adveniō, advenīre, advēnī *arrive*

*adventus, adventūs, m. *arrival*

adversum + *acc. against*

*adversus, adversa, adversum *hostile*, *unfavorable*, *unfortunate*, *undesirable*, *opposite*

* rēs adversae *misfortune*

*adversus +*acc against*

advesperāscit, advesperāscere, advesperāvit *get dark*, *become dark*

*aedificium, aedificiī, n. *building*

*aedificō, aedificāre, aedificāvī, aedificātus *build*

*aeger, aegra, aegrum *sick*, *ill*

Aeolius, Aeolia, Aeolium *Aeolian*

aequātus, aequāta, aequātum *level*, *side by side*

aequē *equally*, *fairly*

*aequor, aequoris, n. *sea*

*aequus, aequa, aequum *equal*, *fair*, *calm*

* aequō animō *calmly*, *in a calm spirit*

aequō discrīmine *at an equal distance*

āēr, āeris, m. *air*

aerārium, aerāriī, n. *treasury*

*aestās, aestātis, f. *summer*

aestimō, aestimāre, aestimāvī, aestimātus *value*

aestuāns, *gen. aestuantis *inflamed*

aestus, aestūs, m. *heat*

aetās, aetātis, f. *age*

aetāte flōrēre *be in the prime of life*

aethēr, aetheris, m. *sky*, *heaven*

afferō, afferre, attulī, adlātus *bring*, *bring news*, *report*

*afficiō, afficere, affēcī, affectus *affect*, *treat*

affīgō, affīgere, affīxī, affīxus – *attach to*, *nail to*

cruce affīgere – *nail to a cross*, *crucify*

*affirmō, affirmāre, affirmāvī *declare*

afflīgō, afflīgere, afflīxī, afflīctus *afflict*, *hurt*, *strike*

affluō, affluere, affluxī *flock to the spot*

*ager, agrī, m. *field*

*aggredior, aggredī, aggressus sum *assail*, *attack*, *make an attempt on*

*agitō, agitāre, agitāvī, agitātus *chase*, *hunt*

*agmen, agminis, n. *column (of people)*, *procession*

*agnōscō, agnōscere, agnōvī, agnitus *recognize*

agnus, agnī, m. *lamb*

*agō, agere, ēgī, āctus *do*, *act*, *drive*

agī *move*, *roll*

* fābulam agere *act in a play*

* grātiās agere *thank*, *give thanks*

iter agere *make one's way*, *travel*

* negōtium agere *do business*, *work*

officium agere *do one's duty*

quid agis? *how are you? how are you doing?*

triumphum agere *celebrate a triumph*

vītam agere *lead a life*

agrestis, agrestis, m. *peasant*

*agricola, agricolae, m. *farmer*

ait *says*, *said*

āla, ālae, f. *wing*

alacriter *eagerly*

Albānus, Albāna, Albānum *Alban*

ālea, āleae, f. *dice*

āles, ālitis, m.f. *bird*

aliās *otherwise*

alibī *elsewhere*

aliēnus, aliēna, aliēnum *belonging to someone else*, *another's*

*aliquandō *sometimes*

aliquantō *somewhat*, *rather*

aliquī, aliqua, aliquod *some*

*aliquis, aliquid *someone*, *something*

aliquot *some*, *several*

*alius, alia, aliud *other*, *another*, *else*

aliī alia *some . . . one thing, some . . . another*, *different people . . . different things*

*aliī . . . aliī *some . . . others*

alius . . . alius *one . . . the other*

in aliud *for any other purpose*
alō, alere, aluī, altus *encourage*
altē *high*
*alter, altera, alterum *the other, another,*
  a second, the second
  alter . . . alter *one . . . the other*
  usque alter *yet another*
altum, altī, n. *deep sea, open sea*
*altus, alta, altum *high deep*
amāns, amantis, m. *lover*
*ambō, ambae, ambō *both*
*ambulō, ambulāre, ambulāvī *walk*
amīca, amīcae, f. *friend, girlfriend,*
  mistress
*amīcitia, amīcitiae, f. *friendship*
  amīcus, amīca, amīcum *friendly*
*amīcus, amīcī, m. *friend*
*āmittō, āmittere, āmīsī, āmissus *lose*
*amō, amāre, amāvī, amātus *love, like*
*amor, amōris, m. *love*
amphitheātrum, amphitheātrī, n.
  amphitheater
*amplector, amplectī, amplexus sum
  embrace, grasp, clasp
amplitūdō, amplitūdinis, f. *stoutness,*
  size
* amplius *more fully, at greater length, any*
  more
* amplissimus, amplissima,
  amplissimum *very great*
decem amplius *more than ten*
*an *or*
* utrum . . . an *whether . . . or*
*ancilla, ancillae, f. *slave-girl, slave-*
  woman
angulus, angulī, m. *corner*
*angustus, angusta, angustum *narrow*
anima, animae, f. *soul, spirit, breath*
*animadvertō, animadvertere,
  animadvertī, animadversus
  notice, take notice of
animal, animālis, n. *animal*
*animus, animī, m. *spirit, soul, mind*
* aequō animō *calmly, in a calm spirit*
  furēns animī *furiously determined, with*
  furious eagerness
* in animō volvere *wonder, turn over in the*
  mind
*annus, annī, m. *year*
*ante (1) +acc. *before, in front of*
ante (2) *before, earlier, in front*

*anteā *before*
antidotum, antiotī, n. *antidote, remedy*
*antīquus, antīqua, antīquum *old,*
  ancient
antrum, antrī, n. *cave*
*ānulus, ānulī, m. *ring*
anus, anūs, f. *old woman*
anxius, anxia, anxium *anxious*
aper, aprī, m. *boar*
*aperiō, aperīre, aperuī, apertus *open,*
  reveal
apertum, apertī, n. *the open*
*appāreō, appārēre, appāruī *appear*
*appellō, appellāre, appellāvī,
  appellātus *call, call out to*
*appropinquō, appropinquāre,
  appropinquāvī +dat. *approach, come*
  near to
*aptus, apta, aptum *suitable*
*apud +acc *among, at the house of, with*
*aqua, aquae, f. *water*
Aquae Sūlis, Aquārum Sūlis, f. pl.
  Bath (city in England)
aquaeductus, aquaeductūs, m.
  aqueduct
Aquārius, Aquāriī, m. *Aquarius*
  (sign of the zodiac)
aquilex, aquilegis, m. *water engineer,*
  hydraulic engineer
Aquilō, Aquilōnis, m. *North Wind*
*āra, ārae, f. *altar*
arātor, arātōris, m. *plowman*
arātrum, arātrī, n. *plow*
arbitror, arbitrārī, arbitrātus sum
  think
*arbor, arboris, f. *tree*
arca, arcae, f. *strong-box, chest, coffin*
*accessō, accessere, accessīvī, accessītus
  summon, send for
architectus, architectī, m. *builder,*
  architect
arcuātus, arcuāta, arcuātum *arched*
arcus, arcūs, m. *arch*
ardenter *passionately*
*ardeō, ardēre, arsī *burn, be on fire*
ardēscō, ardēscere, arsī *catch fire, blaze*
  up
ārea, āreae, f. *courtyard, construction site*
arēna, arēnae, f. *arena; sand*
*argenteus, argentea, argenteum *made*
  of silver

*arma, armōrum, n. pl. *arms, weapons*
armātus, armāta, armātum *armed*
arō, arāre, arāvī, arātus *plow*
arripiō, arripere, arripuī, arreptus
   seize
*arrogantia, arrogantiae, f. *arrogance,
   gall*
*ars, artis, f. *art, skill*
   per artem *deliberately, by design*
   artē *closely*
   artus, artūs, m. *limb*
   as, assis, m. *as (smallest Roman coin)*
*ascendō, ascendere, ascendī *climb, rise*
   ascīscō, ascīscere, ascīvī *adopt*
   asinus, asinī, m. *donkey*
   aspectus, aspectūs, m. *sight*
   asperitās, asperitātis, f. *harshness,
   bitterness*
*aspiciō, aspicere, aspexī *look towards,
   catch sight of*
   assiduē *continually, normally, usually*
   assiduus, assidua, assiduum *continual*
   assignō, assignāre, assignāvī,
   assignātus *attribute, put down to*
   astrologus, astologī, m. *astrologer*
*at *but, yet*
   āter, ātra, ātrum *black*
   Athēnae, Athēnārum, f. pl *Athens*
   āthlēta, āthlētae, m. *athlete*
*atque *and*
*ātrium, ātriī, n. *atrium, entrance room,
   hall*
   ātrōx, gen. ātrōcis *violent, horrible*
   attollō, attollere *lift, raise*
   sē attollere *raise itself, rise up*
   attollor, attolī *rise*
*attonitus, attonita, attonitum
   astonished
   attulī *see* afferō
*auctor, auctōris, m. *creator, originator,
   person responsible*
*auctōritās, auctōritātis, f. *authority*
   auctus *see* augēre
*audācia, audāciae, f. *boldness, audacity*
*audāx, gen. audācis *bold daring*
*audeō, audēre *dare*
*audiō, audīre, audīvī, audītus *hear*
   audītor, audītōris, m. *listener, (pl.)
   audience*
   audītōrium, audītōriī, n. *auditorium,
   hall (used for public readings)*

*auferō, auferre, abstulī, ablātus *take
   away, steal*
*augeō, augēre, auxī, auctus *increase,
   exaggerate*
*aula, aulae, f. *palace*
   aura, aurae, f. *breeze, air*
*aureus, aurea, aureum *golden, made of
   gold*
   aurīga, aurīgae, m. *charioteer*
*auris, auris, f. *ear*
*aurum, aurī, n. *gold*
*aut *or*
   aut . . . aut *either . . . or*
*autem *but*
   auxiliāris, auxiliāre *additional*
*auxilium, auxiliī, n. *help*
* auxiliō esse *be a help, be helpful*
*avārus, avārī, m. *miser*
   avē atque valē *hail and farewell*
   avēna, avēnae, f. *reed*
   āvertō, āvertere, āvertī, āversus *avert,
   turn away*
*avidē *eagerly*
   avidus, avida, avidum *eager*
*avis, avis, f. *bird*
   āvius, āvia, āvium *pathless*
   avunculus, avunculī, m. *uncle*
   avus, avī, m. *grandfather*
   axis, axis, m. *(arched) vault of heaven*

b

   baculum, baculī, n. *stick, staff*
   balneum, balneī, n. *bath*
   barba, barbae, f. *beard*
   barbarus, barbara, barbarum
   barbarian
*barbarus, barbarī, m. *barbarian*
   basilica, basilicae, f. *court building*
   bāsiō, bāsiāre, bāsiāvī *kiss*
   basis, basis, f. *base, pedestal*
   bāsium, bāsiī, n. *kiss*
   beātus, beāta, beātum *prosperous,
   wealthy*
*bellum, bellī, n. *war*
* bellum gerere *wage war, campaign*
   bellus, bella, bellum *pretty*
*bene *well*
   bene velle *like, be friendly*
* optimē *very well*

*beneficium, beneficiī, n. *act of kindness, favor*

benignitās, benignitātis, f. *kindness, concern, kindly interest*

*benignus, benigna, benignum *kind*

bēstia, bēstiae, f. *wild animal, beast*

bibliothēca, bibliothēcae, f. *library*

*bibō, bibere, bibī *drink*

bifurcum, bifurcī, n. *fork of the thighs, crotch*

bis *twice*

Bīthȳnī, Bīthȳnōrum, m. pl. *Bithynians*

blandior, blandīrī, blandītus sum *coax*

blanditiae, blanditiārum, f.pl. *flatteries*

*bonus, bona, bonum *good*

* bona, bonōrum, n.pl. *goods, property*

* melior, melius *better*

melius est *it would be better*

* optimus, optima, optimum *very good, excellent, best*

Boōtēs, Boōtae, m. *Herdsman (constellation)*

Borestī, Borestōrum, m.pl. *the Boresti people*

bōs, bovis, m. *ox, bull*

*bracchium, bracchiī, n. *arm*

*brevis, breve *short, brief, shallow*

breviter *briefly*

Britannī, Britannōrum, m.pl. *Britons*

Britannia, Britanniae, f. *Britain*

c

C. = Gāius

cachinnō, cachinnāre, cachinnāvī *laugh, cackle*

*cadō, cadere, cecidī *fall, die*

*caecus, caeca, caecum *blind; invisible, unseen, impenetrable*

*caedēs, caedis, f. *murder, slaughter*

*caedō, caedere, cecīdī, caesus *kill*

caelebs, caelibis, m. *widower*

*caelum, caelī, n. *sky, heaven*

caeruleus, caerulea, caeruleum *blue, from the deep blue sea, dark, dark blue, dark green*

Caesarēs, Caesarum, m.pl. *the Caesars (family of the first Roman emperors)*

caesūra, caesūrae, f. *cutting*

Calēdonia, Calēdoniae, f. *Scotland*

Calēdoniī, Calēdoniōrum, m.pl. *Caledonians (Scottish tribespeople), Scots*

cālīgō, cālīginis, f. *darkness, gloom, fume*

callidē *cleverly*

calliditās, calliditātis, f. *cleverness, shrewdness*

*callidus, callida, callidum *smart, clever, cunning, shrewd*

calvitium, calvitiī, n. *baldness*

camera, camerae, f. *ceiling*

*campus, campī, m. *plain, ground*

candēns, *gen.* candentis *gleaming white*

*candidus, candida, candidum *bright, shining, gleaming white*

*canis, canis, m. *dog*

*cantō, cantāre, cantāvī *sing, chant*

cānus, cāna, cānum *white*

capāx, *gen.* capācis *liable to, full of*

capella, capellae, f. *she-goat*

*capillī, capillōrum, m.pl. *hair*

*capiō, capere, cēpī, captus *take, catch, capture*

capitālis, capitāle *capital, death*

capitālis poena *capital punishment, death penalty*

Capitōlium, Capitōliī, n. *Capitol*

Capreae, Capreārum, f.pl. *Capri*

*captīvus, captīvī, m. *prisoner, captive*

captō, captāre, captāvī, captātus *try to catch*

capulus, capulī, m. *handle*

*caput, capitis, n. *head*

*carcer, carceris, m. *prison*

*careō, carēre, caruī + *abl.* *lack, be without*

carīna, carīnae, f. *keel, ship*

*carmen, carminis, n. *song, poem*

carnifex, carnificis, m. *executioner*

carpō, carpere, carpsī, carptus *pluck, seize, crop; hasten upon, hasten through, fly through*

*cārus, cāra, cārum *dear*

casa, casae, f. *small house, cottage*

*castīgō, castīgāre, castīgāvī, castīgātus *scold*

*castra, castrōrum, n.pl. *camp*

*cāsus, cāsūs, m. *misfortune, chance, fate; fall*

*catēna, catēnae, f. *chain*

caterva, catervae, f. *band, group, squadron*

catulus, catulī, m. *cub*

caupō, caupōnis, m. *innkeeper*

*causa, causae, f. *reason, cause; case (of law)*

  causam dīcere *plead a case*

  causam īnferre *make an excuse, invent an excuse*

*cautē *cautiously*

*caveō, cavēre, cāvī *beware*

caverna, cavernae, f. *cave, cavern*

cavō, cavāre, cavāvī, cavātus *hollow out*

cecidī *see* cadō

cecīdī *see* caedō

*cēdō, cēdere, cessī *give in, yield*

*celebrō, celebrāre, celebrāvī, celebrātus *celebrate*

*celeriter *quickly, fast*

  quam celerrimē *as quickly as possible*

*cēlō, cēlāre, cēlāvī, cēlātus *hide*

celsus, celsa, celsum *high*

*cēna, cēnae, f. *dinner*

*cēnō, cēnāre, cēnāvī *eat dinner, dine*

centēnī, centēnae, centēna *a hundred at a time*

*centum *a hundred*

*centuriō, centuriōnis, m. *centurion*

cēnula, cēnulae, f. *little supper*

cēpī *see* capiō

*cēra, cērae, f. *wax, wax tablet*

*certāmen, certāminis, n. *struggle, contest, fight*

certē *certainly, at least*

*certō, certāre, certāvī *compete*

*certus, certa, certum *certain, infallible*

* prō certō habēre *know for certain*

cervīcal, cervīcālis, n. *pillow*

*cēterī, cēterae, cētera *the others, the rest*

cēterum *but*

chorus, chorī, m. *chorus, choir*

*cibus, cibī, m. *food*

*cinis, cineris, m. *ash*

circā + *acc. around*

circuit= circumit

*circum +*acc. around*

circumeō, circumīre, circumiī *go round*

circumflectō, circumflectere, circumflexī, circumflexus *turn*

  circumflectere cursum *turn one's course around*

circummingo, circummingere, circummīnxī *urinate around*

circumsiliō, circumsilīre *hop around*

circumsistō, circumsistere, circumstetī *take up positions around*

*circumspectō, circumspectāre, circumspectāvī *look around*

circumvehor, circumvehī, circumvectus sum *sail around*

*circumveniō, circumvenīre, circumvēnī, circumventus *surround*

circumvolūtor, circumvolūtārī, circumvolūtātus sum *roll over*

circus, circī, m. *circus, stadium*

citō *quickly*

*cīvis, cīvis, m.f. *citizen*

*clādēs, clādis, f. *disaster*

*clam *secretly, in private*

*clāmō, clāmāre, clāmāvī *shout*

*clāmor, clāmōris, m. *shout, uproar*

clāritās, clāritātis, f. *brightness*

*clārus, clāra, clārum *famous, distinguished, splendid; clear, bright, loud*

classis, classis, f. *fleet*

  praefectus classis *admiral of the fleet*

*claudō, claudere, clausī, clausus *shut, close, block, conclude, complete, cut off*

clāvus, clāvī, m. *tiller, helm*

*cliēns, clientis, m. *client*

clīvus, clīvī, m. *slope*

cloāca, cloācae, f. *drain*

Cn. = Gnaeus

coāctus *see* cōgō

*coepī *I began*

coeptum, coeptī, n. *work, undertaking*

*cōgitō, cōgitāre, cōgitāvī *think, consider*

cognāta, cognātae, f. *relative (by birth)*

cognitiō, cognitiōnis, f. *trial*

  cognitiō senātūs *trial by the senate*

cognōmen, cognōminis, n. *surname, additional name*

*cognōscō, cognōscere, cognōvī, cognitus *get to know, find out*

*cōgō, cōgere, coēgī, coāctus *force, compel*

*cohors, cohortis, f. *cohort*

collātiō, collātiōnis, f. *comparison*

collēgium, collēgiī, n. *brigade, guild*

*colligō, colligere, collēgī, collēctus *gather, collect, assemble, rally; suppose, imagine*

collis, collis, m. *hill*
*colloco, collocāre, collocāvī, collocātus
  place, put
*colloquium, colloquiī, n. *talk, chat*
colloquor, colloquī, collocūtus sum
  talk, chat
collum, collī, n. *neck*
colō, colere, coluī, cultus *seek favor of,
  make friends with; worship*
colōnus, colōnī, m. *tenant-farmer*
coma, comae, f. *hair*
*comes, comitis, m.f. *comrade, companion*
cōmiter *politely, courteously*
*comitor, comitārī, comitātus sum
  accompany
*commemorō, commemorāre,
  commemorāvī, commemorātus *talk
  about, mention, recall*
*commendō, commendāre,
  commendāvī, commendātus
  recommend
commentārius, commentāriī, m.
  notebook
commercium, commerciī, n. *commercial
  transaction*
commisceō, commiscēre, commiscuī,
  commixtus *mingle with*
committō, committere, commīsī,
  commissus *commit, begin*
commodē *appropriately*
*commodus, commoda, commodum
  convenient
*commōtus, commōta, commōtum
  *moved, upset, affected, alarmed, excited,
  distressed, overcome*
commūnis, commūne *shared (by two or
  more people)*
in commūne *for the general advantage,
  for all*
*comparō, comparāre, comparāvī,
  comparātus *obtain; compare*
compellō, compellere, compulī,
  compulsus *drive, compel*
compīlō, compīlāre, compīlāvī,
  compīlātus *rob*
complector, complectī, complexus sum
  embrace
*compleō, complēre, complēvī,
  complētus *fill*
complexus, complexūs, m. *embrace*
*complūrēs, complūra *several*

*compōnō, compōnere, composuī,
  compositus *put together, arrange,
  settle, mix, compose, make up, construct,
  reunite, reorganize*
compositus, composita, compositum
  composed, steady
*comprehendō, comprehendere,
  comprehendī, comprehēnsus *arrest,
  seize*
compulsus *see* compellō
cōnātur *see* cōnor
concavus, concava, concavum *hollow*
concidō, concidere, concidī *collapse*
concipiō, concipere, concēpī,
  conceptus *take*
  concipere flammās *burst into flames*
concitō, concitāre, concitāvī,
  concitātus *rouse to anger, enrage*
conclāve, conclāvis, n. *room*
condiciō, condiciōnis, f. *status*
condō, condere, condidī, conditus
  hide, bury
sē condere *bring oneself to rest*
*condūcō, condūcere, condūxī,
  conductus *hire*
cōnfarreātiō, cōnfarreātiōnis, f.
  marriage ceremony
*cōnficiō, cōnficere, cōnfēcī, cōnfectus
  finish, finish off, murder
* cōnfectus, cōnfecta, cōnfectum
  finished, worn out, exhausted, overcome
*cōnfīdō, cōnfīdere + dat *trust, put trust;
  be sure, be confident*
cōnfīgō, cōnfīgere, cōnfīxī, cōnfīxus
  stab, skewer
cōnflīctō, cōnflīctāre, cōnflīctāvī,
  cōnflīctātus *strike violently*
sē cōnflīctāre *torment oneself*
*coniciō, conicere, coniēcī, coniectus
  hurl, throw
*coniungō, coniungere, coniūnxī,
  coniūnctus *join*
*coniūnx, coniugis, f. *wife*
*coniūrātiō, coniūrātiōnis, f. *plot,
  conspiracy*
*coniūrō, coniūrāre, coniūrāvī,
  coniūrātus *plot, conspire*
*cōnor, cōnārī, cōnātus sum *try*
*cōnscendō, cōnscendere, cōnscendī
  climb on, embark on, go on board, mount

cōnscientia, cōnscientiae, f. *awareness, knowledge*

cōnscīscō, cōnscīscere, cōnscīvī *inflict*
mortem sibi cōnscīscere *commit suicide*

cōnscius, cōnsciī, m. *accomplice, member of the plot*

cōnsecrō, cōnsecrāre, cōnsecrāvī,
cōnsecrātus *dedicate*

cōnsēnsus, cōnsēnsūs, m. *agreement*

*cōnsentiō, cōnsentīre, cōnsēnsī *agree*

cōnsequor, cōnsequī, cōnsecūtus sum
follow, chase

cōnsīderātus, cōnsīderāta,
cōnsīderātum *careful, well-considered*

cōnsīdō, cōnsīdere, cōnsēdī *sit down*

*cōnsilium, cōnsiliī, n. *plan, idea, advice; council*

*cōnsistō, cōnsistere, cōnstitī *stand one's ground, stand firm, halt, stop*

cōnsōlor, cōnsōlārī, cōnsōlātus sum
console

cōnspectus, cōnspectūs, m. *sight*

*cōnspiciō, cōnspicere, cōnspexī,
cōnspectus *catch sight of*

*cōnspicor, cōnspicārī, cōnspicātus sum
catch sight of

cōnspīrātī, cōnspīrātōrum, m.pl.
conspirators

cōnspīrātiō, cōnspīrātiōnis, f.
conspiracy

cōnstat, cōnstāre, cōnstitit *be agreed*

* satis cōnstat *it is generally agreed*

*cōnstituō, cōnstituere, cōnstituī,
cōnstitūtus *decide; set up, place*

cōnstringō, cōnstringere, cōnstrīnxī,
cōnstrictus *tie down*

cōnsuēscō, cōnsuēscere, cōnsuēvī
become accustomed

cōnsuēvī *I am accustomed, it is my habit to*

cōnsuētūdō, cōnsuētūdinis, f. *custom*

*cōnsul, cōnsulis, m. *consul (highest elected official of Roman government)*

cōnsulāris, cōnsulāris, m. *ex-consul*

*cōnsulātus, cōnsulātūs, m. *the office of consul, consulship*

*cōnsulō, cōnsulere, cōnsuluī,
cōnsultus *consult, take thought for, give consideration to*

*cōnsūmō, cōnsūmere, cōnsūmpsī,

cōnsūmptus *eat, destroy*

cōnsurgō, cōnsugere, cōnsurrēxī *jump up*

*contemnō, contemnere, contempsī,
contemptus *reject, despise, disregard*

contemptus, contempta, contemptum
despicable

*contendō, contendere, contendī *hurry*

*contentus, contenta, contentum
satisfied

contineō, continēre, contigī,
contāctus *touch*

contigit nōbis ut . . . *it was our good fortune that . . ., we had the good fortune to . . .*

continuō *immediately*

continuus, continua, continuum
continuous, on end

*contrā (1) +acc. *against*

contrā (2) *in reply, opposite, in the opposite direction, on the other hand*

contrahō, contrahere, contrāxī,
contractus *draw together, bring together, assemble*

supercilia contrahere *draw eyebrows together, frown*

contrārius, contrāria, contrārium
opposite, contrary

contumēlia, contumēliae, f. *insult, abuse*

conturbō, conturbāre, conturbāvī,
conturbātus *mix up, lose count of*

contus, contī, m. *pole, rod*

convalēscō, convalēscere, convaluī
get better, recover

*conveniō, convenīre, convēnī *come together, gather meet*

in manum convenīre *pass into the hands of*

*convertō, convertere, convertī,
conversus *turn, divert*

sē convertere *turn*

convertor, convertī, conversus sum
turn

convīvālis, convīvāle *for dining*

convocō, convocāre, convocāvī,
convocātus *call together*

coorior, coorīrī, coortus sum *break out*

*cōpiae, cōpiārum, f.pl. *forces*

*coquō, coquere, coxī, coctus *cook*

*coquus, coquī, m. *cook*
corniculārius, corniculāriī, m. *staff-officer*
cornū, cornūs, n. *horn*
*corōna, corōnae, f. *garland, wreath*
*corpus, corporis, n. *body*
corripiō, corripere, corripuī, correptus *seize, scold*
corrumpō, corrumpere, corrūpī, corruptus *corrupt*
Cōrus, Cōrī, m. *Northwest Wind*
*cotīdiē *every day*
*crās *tommorrow*
crassus, crassa, crassum *thick, dense*
crāstinus, crāstina, crāstinum *tomorrow's*
crēber, crēbra, crēbrum *frequent*
*crēdō, crēdere, crēdidī + *dat.* *trust, believe, have faith in*
cremō, cremāre, cremāvī, cremātus *cremate, burn, destroy by fire*
*creō, creāre, creāvī, creātus *make, create*
*crēscō, crēscere, crēvī, crētus *grow*
*crīmen, crīminis, n. *charge*
crīnēs, crīnium, m.pl. *hair*
crododīlus, crocodīlī, m. *crocodile*
cruciō, cruciāre, cruciāvī, cruciātus *torture, torment*
*crūdēlis, crūdēle *cruel*
crūdēliter *cruelly*
cruentō, cruentāre, cruentāvī, cruentātus *stain with blood*
cruentus, cruenta, cruentum *bloody*
crūs, crūris, n. *leg*
crux, crucis, f. *cross*
  cruce affīgere *nail to a cross, crucify*
cubiculārius, cubiculāriī, m. *bedroom-attendant*
*cubiculum, cubiculī, n. *bedroom*
cubitō, cubitāre, cubitāvī *lie down, rest*
cuiuscumque *see* quīcumque
culīna, culīnae, f. *kitchen*
culmen, culminis, n. *roof*
*culpa, culpae, f. *blame, fault*
  illīus culpā *through her fault, thanks to her*
*culpō, culpāre, culpāvī *blame*
*cum (1) *when since, because, although*
*cum (2) +*abl.* *with*

mēcum *with me*
cumba, cumbae, f. *boat*
cūnctanter *slowly, hesitantly*
cūnctor, cūnctārī, cūnctātus sum *delay, hesitate*
cūnctus, cūncta, cūnctum *all*
cupiditās, cupiditātis, f. *desire*
cupīdō, cupīdinis, f. *desire*
Cupīdō, Cupīdinis, m. *Cupid (god of love)*
cupidus, cupida, cupidum *eager, passionate*
*cupiō, cupere, cupīvī *want*
*cūr? *why?*
*cūra, cūrae, f. *care, trouble, bother*
* cūrae esse *be a matter of concern*
cūrātor, cūrātōris, m. *supervisor, superintendent*
*cūria, cūriae, f. *senate-house*
*cūrō, cūrāre, cūrāvī *take care of, supervise*
  cūrandum est *steps must be taken*
  nihil cūrō *I don't care*
*currō, currere, cucurrī *run, race, row, go, fly*
cursim *rapidly*
*cursus, cursūs, m. *course, flight*
  circumflectere cursum *turn one's course around*
  rērum cursus *course of events*
curvāmen, curvāminis, n. *curve*
cuspis, cuspidis, f. *point*
*custōdiō, custōdīre, custōdīvī, custōdītus *guard*
*custōs, custōdis, m. *guard*

d

dā, dabō *see* dō
damnātiō, damnātiōnis, f. *condemnation*
*damnō, damnāre, damnāvī, damnātus *condemn*
damnōsus, damnōsa, damnōsum *ruinous, fatal*
datus *see* dō
*dē + *abl.* *from, down from; about, over*
dē diē *before noon*
*dea, deae, f. *goddess*

*dēbeō, dēbēre, dēbuī, dēbitus *owe;
  ought, should, must*
*decem *ten*
decēns, *gen.* decentis *handsome*
dēcernō, dēcernere, dēcrēvī, dēcrētus
  vote, decree
*decet, decēre, decuit *be proper*
*dēcidō, dēcidere, dēcidī *fall down*
*decimus, decima, decimum *tenth*
*dēcipiō, dēcipere, dēcēpī, dēceptus
  deceive, trick
*decōrus, decōra, decōrum *right, proper*
decuriō, decuriōnis, m. *supervisor*
dēcurrō, dēcurrere, dēcurrī *run down,
  speed, race*
decus, decoris, n. *glory*
dēdecus, dēdecoris, n. *disgrace*
dedī *see* dō
dēdō, dēdere, dēdidī, dēditus *give up*
  sē dēdere *surrender, give oneself up*
dēdūcō, dēdūcere, dēdūxī, dēductus
  escort, lead away
dēeram *see* dēsum
*dēfendō, dēfendere, dēfendī, dēfēnsus
  defend
dēfēnsiō, dēfēnsiōnis, f. *defense*
dēferō, dēferre, dētulī, dēlātus *carry
  away*
*dēfessus, dēfessa, dēfessum *exhausted,
  tired out*
dēficiō, dēficere, dēfēcī *fail, die away*
dēfigō, dēfigere, dēfīxī, dēfīxus *fix*
dēfīxiō, dēfīxiōnis, f. *curse*
dēflectō, dēflectere, dēflexī *turn aside,
  turn off the road*
dēfōrmis, dēfōrme *ugly, inelegant,
  disfigured*
dēfūnctus, dēfūncta, dēfūnctum *dead*
dēgredior, dēgredī, dēgressus sum
  come down
dēhinc *henceforth, accordingly*
dēhīscō, dēhīscere *gape open*
*dēiciō, dēicere, dēiēcī, dēiectus *throw
  down, throw*
dēiectus, dēiecta, dēiectum
  disappointed, downcast
dein = deinde
*deinde *then*
dēlābor, dēlābī, dēlāpsus sum *fall into*
dēlātus *see* dēferō
*dēlectō, dēlectāre, dēlectāvī,

dēlectātus *delight, please*
*dēleō, dēlēre, dēlēvī, dēlētus *destroy*
dēliciae, dēliciārum, f.pl. *darling*
dēligō, dēligāre, dēligāvī, dēligātus
  bind, tie, tie up, moor
dēligō, dēligere, dēlēgī, dēlectus
  choose, select
dēmānō, dēmānāre, dēmānāvī *flow down*
dēmissus, dēmissa, dēmissum *low*
*dēmittō, dēmittere, dēmīsī, dēmissus
  let down, lower
*dēmōnstrō, dēmōnstrāre, dēmōnstrāvī,
  dēmōnstrātus *point out, show*
*dēmum *at last*
* tum dēmum *then at last, only then*
*dēnique *at last, finally*
dēns, dentis, m. *tooth, tusk*
*dēnsus, dēnsa, dēnsum *thick*
*dēpōnō, dēpōnere, dēposuī, dēpositus
  put down, take off, give up, abandon
dēprehendō, dēprehendere,
  dēprehendī, dēprehēnsus *discover*
dēprendō =dēprehendō
*dērīdeō, dērīdēre, dērīsī, dērīsus *mock,
  make fun of, be able to laugh*
dēripiō, dēripere, dēripuī, dēreptus
  tear down
dērīsus, dērīsūs, m. *joke*
dērīsuī esse *be a joke*
*descendō, dēscendere, dēscendī *go
  down, come down*
dēscrībō, dēscrībere, dēscrīpsī,
  dēscrīptus *copy*
*dēserō, dēserere, dēseruī, dēsertus
  desert, leave behind
dēsīderium, dēsīderiī, n. *loss, longing*
*dēsiliō, dēsilīre, dēsiluī *jump down*
*dēsinō, dēsinere *end, cease*
dēsistō, dēsistere, dēstitī *stop*
dēspērātiō, dēspērātiōnis, f. *despair*
*dēspērō, dēspērāre, dēspērāvī *despair,
  give up*
dēstinātus, dēstināta, dēstinātum
  determined
dēstinō, dēstināre, dēstināvī,
  dēstinātus *intend, mark out as, name as*
dēstitūtiō, dēstitūtiōnis, f. *deserting,
  abandoning*
dēstringō, dēstringere, dēstrīnxī,
  dēstrictus *draw out, draw (a sword),
  unsheathe; scrape with a strigil*

dēstruō, dēstruere, dēstrūxī, dēstrūctus
destroy, demolish
dēsum, dēesse, dēfuī *be lacking, be
missing, be unavailable*
dētineō, dētinēre, dētinuī, dētentus
hold back, strand
dētrahō, dētrahere, dētrāxī, dētractus
pull down, take off
dēturbō, dēturbāre, dēturbāvī,
dēturbātus *push, send flying*
*deus, deī, m. *god*
* dī immortālēs! *heavens above!*
dī īnferī *gods of the Underworld*
dī mānēs *the spirits of the dead*
nē illud deī sinant! *heaven forbid!*
Dēva, Dēvae, f. *Chester*
dēvorō, dēvorāre, dēvorāvī, dēvorātus
devour, eat up
dēvoveō, dēvovēre, dēvōvī, dēvōtus
curse
dexter, dextra, dextrum *right, on the
right*
*dextra, dextrae, f. *right hand*
dī *see* deus
diaeta, diaetae, f. *room*
*dīcō, dīcere, dīxī, dictus *say*
causam dīcere *plead a case*
dictus, dicta, dictum *appointed*
male dīcere *insult*
sacrāmentum dīcere *take the military
oath*
dictitō, dictitāre, dictitāvī *keep on saying*
*dictō, dictāre, dictāvī, dictātus *dictate*
dictum, dictī, n. *saying*
didicī *see* discō
*diēs, diēī, m.f. *day*
dē diē *before noon*
diēs fēstus, diēī fēstī, m. *festival,
holiday*
* diēs nātālis, diēī nātālis, m. *birthday*
in diēs *every day, daily*
differō, differre, distulī, dīlātus *postpone,
put off*
*difficilis, difficile *difficult, obstinate*
diffīdō, diffīdere + *distrust*
digitus, digitī, m. *finger, toe*
(sub) dīō *under the open sky*
*dignitās, dignitātis, f. *dignity,
importance, honor, prestige*
*dignus, digna, dignum + abl. *worthy,
appropriate*

*dīligenter *carefully*
*dīligentia, dīligentiae, f. *industry, hard
work*
*dīligō, dīligere, dīlēxī *be fond of*
dīluvium, dīluviī, n. *flood*
*dīmittō, dīmittere, dīmīsī, dīmissus
send away, dismiss, turn, direct
dīrigō, dīrigere, dīrēxī, dīrēctus *steer*
*dīrus, dīra, dīrum *dreadful, awful*
dīs *see* deus
*discēdō, discēdere, discessī *depart, leave*
discernō, discernere, discrēvī,
discrētus *distinguish*
discerpō, discerpere, discerpsī,
discerptus *tear in pieces, mangle*
*discipulus, discipulī, m. *disciple,
follower, student*
*discō, discere, didicī *learn*
discordia, discordiae, f. *strife*
*discrīmen, discrīminis, n. *boundary,
dividing line, distance; crisis*
aequō discrīmine *at an equal distance*
disiciō, disicere, disiēcī, disiectus
scatter, disperse
dispandō, dispandere, dispānsus
spread out
dispār, *gen* disparis *of different length*
dispergō, dispergere, dispersī,
dispersus *scatter*
dispiciō, dispicere, dispexī, dispectus
consider
displiceō, displicēre, displicuī + *dat
displease
*dissentiō, dissentīre, dissēnsī *disagree,
argue*
dissimulō, dissimulāre, dissimulāvī,
dissimulātus *conceal, hide*
dissolūtiō, dissolūtiōnis, f.
disintegration, break-up
dissolvō, dissolvere, dissolvī,
dissolūtus *disperse, dissolve*
distinguō, distinguere, distīnxī,
distīnctus *set off, veneer*
distrahō, distrahere, distrāxī,
distractus *tear apart, tear in two*
distribuō, distribuere, distribuī,
distribūtus *distribute*
distringō, distringere, distrīnxī,
districtus *distract, divert*
distulī *see* differō
*diū *for a long time*

diūtius *any longer*
*dīversus, dīversa, dīversum *different*
*dīves, *gen.* dīvitis *rich*
dīvidō, dīvidere, dīvīsī, dīvīsus *separate*
*dīvitiae, dīvitiārum, f.pl. *riches*
dīvortium, dīvortiī, n. *divorce*
dīvulgō, dīvulgāre, dīvulgāvī,
   dīvulgātus *make known, divulge*
*dīvus, dīvī, m. *god*
dīxī *see* dīcō
*dō, dare, dedī, datus *give, put forward*
* poenās dare *pay the penalty, be punished*
*doceō, docēre, docuī, doctus *teach*
* doctus, docta, doctum *educated,
   skillful, learned, clever*
*doleō, dolēre, doluī *hurt, be in pain;
   grieve, be sad*
dolō, dolōnis, m. *dagger, stiletto*
*dolor, dolōris, m. *pain; grief*
*domina, dominae, f. *lady (of the house),
   mistress*
*dominus, dominī, m. *master (of the
   house), owner*
*domus, domūs, f. *home*
domī *at home*
domum Hateriī *to Haterius' house*
domum redīre *return home*
domum revenīre *return home*
*dōnec *until*
*dōnō, dōnāre, dōnāvī, dōnātus *give*
*dōnum, dōnī, n. *present, gift*
*dormiō, dormīre, dormīvī *sleep, sleep
   through*
dubiē *doubtfully*
nōn dubiē *undoubtedly, clearly*
*dubitō, dubitāre, dubitāvī *hesitate,
   doubt, be doubtful*
nōn dubitō quīn *I do not doubt that*
*dubium, dubiī, n. *doubt*
dubius, dubia, dubium *uncertain,
   doubtful*
ducem *see* dux
*ducentī, ducentae, ducenta *two hundred*
*dūcō, dūcere, dūxī, ductus *lead;
   consider, marry*
uxōrem dūcere *take as a wife, marry*
dulce *sweetly*
*dulcis, dulce *sweet*
*dum *while, until, so long as, provided that*
dumtaxat *not exceeding*
*duo, duae, duo *two*

* duo mīlia *two thousand*
*duodecim *twelve*
*duodēvīgintī *eighteen*
*dūrus, dūra, dūrum *harsh, hard*
*dux, ducis, m. *leader*
dūxī *see* dūcō

e

*ē, ex + *abl.* *from, out of*
ex industriā *on purpose*
eandem *see* īdem
*ecce! *see! look!*
ecquid *whether*
ēdictum, ēdictī, n. *edict, policy,
   statement, regulation*
ēdō, ēdere, ēdidī, ēditus *put on, present,
   dedicate*
ēdūcō, ēdūcāre, ēdūcāvī, ēdūcātus
   bring up, rear
*efferō, efferre, extulī, ēlātus *bring out,
   carry out, carry away*
* ēlātus, ēlāta, ēlātum *thrilled, excited,
   carried away*
*efficiō, efficere, effēcī, effectus *carry out,
   accomplish*
efficere ut *bring it about that, see to it that*
rem efficere *accomplish the task*
*effigiēs, effigiēī, f. *image, statue*
efflāgitō, efflāgitāre, efflāgitāvī *demand
   justice*
effodiō, effodere, effōdī, effossus *dig,
   gouge out*
effringō, effringere, effrēgī, effrāctus
   break down
*effugiō, effugere, effūgī *escape*
*effundō, effundere, effūdī, effūsus *pour
   out*
ēgī *see* agō
*ego, meī *I, me*
mēcum *with me*
meī locō *my place*
*ēgredior, ēgredī, ēgressus sum *go out*
ēgregius, ēgregia, ēgregium *excellent,
   outstanding*
*ēheu! *alas! oh dear!*
*ēiciō, ēicere, ēiēcī, ēiectus *throw out*
eīdem *see* īdem
ēlābor, ēlābī, ēlāpsus sum *escape*
ēlātus *see* efferō

ēlegāns, *gen.* ēlegantis *tasteful, elegant*

ēliciō, ēlicere, ēlicuī, ēlicitus *lure, entice*

*ēligō, ēligere, ēlēgī, ēlēctus *choose, decide*

ēlēcta, ēlēctōrum, n.pl *excerpts, extracts*

ēmendō, ēmendāre, ēmendāvī, ēmendātus *correct*

ēmineō, ēminēre, ēminuī *project*

*ēmittō, ēmittere, ēmīsī, ēmissus *throw, send out*

*emō, emere, ēmī, ēmptus *buy*

ēmoveō, ēmovēre, ēmōvī, ēmōtus *move, clear away, remove*

ēn! *look*

eōdem, eōsdem *see* īdem

*enim *for*

ēnsis, ēnsis, m. *sword*

ēnumerō, ēnumerāre, ēnumerāvī, ēnumerātus *count*

eō *therefore, for this reason*

*eō, īre, iī *go*

* obviam īre + *dat. meet, go to meet*

Ephesius, Ephesia, Ephesium *of Ephesus*

epigramma, epigrammatis, n. *epigram*

*epistula, epistulae, f. *letter*

epulae, epulārum, f.pl. *dishes, feast, banquet*

*eques, equitis, m. *horseman; man of equestrian rank*

equidem *indeed*

*equitō, equitāre, equitāvī *ride (a horse)*

*equus, equī, m. *horse*

ērādō, ērādere, ērāsī, ērāsus *erase*

eram *see* sum

*ergō *therefore*

*ēripiō, ēripere, ēripuī, ēreptus *snatch, tear, rescue, snatch away*

*errō, errāre, errāvī *make a mistake; wander*

longē errāre *make a big mistake*

ērubēscō, ērubēscere, ērubuī *blush*

ērudiō, ērudīre, ērudiī, ērudītus *teach*

ērumpō, ērumpere, ērūpī *break away, break out*

est, estō *see* sum

*et *and*

* et . . . et *both . . . and*

*etiam *even, also*

nōn modo . . . sed etiam *not only . . . but also*

etiamsī *even if, although*

Etruscus, Etruscī, m. *Etruscan*

etsī *although, even if*

*euge! *hurrah!*

euntem *see* eō

*ēvādō, ēvādere, ēvāsī *escape*

ēvānēscō, ēvānēscere, ēvānuī *vanish, die away*

ēvellō, ēvellere, ēvellī, ēvulsus *wrench off, pull out*

ēveniō, ēvenīre, ēvēnī *occur*

ēvertō, ēvertere, ēvertī, ēversus *overturn*

ēvolō, ēvolāre, ēvolāvī *fly out*

ēvolvō, ēvolvere, ēvolvī, ēvolūtus *unroll, open*

ēvomō, ēvomere, ēvomuī, ēvomitus *spit out, spew out*

*ex, ē + *abl. from, out of*

ex industriā *on purpose*

*exanimātus, exanimāta, exanimātum *unconscious*

exanimis, exanime *out of one's mind*

exardeō, exardēre, exarsī *blaze up*

exarmō, exarmāre, exarmāvī, exarmātus *disarm*

excēdō, excēdere, excessī *come out of*

excerpō, excerpere, excerpsī, excerptus *make excerpts*

*excipiō, excipere, excēpī, exceptus *receive, take over, except*

*excitō, excitāre, excitāvī, excitātus *arouse, wake up, awaken, heighten*

*exclāmō, exclāmāre, exclāmāvī *exclaim, shout*

excōgitō, excōgitāre, excōgitāvī, excōgitātus *invent, think up*

excruciō, excruciāre, excruciāvī, excruciātus *torture, torment*

excutiō, excutere, excussī, excussus *examine, investigate; shake off, drive violently off*

exemplar, exemplāris, n. *prototype*

*exemplum, exemplī, n. *example, precedent*

pertinēre ad exemplum *involve a precedent*

*exeō, exīre, exiī *go out*

exequiae, exequiārum, f.pl. *funeral rites*

*exerceō, exercēre, exercuī, exercitus *exercise, practice, train*

*exercitus, exercitūs, m. *army*
exēsus, exēsa, exēsum *porous*
exigō, exigere, exēgī, exāctus *demand, spend*
*exilium, exiliī, n. *exile*
eximō, eximere, exēmī, exēmptus *take away (from), get out*
*exīstimō, exīstimāre, exīstimāvī, exīstimātus *think, consider*
exit *see* exeō
*exitium, exitiī, n. *ruin, destruction*
exitus, exitūs, m. *way out, escape; death*
exonerō, exonerāre, exonerāvī, exonerātus *unburden, relieve*
expavēscō, expavēscere, expāvī *panic*
expediō, expedīre, expedīvī, expedītus *bring out, get out*
sēsē expedīre *prepare oneself, get ready*
expedītiō, expedītiōnis, f. *expedition*
expingō, expingere, expīnxī, expictus *paint, put paint onto*
expleō, explēre, explēvī, explētus *complete, put final touch to*
*explicō, explicāre, explicāvī, explicātus *explain*
explōrātor, explōrātōris, m. *scout, spy*
expōnō, expōnere, exposuī, expositus *unload; set out, explain*
exportō, exportāre, exportāvī, exportātus *carry out*
exsequor, exsequī, exsecūtus sum *carry out, accomplish*
exsistō, exsistere, exstitī *stand out (as), be actually, emerge*
exspatior, exspatiārī, exspatiātus sum *extend, spread out*
*exspectō, exspectāre, exspectāvī, exspectātus *wait for*
exspīrō, exspīrāre, exspīrāvī *die*
*exstinguō, exstinguere, exstīnxī, exstīnctus *extinguish, put out, destroy*
*exstruō, exstruere, exstrūxī, exstrūctus *build*
exsultō, exsultāre, exsultāvī *exult, be triumphant, get excited*
exta, extōrum, n.pl. *entrails*
extendō, extendere, extendī, extentus *stretch out*
exterreō, exterrēre, exterruī, exterritus *frighten away*
extorqueō, extorquēre, extorsī,

extortus *extort, wrest away*
*extrā + *acc. outside*
*extrahō, extrahere, extrāxī, extractus *drag out, pull out, take out*
*extrēmus, extrēma, extrēmum *farthest, end*
extrēma scaena *the edge of the stage*
exulcerātus, exulcerāta, exulcerātum *festering*
exuō, exuere, exuī, exūtus *take off, strip*

f

*faber, fabrī, m. *craftsman, carpenter, workman, fireman*
*fābula, fābulae, f. *play, story*
* fābulam agere *act in a play*
fābulōsus, fābulōsa, fābulōsum *legendary, famous*
facēs *see* fax
faciēs, faciēī, f. *face*
*facile *easily*
*facilis, facile *easy*
*facinus, facinoris, n. *crime*
*faciō, facere, fēcī, factus *make do*
floccī nōn faciō *I don't give a hoot about*
impetum facere *charge, make an attack*
ō factum male! *oh dreadfully done! oh awful deed!*
quid faciam? *what am I to do?*
tantī facere ut *rate . . . so high that*
factiō, factiōnis, f. *organized group*
*factum, factī, n. *deed, achievement*
factus *see* faciō, fīō
facultās, facultātis, f. *opportunity*
fācundē *fluently, eloquently*
fācundus, fācunda, fācundum *fluent, eloquent*
*fallō, fallere, fefellī, falsus *deceive, escape notice of, slip by*
fidem fallere *break one's word*
falsum, falsī, n. *lie, forgery*
*falsus, falsa, falsum *false, untrue, dishonest*
*fāma, fāmae, f. *rumor*
*familia, familiae, f. *household*
*familiāris, familiāris, m. *close friend, relation, relative*
familiāritās, familiāritātis, f. *friendliness*

farreus, farrea, farreum *made from grain*
fās, n. *right*
fascia, fasciae, f. *bandage*
fascinātiō, fascinātiōnis, f. *the evil eye*
Fāstī, Fāstōrum, m.pl. *the list of the*
  consuls
fātum, fātī, n. *fate*
faucēs, faucium, f.pl. *throat*
  fauce *by hunger*
*faveō, favēre, fāvī +*dat*. favor, support*
favor, favōris, m. favor
fax, facis, f. torch
febricula, febriculae, f. *slight fever*
febris, febris, f. *fever*
fēcī *see* faciō
fēcunditās, fēcunditātis, f. *fertility*
fēcundus, fēcunda, fēcundum *fertile,*
  rich
fēlīciter! *good luck!*
fēlīx, gen. fēlīcis *lucky, happy*
fēmina, fēminae, f. woman
fenestra, fenestrae, f. *window*
fera, ferae, f. *beast, wild animal*
ferē *generally*
feriō, ferīre *strike*
ferō, ferre, tulī, lātus bring, carry
ferōciter fiercely
ferōx, gen. ferōcis *fierce, ferocious*
ferrātus, ferrāta, ferrātum *tipped with*
  iron
ferreus, ferrea, ferreum *iron, made of*
  iron
ferrum, ferrī, n. iron, sword
fessus, fessa, fessum tired
festīnō, festīnāre, festīnāvī hurry
fēstus, fēsta, fēstum festival, holiday
fētus, fēta, fētum *having recently given*
  birth
fiam *see* fīo
fictus *see* fingō
fidēlis, fidēle faithful, loyal, reliable,
  trustworthy
fidēliter *faithfully, loyally, reliably*
fidēs, fideī, f. loyalty, trustworthiness
  fidem fallere *break one's word*
  (medius) fidius! *for goodness' sake!*
fīdus, fīda, fīdum loyal, trustworthy
fīgō, fīgere, fīxī, fīxus *fix, fasten, pierce*
figūra, figūrae, f. *figure, shape*
fīlia, fīliae, f. daughter
fīlius, fīliī, m. son

fingō, fingere, finxī, fictus pretend,
  invent, forge
fīnis, fīnis, m. end; starting-place
  fīnēs, fīnium, m.pl. *territory*
fīō, fierī, factus sum be made, be done,
  become, occur
firmē *firmly*
firmo, firmāre, firmāvī, firmātus
  strengthen, establish
firmus, firma, firmum *firm*
fistula, fistulae, f. *pipe*
flamma, flammae, f. flame
  concipere flammās *burst into flames*
flammeum, flammeī, n. *veil*
Flāvius, Flāvia, Flāvium *Flavian*
  gēns Flāvia *the Flavian family*
flāvus, flāva, flāvum *yellow, golden*
flectō, flectere, flexī, flexus *bend*
fleō, flēre, flēvī weep (for)
flētus, flētūs, m. *weeping, tears*
floccī nōn faciō *I don't give a hoot about*
flōreō, flōrēre, flōruī flourish
  aetāte flōrēre *be in the prime of life*
flōs, flōris, m. flower
flūctus, flūctūs, m. wave
flūmen, flūminis, n. river
fluō, fluere, flūxī flow
  fluēns, gen. fluentis *dripping, streaming*
foedus, foeda, foedum *foul, horrible*
fōns, fontis, m. fountain, spring
forās *out of the house*
fore =futūrum esse (*future infinitive of*
  sum)
forēs, forium, f.pl. *door*
fōrma, fōrmae, f. *beauty, shape*
formīdō, formīdinis, f. *fear, terror*
formīdolōsus, formīdolōsa,
  formīdolōsum *alarming*
fōrmō, fōrmāre, fōrmāvī, fōrmātus
  fashion, shape
fors *perhaps*
fortasse perhaps
forte by chance
fortis, forte brave
fortiter bravely
fortuita, fortuitōrum, n.pl. *accidents*
fortūna, fortūnae, f. fortune, luck
fortūnātus, fortūnāta, fortūnātum
  lucky
forum, forī, n. forum, business center
fossa, fossae, f. ditch

Complete Vocabulary

fovea, foveae, f. *pit*
*fragor, fragōris, m. *crash, shout*
*frangō, frangere, frēgī, frāctus *break*
*frāter, frātris, m. *brother*
frāternus, frāterna, frāternum *of a brother, fraternal*
*fraus, fraudis, f. *trick*
fremitus, fremitūs, m. *noise, din*
frēna, frēnōrum, n.pl. *reins*
frequenter *frequently, often*
frētum, frētī, n, *water, sea*
frīgidus, frīgida, frīgidum *cold*
frondēns, *gen.* frondentis *leafy*
frōns, frontis, f. *front, prow, forehead, outward appearance*
*frūmentum, frūmentī, n. *grain*
fruor, fruī, fructus sum + *abl. enjoy*
*frūstrā *in vain*
fūdī *see* fundō
*fuga, fugae, f. *escape, flight*
fugāx, *gen.* fugācis *running away, fleeing*
*fugiō, fugere, fūgī *run away, flee (from)*
fugitīvus, fugitīvī, m. *fugitive, runaway*
fugō, fugāre, fugāvī, fugātus *put to flight*
fuī *see* sum
fulciō, fulcīre, fulsī, fultus *prop up, wedge*
*fulgeō, fulgēre, fulsī *shine, glitter*
fulgor, fulgōris, m. *glare*
fulgur, fulguris, n. *lightning*
fulmen, fulminis, n. *thunderbolt*
fulvus, fulva, fulvum *tawny, light brown*
fūmō, fūmāre, fūmāvī *smoke*
fūmus, fūmī, m. *smoke*
*fundō, fundere, fūdī, fūsus *pour, pour out*
*fundus, fundī, m. *farm; depth*
fūnerō, fūnerāre, fūnerāvī, fūnerātus *cremate*
fūnus, fūneris, n. *funeral, funeral procession, funeral pyre*
*fūr, fūris, m. *thief*
*furēns, *gen.* furentis *furious, in a rage*
furēns animī *furiously determined, with furious eagerness*
fūstis, fūstis, m. *club, stick*
futūrus, futūra, futūrum *future*
futūrus *see* sum

g

gallicinium, gallicinii, n. *cockcrow, dawn*

*gaudeō, gaudēre *be pleased, rejoice, be delighted*
*gaudium, gaudiī, n. *joy*
per gaudium *joyfully*
gelō, gelāre, gelāvī, gelātus *freeze*
*geminī, geminōrum, m.pl. *twins*
geminus, gemina, geminum *twin, the two, twofold, double*
*gemitus, gemitūs, m. *groan*
*gemma, gemmae, f. *jewel, gem*
gena, genae, f. *cheek*
gener, generī, m. *son-in-law*
*gēns, gentis, f. *family, tribe, race*
gēns Flāvia *the Flavian family*
*genū, genūs, n. *knee*
*genus, generis, n. *race, kind*
genus mortāle *the human race*
Germānī, Germānōrum, m.pl. *Germans*
Germānia, Germāniae, f. *Germany*
Germānus, Germāna, Germānum *German*
*gerō, gerere, gessī, gestus *wear; achieve*
* bellum gerere *wage war, campaign*
sē gerere *behave, conduct oneself*
Gerūsia, Gerūsiae, f. *the Gerusia (club for wealthy, elderly men)*
gestiō, gestīre, gestīvī *become restless, leap for joy, gambol*
gladiātor, gladiātōris, m. *gladiator*
gladiātōrius, gladiātōria, gladiātōrium *gladiatorial, gladiators'*
gladiātōrius lūdus *gladiators' (training) camp*
*gladius, gladiī, m. *sword*
*glōria, glōriae, f. *glory*
glōriōsus, glōriōsa, glōriōsum *boastful*
gnārus, gnāra, gnārum + *gen. having knowledge of, familiar with*
gnātus = nātus
gracilis, gracile *graceful*
gracilitās, gracilitātis, f. *thinness*
gradus, gradūs, m. *step*
addere gradum *go forward step by step*
Graecus, Graeca, Graecum *Greek*
grāmen, grāminis, n. *grass*
grandis, grande *awesome, large*
grātia, grātiae, f. *gratitude*
grātiam referre *show gratitude, thank*
grātiae, grātiārum, f.pl. *thanks*
* grātiās agere *thank, give thanks*

grātificor, grātificārī, grātificātus sum *do favors*

grātulātiō, grātulātiōnis, f. *congratulation*

grātulor, grātulārī, grātulātus sum *congratulate*

*grātus, grāta, grātum *acceptable, pleasing*

*gravis, grave *heavy, serious, severe*

*graviter *heavily, soundly, seriously*

gravō, gravāre, gravāvī *load, weigh down*

gremium, gremiī, n. *lap*

gubernāculum, gubernāculī, n. *helm, steering-oar*

gurges, gurgitis, m. *whirlpool, swirling water*

*gustō, gustāre, gustāvī *taste, have a snack*

h

*habeō, habēre, habuī, habitus *have, regard*

* prō certō habēre *know for certain*

*habitō, habitāre, habitāvī *live*

habitus, habitūs, m. *condition, appearance*

hāctenus *this much, so much*

*haereō, haerēre, haesī *stick, cling, linger*

*haesitō, haesitāre, haesitāvī *hesitate*

hama, hamae, f. *fire-bucket*

harundō, harundinis, f. *reed, rod*

*haruspex, haruspicis, m. *diviner, soothsayer*

*hasta, hastae, f. *spear*

*haud *not*

*haudquāquam *not at all*

*hauriō, haurīre, hausī, haustus *drain, drink up*

haustus, haustūs, m. *drinking, drinking-place*

hebes, *gen.* hebetis *weak, poor*

Helicē, Helicēs, f. *Big Bear (constellation)*

*hercle! *by Hercules!*

*hērēs, hērēdis, m.f. *heir*

*heri *yesterday*

hetaeria, hetaeriae, f. *political club*

heu! = ēheu!

hiātus, hiātūs, m. *open jaws*

Hibernī, Hibernōrum, m.pl. *Irish*

Hibernia, Hiberniae, f. *Ireland*

hībernus, hīberna, hībernum *wintry, of winter*

*hīc *here*

*hic, haec, hoc *this*

hī . . . aliī *some . . . others*

hī . . . hī *some . . . others*

hic . . . ille *this one . . . that one, one man . . . another man*

*hiems, hiemis, f. *winter*

hilaris, hilare *in high spirits, merry*

*hinc *from here; then, next*

hiō, hiāre, hiāvī *open the jaws*

hippopotamus, hippopotamī, m. *hippopotamus*

Hispānia, Hispāniae, f. *Spain*

historia, historiae, f. *history*

*hodiē *today*

*homō, hominis, m. *person, man*

homunculus, homunculī, m. *little man, pip-squeak*

*honor, honōris, m. *honor, official position*

*honōrō, honōrāre, honōrāvī, honōrātus *honor*

*hōra, hōrae, f. *hour*

horrendus, horrenda, horrendum *horrifying*

horrēscō, horrēscere, horruī *shudder*

*horreum, horreī, n. *barn, granary*

*hortor, hortārī, hortātus sum *encourage, urge*

*hortus, hortī, m. *garden*

*hospes, hospitis, m. *guest, host*

*hostis, hostis, m.f. *enemy*

*hūc *here, to this place*

hūc . . . illūc *this way . . . that way, one way . . . another way, here and there, up and down*

humilis, humile *low-born, of low class; low-lying*

humus, humī, f. *ground*

* humī *on the ground*

Hymēn, Hymenis, m. *Hymen, god of weddings*

Hymenaeus, Hymenaeī, m. *Hymen, god of weddings*

i

*iaceō, iacēre, iacuī *lie, rest*
*iaciō, iacere, iēcī, iactus *throw*
iactantia, iactantiae, f. *boasting*
*iactō, iactāre, iactāvī, iactātus *throw;
  speak*
*iam *now*
  iam iamque *at any moment now*
  nec iam *no longer*
  nunc iam *now however, as things are now*
*iānua, iānuae, f. *door*
*ibi *there, then, in those days*
  ībō see eō
  ictus, ictūs, m. *blow, shot*
*īdem, eadem, idem *the same*
  idem . . . ac *the same . . . as*
  in idem *for a common purpose, for the
    same purpose*
*identidem *repeatedly*
*ideō *for this reason*
* ideō . . . quod *for the reason that, because*
*igitur *therefore, and so*
*ignārus, ignāra, ignārum *not knowing,
    unaware, unsuspecting*
*ignāvus, ignāva, ignāvum *lazy,
    cowardly*
*ignis, ignis, m. *fire, lighting, heat of the
    sun*
*ignōrō, ignōrāre, ignōrāvī *not know (about)*
*ignōscō, ignōscere, ignōvī + *dat. forgive*
  ignōtus, ignōta, ignōtum *unknown*
  iī see eō
  īlex, īlicis, f. *oak tree*
  īlia, īlium, n.pl. *groin*
  illāc *by that way*
  illaesus, illaesa, illaesum *uninjured*
*ille, illa, illud *that, he, she*
  hic . . . ille *this one . . . that one, one man
    . . . another man*
  nē illud deī sinant! *heaven forbid!*
  illīc *there, in that place*
*illūc *there, to that place*
  hūc . . . illūc *this way . . . that way, one
    way . . . another way, here and there, up
    and down*
  illūcēscō, illūcēscere, illūxī *dawn, grow
    bright*
  illūstris, illūstre *bright*
  imāgō, imāginis, f. *image, picture, bust,
    reflection*

imber, imbris, m. *rain, storm-cloud*
imitor, imitārī, imitātus sum *copy,
    imitate, mime*
*immemor, *gen.* immemoris *forgetful*
immēnsus, immēnsa, immēnsum *vast*
*immineō, imminēre, imminuī + *dat.
    hang over*
immītis, immīte *cruel*
immō *or rather*
*immortālis, immortāle *immortal*
* dī immortālēs! *heavens above!*
*immōtus, immōta, immōtum *still,
    motionless*
impatiēns, *gen.* impatientis *impatient,
    intolerant, incapable*
*impediō, impedīre, impedīvī,
    impedītus *delay, hinder*
impellō, impellere, impulī, impulsus
    push, force
impendium, impendiī, n. *expense,
    expenditure*
impendō, impendere, impendī,
    impēnsus *spend, make use of*
impēnsē *strongly, violently, at great cost*
*imperātor, imperātōris, m. *emperor*
imperfectus, imperfecta, imperfectum
    unfinished
*imperium, imperiī, n. *power, empire,
    rule, reign*
*imperō, imperāre, imperāvī +. *dat.
    order, command; be emperor*
impetrō, impetrāre, impetrāvī *obtain*
*impetus, impetūs, m. *attack*
  impetum facere *charge, make an attack*
implicō, implicāre, implicāvī,
    implicātus *implicate, involve*
*impōnō, impōnere, imposuī, impositus
    impose, put into, put onto
impotēns, *gen.* impotentis *helpless,
    powerless*
imprimō, imprimere, impressī,
    impressus *press*
improbus, improba, improbum
    wicked, relentless
imprōvīsus, imprōvīsa, imprōvīsum
    unexpected, unforeseen
imprūdenter *stupidly, foolishly*
impudentia, impudentiae, f.
    shamelessness
impulī, impulsus see impellō
impūrus, impūra, impūrum *immoral*

īmus, īma, īmum *lowest, bottom*
*in (1) + *acc.* *into, onto, against*
  in aliud *for any other purpose*
  in commūne *for the general advantage,*
    for all
  in diēs *every day, daily*
  in idem *for a common purpose, for the*
    same purpose
  in mentem venīre *occur, come to mind*
  in perpetuum *forever*
  in rem subitam *to meet the sudden crisis*
  in remedium *as a cure*
*in (2) + *abl.* *in, on*
* in animō volvere *wonder, turn over in*
    the mind
  in prīmīs *in the first place, in particular*
  in proximō *nearby*
*inānis, ināne *empty, meaningless*
incautus, incauta, incautum *unwary*
*incēdō, incēdere, incessī *march, stride*
*incendium, incendiī, n. *fire, blaze*
*incendō, incendere, incendī,
  incēnsus *burn, set fire to*
*incēnsus, incēnsa, incēnsum *inflamed,*
  angered
incertus, incerta, incertum *uncertain*
incestum, incestī, n. *immorality,*
  unchastity
*incidō, incidere, incidī *fall*
incīdō, incīdere, incīsī, incīsus *cut open*
*incipiō, incipere, incēpī, inceptus *begin*
*incitō, incitāre, incitāvī, incitātus *urge*
  on, encourage
inclīnō, inclīnāre, inclīnāvī,
  inclīnātus *lean*
inclūdō, inclūdere, inclūsī, inclūsus
  shut up, confine
incohō, incohāre, incohāvī, incohātus
  begin
*incolumis, incolume *safe*
incurrō, incurrere, incurrī *run onto,*
  collide with, bump into
*inde *then*
*indicium, indiciī, n. *sign, evidence*
indignē *unfairly*
indignor, indignārī, indignātus sum
  feel shame, think it shameful
indulgeō, indulgēre, indulsī + *dat.* *give*
  way
*induō, induere, induī, indūtus *put on*
  indūtus, indūta, indūtum *dressed*

industria, industriae, f. *hard work*
  ex industriā *on purpose*
inedia, inediae, f. *starvation*
inelegāns, *gen.* inelegantis *unattractive*
ineptiō, ineptīre *be silly, be a fool*
ineptus, inepta, ineptum *silly*
ineram *see* īnsum
inermis, inerme *unarmed, disarmed*
inertia, inertiae, f. *laziness, idleness*
*īnfāns, īnfantis, m. *baby, child*
*īnfēlīx, *gen.* īnfēlīcis *unlucky*
īnferiae, īnferiārum, f.pl. *tribute to the*
  dead
īnferior, īnferius *lower, further*
  downstream
*īnferō, īnferre, intulī, inlātus *bring in,*
  bring on, bring against
  causam īnferre *make an excuse, invent an*
  excuse
īnferus, īnfera, īnferum *of the*
  Underworld
  dī īnferī *gods of the Underworld*
*īnfestus, īnfesta, īnfestum *hostile,*
  dangerous
īnfitior, īnfitiārī, īnfitiātus sum *deny*
ingeminō, ingemināre, ingemināvī
  redouble
*ingenium, ingeniī, n. *character,*
  inclination, talent
*ingēns, *gen.* ingentis *huge*
ingravēscō, ingravēscere *grow worse*
*ingredior, ingredī, ingressus sum *enter*
inguen, inguinis, n. *groin*
inhaereō, inhaerēre, inhaesī *stick in*
inhorrēscō, inhorrēscere, inhorruī
  shudder
*iniciō, inicere, iniēcī, iniectus *throw in*
iniectus, iniectūs, m. *placing, touch*
*inimīcus, inimīcī, m. *enemy*
inīquus, inīqua, inīquum *unfair,*
  narrow, dangerous
*initium, initiī, n. *beginning*
*iniūria, iniūriae, f. *injustice, injury*
iniūstē *unfairly*
iniūstus, iniūsta, iniūstum *unjust*
inlātus *see* īnferō
inlēctus, inlēcta, inlēctum *unread*
innatō, innatār, innatāvī *dive in*
innītor, innītī, innīxus sum *lean on,*
  lean, rest
innocēns, *gen.* innocentis *innocent*

innocentia, innocentiae, f. *innocence*
innocuē *harmlessly*
*inopia, inopiae, f. *shortage, scarcity,*
poverty
inquiētus, inquiēta, inquiētum
unsettled
*inquit *says, said*
inquam *I said*
inquis *you say*
*īnsānus, īnsāna, īnsānum *insane, crazy*
īnscrībō, īnscrībere, īnscrīpsī,
īnscrīptus *write, inscribe*
īnserō, īnserere, īnseruī, īnsertus *insert*
*īnsidiae, īnsidiārum, f.pl. *trap, ambush*
*īnspiciō, īnspicere, īnspexī, īnspectus
look at, inspect, examine, search
īnstīgō, īnstīgāre, īnstīgāvī, īnstīgātus
urge on
īnstituō, īnstituere, īnstituī, īnstitūtus
set up
īnstō, īnstāre, īnstitī *be pressing,*
threaten, harass
īnstrūmentum, īnstrūmentī, n.
equipment
*īnstruō, īnstruere, īnstrūxī, īnstrūctus
draw up, set up, equip, fit (with wings)
sē īnstruere *draw oneself up*
*īnsula, īnsulae, f. *island; apartment*
building
*īnsum, inesse, īnfuī *be in, be inside*
integer, integra, integrum *intact,*
uninjured
*intellegō, intellegere, intellēxī,
intellēctus *understand*
*intentē *intently*
intentiō, intentiōnis, f. *effort*
intentus, intenta, intentum *intent*
*inter + *acc. among, during*
inter sē *among themselves, with each other*
intercipiō, intercipere, intercēpī,
interceptus *steal*
interdiū *during the day*
interdum *sometimes, occasionally*
*intereā *meanwhile*
intereō, interīre, interiī, interitus *wear*
away, wear out
*interficiō, interficere, interfēcī,
interfectus *kill*
intericiō, intericere, interiēcī,
interiectus *insert, hide inside*
*interim *meanwhile*

interior *on the inside*
interior, interius *inner*
interpellātiō, interpellātiōnis, f.
interruption
interpellō, interpellāre, interpellāvī
interrupt
interrogō, interrogāre, interrogāvī,
interrogātus *question*
intersum, interesse, interfuī + *dat. be*
present at
intervallum, intervallī, n. *space between*
*intrā + *acc. inside, during*
intremō, intremere, intremuī *shake*
*intrō, intrāre, intrāvī *enter*
intulī *see *īnferō
intus *inside*
inultus, inulta, inultum *unavenged*
invalēscō, invalēscere, invaluī *become*
strong
invalidus, invalida, invalidum *weak*
invehor, invehī, invectus sum *sail in*
*inveniō, invenīre, invēnī, inventus *find*
investīgō, investīgāre, investīgāvī,
investīgātus *investigate*
invicem *in turn, each other, together*
*invideō, invidēre, invīdī + *dat. envy, be*
jealous of, begrudge, cast an evil eye
*invidia, invidiae, f. *jealousy, envy,*
unpopularity
*invītō, invītāre, invītāvī, invītātus
invite
*invītus, invīta, invītum *unwilling,*
reluctant
involvō, involvere, involvī, involūtus
envelop, swallow up
iocor, iocārī, iocātus sum *joke*
iocōsum, iocōsī, n. *moment of fun,*
moment of pleasure
*iocus, iocī, m. *joke*
Iovis *see *Iuppiter
*ipse, ipsa, ipsum *himself, herself, itself;*
master, mistress
*īra, īrae, f. *anger*
īrāscor, īrāscī, īrātus sum + *dat. become*
angry with
*īrātus, īrāta, īrātum *angry*
īre *see *eō
irrigō, irrigāre, irrigāvī, irrigātus *water*
*irrumpō, irrumpere, irrūpī *burst in,*
burst into
*is, ea, id *he, she, it; that*

id quod *what*
**iste, ista, istud *that*
it *see* eō
**ita *in this way*
sīcut . . . ita *just as . . . so*
ita vērō *yes*
Ītalia, Ītaliae, f. *Italy*
**itaque *and so*
item *likewise, also*
**iter, itineris, n. *journey, progress*
iter agere *make one's way, travel*
**iterum *again*
nōn iterum *never again*
**iubeō, iubēre, iussī, iussus *order*
**iūdex, iūdicis, m. *judge*
iūdicium, iūdiciī, n. *judgment*
**iūdicō, iūdicāre, iūdicāvī, iūdicātus
judge
**iungō, iungere, iūnxī, iūnctus *join*
iūnctus *side by side*
Iūnō, Iūnōnis, f. *Juno (goddess of
marriage)*
Iūnōnius, Iūnōnia, Iūnōnium *sacred to
Juno*
Iuppiter, Iovis, m. *Jupiter (god of the
sky, greatest of Roman gods)*
iūrgium, iūrgiī, n. *argument, dispute*
iūrō, iūrāre, iūrāvī *swear*
iūs, iūris, n. *right, privilege*
iussī *see* iubeō
**iussum, iussī, n. *order,
instruction*
iussū Imperātōris *at the Emperor's order*
iūstus, iūsta, iūstum *proper, right, fair*
iūstius erat *it would have been fairer,
more proper*
iuvencus, iuvencī, m. *bullock, young bull*
iuvenīlis, iuvenīle *youthful*
**iuvenis, iuvenis, m. *young man*
iuventa, iuventae f. *youth*
**iuvō, iuvāre, iūvī, iūtus *help, assist,
please*
**iuxtā + *acc. *next to*
iuxtā *side by side*

k

Kal. = Kalendās
Kalendae, Kalendārum, f.pl. *Kalends,
1st day of each month*

l

L. = Lūcius
labellum, labellī, n. *lip*
**labor, labōris, m. *work*
**lābor, lābī, lāpsus sum *fall, glide; pass
by, slide by*
**labōrō, labōrāre, labōrāvī *work*
lacerō, lacerāre, lacerāvī, lacerātus
tear apart
lacertus, lacertī, m. *arm, muscle*
**lacrima, lacrimae, f. *tear*
**lacrimō, lacrimāre, lacrimāvī *weep, cry*
lacus, lacūs, m. *lake*
**laedō, laedere, laesī, laesus *harm*
laetē *happily*
**laetus, laeta, laetum *happy*
laevus, laeva, laevum *left*
laevā parte *on the left hand*
lagōna, lagōnae, f. *bottle*
lāna, lānae, f. *wool*
langueō, languēre *feel weak, feel sick*
lāniger, lānigerī, m.f. *woolly one, lamb*
lanius, laniī, m. *butcher*
lapideus, lapidea, lapideum *made of
stone*
**lapis, lapidis, m. *stone*
Larēs, Larum, m.pl. *guardian spirits,
household gods*
lārva, lārvae, f. *ghost*
lassō, lassāre, lassāvī, lassātus *tire,
weary*
lātē *widely*
latebrae, latebrārum, f.pl. *hiding-place*
**lateō, latēre, latuī *lie hidden*
Latīnus, Latīna, Latīnum *Latin*
**latrō, latrōnis, m. *robber*
lātrō, lātrāre, lātrāvī *bark*
**latus, lateris, n. *side*
**lātus, lāta, lātum *wide*
**laudō, laudāre, laudāvī, laudātus
praise
**laus, laudis, f. *praise, fame*
**lavō, lavāre (*sometimes* lavere), lāvī,
lautus *wash, bath*
**lectīca, lectīcae, f. *sedan-chair*
lēctor, lēctōris, m. *reader, slave who read
aloud*
**lectus, lectī, m. *couch, bed*
**lēgātus, lēgātī, m. *commander*
lēgem *see* lēx

*legiō, legiōnis, f. legion
*legō, legere, lēgī, lēctus read; choose,
    conscript, gather up
 lēgō, lēgāre, lēgāvī, lēgātus bequeath
 lēniō, lēnīre, lēnīvī, lēnītus soothe, calm
    down
*lēniter gently
*lentē slowly
 lentus, lenta, lentum supple, slow
 lēnunculus, lēnunculī, m. small boat
*leō, leōnis, m. lion
*levis, leve light, slight, trivial, changeable,
    inconsistent, worthless
 levō, levāre, levāvī, levātus raise, lift up
*lēx, lēgis, f. law
 libellus, libellī, m. little book
    ā libellīs in charge of petitions to the
    Emperor, private secretary
*libenter gladly
*liber, librī, m. book
*līberālis, līberāle generous, liberal
    līberālia studia liberal studies
*līberī, līberōrum, m.pl. children
*līberō, līberāre, līberāvī, līberātus free,
    set free
*lībertās, lībertātis, f. freedom
*lībertus, lībertī, m. freedman, ex-slave
 lībrō, lībrāre, lībrāvī, lībrātus balance
 librum see liber
 lībum, lībī, n. cake
*licet, licēre be allowed
* mihi licet I am allowed
    licet although
*līmen, līminis, n. threshold, doorway
 līmes, līmitis, m. course
 līmus, līmī, m. mud
*lingua, linguae, f. tongue, language
 linteum, linteī, n. linen cloth, towel
 līnum, līnī, n. thread
 liqueō, liquēre, līquī flow
 liquidus, liquida, liquidum liquid
 liquor, liquōris, m. water
*littera, litterae, f. letter (of alphabet)
* litterae, litterārum, f.pl. letter, letters
    (correspondence), literature
*lītus, lītoris, n. seashore, shore
 locō, locāre, locāvī, locātus place
*locus, locī, m. place
    meī locō in my place
    locus nātālis, locī nātālis, m. place of
    birth, native land

*longē far, a long way
    longē errāre make a big mistake
 longinquus, longinqua, longinquum
    distant
*longus, longa, longum long
*loquor, loquī, locūtus sum speak
 lūcem see lūx
 lūceō, lūcēre, lūxī shine
 Lucrīnus lacus, Lucrīnī lacūs, m. the
    Lucrine lake
 lūctor, lūctārī, lūctātus sum struggle
*lūdō, lūdere, lūsī, lūsus play
*lūdus, lūdī, m. game
    gladiātōrius lūdus gladiators'
    (training) camp
*lūgeō, lūgēre, lūxī lament, mourn
*lūmen, lūminis, n. light
    lūmina, lūminum, n.pl. eyes
*lūna, lūnae, f. moon
 lupus, lupī, m. wolf
 lūscus, lūsca, lūscum one-eyed
 lūsus, lūsūs, m. play, games
*lūx, lūcis, f. light, daylight

m

 M. = Marcus
 M'. = Mānius
 māchināmentum, māchināmentī, n.
    machine, contraption
 madēscō, madēscere, maduī become wet
 madidus, madida, madidum soaked
    through
*magister, magistrī, m. master, foreman,
    pilot
*magistrātus, magistrātūs, m. public
    official
 magnificus, magnifica, magnificum
    splendid, magnificent
*magnopere greatly
* magis more
* maximē very greatly, very much, most of
    all, in particular
*magnus, magna. magnum big, large,
    great
    maior, maius bigger, larger, greater
* maximus, maxima, maximum very
    big, very large, very great, greatest
    Pontifex Maximus Chief Priest
*male badly, unfavorably

male dīcere *insult*
ō factum male! *oh dreadfully done! oh awful deed!*
vōbīs male sit *curses on you*
*mālō, mālle, māluī *prefer*
mālum, mālī, n. *apple*
*malus, mala, malum *evil, bad*
* pessimus, pessima, pessimum *very bad, worst*
*mandātum, mandātī, n. *instruction, order*
*mandō, mandāre, mandāvī, mandātus *order, entrust, hand over*
*māne *in the morning*
*maneō, manēre, mānsī *remain, stay*
mānēs, mānis, m. *departed spirit*
dī mānēs *the spirits of the dead*
manicae, manicārum, f.pl. *long sleeves*
manifestus, manifesta, manifestum *clear*
mānō, mānāre, mānāvī *flow, be wet*
multum mānāns *drenched*
*manus, manūs, f. *hand; band*
in manum convenīre *pass into the hands of*
manus ultima *final touch*
*mare, maris, n. *sea*
margarītum, margarītī, n. *pearl*
maritīmus, maritīma, maritīmum *seaside, by the sea*
*marītus, marītī, m. *husband*
marmor, marmoris, n. *marble*
Mārtiālis, Mārtiāle *of Martial*
massa, massae, f. *block*
Massicus, Massica, Massicum *Massic*
*māter, mātris, f. *mother*
mathēmaticus, mathēmaticī, m. *mathematician, astrologer*
mātrimōnium, mātrimōniī, n. *marriage*
mātrōna, mātrōnae, f. *lady*
mātūrō, mātūrāre, mātūrāvī, mātūrātus *hasten*
mātūtīnus, mātūtīna, mātūtīnum *morning*
maximē *see* magnopere
maximus *see* magnus
mē *see* ego
meātus, meātūs, m. *movement, passage*
medicāmentum, medicāmentī, n. *ointment, medicine, drug*

medicīna, medicīnae, f. *medicine*
*medicus, medicī, m. *doctor*
*meditor, meditārī, meditātus sum *consider*
*medius, media, medium *middle*
medius fidius! *for goodness sake!*
meī *see* ego
mel, mellis, n. *honey*
melior *see* bonus
mellītus, mellīta, mellītum *sweet as honey*
*meminī, meminisse *remember*
memor, *gen.* memoris *remembering, mindful of*
memoria, memoriae, f. *memory*
*mendāx, mendācis, m. *liar*
mendāx, *gen.* mendācis *lying, deceitful*
*mēns, mentis, f. *mind*
in mentem venīre *occur, come to mind*
*mēnsa, mēnsae, f. *table*
*mēnsis, mēnsis, m. *month*
mēnsor, mēnsōris, m. *surveyor*
mēnsūra, mēnsūrae, f. *measurement*
*mentior, mentīrī, mentītus sum *lie, tell a lie*
*mercātor, mercātōris, m. *merchant*
mereō, merēre, meruī *deserve*
* meritus, merita, meritum *deserved, well-deserved*
mergō, mergere, mersī, mersus *submerge*
merīdiēs, merīdiēī, m. *noon*
meritō *deservedly, rightly*
mēta, mētae, f. *turning-point*
metallum, metallī, n. *a mine*
*metuō, metuere, metuī *be afraid, fear*
*metus, metūs, m. *fear*
*meus, mea, meum *my, mine*
mī Lupe *my dear Lupus*
mī Secunde *my dear Secundus*
mī = mihi
mihi *see* ego
*mīles, mīlitis, m. *soldier*
mīliārium, mīliāriī, n. *milestone*
mīlitō, mīlitāre, mīlitāvī *be a soldier*
*mīlle *a thousand*
* mīlia *thousands*
minae, minārum, f.pl. *threats*
mināx, *gen.* minācis *threatening*
*minimē *no, least, very little*

minimus *see* parvus

minister, ministrī, m. *servant, agent*

minor *see* parvus

*minor, minārī, minātus sum + *dat.*
threaten

minus *see* paulum

minūtus, minūta, minūtum *small*

*mīrābilis, mīrābile *marvelous, strange,*
wonderful .

*mīror, mīrārī, mīrātus sum *admire,*
wonder at

mīrus, mīra, mīrum *extraordinary*

misceō, miscēre, miscuī, mixtus *mix,*
share

misellus, misella, misellum *wretched*
little

*miser, misera, miserum *miserable,*
wretched, sad

miserātiō, miserātiōnis, f. *pity,*
compassion

misereor, miserērī, miseritus sum *pity*

misericors, *gen.* misericordis *tender-*
hearted, full of pity

*mittō, mittere, mīsī, missus *send*

moderātiō, moderātiōnis, f. *moderation,*
caution

modestus, modesta, modestum *modest*

modicus, modica, modicum *ordinary,*
little

*modo *just, now, only, just now*

* modo . . . modo *now . . . now,*
sometimes . . . sometimes

nōn modo . . . sed etiam *not only . . .*
but also

*modus, modī, m. *manner, way, kind*

* quō modō? *how? in what way?*

moechus, moechī, m. *lover, adulterer*

moenia, moeniōrum, n.pl. *city walls*

mōlēs, mōlis, f. *bulk; embankment,*
sea-wall

molestus, molesta, molestum
troublesome

molliō, mollīre, mollīvī, mollītus
soothe, soften

*mollis, molle *soft, gentle*

molliter *gently, leniently*

*moneō, monēre, monuī, monitus *warn,*
advise

monitus, monitūs, m. *warning, advice*

*mōns, montis, m. *mountain*

mōns Palātīnus *the Palatine hill*

summus mōns *the top of the mountain*

monumentum, monumentī, n.
monument, tomb

*mora, morae, f. *delay, slow place*

morbidus, morbida, morbidum *liable*
to disease

*morbus, morbī, m. *illness*

mordeō, mordēre, momordī, morsus
bite

*morior, morī, mortuus sum *die*
morere! *die!*

* mortuus, mortua, mortuum *dead*

*moror, morārī, morātus sum *delay,*
hold steady

*mors, mortis, f. *death*

mortem obīre *die*

mortem sibi cōnscīscere *commit suicide*

morsus, morsūs, m. *bite, fangs*

mortālis, mortāle *mortal*

genus mortāle *the human race*

mortuus *see* morior

*mōs, mōris, m. *custom*

mōtus, mōtūs, m. *movement*

*moveō, movēre, mōvī, mōtus *move,*
influence

mōtus, mōta, mōtum *moved, moving*

*mox *soon*

*mulier, mulieris, f. *woman*

multiplicō, multiplicāre, multiplicāvī,
multiplicātus *increase greatly*

*multitūdō, multitūdinis, f. *crowd*

*multō *much*

multum *much*

multum mānāns *drenched*

*multus, multa, multum *much*

* multī *many*

plūrēs, plūra *many, several*

* plūrimī, plūrimae, plūrima *very many*

* plūrimus, plūrima, plūrimum *most*

* plūs, *gen.* plūris *more*

quid multa? *in brief, in short*

quid plūra? *why say more?*

mūnīmentum, mūnīmentī, n. *protection*

mūniō, mūnīre, mūnīvī, mūnītus
protect, immunize

*mūnus, mūneris, n. *gift*

*mūrus, mūrī, m. *wall*

musca, muscae, f. *fly*

musicus, musicī, m. *musician*

mūtātiō, mūtātiōnis, f. *change*

*mūtō, mūtāre, mūtāvī, mūtātus *change*

vestem mūtāre *put on mourning clothes*
mūtus, mūta, mūtum *silent*

n

*nam *for*
nancīscor, nancīscī, nactus sum *seize*
nārrātiō, nārrātiōnis, f. *narration*
*nārrō, nārrāre, nārrāvī, nārrātus *tell,
relate*
*nāscor, nāscī, nātus sum *be born*
nātū maximus *eldest*
septuāgintā annōs nātus *seventy years
old*
trēdecim annōs nāta *thirteen years old*
nāsus, nāsī, m. *nose*
nat *see* nō
nātālis, nātāle *native*
* diēs nātālis, diēī nātālis, m. *birthday*
locus nātālis, locī nātālis, m. *place of
birth, native land*
natō, natāre, natāvī *swim*
nātūra, nātūrae, f. *nature*
nātus *see* nāscor
nātus, nātī, m. *son*
naufragium, naufragiī, n. *shipwreck*
*nauta, nautae, m. *sailor*
nauticus, nautica, nauticum *made by
sailors*
nāvigātiō, nāvigātiōnis, f. *voyage*
*nāvigō, nāvigāre, nāvigāvī *sail*
*nāvis, nāvis, f. *ship*
*nē *that . . . not, so that . . . not, in order
that . . . not*
nē deī illud sinant! *heaven forbid!*
* nē quid *lest anything, in case anything*
* nē . . . quidem *not even*
* nē quis *lest anyone, in case anyone, that
anyone, that nobody*
nebula, nebulae, f. *mist*
*nec *and not, nor*
nec iam *no longer*
* nec . . . nec *neither . . . nor*
necessārius, necessāria, necessārium
necessary
*necesse *necessary*
necessitās, necessitātis, f. *need*
*necō, necāre, necāvī, necātus *kill*
*neglegēns, *gen.* neglegentis *careless*
neglegentia, neglegentiae, f. *carelessness*

*neglegō, neglegere, neglēxī, neglēctus
neglect
*negō, negāre, negāvī, negātus *deny, say
that . . . not*
*negōtium, negōtiī, n. *business*
* negōtium agere *do business, work*
*nēmō *no one, nobody*
nūllīus *of nobody*
nempe *surely, of course*
Neptūnus, Neptūnī, m. *Neptune (god of
the sea)*
*neque *and not, nor*
* neque . . . neque *neither . . . nor*
nēquīquam *in vain*
Nēreis, Nēreidis, f. *sea-nymph*
*nescio, nescīre, nescīvī *not know*
nescio quid *an "I-don't-know-what,"
something*
nēve *and that . . . not*
nex, necis, f. *slaughter, murder*
nī = nisi
Nīcomēdēnsēs, Nīcomēdēnsium, m.pl.
people of Nicomedia
nīdus, nīdī, m. *nest*
*niger, nigra, nigrum *black*
*nihil *nothing*
nihil cūrō *I don't care*
nihil opus est *there is no need*
nihil vōcis *no voice*
*nihilōminus *nevertheless*
Nīlus, Nīlī, m. *the river Nile*
nimbus, nimbī, m. *rain-cloud*
*nimis *too*
*nimium *too much*
*nisi *except, unless*
nītor, nītī, nīxus sum *lean*
niveus, nivea, niveum *snow-white*
nix, nivis, f. *snow*
nō, nāre, nāvī *swim*
*nōbilis, nōbile *noble, of noble birth*
nōbīs *see* nōs
*noceō, nocēre, nocuī + *dat.* *hurt*
nocte *see* nox
*nōlō, nōlle, nōluī *not want*
nōlī, nōlīte *do not, don't*
nōllem *I would not want*
*nōmen, nōminis, n. *name*
nōminō, nōmināre, nōmināvī,
nōminātus *name, mention by name*
*nōn *not*
nōn dubiē *undoubtedly, clearly*

nōn iterum *never again*
nōn sī *not even if*
nōn temerē *rarely, not without good reason*
*nōnāgintā *ninety*
*nōndum *not yet*
*nōngentī, nōngentae, nōngenta *nine hundred*
*nōnne? *surely?*
*nōnnūllī, nōnnūllae, nōnnūlla *some, several*
nōnnumquam *sometimes*
*nōnus, nōna, nōnum *ninth*
nōrat = nōverat
*nōs *we, us*
nōscitō, nōscitāre, nōscitāvī, nōscitātus *recognize*
nōsse = nōvisse
*noster, nostra, nostrum *our*
notābilis, notābile *noteworthy, memorable*
notārius, notāriī, m. *shorthand writer, stenographer*
nōtitia, nōtitiae, f. *notice*
*nōtus, nōta, nōtum *known, well-known, famous*
Notus, Notī, m. *South Wind*
*novem *nine*
*nōvī *I know*
novissimē *last, most recently*
novō, novāre, novāvī, novātus *change, revolutionize*
*novus, nova, novum *new*
*nox, noctis, f. *night, darkness*
*nūbēs, nūbis, f. *cloud*
*nūbō, nūbere, nūpsī + *dat. *marry*
nūdus, nūda, nūdum *bare*
nūgae, nūgārum, f.pl. *nonsense, foolish talk*
nūllīus *see* nēmō
*nūllus, nūlla, nūllum *not any, no, not at all*
*num? *(1) surely . . . not?*
*num *(2) whether*
*numerō, numerāre, numerāvī, numerātus *count*
*numerus, numerī, m. *number*
numerī, numerōrum, m.pl. *military units*
nummus, nummī, m. *sesterce coin*
*numquam *never*
*nunc *now*

nunc iam *now however, as things are now*
*nūntiō, nūntiāre, nūntiāvī, nūntiātus *announce*
*nūntius, nūntiī, m. *messenger, message, news*
*nūper *recently*
nūpsī *see* nūbō
nūptiae, nūptiārum, f.pl. *wedding, marriage*
nūptiālis, nūptiāle *wedding, marriage*
tabulae nūptiālēs *marriage contract, marriage tablets*
nūptūrus *see* nūbō
*nusquam *nowhere*
nūtō, nūtāre, nūtāvī *sway to and fro, shake*
nūtrīx, nūtrīcis, f. *nurse*

O

ob + *acc. *on account of, because of*
obdūcō, obdūcere, obdūxī, obductus *cover over, close up*
obdūrō, obdūrāre, obdūrāvī *be firm*
obeō, obīre, obiī *meet, go to meet*
mortem obīre *die*
obēsitās, obēsitātis, f. *corpulence, fatness*
obēsus, obēsa, obēsum *fat*
*obiciō, obicere, obiēcī, obiectus *present, put in the way of, expose to*
obiectō, obiectāre, obiectāvī, obiectātus *ascribe*
oblātus *see* offerō
oblīdō, oblīdere, oblīsī, oblīsus *crush*
*oblīvīscor, oblīvīscī, oblītus sum *forget*
obscēnus, obscēna, obscēnum *obscene, disgusting*
*obscūrus, obscūra, obscūrum *dark, gloomy*
observō, observāre, observāvī, observātus *notice, observe*
obses, obsidis, m.f. *hostage*
obstinātē *stubbornly*
obstinātus, obstināta, obstinātum *stubborn*
obstipēscō, obstipēscere, obstipuī *gape in amazement*
*obstō, obstāre, obstitī + *dat *obstruct, block the way*

obstringō, obstringere, obstrīnxī,
  obstrictus bind (with oath of loyalty)
obstruō, obstruere, obstrūxī,
  obstrūctus block the way through
*obstupefaciō, obstupefacere,
  obstupefēcī, obstupefactus amaze,
  stun
obterō, obterere, obtrīvī, obtrītus
  trample to death
obtineō, obtinēre, obtinuī, obtentus
  hold
obtulī see offerō
obversor, obversārī, obversātus sum
  walk to and fro
*obviam eō, obviam īre, obviam iī + dat.
  meet, go to meet
obvius, obvia, obvium encountering, meeting
obvolvō, obvolvere, obvolvī,
  obvolūtus wrap up
*occāsiō, occāsiōnis, f. opportunity
*occīdō, occīdere, occīdī, occīsus kill
occidō, occidere, occidī set
*occupātus, occupāta, occupātum busy
*occupō, occupāre, occupāvī, occupātus
  seize, take over
*occurrō, occurrere, occurrī meet
ocellus, ocellī, m. poor eye, little eye
*octāvus, octāva, octāvum eighth
*octingentī, octingentae, octingenta
  eight hundred
*octō eight
Octōber, Octōbris, Octōbre October
*octōgintā eighty
*oculus, oculī, m. eye
*ōdī I hate
odiōsus, odiōsa, odiōsum hateful
*odium, odiī, n. hatred
* odiō esse be hateful
odor, odōris, m. smell
odōrātus, odōrāta, odōrātum sweet-
  smelling
*offendō, offendere, offendī, offēnsus
  displease, offend
*offerō, offerre, obtulī, oblātus offer
*officium, officiī, n. duty, task
officium agere do one's duty
oleum, oleī, n. oil
olfactus, olfactūs, m. smell
*ōlim once, some time ago, sometimes
omitto, omittere, omīsī, omissus drop,
  leave out, omit, abandon

*omnīnō completely
*omnis, omne all, every
  omnia all, everything
opera, operae, f. work, attention
  tuā operā by your doing, because of you
operiō, operīre, operuī, opertus cover,
  bury, shut
operis see opus
*opēs, opum, f.pl. money, wealth
opifex, opificis, m. inventor, craftsman
opisthographus, opisthographa,
  opisthographum written on both sides
*oportet, oportēre, oportuit be right
  nōs oportet we must
*oppidum, oppidī, n. town
oppleō, opplēre, opplēvī, opplētus fill
*opprimō, opprimere, oppressī,
  oppressus crush
*oppugnō, oppugnāre, oppugnāvī,
  oppugnātus attack
optimē see bene
optimus see bonus
*optō, optāre, optāvī, optātus pray for,
  long for
*opus, operis, n. work, construction,
  building
  nihil opus est there is no need
* opus est + abl. there is need of
  testāceum opus brick work
ōra see ōs
*ōrātiō, ōrātiōnis, f. speech
  ōrātiō solūta prose speech
ōrātor, ōrātōris, m. speaker (in court),
  pleader
orba, orbae, f. (female) orphan
*orbis, orbis, m. globe
* orbis terrārum world
orbitās, orbitātis, f. childlessness
orbus, orba, orbum bereaved, orphaned
Orcus, Orcī, m. the Underworld, Hell
*ōrdō, ōrdinis, m. row, line
Ōrīōn, Ōrīonis, m. Orion, the Hunter
  (constellation)
*orior, orīrī, ortus sum rise, rise up, arise
*ōrnō, ōrnāre, ōrnāvī, ōrnātus decorate
ōrnātus, ōrnāta, ōrnātum decorated,
  elaborately furnished
*ōrō, ōrāre, ōrāvī beg
*ōs, ōris, n. face, mouth
os, ossis, n. bone
*ōsculum, ōsculī, n. kiss

*ostendō, ostendere, ostendī, ostentus
  show
*ōtiōsus, ōtiōsa, ōtiōsum idle, on vacation
*ōtium, ōtiī, n. leisure
  per ōtium at leisure, free from care
Ovidiānus, Ovidiāna, Ovidiānum of Ovid
ovis, ovis, f. sheep

p

pācem see pāx
pacīscor, pacīscī, pactus sum exchange,
  bargain
pācō, pācāre, pācāvī, pācātus pacify,
  make peaceful
*paene nearly, almost
paenitentia, paenitentiae, f. repentance,
  change of heart
palam openly
Palātīnus, Palātīna, Palātīnum
  Palatine
  mōns, Palātīnus the Palatine hill
*pallēscō, pallēscere, palluī grow pale
*pallidus, pallida, pallidum pale
palma, palmae, f. palm, hand
pānis, pānis, m. bread
panthēra, panthērae, f. panther
*pār, gen. paris equal
*parātus, parāta, parātum ready,
  prepared
*parcō, parcere, pepercī + dat. spare
*parēns, parentis, m.f. parent
  parentēs, parentum, m.f.pl. ancestors,
  forefathers
*pāreō, pārēre, pāruī + dat. obey
pariēs, parietis, m. wall, side (of couch)
pario, parere, peperī, partus gain, win
pariter equally, at the same time
*parō, parāre, parāvī, parātus prepare
*pars, partis, f. part, direction
  laevā parte on the left hand
  summā suī parte from its highest part,
  from the top downwards
parsimōnia, parsimōniae, f. economy,
  thriftiness
*parum too little, not . . . enough
*parvus, parva, parvum small
  minor, gen. minōris less, smaller
* minimus, minima, minimum very
  little, least

passer, passeris, m. sparrow
passim everywhere
passus, passa, passum loose, disheveled
passus see patior
pāstor, pāstōris, m. shepherd
*patefaciō, patefacere, patefēcī,
  patefactus reveal
pateō, patēre, patuī lie open
*pater, patris, m. father
patientia, patientiae, f. patience
*patior, patī, passus sum suffer, endure,
  allow
*patria, patriae, f. country, homeland
patrimōnium, patrimōniī, n. fortune,
  inheritance
patrius, patria, patrium of the father
patrō, patrāre, patrāvī, patrātus
  accomplish, commit
*patrōnus, patrōnī, m. patron
*paucī, paucae, pauca few, a few
*paulātim gradually
*paulīsper for a short time
*paulō a little
*paulum a little, slightly, to a slight extent
* minus less
*pauper, gen. pauperis poor
*pavor, pavōris, m. panic
*pāx, pācis, f. peace
peccō, peccāre, peccāvī do wrong, be to
  blame
*pectus, pectoris, n. chest, breast, heart
*pecūnia, pecūniae, f. money, sum of
  money
pecus, pecoris, n. sheep
pedem see pēs
*peditēs, peditum, m.pl. foot soldiers,
  infantry
pelagus, pelagī, n. sea
*pendeō, pendēre, pependī hang
penes + acc. with
penna, pennae, f. feather, wing
pepercī see parcō
*per + acc. through, along
  per artem deliberately, by design
  per gaudium joyfully
  per ōtium at leisure, free from care
peragō, peragere, perēgī, perāctus
  finish
percipiō, percipere, percēpī, perceptus
  take hold of, get a grip on
percussor, percussōris, m. assassin

percutiō, percutere, percussī,
percussus *strike*
*perdō, perdere, perdidī, perditus
destroy, waste, lose
perditus, perdita, perditum *completely
lost, gone forever*
perdūcō, perdūcere, perdūxī,
perductus *bring, carry, continue*
*pereō, perīre, periī *die, perish*
perferō, perferre, pertulī, perlātus
bring, endure
*perficiō, perficere, perfēcī, perfectus
finish
*perfidia, perfidiae, f. *treachery*
*perfidus, perfida, perfidum
treacherous, untrustworthy
*perīculōsus, perīculōsa, perīculōsum
dangerous
*perīculum, perīculī, n. *danger*
periī *see* pereō
perinde *in the same manner*
perinde . . . quam *as much . . . as*
*perītus, perīta, perītum *skillful*
permisceō, permiscēre, permiscuī,
permixtus *mix with*
*permōtus, permōta, permōtum
alarmed, disturbed
perōsus, perōsa, perōsum *hating*
perperam *incorrectly*
perpetuus, perpetua, perpetuum
perpetual
in perpetuum *forever*
perseverō, perseverāre, perseverāvī
continue
perstō, perstāre, perstitī *persist*
*persuādeō, persuādēre, persuāsī+ *dat.*
persuade
*perterritus, perterrita, perterritum
terrified
pertinācia, pertināciae, f. *obstinacy,
determination*
pertineō, pertinēre, pertinuī *concern*
pertinēre ad exemplum *involve a
precedent*
*perturbō, perturbāre, perturbāvī,
perturbātus *disturb, alarm*
*perveniō, pervenīre, pervēnī *reach,
arrive at*
pervigilō, pervigilāre, pervigilāvī *sit up
all night, stay awake all night*
*pēs, pedis, m. *foot, paw*

pessimus *see* malus
*pestis, pestis, f. *pest, rascal*
*petō, petere, petīvī, petītus *head for,
attack; seek, beg for, ask for*
phengītēs, phengītae, m. *phengite,
oxyx-like stone*
phōca, phōcae, f. *seal*
*pietās, pietātis, f. *duty, piety, family
feeling (respect for (1) the gods,
(2) homeland, (3) family)*
pignus, pignoris, n. *hostage*
pignora, pignorum, n.pl. *children*
pinguis, pingue *plump*
pīnus, pīnī, f. *pine tree, boat (made of
pine wood)*
pīpiō, pīpiāre, pīpiāvī *chirp, peep*
piscis, piscis, m. *fish*
pius, pia, pium *good, pious, respectful to
the gods*
*placeō, placēre, placuī + *dat.* *please,
suit*
placuit *it was decided*
placidus, placida, placidum *calm,
peaceful*
plānus, plāna, plānum *level, flat*
*plaudō, plaudere, plausī, plausus
applaud, clap
*plaustrum, plaustrī, n. *wagon, cart*
plausus, plausūs, m. *applause*
*plēnus, plēna, plēnum *full*
*plērīque, plēraeque, plēraque *most,
the majority*
plērumque *generally*
plōrātus, plōrātūs, m. *weeping*
plūma, plūmae, f. *feather*
plumbum, plumbī, n. *lead*
plūra, plūrēs, plūs *see* multus
plūrimī *see* multus
*pōculum, pōculī, n. *cup (often for wine)*
*poena, poenae, f. *punishment*
capitālis poena *capital punishment,
death penalty*
* poenās dare *pay the penalty, be punished*
*poēta, poētae, m. *poet*
*polliceor, pollicērī, pollicitus sum
promise
pollex, pollicis, m. *thumb*
*pompa, pompae, f. *procession*
*pondus, ponderis, n. *weight*
*pōnō, pōnere, posuī, positus *put, place,
put up, serve*

*pōns, pontis, m. *bridge*
*pontifex, pontificis, m. *priest*
  Pontifex Maximus *Chief Priest*
  pontus, pontī, m. *sea*
  poposcī *see* poscō
  populāris, populāre *ordinary*
  populus, populī, m. *people*
  porrigō, porrigere, porrēxī, porrēctus
    stretch out, hand to
*porta, portae, f. *gate*
  porticus, porticūs, f. *colonnade*
*portō, portāre, portāvī, portātus *carry*
*portus, portūs, m. *harbor, port*
*poscō, poscere, poposcī *demand, ask for*
  positus *see* pōnō
*possideō, possidēre, possēdī, possessus
    possess
*possum, posse, potuī *can, be able*
*post + *acc. *after, behind*
*posteā *afterwards*
  postis, postis, m. *door, doorpost*
*postquam *after, when*
*postrēmō *finally, lastly*
  postrēmus, postrēma, postrēmum *last*
*postrīdiē *(on) the next day*
*postulō, postulāre, postulāvī,
    postulātus *demand*
  posuī *see* pōnō
*potēns, *gen. potentis *powerful*
  potes *see* possum
*potestās, potestātis, f. *power*
  in potestātem redigere *bring under the
    control*
  potis, pote *possible*
    quī potis est? *how is that possible? how
    can that be?*
  pōtiuncula, pōtiunculae, f. *little drink*
  potius *rather*
  potuī *see* possum
  prae + *abl. *instead of, rather than*
*praebeō, praebēre, praebuī, praebitus
    provide
*praeceps, *gen. praecipitis *headlong*
  praeceptum, praeceptī, n. *instruction*
  praecipiō, praecipere, praecēpī,
    praeceptus *instruct, order*
  praecipitō, praecipitāre, praecipitāvī
    hurl
  praecipuē *especially*
  praecipuus, praecipua, praecipuum
    special

*praecō, praecōnis, m. *herald, announcer*
  praecurrō, praecurrere, praecucurrī
    go on ahead, run ahead
  praeda, praedae, f. *booty, plunder*
  praedīcō, praedīcere, praedīxī,
    praedictus *foretell, predict*
  praedium, praediī, n. *estate, property*
*praefectus, praefectī, m. *commander*
  praefectus classis *admiral of the fleet*
  praefectus praetōriō *commander of the
    praetorian guard*
*praeficiō, praeficere, praefēcī,
    praefectus *put in charge*
  praenūntius, praenūntiī, m. *forerunner,
    warning sign*
*praemium, praemiī, n. *prize, reward, profit*
  praepositus, praeposita, praepositum
    + *dat. *put in charge of*
*praesēns, *gen. praesentis *present, ready*
  ad praesēns *for the present, for the
    moment*
  praesentia, praesentiae, f. *presence*
*praesertim *especially*
*praesidium, praesidiī, n. *protection*
*praestō, praestāre, praestitī *show,
    display*
*praesum, praeesse, praefuī + *dat. *be in
    charge of*
  praesūmō, praesūmere, praesūmpsī,
    praesūmptus *take in advance*
*praeter + *acc. *except*
*praetereā *besides*
*praetereō, praeterīre, praeteriī *pass by,
    go past*
  praetōriānus, praetōriāna,
    praetōriānum *praetorian (belonging to
    emperor's bodyguard)*
  praetōrium, praetōriī, n. *the praetorian
    guard*
  praefectus praetōriō *commander of the
    praetorian guard*
  praevaleō, praevalēre, praevaluī
    prevail, be uppermost
  prandeō, prandēre, prandī *lunch, have
    lunch*
  prātum, prātī, n. *meadow*
*prāvus, prāva, prāvum *evil*
*precēs, precum, f.pl. *prayers*
  precēs adhibēre *offer prayers*
*precor, precārī, precātus sum *pray (to),
    plead*

*premō, premere, pressī, pressus *push,
press, crush
prēnsō, prēnsāre, prēnsāvī, prēnsātus
take hold of, grab
*pretiōsus, pretiōsa, pretiōsum
expensive, precious
*pretium, pretiī, n. *price*
prīdiē *the day before*
prīdiē quam . . . *the day before* . . .
prīmō *at first*
prīmum *first, for the first time*
cum prīmum *as soon as*
*prīmus, prīma, prīmum *first*
in prīmīs *in the first place, in particular*
*prīnceps, prīncipis, m. *chief, chieftain,
emperor*
prīncipātus, prīncipātūs, m. *principate,
reign*
*prīncipia, prīncipiōrum, n.pl.
headquarters
*prior, prius *first, in front, earlier*
prīscus, prīsca, prīscum *ancient*
*prius *earlier, before now*
*priusquam *before, until*
prīvātus, prīvāta, prīvātum *private*
*prō + abl. *in front of, for, in return for, as,
instead of*
* prō certō habēre *know for certain*
*probō, probāre, probāvī, probātus
*prove, examine (e.g. at time of enrollment),
approve*
*prōcēdō, prōcēdere, prōcessī *advance,
proceed*
procella, procellae, f. *violent wind*
prōcērus, prōcēra, prōcērum *tall*
*procul *far off*
*prōcumbō, prōcumbere, prōcubuī *fall
down*
prōcūrātor, prōcūrātōris, m. *manager*
prōcūrō, prōcūrāre, prōcūrāvī *to serve
as governor*
prōcurrō, prōcurrere, prōcurrī *project*
prōdesse *see* prōsum
prōditor, prōditōris, m. *betrayer,
informer*
*prōdō, prōdere, prōdidī, prōditus
betray
prōdūcō, prōdūcere, prōdūxī,
prōductus *bring forward, bring out,
prolong, continue*
*proelium, proeliī, n. *battle*

profēstus, profēsta, profēstum *working,
not kept as a holiday*
*proficīscor, proficīscī, profectus sum
set out
profiteor, profitērī, professus sum
declare, claim
prōfluō, prōfluere, prōflūxī *flow, flow out*
prōfluvium, prōfluviī, n. *flow*
*prōgredior, prōgredī, prōgressus sum
advance
*prohibeō, prohibēre, prohibuī,
prohibitus *prevent*
prōiciō, prōicere, prōiēcī, prōiectus
cast (as an offering)
prōlēs, prōlis, f. *offspring, brood*
prōmissum, prōmissī, n. *promise*
*prōmittō, prōmittere, prōmīsī,
prōmissus *promise*
prōmptus, prōmpta, prōmptum *quick*
prōmunturium, prōmunturiī, n.
promontory
prōnūntiō, prōnūntiāre, prōnūntiāvī,
prōnūntiātus *proclaim, preach,
announce, pronounce*
prōnus, prōna, prōnum *easy*
*prope *near*
properō, properāre, properāvī *hurry*
propinquus, propinquī, m. *relative*
prōpōnō, prōpōnere, prōposuī,
prōpositus *propose, put forward*
prōpositum, prōpositī, n. *intention,
resolution*
proprius, propria, proprium *right,
proper; one's own, that belongs to one*
*propter + acc. *because of*
proptereā *for that reason*
prōra, prōrae, f. *prow*
prōsequor, prōsequī, prōsecūtus sum
follow, escort
prōsiliō, prōsilīre, prōsiluī *leap forward,
jump*
prōsum, prōdesse, prōfuī + dat. *benefit*
quid prōderit? *what good will it do?*
prōtegō, prōtegere, prōtēxī, prōtēctus
protect
prōtendō, prōtendere, prōtendī,
prōtentus *thrust forward*
prōtinus *immediately*
prout *according as*
prōvideō, prōvidēre, prōvīdī, prōvīsus
foresee, see in front

*prōvincia, prōvinciae, f. *province*
*proximus, proxima, proximum *nearest,*
   next to, very close, last
   in proximō *nearby*
prūdēns, *gen.* prūdentis *shrewd,*
   intelligent, sensible
prūdenter *prudently, sensibly*
*prūdentia, prūdentiae, f. *prudence,*
   good sense, shrewdness
Prūsēnsēs, Prūsēnsium, m.pl. *people of*
   Prusa
pūblicō, pūblicāre, pūblicāvī,
   pūblicātus *confiscate*
*pūblicus, pūblica, pūblicum *public*
pudīcitia, pudīcitiae, f. *chastity, virtue,*
   purity
pudīcus, pudīca, pudīcum *chaste,*
   virtuous
*puella, puellae, f. *girl*
*puer, puerī, m. *boy*
pugillārēs, pugillārium, m.pl. *notebook*
pugiō, pugiōnis, m. *dagger*
*pugna, pugnae, f. *fight*
*pugnō, pugnāre, pugnāvī *fight*
*pulcher, pulchra, pulchrum *beautiful*
pulchritūdō, pulchritūdinis, f. *beauty*
*pulsō, pulsāre, pulsāvī, pulsātus *hit,*
   knock on, whack, punch
pulvīnus, pulvīnī, m. *cushion, pillow*
pūmex, pūmicis, m. *pumice-stone*
pūmiliō, pūmiliōnis, m. *dwarf*
*pūniō, pūnīre, pūnīvī, pūnītus *punish*
puppis, puppis, f. *stern*
pūriter *decently, with clean water*
pūrus, pūra, pūrum *pure, clean, spotless*
*putō, putāre, putāvī *think*

q

quā *where*
quadrāgēsimus, quadrāgēsima,
   quadrāgēsimum *fortieth*
*quadrāgintā *forty*
quadrātus, quadrāta, quadrātum
   squared, in blocks
quadrīga, quadrīgae, f. *chariot*
*quadringentī, quadringentae,
   quadringenta *five hundred*

quaedam *see* quīdam
*quaerō, quaerere, quaesīvī, quaesītus
   search for, look for
quaesō *I beg,* i.e. *please*
*quālis, quāle *what sort of*
*quam *(1) how*
   tam . . . quam *as . . . as*
*quam *(2) than*
   perinde . . . quam *as much as*
   prīdiē quam . . . *the day before* . . .
   quam celerrimē *as quickly as possible*
quamdiū *as long as*
*quamquam *although, however*
quamvīs *although*
*quandō? *when?*
quandoquidem *seeing that, since*
*quantus, quanta, quantum *how big*
   quantum *as, as much as, as far as*
   quantum est *as much as there is*
*quārē? *why?*
quārē *and so, wherefore*
*quārtus, quārta, quārtum *fourth*
*quasi *as if, like*
quassō, quassāre, quassāvī, quassātus
   shake violently
quater *four times*
quatiō, quatere *shake, flap*
*quattuor *four*
*quattuordecim *fourteen*
*-que *and*
   -que . . . -que *both . . . and*
quendam *see* quīdam
querēla, querēlae, f. *complaint*
*queror, querī, questus sum *lament,*
   complain about
questus, questūs, m. *lamentation, cry of*
   grief
*quī, quae, quod *who, which, some*
   id quod *what*
   quod sī *but if*
qui? quae? quod? *which? what? how?*
   quī potis est? *how is that possible? how*
   can that be?
*quia *because*
quicquam *see* quisquam
quicquid *see* quisquis
quīcumque, quaecumque,
   quodcumque *whoever, whatever, any*
   whatever
quid *see* quis
quid? *see* quis?

*quīdam, quaedam, quoddam *one, a certain*
*quidem *indeed*
* nē . . . quidem *not even*
  quidquid *see* quisquis
*quiēs, quiētis, f. *rest*
  quiēscō, quiēscere, quiēvī *rest*
  quiētus, quiēta, quiētum *quiet, peaceful*
  quīlibet, quaelibet, quodlibet *anyone at all, anything at all*
*quīndecim *fifteen*
*quīngentī, quīngentae, quīngenta *five hundred*
*quīnquāgintā *fifty*
*quīnque *five*
*quīntus, quīnta, quīntum *fifth*
*quis? quid? *who? what?*
  quid agis? *how are you? how are you doing?*
  quid faciam? *what am I to do?*
  quid multa? *in brief, in short*
  quid plūra? *why say more?*
  quid prōderit? *what good will it do?*
  quis, quid *anyone, anything*
* nē quid *lest anything, in case anything*
* nē quis *lest anyone, in case anyone, that anyone, that nobody*
  nescio quid *an "I-don't-know-what," something*
* sī quid *if anything*
* sī quis *if anyone*
*quisquam, quicquam *or* quidquam *anyone, anything*
*quisque, quaeque, quodque *each one, every one*
  usque quāque *on every possible occasion*
  ut quisque *as soon as each one*
*quisquis *whoever*
* quidquid *or* quicquid *whatever, whatever possible*
  quidquid est *whatever is happening*
  quō *in order that*
*quō? *where? where to?*
*quō modō? *how? in what way?*
*quod *because*
* ideō quod *for the reason that, because*
  quōdam *see* quīdam
  quodcumque *see* quīcumque
*quondam *one day, once, sometimes*
*quoniam *since*
*quoque *also, too*

quōsdam *see* quīdam
*quot? *how many?*
*quotiēns *whenever*

r

rapidus, rapida, rapidum *rushing, racing, blazing, consuming*
*rapiō, rapere, rapuī, raptus *seize, grab*
  rārō *rarely, seldom*
  rārus, rāra, rārum *occasional, far apart*
  ratiō, ratiōnis, f. *reason*
*ratiōnēs, ratiōnum, f.pl. *accounts*
  ratis, ratis, f. *boat*
  rē *see* rēs
  rebellō, rebellāre, rebellāvī *rebel, revolt*
  rēbus *see* rēs
  recēns, *gen.* recentis *recent*
*recipiō, recipere, recēpī, receptus *recover, take back*
  recitātiō, recitātiōnis, f. *recital, public reading*
*recitō, recitāre, recitāvī, recitātus *recite, read out*
*rēctē *rightly, properly*
  rēctor, rēctōris, m. *helmsman*
*recumbō, recumbere, recubuī *lie down, recline*
*recūsō, recūsāre, recūsāvī, recūsātus *refuse*
*reddō, reddere, reddidī, redditus *give back, restore, make*
  sē reddere *return, go back*
  ribi reddī *be restored to one's senses, be restored to oneself*
*redeō, redīre, rediī *return, go back, come back*
  redigō, redigere, redēgī, redāctus *bring*
  in potestātem redigere *bring under the control*
*redūcō, redūcere, redūxī, reductus *lead back*
*referō, referre, rettulī, relātus *bring back, carry, deliver, tell, report*
  grātiam referre *show gratitude, thank*
  rem referre *report the event*
  victōriam referre *win a victory*
  rēfert, rēferre, rētulit *make a difference*
*reficiō, reficere, refēcī, refectus *repair*
  refectus sum *I got over, recovered*

*rēgīna, rēgīnae, f. *queen*
*regiō, regiōnis, f. *region*
rēgis *see* rēx
*rēgnum, rēgnī, n. *kingdom*
*regō, regere, rēxī, rēctus *rule*
*regredior, regredī, regressus sum *go back, return*
reiciō, reicere, reiēcī, reiectus *reject*
*relēgō, relēgāre, relēgāvī, relēgātus *exile*
*relinquō, relinquere, relīquī, relictus *leave*
reliquiae, reliquiārum, f.pl. *remains*
*reliquus, reliqua, reliquum *remaining, the rest*
relūceō, relūcēre, relūxī *blaze, shine out*
relūcēscō, relūcēscere, relūxī *become light again*
rem *see* rēs
remacrēscō, remacrēscere, remacruī *shrink into thinness, become, spindly*
remaneō, remanēre, remānsī *stay behind*
*remedium, remediī, n. *cure*
rēmigium, rēmigiī, n. *oars, wings*
rēmigō, rēmigāre, rēmigāvī *row*
remittō, remittere, remīsī, remissus *send back*
rēmus, rēmī, m. *oar*
renīdeō, renīdēre *grin, smirk, smile*
renovō, renovāre, renovāvī, renovātus *renew, repeat, resume*
repellō, repellere, reppulī, repulsus *repel push back*
repulsus, repulsa, repulsum *repelled, taken aback*
*repentē *suddenly*
repentīnus, repentīna, repentīnum *sudden*
*reperiō, reperīre, repperī, repertus *find*
repetō, repetere, repetīvī, repetītus *seek again, repeat, claim, recall*
reprehendō, reprehendere, reprehendī, reprehēnsus *blame, criticize*
repudiō, repudiāre, repudiāvī, repudiātus *divorce, reject*
*requīrō, requīrere, requīsīvī, requīsītus *ask, seek, search for, go looking for*
*rēs, reī, f. *thing, business*

in rem subitam *to meet the sudden crisis*
* rē vērā *in fact, truly, really*
rem administrāre *manage the task*
rem cōgitāre *consider the problem*
rem efficere *accomplish the task*
rem nārrāre *tell the story*
rem referre *report the event*
rērum cursus *course of events*
* rēs adversae *misfortune*
resīdō, resīdere, resēdī *sit down, sink down*
*resistō, resistere, restitī + *dat. *resist*
resonō, renonāre, resonāvī *resound*
resorbeō, resorbēre *suck back*
respectō, respectāre, respectāvī *look towards, count on, keep an eye on*
*respiciō, respicere, respexī *look at, look upon, look back, look up*
respīrō, respīrāre, respīrāvī *recover, revive, recover one's breath, get one's breath back*
*respondeō, respondēre, respondī *reply*
respōnsum, respōnsī, n. *answer*
rēspūblica, reīpūblicae, f. *"the republic"*
restituō, restituere, restituī, restitūtus *restore*
restrictus, restricta, restrictum *pinched*
resūmō, resūmere, resūmpsī, resūmptus *pick up again*
resupīnus, resupīna, resupīnum *thrown back*
*retineō, retinēre, retinuī, retentus *keep, hold back, restrain, check*
rettulī *see* referō
reus, reī, m. *defendant, accused (of)*
vōtī reus *bound by one's vow, in payment of one's vow*
*reveniō, revenīre, revēnī *come back, return*
*revertor, revertī, reversus sum *turn back, return*
*revocō, revocāre, revocāvī, revocātus *recall, call back, recover, make (someone) go back*
revomō, revomere, revomuī *vomit up*
*rēx, rēgis, m. *king*
rēxī *see* regō
rhētor, rhētoris, m. *teacher*
*rīdeō, rīdēre, rīsī *laugh, smile*
rīdiculus, rīdicula, rīdiculum *ridiculous, silly*

*rīpa, rīpae, f. *river bank*
rīsus, rīsūs, m. *smile*
rīte *properly*
rīvus, rīvī, m. *stream*
*rogō, rogāre, rogāvī, rogātus *ask*
rogus, rogī, m. *pyre*
Rōma, Rōmae, f. *Rome*
Rōmānī, Rōmānōrum, m.pl. *Romans*
Rōmānus, Rōmāna, Rōmānum *Roman*
rōstrum, rōstrī, n. *prow*
rubeō, rubēre *be red*
rubor, rubōris, m. *redness, high color*
ruīna, ruīnae, f. *ruin, wreckage, collapse*
rūmor, rūmōris, m. *rumor*
   rūmōrēs, rūmōrum, m.pl. *gossip,*
   rumors
*rumpō, rumpere, rūpī, ruptus *break,*
   split, burst, rupture
*ruō, ruere, ruī *rush, collapse, charge*
rūpēs, rūpis, f. *rock, crag*
*rūrsus *again*
*rūs, rūris, n. *country, countryside*
rūsticus, rūstica, rūsticum *country, in*
   the country, of a country man
   vīlla rūstica *house in the country*

S

Sabīnus, Sabīnī, m. *Sabine*
*sacer, sacra, sacrum *sacred*
*sacerdōs, sacerdōtis, m. *priest*
sacerdōtium, sacerdōtiī, n. *priesthood*
sacrāmentum, sacrāmentī, n. *oath*
   sacrāmentum dīcere *take the military*
   oath
sacrārium, sacrāriī, n. *shrine*
sacrificium, sacrificiī, n. *offering,*
   sacrifice
sacrificō, sacrificāre, sacrificāvī,
   sacrificātus *sacrifice*
*saepe *often*
*saeviō, saevīre, saeviī *be in a rage*
*saevus, saeva, saevum *savage, cruel*
*sagitta, sagittae, f. *arrow*
salsus, salsa, salsum *salty*
saltem *at least*
*saltō, saltāre, saltāvī *dance*
salūbris, salūbre *comfortable*
*salūs, salūtis, f. *safety, health*
   salūtem dīcere *sends good wishes*

*salūtō, salūtāre, salūtāvī, salūtātus
   greet
*salvē! salvēte! *hello!*
sandapila, sandapilae, f. *bier (for a poor*
   person)
*sānē *obviously*
*sanguis, sanguinis, m. *blood*
sānō, sānāre, sānāvī, sānātus *heal, cure,*
   treat
*sapiēns, *gen. sapientis *wise*
sapienter *wisely*
satietās, satietātis, f. *gorging, eating*
   one's fill; disgust, weariness (with killing)
*satis *enough*
* satis cōnstat *it is generally agreed*
*saxum, saxī, n. *rock*
scaena, scaenae, f. *stage, scene*
   extrēma scaena *the edge of the stage*
scalpō, scalpere, scalpsī, scalptus
   scratch
scapha, scaphae, f. *small boat*
*scelestus, scelesta, scelestum *wicked,*
   wretched
*scelus, sceleris, n. *crime*
scīlicet *obviously*
*scindō, scindere, scidī, scissus *tear,*
   tear up, cut up, cut open, carve
*sciō, scīre, scīvī *know*
scopulus, scopulī, m. *reef, rock*
*scrībō, scrībere, scrīpsī, scrīptus *write*
sculptor, sculptōris, m. *sculptor*
scurrīlis, scurrīle *obscene, dirty*
*sē *himself, herself, themselves*
   inter sē *among themselves, with each other*
   sēcum *with him, with her, with them*
sēcessus, sēcessūs, m. *retreat*
*secō, secāre, secuī, sectus *cut*
sēcrētō *in solitude, in secret*
sēcrētus, sēcrēta, sēcrētum *secret*
sector, sectārī, sectātus sum *chase after*
*secundus, secunda, secundum *second*
   tempestās secunda *favorable weather*
   ventus secundus *favorable, following*
   wind
secūris, secūris, f. *axe*
sēcūritās, sēcūritātis, f. *unconcern, lack*
   of anxiety
*sēcūrus, sēcūra, sēcūrum *without a care*
secūtus *see* sequor
*sed *but*
*sēdecim *sixteen*

*sedeō, sedēre, sēdī *sit*
*sēdēs, sēdis, f. *seat*
sēdō, sēdāre, sēdāvī, sēdātus *quell,*
    calm down
seges, segetis, f. *crop, harvest*
sēgnis, sēgne *timid, unenterprising*
sēiūnctus, sēiūncta, sēiūnctum *separate*
*sella, sellae, f. *chair, sedan-chair*
semel *once*
sēmiustus, sēmiusta, sēmiustum *half-*
    burned
*semper *always*
*senātor, senātōris, m. *senator*
senātus, senātūs, m. *senate*
    cognitiō senātūs *trial by the senate*
senēscō, senēscere, senuī *grow old*
*senex, senis, m. *old man*
senīlis, senīle *old*
senior, senius *older, elder, elderly*
sēnsus, sēnsūs, m. *feeling, sense*
*sententia, sententiae, f. *opinion, sentence*
*sentiō, sentīre, sēnsī, sēnsus *feel, notice*
sēparō, sēparāre, sēparāvī, sēparātus
    break off
*sepeliō, sepelīre, sepelīvī, sepultus *bury*
*septem *seven*
*septendecim *seventeen*
*septimus, septima, septimum *seventh*
*septingentī, septingentae, septingenta
    seven hundred
*septuāgintā *seventy*
*sepulcrum, sepulcrī, n. *tomb*
sepultūra, sepultūrae, f. *burial*
sepultus, sepultī, m. *one who is buried*
*sequor, sequī, secūtus sum *follow*
*serēnus, serēna, serēnum *calm clear*
*sermō, sermōnis, m. *conversation*
sērō *late, after a long time*
*serviō, servīre, servīvī + dat. *serve (as a*
    slave)
*servō, servāre, servāvī, servātus *save,*
    look after
*servus, servī, m. *slave*
*sescentī, sescentae, sescenta *six hundred*
sēsē = sē
sēstertius, sēstertiī, m. *sesterce (coin)*
Sētīnus, Sētīna, Sētīnum *Setian*
sevērē *severely*
sevēritās, sevēritātis, f. *strictness,*
    severity
*sevērus, sevēra, sevērum *severe, strict*

*sex *six*
*sexāgintā *sixty*
*sextus, sexta, sextum *sixth*
*sī *if*
    nōn sī *not even if*
    quod sī *but if*
* sī quid *if anything*
* sī quis *if anyone*
sibi *see* sē
sibilō, sibilāre, sibilāvī *hiss*
*sīc *thus, in this way, in the same way*
siccus, sicca, siccum *dry*
*sīcut *like*
    sīcut . . . ita *just as . . . so*
sīdus, sīderis, n. *star*
significō, significāre, significāvī,
    significātus *mean, indicate*
signō, signāre, signāvī, signātus *sign,*
    seal
*signum, signī, n. *sign, seal, signal*
*silentium, silentiī, n. *silence*
sileō, silēre, siluī *be silent*
*silva, silvae, f. *woods, forest*
sim *see* sum
*similis, simile + dat. *similar*
*simul *at the same time, as soon as*
*simulac, simulatque *as soon as*
simulātiō, simulātiōnis, f. *pretense,*
    play-acting
*simulō, simulāre, simulāvī, simulātus
    pretend
*sine + abl. *without*
sinister, sinistra, sinistrum *left*
sinō, sinere, sīvī, situs *allow*
    nē illud deī sinant! *heaven forbid!*
sīpō, sīpōnis, m. *fire-pump*
sistō, sistere, stitī *stop, halt*
sitiō, sitīre, sitīvī *be thirsty*
sitis, sitis, f. *thirst*
socia, sociae, f. *companion, partner*
*socius, sociī, m. *companion, partner*
*sōl, sōlis, m. *sun, day*
*soleō, solēre *be accustomed*
    solitus, solita, solitum *common, usual*
sōlitūdō, sōlitūdinis, f. *lonely place,*
    abandoned area
sollemnis, sollemne *solemn, traditional*
sollemniter *solemnly*
sollicitō, sollicitāre, sollicitāvī,
    sollicitātus *worry*
sollicitūdō, sollicitūdinis, f. *anxiety*

*sollicitus, sollicita, sollicitum *worried, anxious*

sōlor, sōlārī, sōlātus sum *relieve, mitigate*

sōlum *only*

*sōlus, sōla, sōlum *alone, lonely, only, on one's own*

*solvō, solvere, solvī, solūtus *loosen, untie, cast off*

somniō, somniāre, somniāvī *dream*

*somnus, somnī, m. *sleep*

*sonitus, sonitūs, m. *sound*

sonō, sonāre, sonuī *sound*

sonāns, *gen.* sonantis *resounding, loud*

*sordidus, sordida, sordidum *dirty*

*soror, sorōris, f. *sister*

*sors, sortis, f. *lot, fate, one's lot*

*spargō, spargere, sparsī, sparsus *scatter, spread*

spatiōsus, spatiōsa, spatiōsum *huge*

*spatium, spatiī, n. *space, distance*

spē *see* spēs

*speciēs, speciēī, f. *appearance*

speciōsus, speciōsa, speciōsum *impressive*

*spectāculum, spectāculī, n. *show, spectacle*

spectātor, spectātōris, m. *spectator*

* spectō, spectāre, spectāvī, spectātus *look at, watch*

speculor, speculārī, speculātus sum *spy out*

*spernō, spernere, sprēvī, sprētus *despise, reject, ignore, disobey, disregard*

*spērō, spērāre, spērāvī *hope, expect*

*spēs, speī, f. *hope*

spīritus, spīritūs, m. *breathing*

splendidus, splendida, splendidum *splendid, impressive*

splendor, splendōris, m. *brightness, brilliance*

spoliō, spoliāre, spoliāvī, spoliātus *deprive*

sportula, sportulae, f. *handout (gift of food or money)*

spūmō, spūmāre, spūmāvī *foam*

st! *ssh! hush!*

stābam *see* stō

*statim *at once*

*statiō, statiōnis, f. *post*

statua, statuae, f. *statue*

statūra, statūrae, f. *height*

stēla, stēlae, f. *stone slab, tombstone*

*sternō, sternere, strāvī, strātus *lay low, knock over*

*stilus, stilī, m. *pen (pointed stick for writing on wax tablet), stylus*

stirps, stirpis, f. *stem*

stīva, stīvae, f. *plow-handle*

*stō, stāre, stetī *stand, lie at anchor*

*stola, stolae, f. *(long) dress*

stomachus, stomachī, m. *esophagus, windpipe*

*strēnuē *hard, energetically*

*strepitus, strepitūs, m. *noise, din*

stringō, stringere, strīnxī, strictus *draw, unsheathe*

*studeō, studēre, studuī *study*

*studium, studiī, n. *enthusiasm, shout of support, cheer; study*

līberālia studia *liberal studies*

*stultus, stulta, stultum *stupid, foolish*

*suādeō, suādēre, suāsī = dat. *advise, suggest*

*suāvis, suāve *sweet*

*suāviter *sweetly*

*sub (1) + acc. *under, to the depths of*

*sub (2) + abl. *under, beneath*

sub dīō *under the open sky*

subeō, subīre, subiī *approach, come up, take over*

subinde *regularly*

*subitō *suddenly*

subitus, subita, subitum *sudden*

in rem subitam *to meet the sudden crisis*

sublevō, sublevāre, sublevāvī, sublevātus *remove, relieve*

subrīdeō, subrīdēre, subrīsī *smile, smirk*

subsellium, sellliī, n. *bench (for prisoner in court)*

subsistō, subsistere, substitī *halt, stop, stay*

suburbānum, suburbānī, n. *suburban home*

suburgeō, suburgēre *drive up close*

*subveniō, subvenīre, subvēnī + dat. *help, come to help*

successor, successōris, m. *successor*

successus, successūs, m. *success*

sūdor, sūdōris, m. *sweat*

sufficiēns, *gen.* sufficientis *enough, sufficient*

suffodiō, suffodere, suffōdī, suffossus
stab
suī *see* sē
sulcō, sulcāre, sulcāvī *plow through*
sulphur, sulphuris, n. *sulphur*
*sum, esse, fuī *be*
estō! *be!*
summa, summae, f. *full responsibility,*
supreme command
summergō, summergere, summersī,
summersus *sink, dip*
summoveō, summovēre, summōvī,
summōtus *dismiss, remove*
*summus, summa, summum *highest,*
greatest, top
summā suī parte *from its highest part,*
from the top downwards
summus mōns *the top of the mountain*
sūmō, sūmere, sūmpsī, sūmptus *take*
*sūmptuōsus, sūmptuōsa, sūmptuōsum
expensive, lavish, costly
suōpte = suō
super + *acc. on, during*
superbē *arrogantly*
*superbus, superba, superbum
arrogant, proud
supercilia, superciliōrum, n.pl.
eyebrows
supercilia contrahere *draw eyebrows*
together, frown
superior, superius *higher, further*
upstream
*superō, superāre, superāvī, superātus
overcome, overpower, surpass, achieve, win
superpōnō, superpōnere, superposuī,
superpositus *place on*
superstes, superstitis, m. *survivor*
superstitiōsē *superstitiously, with*
superstitious reverence
*supersum, superesse, superfuī *survive,*
remain, be left
suppliciter *like a suppliant, humbly*
supplicium, suppliciī, n. *punishment,*
penalty
supplicium ultimum *death penalty*
supprimō, supprimere, suppressī,
suppressus *staunch, stop flow*
*suprā + *acc. over, on top of*
suprēmus suprēma, suprēmum *last*
*surgō, surgere, surrēxī *get up, rise,*
grow up, be built up

*suscipiō, suscipere, suscēpī, susceptus
undertake, take on
suspiciō, suspicere, suspexī,
suspectus *suspect*
suspīciō, suspīciōnis, f. *suspicion*
suspīciōsus, suspīciōsa, suspīciōsum
suspicious
*suspicor, suspicārī, suspicātus sum
suspect
sustulī *see* tollere
susurrō, susurrāre, susurrāvī *whisper,*
mumble
*suus, sua, suum *his, her, their, his own*
suī, suōrum, m.pl. *his men, his family,*
their families

t

T. = Titus
*taberna, tabernae, f. *store, inn*
tābēscō, tābēscere, tābuī *melt*
tablīnum, tablīnī, n. *study*
tabula, tabulae, f. *tablet, writing-tablet*
tabulae nūptiālēs *marriage contract,*
marriage tablets
*taceō, tacēre, tacuī *be silent, be quiet*
tacē! *shut up! be quiet!*
*tacitē *quietly, silently*
*tacitus, tacita, tacitum *quiet, silent, in*
silence
*taedet, taedēre *be tiring*
*tālis, tāle *such*
*tam *so*
tam . . . quam *as . . . as*
*tamen *however*
*tamquam *as, like*
*tandem *at last*
vix tandem *at long last*
*tangō, tangere, tetigī, tāctus *touch, move*
*tantum *only*
*tantus, tanta, tantum *so great, such a*
great
tantī esse *be worth*
tantī facere ut *rate . . . so high that*
tantum *so much, such a great number*
tardē *late, slowly*
*tardus, tarda, tardum *late, slow*
taurus, taurī, m. *bull*
tē *see* tū
*tēctum, tēctī, n. *ceiling, roof, building*

*tegō, tegere, tēxī, tēctus *cover*
*tellūs, tellūris, f. *land, earth*
temerē *without good reason*
nōn temerē *rarely, not without good reason*
*tempestās, tempestātis, f. *storm, weather*
tempestās secunda *favorable weather*
*templum, templī, n. *temple*
*temptō, temptāre, temptāvī, temptātus *try, put to the test*
*tempus, temporis, n. *time*
tendō, tendere, tetendī, tentus *strain, strive, stretch out*
*tenebrae, tenebrārum, f.pl. *darkness*
tenebricōsus, tenebricōsa, tenebricōsum *dark, shadowy*
*teneō, tenēre, tenuī, tentus *hold, keep to, hold on to, occupy, possess, be upon, hold back*
tener, tenera, tenerum *tender, helpless*
*tenuis, tenue *thin, subtle*
tenuō, tenuāre, tenuāvī, tenuātus *thin out*
tergō, tergere, tersī, tersus *rub down*
*tergum, tergī, n. *back*
*terra, terrae, f. *ground, land*
orbis terrārum *world*
*terreō, terrēre, terruī, territus *frighten*
terrestris, terrestre *on land*
terribilis, terribile *terrible*
terror, terrōris, m. *terror*
*tertius, tertia, tertium *third*
testāceum opus, testāceī operis, n. *brick work*
*testāmentum, testāmentī, n. *will*
testimōnium, testimōniī, n. *evidence*
*testis, testis, m.f. *witness*
testor, testārī, testātus sum *call to witness*
tētē = tē
tetigī *see* tangere
Teucrī, Teucrōrum, m.pl. *Trojans*
theātrum, theātrī, n. *theater*
thermae, thermārum, f.pl. *baths*
Tiberis, Tiberis, m. *river Tiber*
tibi *see* tū
tībia, tībiae, f. *pipe*
Tīburs, Tīburtis, m. *man from Tibur*
*timeō, timēre, timuī *be afraid, fear*
timidē *fearfully*

timidus, timida, timidum *fearful, frightened*
*timor, timōris, m. *fear*
tintinō, tintināre, tintināvī *ring*
tīrō, tīrōnis, m. *recruit*
titulus, titulī, m. *advertisement, slogan, inscription, label*
toga, togae, f. *toga*
*tollō, tollere, sustulī, sublātus *raise, lift up, hold up; remove, do away with*
tōnsor, tōnsōris, m. *barber*
tormentum, tormentī, n. *torture*
torpeō, torpēre *be paralyzed*
torqueō, torquēre, torsī, tortus *torture, twist, turn*
*tot *so many*
totidem *the same number*
*tōtus, tōta, tōtum *whole*
tractō, tractāre, tractāvī, tractātus *handle, touch*
*trādō, trādere, trādidī, trāditus *hand over*
trādunt *they say, people say*
*trahō, trahere, trāxī, tractus *drag, draw on, urge on, draw, derive*
trāiciō, trāicere, trāiēcī, trāiectus *stab*
tranquillum, tranquillī, n. *calm weather*
*trāns + acc. *across*
*trānseō, trānsīre, trānsiī, trānsitus *cross*
trānsferō, trānsferre, trānstulī, trānslātus *transfer, put*
trānsigō, trānsigere, trānsēgī, trānsāctus *end*
trānsitus, trānsitūs, m. *crossing*
*trecentī, trecentae, trecenta *three hundred*
*trēdecim *thirteen*
tremō, tremere, tremuī *tremble, shake*
tremor, tremōris, m. *trembling, tremor*
tremulus, tremula, tremulum *quivering*
trepidātiō, trepidātiōnis, f. *panic, terror*
trepidō, trepidāre, trepidāvī *tremble*
*trēs, tria *three*
trēs adeō *as many as three, three entire*
*tribūnus, tribūnī, m. *tribune (high-ranking officer)*
tribūtum, tribūtī, n. *tribute, tax*
triclīnium, triclīniī, n. *dining-room*
tridēns, tridentis, m. *trident*
triērarchus, triērarchī, m. *naval captain*

*trīgintā *thirty*
*trīstis, trīste *sad*
triumphālis, triumphāle *triumphal*
triumphus, triumphī, m. *triumph*
  triumphum agere *celebrate a triumph*
Trucculēnsis, Trucculēnse
  Trucculensian
trucīdō, trucīdāre, trucīdāvī,
  trucīdātus *slaughter*
trudis, trudis, f. *pole*
*tū, tuī *you (singular)*
*tuba, tubae, f. *trumpet*
tueor, tuērī, tuitus sum *watch over,*
  protect
tulī *see* ferō
*tum *then*
* tum dēmum *then at last, only then*
tumidus, tumida, tumidum *swollen*
*tumultus, tumultī, m. *riot*
tunc *then*
tundō, tundere *beat, buffet*
*turba, turbae, f. *crowd*
turbātus, turbāta, turbātum *confused*
turbulentus, turbulenta, turbulentum
  rowdy, disorderly, disturbed, muddy
turgidulus, turgidula, turgidulum
  swollen
turpis, turpe *shameful*
*tūtus, tūta, tūtum *safe*
*tuus, tua, tuum *your (singular), yours*

u

*ubi *where, when*
ubicumque *wherever*
*ubīque *everywhere*
*ulcīscor, ulcīscī, ultus sum *avenge, take*
  revenge on, take vengeance
*ūllus, ūlla, ūllum *any*
ulmus, ulmī, f. *elm-tree*
*ultimus, ultima, ultimum *farthest, last,*
  at the edge
  manus ultima *final touch*
  supplicium ultimum *death penalty*
*ultiō, ultiōnis, f. *revenge*
*ultrā *more, further, beyond*
ultrō *of one's own accord*
ululātus, ululātūs, m. *shriek*

ululō, ululāre, ululāvī *howl*
Umber, Umbrī, m. *Umbrian*
*umbra, umbrae, f. *shadow, ghost*
*umerus, umerī, m. *shoulder*
ūmidus, ūmida, ūmidum *rainy, stormy*
*umquam *ever*
ūnā *with him*
* ūnā cum + abl. *together with*
*unda, undae, f. *wave*
*unde *from where*
*ūndecim *eleven*
*ūndēvīgintī *nineteen*
*undique *on all sides*
unguis, unguis, m. *claw*
*unguō, unguere, ūnxī, ūnctus *anoint,*
  smear
ūnicus, ūnica, ūnicum *one and only*
ūnivira, ūnivirae, f. *woman who has had*
  only one husband
*ūnus, ūna, ūnum *one, a single*
urbānus, urbāna, urbānum *chic,*
  fashionable, refined; city-dweller, man
  from Rome
*urbs, urbis, f. *city*
urgeō, urgēre *pursue, press upon*
ūrō, ūrere, ussī, ustus *burn*
usquam *anywhere*
usque (1) *continually*
  usque quāque *on every possible occasion*
usque (2) + acc. *as far as*
  usque adhūc *until now, up to this time*
  usque alter *yet another*
ūsus, ūsūs, m. *use*
  ūsuī esse *be of use*
ūsus *see* ūtor
*ut *(1) as, like, as soon as, when*
  ut quisque *as soon as each one*
*ut *(2) that, so that, in order that*
*uterque, utraque, utrumque *each, both,*
  each of two
utrīque *both groups of people*
uterus, uterī, m. *womb*
*ūtilis, ūtile *useful*
ūtilitās, ūtilitātis, f. *usefulness*
utinam *would that! if only!*
*ūtor, ūtī, ūsus sum + abl. *use*
utrimque *on each side*
*utrum *whether*
* utrum . . . an *whether . . . or*
*uxor, uxōris, f. *wife*
  uxōrem dūcere *take as a wife, marry*

V

vavō, vacāre, vacāvī *be unoccupied*

*vacuus, vacua, vacuum *empty*

vadum, vadī, n. *water*

vae tē! *alas for you!*

vāgītus, vāgītūs, m. *wailing, crying*

vagor, vagārī, vagātus sum *spread, go around, wander*

vagus, vaga, vagum *wandering*

*valdē *very much, very*

*valē *good-by, farewell*

  avē atque valē *hail and farewell*

valedīcō, valedīcere, valedīxī *say good-by*

valeō, valēre, valuī *be well, feel well, thrive, prosper*

valētūdō, valētūdinis, f. *health, ill-health, sickness*

*validus, valida, validum *strong*

varius, varia, varium *different, various*

vāstus, vāsta, vāstum *great, large, enormous*

-ve *or*

*vehementer *violently, loudly*

vehiculum, vehiculī, n. *carriage*

*vehō, vehere, vexī, vectus *carry*

vehor, vehī, vectus sum *be carried (e.g. by horse or ship), travel*

*vel *or*

* vel . . . vel *either . . . or*

velim, vellem *see* volō

*velut *like*

vēna, vēnae, f. *vein*

vēnālīcius, vēnālīciī, m. *slave-dealer*

*vēnātiō, vēnātiōnis, f. *hunt*

vēnātus, vēnātūs, m. *catch (from the hunt)*

*vēndō, vēndere, vēndidī, vēnditus *sell*

*venēnum, venēnī, n. *poison*

*venia, veniae, f. *mercy*

*veniō, venīre, vēnī *come, come forward*

  in mentem venīre *occur, come to mind*

vēnor, vēnārī, vēnātus sum *hunt*

venter, ventris, m. *stomach, womb*

ventitō, ventitāre *often go, go repeatedly*

*ventus, ventī, m. *wind*

Venus, Veneris, f. *Venus (goddess of love)*

venustās, venustātis, f. *charm*

venustus, venusta, venustum *tender-hearted, loving*

*verberō, verberāre, verberāvī,

verberātus *strike, beat*

*verbum, verbī, n. *word*

vērē *truly*

verēcundia, verēcundiae, f. *shyness*

*vereor, verērī, veritus sum *be afraid, fear*

vēritās, vēritātis, f. *truth*

*vērō *indeed*

verrūca, verrūcae, f. *wart*

versipellis, versipellis, m. *werewolf*

versus, versūs, m. *verse, line of poetry*

vertex, verticis, m. *top, peak*

*vertō, vertere, vertī, versus *turn, churn up*

  sē vertere *turn around*

vērum *but*

*vērum, vērī, n. *truth*

*vērus, vēra, vērum *true, real*

* rē vērā *in fact, truly, really*

vespillō, vespillōnis, m. *undertaker*

*vester, vestra, vestrum *your (plural)*

*vestīmenta, vestīmentōrum, n.pl. *clothes*

*vestis, vestis, f. *clothing*

  vestem mūtāre *put on mourning clothes*

*vetus, *gen.* veteris *old*

  veterēs, veterum, m.pl. *old-timers*

vetustās, vetustātis, f. *length, duration*

*vexō, vexāre, vexāvī, vexātus *annoy*

vexātus, vexāta, vexātum *confused, in chaos*

*via, viae, f. *street, way*

viātor, viātōris, m. *traveler*

vicārius, vicāriī, m. *substitute*

vīcīnia, vīcīniae, f. *nearness*

*vīcīnus, vīcīnī, m. *neighbor*

victima, victimae, f. *victim*

*victor, victōris, m. *victor, winner*

victōria, victōriae, f. *victory*

  victōriam, referre *win a victory*

victus *see* vincere

*videō, vidēre, vīdī, vīsus *see*

*videor, vidērī, vīsus sum *seem*

vigilō, vigilāre, vigilāvī *stay awake, keep watch*

*vīgintī *twenty*

vīlicus, vīlicī, m. *overseer, manager*

*vīlis, vīle *cheap*

*vīlla, vīllae, f. *villa, (large) house*

*vinciō, vincīre, vīnxī, vīnctus *bind, tie up*

*vincō, vincere, vīcī, victus *conquer, win, be victorious, outweigh*
victī, victōrum, m.pl. *the conquered*
*vinculum, vinculī, n. *fastening, chain*
vindicō, vindicāre, vindicāvī, vindicātus *avenge*
*vīnum, vīnī, n. *wine*
violentia, violentiae, f. *violence*
vīpera, vīpperae, f. *viper*
*vir, virī, m. *man*
*virgō, virginis, f. *virgin*
viridis, viride *green*
*virtūs, virtūtis, f. *courage, virtue*
*vīs, f. *force, violence*
* vīrēs, vīrium, f.pl. *forces, strength*
vīs *see* volō
vīsitō, vīsitāre, vīsitāvī, vīsitātus *visit*
vīsō, vīsere, vīsī *come to visit*
vīsus *see* videō
*vīta, vītae, f. *life*
vītam agere *lead a life*
vītābundus, vītābunda, vītābundum *avoiding*
*vitium, vitiī, n. *sin, fault, failure, vice*
*vītō, vītāre, vītāvī, vītātus *avoid*
*vituperō, vituperāre, vituperāvī, vituperātus *find fault with, curse, criticize*
*vīvō, vīvere, vīxī *live, be alive*
*vīvus, vīva, vīvum *alive, living*
*vix *hardly, scarcely, with difficulty*
vix tandem *at long last*
vōbīs *see* vōs
vōcem *see* vōx

*vocō, vocāre, vocāvī, vocātus *call*
volātus, volātūs, m. *flying, flight*
*volō, velle, voluī *want*
bene velle *like, be friendly*
velim *I would like*
vellem *I would be willing*
volō, volāre, volāvī *fly*
volt = vult
volucer, volucris, volucre *winged, swift*
volucris, volucris, f. *bird*
volūmen, volūminis, n. *volume, book*
voluntārius, voluntāriī, m. *volunteer*
*volvō, volvere, volvī, volūtus *turn, set rolling, turn to billows, send rolling upwards*
* in animō volvere *wonder, turn over in the mind*
vōmer, vōmeris, m. *plowshare*
*vōs *you (plural)*
vōbīscum *with you (plural)*
vōtum, vōtī, n. *vow*
vōtī reus *bound by one's vow, in payment of one's vow*
*vōx, vōcis, f. *voice*
vulgō, vulgāre, vulgāvī, vulgātus *make known*
vulgus, vulgī, n. *the ordinary man, common man*
*vulnerō, vulnerāre, vulnerāvī, vulnerātus *wound, injure*
*vulnus, vulneris, n. *wound*
vult *see* volō
*vultus, vultūs, m. *expression, face*

Index of Authors, Characters, Cultural and Political Topics, and Works

Numbers refer to pages; numbers in boldface refer to pages with illustrations.

Acerronia, friend of Agrippina 264–66
Achaians (= Greeks) 250–55
Achilles (or Achilleus), Greek hero
  250–61
Acts of the Apostles 135
Admetos, father of Eumelos 250–55
adultery, charges of 46, 215, 217
aedīlis 47
Aeneas, Trojan hero 150, 177, 236–39
Aeneid **139**, 150–54, 177, 232, 236–50
  see also Vergil
Aesop, Greek fabulist 140
Africa, province 177, 242, 338
Agamemnon, Greek king 250, 255
Agricola, governor of Britain 50, 132,
  134–35, 136–37, 232, 342–45
Agricola
  see Tacitus
Agrippina, mother of Nero 257–270,
  275–277
Aithe, borrowed mare of Menelaos
  250–55
Alban hills, in Latium, southeast of
  Rome 346–47
Alcantara, Roman bridge in Spain **275**
Alexandria, city in Egypt, 346, 348
Allegrini, painter **188**, 194
Alps, mountains in Europe 211
Amastris, city in Bithynia 136
amīcī of the Emperor 45–46, 277
  see also Crispus, Fuscus, Glabrio,
  Messalinus, Veiento
Amymone, wife of Marcus 71
Anchises, father of Aeneas 236
Anicetus, freeman of Nero 260–62, 266,
  268–70, 277
annual games, abolished in Gaulish
  town 46
Antilochos, son of hero Nestor 250–55
Antipater, divorced husband of Zois 175

Antony, Roman general 157
apodyterium in country villas 12–14
Apollo, god 250–51
appeal by condemned to emperor 46
Arabia, province 133, 211
Arcanum 71
Argiletum street 88
Ars Amatoria, displeasing to Augustus
  89
  see also Ovid
Ascletarion, astrologer 348, 350
Athene, goddess 250–52
Athens, Greek city 180, **245**
Atreus, father of Agamemnon and
  Menelaos 250, 253
Auden W.H., British poet 194
  Musée des Beaux Arts 194
auditorium used for recitatio 29
augur, title of Pliny 50
Augustine, Saint 90
Augustus, Emperor 29, 157, 168, 175,
  274, **279**
Aulus Fabricius Veiento
  see Veiento
Aurelius, friend of Catullus 211
Ayrton, Michael, artist and author
  183, 194

Baiae, resort on Bay of Naples 217, 223,
  261–62
basilica court site 108
Basilica Julia **45**
Bauli, site of Agrippina's villa 261–62
birthrate, decline in 69
Bithynia, province of Asia Minor 112,
  111–137, 157, 276
book, physical appearance of 31, 89
  cost of 88
  sellers of 88
Bootes, constellation 184

Boresti, tribe in Scotland 344–45
Britannia (Britain), province 132–33,
136–7, 157, 211, 342–45
Britannicus, son of Claudius 259
Bruegel, Pieter, Flemish painter 194–
95, **196**
Burrus, commander of praetorian
guard 258, 266, 268

Caelius, lover of Clodia 215–17, 232
Caesar, Roman general and politician
157, 166, 211, 274
caldarium, in country villas 12–14
Caligula, Emperor 279
Calpurnia, wife of Pliny 69–70
Calymne, Aegean island 180, 188
Campania, region of Italy 222–23
Capitolium, temple of Jupiter, Juno,
and Minerva 350
Capreae (Capri), island in Bay of
Naples 223–24
Carthage, city in northern Africa 150,
157
war with 109
Catullus, Roman lyric poet 142–44,
157, 200–12
Centaur, ship 237–47
centumviri, court of (inheritance cases)
71
Chatti, tribe in Germany 345
Chimaera, ship 237–47
Cicero, Roman orator and politician
215–17, 232
describes sister-in-law 71
civil cases
see legacy disputes, property damage
Claudius, Emperor 125, 157, 258, 259,
279
disastrous recitatio by 30
Claudius Epaphroditus
see Epaphroditus
Clemens, senator and relative of
Domitian 54–55, 348
clients, legal problems of 108
Cloanthus, Trojan captain 237–47
Clodia, Roman matron, probably =
Lesbia 215–17
Clodianus, staff officer of Domitian
352–53
Clodius, brother of Clodia 215

Cogidubnus, death of 96, 98, 101
coloni, "tenant farmers" of Pliny 15
consilium, emperor's "council" 45–7,
277
conspiracy against an emperor 95
consul, duties of 48
Cornelius Tacitus
see Tacitus
courts of law 106–9
Crepereius Gallus, friend of Agrippina
264
Crete, large island south of Greece 150,
180–81, 194
Crispus, senator and ex-consul 37–40
Cupid, god 205–6
curator Tiberis, title of Pliny 50
cursus honorum 47–49
Cyclops, one-eyed giant 243

Dacia, province in Balkans 132–33
Daedalus, mythical Greek inventor
179–90, 194
Delos, Aegean island 180, 188
Diaulos, undertaker ridiculed by
Martial 20
Dido, Carthaginian queen 150, 177
Dio, Greek writer 277
Diomedes, Greek hero 250–55
Domitia Augusta, wife of Emperor
Domitian 96
Domitian, Emperor, *passim* 35–46, 157,
275, 342–53
Domitianus, Emperor
see Domitian
Domitianus, son of Clemens and
adopted son of Domitian 350
Domitilla, sister of Domitian 352
dos "dowry" 175
Dryden, John, British poet and
translator 152

education, literature in 90–92
Education of an Orator
see Quintilian
Egnatius, character in poem of Catullus
142–43
Egypt, province 132–33
election bribery (*quaestio*) 106
emperor, duties of 274–78
emperor's heir, selection of 46
Epaphroditus, freedman of Nero and

Domitian 348–49

Ephesian matron
see Petronius

Ephesus, city in province of Asia
112–13, 161

equestrian rank, offices of 46

Eumelos, Greek hero 250–51

Eutrapelus, barber in poem by Martial 146

Festus, Roman governor of Judaea 135

Fidentinus, poet lampooned by Martial
20

fishing 14

Fitzgerald, Robert, American poet
152–3

flammeum "bridal veil" 68

Flavia Domitilla, granddaughter of
Vespasian and relative of Domitian
56, 61–63

Flavian family
see gens Flavia

Flavius Clemens
see Clemens

forgery (*quaestiō*) 106

frigidarium, in country villas 12

Fry, Christopher, British playwright 160
A Phoenix Too Frequent 160

Furius, friend of Catullus 211

Fuscus, commander of praetorian
guard 40

Gaius Helvidius Lupus
see Lupus

Gaius Petronius Arbiter
see Petronius

Gaius Plinius Caecilius Secundus
see Pliny (the Younger)

Gaius Salvius Liberalis
see Salvius

Gaius Valerius Catullus
see Catullus, lyric poet

Galba, governor of Hispania
Tarraconensis and later Emperor 42

gens Flavia, family of Emperors
Vespasian, Titus, and Domitian 350

Germania (Germany), province 344–
45, 350

Germanicus, father of Agrippina 266

Gerusia, club for elderly men 125

Glabrio, supporter of Agricola 2–4,
6–8, 41–2

Gnaeus Iulius Agricola
see Agricola

Graupius, mountain in Scotland 342–45

Greece 242

Gyas, Trojan captain 237–47

Hadrian, Emperor 277
villa of at Tibur 12

Haterius, client and brother-in-law of
Salvius 102

Hector, Trojan hero 242

Helice, constellation 184

Helvidius, son of C. Helvidius Lupus 8,
56–59, 64

Herculaneum, **201**, **205**

Hispania (Tarraconensis), province of
Spain 145, **275**, 336–37

Histories
see Tacitus

Homer, Greek poet 154
Odyssey 250
Iliad 250

Horace, lyric poet 26

hunting methods 13–14

hypocaust, in country villas 12

Icarus, son of Daedalus 179–90, 194,
195, **196**

Iliad
see Homer

India 211

Ionian sea 242

Isis, goddess 125

iūdex "judge" 106

Iulia
see Julia

iūnctiō dextrārum, wedding ritual 68

Iuppiter
see Jupiter

Jesus 132

Jove
see Jupiter

Judaea, province 132–34

Julia, daughter of Titus and niece of
Domitian 352–53

Julius Caesar
see Caesar

Juno, goddess 63, 188–89

Jupiter, Roman god 206, 350

jurors 108

murder (*quaestiō*) 106
Musée des Beaux Arts (Auden) 194
Myropnoüs, dwarf pipe-player 96, 103

Nash, Ogden, American poet 84
Natural History (*Historia Naturalis*)
  see Pliny (the Elder)
Neleus, grandfather of Antilochos 250
Neptune, god of the sea 242
Nero, Emperor 135, 160, 257–68, 275–
  77, 348–49
Nerva, Emperor 279
Nestor, father of Antilochos 250, 252
Nicaea, city in Bithynia 112, 136
Niceros, fictional narrator of werewolf
  story 334–35
Nicomedia, city in Bithynia, 112, 119–
  21, 125–29, 136
Nile (Nilus), river of Egypt 211, 340–41

Octavia, sister of Augustus 29
Octavian
  see Augustus
Odyssey
  see Homer
Orcus, (god of) the Underworld 205,
  334
Orion, constellation 184
Ovid, Roman poet 149, 154, 157, 180–
  95, 232, 248
  Ars Amatoria 149, 232
  Metamorphoses 149, 180–90, 232

Palātīna domus, palace of Domitian on
  Palatine hill 350
Palatine hill 20–21
Palinurus, Trojan helmsman 150–51
Panopea, sea-nymph 246
Papylus, character in poem by Martial
  145
Parker, Dorothy, American poet
Paros, Aegean island 180, 188
Parthenius, freedman and chamberlain
  of Domitian 350–53
Parthia 211
Patroklos, friend of Achilles 250
patrons 28–9, 88
Paul, St. 134
Paula, character in poem by Martial
  146
Penelope, wife of Odysseus 149

Pergama
  see Troy
Pergamum, city in province of Asia
  112–13
Persia 211
Petronius, Roman author 160–63, 232,
  334–35
  Satyrica 160–63, 232, 334–35
Phaedrus, Roman fabulist 140–41, 157,
  160
Phoenix Too Frequent, 160
Phoibos Apollo
  see Apollo
Phoinix, judge of Greek games 251
Phorcus, sea-god 246–47
Phyllis, nurse of Domitian and Julia
  348, 352
Pilate, governor of Judaea 132
Plaugus, performances of 89
Pliny (the Elder) 221–25, 226–27, 337–
  43
  Natural History 337–41
Pliny (the Younger) 12–15, 36–7, 46,
  48, 49–51, 111–37, 145, 157, 173,
  221–28, 232, 276, 336–37, 340–43
Polla, daughter of Clemens and Flavia
  55, 56, 58–59, 61–65
Pompeii, city in Campania **185**, 194,
  223, **224**, 341
Pompey, Roman general, 157, 166
Pomponia, wife of Quintus Cicero 70
Ponponianus, friend of Pliny (the
  Elder) 340–41
Pontilianus, poet lampooned by
  Martial 19
Pontius Pilatus
  see Pilate
Pontus, province in Asia Minor 112,
  133
Poppaea Sabina, wife of Nero 258–59
Portunus, god of harbors 211
praefātiō, opening of recitatio 30
praefectus aerāriī Sāturnī, title of Pliny 50
praetor, title of Agricola and Pliny 48
  legal inquiries of 106
praetorian guard 46
Pristis, ship 237–47
Propertius, Roman elegiac poet 154,
  191
property damage 106
prosecutor, private individual 108

Prusa, city in Bithynia 112, 113, 136
Publius, younger son of Clemens and Flavia and adopted son of Domitian 74–78
Publius Cornelius Fuscus
  see Fuscus
Publius Ovidius Naso
  see Ovid
Publius Vergilius Maro
  see Vergil
Pudicitia, temple of 177

quaestiōnēs, types of 106
  see also adultery, election bribery, forgery, misconduct, murder, treason
quaestor, title of Agricola and Pliny 47
Quintilian, Roman rhetor 54–55
  The Education of an Orator 90
Quintus, accuser of Salvius 98–9, 104
Quintus, silly lover described by Martial 25
Quintus Caecilius Iucundus
  see Quintus, accuser of Salvius
Quintus Cicero 70
Quintus Haterius Latronianus
  see Haterius
Quintus Lucretius Vespillo
  see Vespillo
Quintus Vibius Crispus
  see Crispus

reading aloud, silently 90
recitationes 28–31, 54, 89
rhetor **89**, 54
Rufilla, wife of Salvius 100–2

Sabidius, enemy of Martial 18
Sabinus, consul and brother of Clemens 54
Sallust, Roman historian 268
Salvius, senator, iuridicus, and later consul 135
Samos, Aegean island 180, 188
Saturnalia 13
Satur, supervisor of Domitian's bedroom-attendants 351–52
Satyrica, see Petronius
schools 89–92
Scotland 112, 134, 135, 137, 342–45
Scylla, ship 237–47
Scythia 211

Secundus
  see Pliny (the Younger)
Sempronius Caelianus, Roman official 122–23
senate, elections by 47
senatorian rank 46
senators, trial by fellow 107
Seneca, tutor of Nero 30, 258, 266–268
sententia in a meeting of emperor's *cōnsilium* 46–47
Sergestus, Trojan captain 237–47
Servius Sulpicius Galba
  see Galba
Setina, type of wine, 145
Sextus, man with ugly face 23
Sicily, island south of Italy 132–33, **216**, 236
Spain, see Hispania
Sparsus, fifty-five-year-old senator 55, 56, 58, 61–65, 67–8
spōnsālia "betrothal" 67
Spurius Carvilius, Roman senator 174
Stabiae, town on Bay of Naples 223, 340–42
Stephanus, freedman and financial manager of Domitilla 348–352
Sthenelos, companion of Diomedes 250, 254
Subura 88
Suetonius, Roman historian 274–75, 347–53
  Lives of the Emperors 274, 347–53
Symmachus, doctor ridiculed by Martial 24

Tacitus, Roman historian 136–37, 221, 232, 258–70, 274, 277, 342–45
  Agricola 136–37, 232, 242–45
  Annals 258–70, 274
  Histories 274
Tentyritae, tribe of pygmies 340
tepidarium, in country villas 12–14
Teucri
  see Trojans
Thais, character in poem by Martial 190
Tiberius, Emperor 258, 348–49
Tiberius Claudius Cogidubnus
  see Cogidubnus
Tibullus, Roman elegiac poet 154
Tibur 12

Index of Grammatical Topics

Key: AL = About the Language; RvG = Review Grammar; RfG = Reference Grammar

Page references are given first, with paragraph references (i.e. references to numbered sections in the language notes and the Review Grammar) following in boldface; Roman numerals following page numbers denote sections in the Reference Grammar, which are sometimes followed by paragraph references.

In general, AL references are only to the *first* language note in this Unit on the grammatical topic in question: in a few cases, additional pages are cited.

of the whole RvG 311.**3**.3a, b
gerund RvG 302.**10**
  ablative of AL 170.**2–3**; RvG 324.**1**;
    RfG 332.XI.**1**
  genitive of AL 170.**2–3**; RvG 324.**1**;
    RfG 332.XI.**1**
  with **ad** (purpose) AL 104.**2–3**,
    170.**1**,**3**; RvG 324.**1**; RfG 332.XI.**1**
gerundive RvG 302.**11**
  of obligation AL 103.**1**; RvG 325.**3**
  with **ad** + noun (purpose) AL 104.**2**,
    118.**1**,**3**; RvG 324.**2**; RfG 332.XI.**2**
historical infinitive AL 268.**2–3**
historical present AL. 186.**1–4**;
    RvG 295.**4**
  with **dum** (*while*) RvG 326.**1**
indirect statement RvG 319–21.**1**, **4**;
    RfG 330–31.IX. **1–2**
  position of leading verb AL 172–73.
    1–3
  with forms of **nego** RvG 320.**2**;
    RfG 331.**1**
  with future infinitive AL 57.**1**, **3**
  with perfect active infinitive AL 38.**1**,
    3
  with perfect leading verb AL 99.**2**
  with perfect passive infinitive AL 43.**1**,
    3
  with present leading verb AL 10–
    11.**2–3**; 99.**1**
  with present passive infinitive
    AL 10.**2**
  without leading verb RvG 321.**6**
infinitive
  deponent future RvG 306.**6**
  deponent perfect RvG 306.**5**
  deponent present RvG 306.**4**
  future active RvG 301.**9**
  historical AL 268.**2–3**
  irregular future RvG 301.**4**
  irregular perfect RvG 301.**4**
  irregular present RvG 301.**4**
  perfect active RvG 301.**7**
  perfect passive RvG 301.**8**
  present active RvG 301.**5**
  present passive RvG 301.**6**
intensive pronouns (**ipse**) RvG 291.**5**
locative case RvG 314.**8**
longer sentences RvG 326–27. **1–2**,
    4–5
malo (**malle**)

indicative RvG 307.**1**
subjunctive RvG 308.**3**
nominative case RvG 311.**1**
nouns RvG 284–85.**1–6**
  plural with singular meaning AL 248.**1**
nolo (**nolle**)
  indicative RvG 307.**1**
  subjunctive RvG 308.**3**
omission of verbs
  of forms of **esse** AL 23.**2–3**
  in parallel clauses AL 190–91.**1–5**
participles RvG 315.**1–4**
  deponent future RvG 306.**3**
  deponent perfect active RvG 306.**2**
  deponent present RvG 306.**1**
  future RvG 301.**4**
  perfect passive RvG 301.**3**
  present RvG 301.**2**
passive verbs
  future AL 79.**2–4**
  imperfect AL 79.**2–4**; 164–65.**2–3**
  present AL 5–6.**1**, 65.**1**
  facior (=**fieri** and **factus esse**)
    AL 124–25.**2**,**4**; RvG 310.**6**
  feror (**ferri**)
    indicative RvG 309.**5**
    subjunctive RvG 310.**5**
personal pronouns (**ego, tu,** etc.)
    RvG 290.**1**
possum (**posse**)
  indicative RvG 307.**1**
  subjunctive RvG 308.**3**
pronouns RvG 290–92.**1–9**
  see also demonstrative pronouns;
    determinative pronouns; **idem**;
    intensive pronouns; personal
    pronouns; reflexive pronouns; relative
    pronouns
purpose clauses RvG 316.**3**
questions
  direct deliberative AL 263.**1**,**3**
  indirect RvG 316.**2**
  indirect deliberative AL 263.**2–3**
reflexive pronouns (**se**) RvG 290.**2**
relative pronouns
  (**qui**) RvG 292.**8**
  position of antecedents AL 208–9.**1–**
    3; RvG 292–93.**9**
result clauses RvG 317.**5**
subjunctive of the verb RvG 316–19.
    1–6, 8–9, 11–13

in subordinate clauses in indirect
statement RvG 317.**4**; RfG 331.**2**
imperfect passive AL 164.**1–2**
jussive AL 204.**1–3**; RvG 318.**9**;
RfG 330.VIII
perfect active AL 60.**2**, **4–5**
perfect passive AL 271–72.**2–4**
pluperfect passive AL 225.**2–3**
present active AL 22–23.**2–5**
present passive AL 129–30.**1–2**
with **dum** (*until*) RvG 317.**6**
with **priusquam** (*before*) RvG 317.**6**
see also commands, indirect; **cum**-
clauses; fearing clauses; purpose
clauses; result clauses; questions,
indirect; subjunctive of the verb,
jussive
sum (**esse**)
indicative RvG 307.**1**
subjunctive RvG 308.**3**
verbs, irregular RvG 307–8.**1**, **3–4**

see also **eō, ferō, mālō, nōlō, possum,
sum, volō**
verbs, non-finite forms (verbals)
see commands, gerund, gerundive,
infinitive, participles
verbs, omission of
see omission of verbs
verbs, regular
forms other than finite RvG 300–2.**1–
11**
indicative active RvG 294–95.**1, 3, 5,
6**
indicative passive RvG 296–98.**1**, **4**
subjunctive active RvG 298.**1–4**
subjunctive passive RvG 299.**1–4**
see also gerund, gerundive, infinitive,
participles
vocative case RvG 311.**2**
volō (**velle**)
indicative RvG 307.**1**
subjunctive RvG 308.**3**

Quick References to Grammatical Information

Time Chart

A.D.		ROME AND ITALY	WORLD	A.D.
14		Tiberius becomes Emperor		14
c. 29			Crucifixion of Jesus	c. 29
35–?	Quintilian; – *The Education of an Orator*			35–?
37		Caligula becomes Emperor		37
c. 40–c.104	Martial; – *Epigrams*			c. 40–c.104
41		Claudius becomes Emperor		41
42		St. Peter brings Christianity to Rome		42
43	Britain becomes province of Rome			43
45–57			Missionary journeys of St. Paul	45–57
54		Nero becomes Emperor		54
c. 55–c. 116	Tacitus; – prose *Annales*			c. 55–c. 116
c. 61–c. 112	Pliny the Younger; – *Letters*			c. 61–c. 112
64		Great Fire at Rome; Persecution of Christians by Nero		64
69		Year of Four Emperors; Vespasian becomes Emperor		69
70			Romans sack Jerusalem and Temple	70
79		Titus becomes Emperor; August 24: Vesuvius erupts		79
81		Domitian becomes Emperor		81
96		Nerva becomes Emperor		96
98		Trajan becomes Emperor		98
117		Hadrian becomes Emperor		117
313			Emperor Constantine officially supports Christianity in Roman Empire	313
330			Capital of Roman Empire moved to Constantinople	330

Date	Event	Event
410	Visigoths sack Rome	
	Rome formally renounces Britain	
476	Last Emperor of Rome deposed	
570		Birth of Mohammed
c. 643		Arabs conquer Egypt
800		Charlemagne crowned Emperor of Holy Roman Empire
800–1100	Period of turmoil in Italy	
1143	Rome becomes an independent city-state	
1265–1321	Dante; – *Divine Comedy*	
c. 1400	The Renaissance begins in Italy	
1453		Turks capture Constantinople
1492		Columbus arrives in America
1497		Cabot explores Canada
1521		Reformation begins
1620		Pilgrims land at Plymouth, Mass.
1776		United States declare their Independence
1806		End of Holy Roman Empire
1815		Napoleon finally defeated at Waterloo
1861	Victor Emmanuel II becomes King of a united Italy	
1863		Lincoln emancipates American slaves
1867		Canada becomes a Dominion
1914–1918		First World War
1931		Canada becomes a Commonwealth nation
1939–1945		Second World War
1946	Italy becomes a Republic